Mexican American Youth Organization

MEXICAN AMERICAN YOUTH ORGANIZATION

Avant-Garde of the Chicano Movement in Texas

Armando Navarro

Foreword by Mario C. Compean

 University of Texas Press
Austin

*This book is dedicated to
the memory of my parents,
Silvestre and Altagracia Navarro,
who gave me life, love, and support
in my efforts to improve the quality
of our people's lives*

Copyright © 1995 by the University of Texas Press
All rights reserved
Printed in the United States of America
First edition, 1995

Requests for permission to reproduce material from this work
should be sent to Permissions, University of Texas Press,
Box 7819, Austin, TX 78713-7819.

⊗ The paper used in this publication meets the minimum
requirements of American National Standard for Information
Sciences—Permanence of Paper for Printed Library Materials,
ANSI Z39.48-1984.

LIBRARY OF CONGRESS CATALOGING-IN-PUBLICATION DATA

Navarro, Armando, 1941–
    Mexican American youth organization : avant-garde of the
Chicano movement in Texas / Armando Navarro. — 1st ed.
        p.   cm.
    Includes bibliographical references (p.   ) and index.
    ISBN 0-292-75556-2 (cloth : acid-free paper). —
    ISBN 0-292-75557-0 (paper : acid-free paper)
        1. MAYO (Organization)   2. Mexican American youth—
Texas—Political activity.   I. Title.
F395.M5N39   1995
323.3'52'08968720764—dc20   94-39569

Contents

Tables

Foreword

Armando Navarro has made a major contribution to the scholarship on the Chicano Movement (*el movimiento*) with this book-length study of the Mexican American Youth Organization (MAYO). As is the case with a number of studies of *el movimiento*, Navarro's work (originally done two decades ago) remained buried in the library stacks, touched only by emerging and established scholars. In Navarro's perspective and analysis, MAYO was the vanguard of *el movimiento* in Texas. It is nevertheless remarkable that although several works were published previously on *el movimiento* in Texas, no book-length study of MAYO's presence in Chicana/o history appeared before Navarro's work.

Prof. Navarro has produced a study rich in historical detail. He presents a synthesis of the historical forces and antecedents that provided the context for the emergence of both *el movimiento* and the Chicano youth movement. His use of the concepts of exogenous and endogenous antagonisms provides an analytical framework that locates the emergence of both movements in the biography of Chicana/o oppression and domination at the hands of the U.S. institutional apparatus and society, which became deeply entrenched during the century that preceded their emergence. His case study of MAYO, moreover, provides even richer historical detail that captures a deep understanding of this era in Chicana/o political and social history in Texas.

The MAYO activists very consciously and deliberately set out to build the ideological and power base to empower the Chicano people. They immersed themselves intensely and meticulously in the task and struggle to "liberate" Chicanas and Chicanos in Texas from over a century of oppression and domination at the hands of what they called the "gringo" system. The issue of how successful MAYO was in accomplishing this goal, as is the case with La Raza Unida party in Texas, will remain an open question for some time to come. Nonetheless, what is certain is that both MAYO and, subsequently, La Raza Unida were unique and potent forces that forced Texas to make the transition from a primitive state, in terms of its political and cultural development, to a more open civilized society in which Chicanos/as enjoy more political freedom and participation. However, it would be naive, at best, for me to claim that Chicano/as in Texas and in the nation are not still bound by the chains of oppression. One has only to look at the rampant racism that has reemerged in the 1980s and 1990s and the high rates of educational failure and poverty that pervade the Chicana/o communities throughout the land, as Navarro suggests in the epilogue, to realize the falseness of such a claim.

Navarro has produced a valuable study in another sense. Its rich historical detail has tremendous value for both scholars and the younger Chicana/o generations. It is a valuable resource especially for today's Chicana/o youth because it provides an excellent means for them to develop a historical knowledge base of the generation that preceded them. For most of the past fifteen years, the forces that have sought to erase our Chicana/o identity, our identity as a people (and thus some of the important accomplishments of *el movimiento*), have been quite successful. We have in our midst individuals, youths and adults, who trot the Chicano/a landscape calling themselves "Hispanics" and speaking of their "Hispanic" Raza. This sad state of affairs derives, in part, from the mainstream media, politicians, and government officials. It emanates also from some of "our" leaders and scholars who find it too easy to willingly traverse the path of political and material expediency. Thus, Navarro's book will allow some of our "elders" who left *el movimiento* to recapture their historical memory and, perhaps, even return home. In the past two or three years, moreover, the emergence of a new generation of Chicana/o warriors has become increasingly visible, particularly in the Midwest and in California. Navarro poses to them the challenge of picking up where their elders left off and continuing the struggle for Chicano/a liberation. Venceremos!

Mario C. Compean

Preface

Overview of the Book

No other period in American political history produced as many diverse social movements as did the epoch of protest. For purposes of analysis, I will define this era as beginning in 1955 with the Montgomery bus boycott and concluding in 1972 with the decline of most of the movements that had emerged during the preceding seventeen years. The vortex of discontent led American politics into a dynamic, tumultuous, and radical epoch that generated divergent reform and radical social movements—the civil rights, New Left, Vietnam antiwar, Black Power, and Chicano movements.[1] Furthermore, out of the dynamism of the Chicano movement (CM), the Chicano Youth Movement (CYM) and the Mexican American Youth Organization (MAYO) emerged. Using protest strategies and tactics, these movements audaciously challenged the prevailing American social order's creed, institutions, policies, and even culture.

The epoch of protest was particularly significant for Chicanos because it unleashed the historical forces that gave rise to the CM. As will be explained, the CM was a product of exogenous (external) and endogenous (internal) antagonisms. These antagonisms caused an unprecedented contagion of activism, militancy, and radicalism. The barrios of Aztlan[2] came alive with a spirit of activism, a plethora of new leaders and organizations, a cultural renaissance, and an unequivocal determination to break free from the yoke of poverty, powerlessness, and injustice. "Social change," "Viva la raza," and "Chicano Power," among others, were terms that embellished the movement's cultural-nationalist rhetoric. For some the CM was a reformist call for inclusion in the "American dream" connoting change, equal opportunity, cultural pluralism, and empowerment. For others, however, the CM was a radical repudiation of this nation's political and economic systems in favor of the establishment of a Chicano nation, Aztlan. Added to these two extremes were other perceptions of what "La Causa" meant, rendering the Chicano movement heterogeneous in makeup and direction.

The CM produced a submovement, the CYM. No other sector within the CM contributed more to its "militantization" than the CYM did. It was the youth in the barrios and universities of Aztlan that became the avant-garde of the CM. Although other sectors were involved (e.g., campesinos, workers, professionals, etc.), it was the youths who became the most powerful, energizing force of activism, radicalism, and change. Through their dedication, sacrifice, and idealism, they helped awaken and politicize a Chicano community caught in a quasi slumber of internal colonialism. It was Chicano youths who joined the other youths of America to create an unprecedented epoch of protest, militancy, and extralegal radical activism. Thus, the CYM as a progeny of the CM influenced the emergence and formation of MAYO.

The CM gave life to MAYO in the fertile ground of Texas. Through its constituency of both students and barrio youth, MAYO became one of the most activist and change-oriented groups to emerge during the epoch of protest. Numerous Chicano student and youth groups were formed during this era, but none equaled MAYO's audacity, militancy, and zeal for change. Its "creativity of action" was indicative of the many issues it dealt with, such as education, political empowerment, and various community social problems. No other Chicano organization was more involved in educational reform than was MAYO. This was illustrated in the many school boycotts it initiated during the late sixties and early seventies. In addition, MAYO demonstrated "creativity of action toward political empowerment by playing a principal role in organizing the Raza Unida party (RUP) in Texas. In fact, its role as precursor to the RUP created the circumstances that led to MAYO's demise in 1972.

Organization of the Book

The book is an in-depth case study on MAYO. It consists of an introduction, chapters on the CM and CYM, five chapters that constitute the body of the study on MAYO, and an epilogue. In addition, an appendix contains documents germane to the case study.

The introduction provides a brief and general overview of theories on social movements, synthesizing the literature on the various theories that purport to explain the causes of social movements. Moreover, it sets forth a paradigm on the etiology of the CM as a basis of analysis. The paradigm attributes the CM's emergence to exogenous and endogenous antagonisms. Because MAYO was a creation primarily of endogenous antagonisms, instances of the former category are merely mentioned and not examined, whereas endogenous antagonisms are thoroughly analyzed in the ensuing two chapters.

Chapter 1 provides a historical analysis on the various endogenous antagonisms that played a significant role in fostering the climate for change necessary to produce the CM, CYM, and MAYO. Each contributing endogenous antagonism is identified, and a brief but thorough historical analysis is provided. The chapter includes analyses of the CM's history of resistance, the impact of the immigration exodus, and Chicano demographic spread, as well as a socioeconomic profile of the Chicano community during the epoch of protest. Furthermore, the analysis includes the submovements of Reies Lopez Tijerina, Cesar Chavez, and Rodolfo "Corky" Gonzales. Together, these antagonisms catalyzed the formation of the CM.

The Chicano Youth Movement is the topic of Chapter 2. In itself, the CYM became a major endogenous antagonism to the CM. This chapter examines the following historical antecedents to the CYM: the historical roots of the CYM (1920s and 1930s); the emergence of the Mexican-American Movement in the late thirties to its demise in 1952; the changing conditions of the United States following World War II; and the calm-before-the-storm years (early sixties) that helped set the stage for the emergence of the CYM in 1967.

With the preceding chapters serving as a theoretical and historical framework for the analysis of MAYO, Chapter 3 introduces MAYO as an organization. It provides a historical analysis of MAYO's creation by five young Chicano activists called Los Cinco. Beyond examining MAYO's views on what Los Cinco called the "gringo power structure" of Texas, the chapter examines MAYO's purpose, goals, and objectives; pragmatic quasi ideology; unconventional protest strategies and tactics; decentralized structure; collective leadership; and gender factor, as well as the role of its organizing newspapers.

In Chapter 4 I examine MAYO's perspective on educational change. Integral to the analysis is the proposition that no other Chicano organization during the epoch of protest was as active and committed to bringing about educational change as MAYO was. To illustrate this point, I provide mini–case studies of three MAYO-induced school boycotts: Edcouch-Elsa (1968), Kingsville (1969), and Crystal City (1969–1970). Of the numerous school walkouts MAYO was involved in, these three were the most important in catapulting it into its role as the avant-garde of the CM in Texas.

MAYO's early social change activities, its participation in conferences, and its struggle to acquire resources for its organizing efforts are examined in Chapter 5. A brief account is provided of the Del Rio incident, which resulted in attacks on MAYO by some of its adversaries and its loss of financial resources. The implications of Jose Angel Gutierrez's infamous "Kill the Gringo" press conference statement are also examined. This chapter shows how MAYO was able to intensify its social change efforts in spite of being under severe scrutiny and attack.

In Chapter 6 I examine MAYO's political empowerment agenda. In particular, the chapter traces Gutierrez's efforts to convince MAYO's leaders that their organization should form a Chicano political party in Texas. In addition, a brief account of MAYO's involvement in the 1969 San Antonio City Council elections is presented. MAYO ran candidates under the guise of the "Committee for *Barrio* Betterment" against the Anglo-controlled political machine of the "Good Government League," an effort that served as preparation for MAYO's most comprehensive political empowerment and community control plan of action, the Winter Garden Project. A short case study is provided on its implementation, which resulted in the second Crystal City electoral revolt and the emergence of the RUP.

Chapter 7 analyzes how MAYO's success in forming the RUP in Texas actually led to its own demise. Specifically, the chapter examines the genesis of the RUP, the Winter Garden Project electoral revolt, and the decline and demise of MAYO in 1972.

Finally, the epilogue highlights MAYO's unique orientation and explains its contributions both to Texas and to Chicano political history. The MAYO leaders and spokespersons whom I interviewed present their perspectives on MAYO's contributions to Chicanos in Texas and Aztlan and the reasons for the organization's decline. A brief analysis is provided on the era following the epoch of protest, the "Vivo Yo Generation," and the implications of resurrecting the CM in the nineties.

Research Methodology

This case study of MAYO presents the most extensive research yet done on the subject. A large portion of the research was conducted in 1973 while I was working on my dissertation, "El Partido de la Raza Unida in Crystal City: A Peaceful Revolution." The dissertation was a case study of the RUP and its "political takeover" of Crystal City's city council and school board. However, it also dealt with MAYO. In fact, it included four chapters that examined numerous aspects of MAYO's history, development, and role in the formation of the RUP. The dissertation was actually two case studies in one.

As for the research methodology, the present case study on MAYO relies on both primary and secondary sources. Specifically, I used four research methods: (1) in-depth interviews; (2) documentary content analysis; (3) participant observations; and (4) consultation of numerous secondary sources such as articles and newspapers. In 1973 I conducted fifty-one in-depth interviews with RUP's leaders in Crystal City and statewide. To update the research on MAYO, I conducted an additional eighteen interviews in 1993. I interviewed MAYO's four founders (Jose Angel Gutierrez, Mario Compean, Nacho Perez, and Juan Patlan), as well as the last MAYO state chairperson, Alberto Luera, and national chairperson, Carlos Guerra. Other MAYO leaders, such as Lupe Youngblood, Rudy "Flaco" Rodriguez, Edgar Lozano, and Daniel Bustamante, were also interviewed. To ascertain the role that Chicanas played in MAYO's development, I interviewed the following MAYO spokespersons: Luz Gutierrez, Rosie Castro, Choco Meza, Viviana Santiago, Juanita Bustamante, and Irma Mireles.

I used content analysis for primary sources such as documents, letters, diaries, position papers, and so on. While conducting research on the RUP and MAYO, I lived in Crystal City for four months in 1973. During that time Jose Angel Gutierrez gave me access to the RUP archives. In addition, as a participant/observer I was given the opportunity to attend numerous meetings, social functions, rallies, and press conferences both in Crystal City and in San Antonio. Finally, I thoroughly researched the literature on both RUP and MAYO, consequently incorporating numerous secondary sources such as books and articles into the study.

In researching and writing this case study on MAYO, I sought to be as thorough as possible in presenting an accurate account of its rise and fall. This is the most comprehensive study done on MAYO to date. However, under no circumstances am I stating that this is *the* definitive study. Although my research covers many topics related to MAYO, much more research is needed to recapture the full breadth of its activities and contributions to the Chicano struggle for empowerment and change in Texas and throughout Aztlan.

Acknowledgments

I am indebted to a number of people for both their inspiration and their assistance in the preparation of this study. I am indebted for inspiration to those Chicanos and Chicanas who have struggled to empower the Chicano community and improve its quality of life. I thank leaders such as Reies Lopez Tijerina, Cesar Chavez, Rodolfo "Corky" Gonzales, and Jose Angel Gutierrez, who through their struggles influenced my decision to become an "activist social engineer" in the late sixties.

But I am especially beholden to Jose Angel Gutierrez for the generous assistance and support he gave to me and my family during our four-month stay in Crystal City in 1973. While I was in Crystal City, he and his former wife, Luz, and numerous other RUP and MAYO leaders and supporters made it possible for me to have access to people and information that allowed me to complete my research. My thanks to the people of Crystal City, who treated me and my family as if we were *familia* and not strangers from California. I want to thank Alberto Luera, Mario Compean, and the other MAYO leaders and spokespersons for their accessibility and willingness to be interviewed and reinterviewed.

I am also grateful for the patience of and sacrifices made by my wife, Maria, who typed my dissertation, and my children, Armando III, Maria Antonieta, Miguel Antonio, Orlando, and Xavier Angel. In addition, my thanks go to my brother Alfonso, sisters Delia, Gloria, and Lydia, nieces and nephews, and uncles, who have always been a source of support and encouragement. I cannot forget my friends, who have for many years stood by me through both the good and the hard times, but especially through the latter.

Moreover, my acknowledgments could not be complete without making reference to the people who, through their input and work, made the completion of this study possible. To scholars Rudy Acuña, Carlos Muñoz, and Ronald Chilcote I wish to express my heartfelt appreciation for their invaluable suggestions, which improved the quality of this book. My personal appreciation and gratitude go to Mary Ann Gonzales for the countless hours she spent in editing and preparing the manuscript. My sincere thanks to Marcela Ruiz, who typed and retyped the manuscript, and Pamela Norman, who assisted Mary Ann in editing and preparing the final manuscript.

I want to acknowledge also various persons at the University of California at Riverside for the support and encouragement given to me. I am truly obliged to the Ethnic Studies Department chairperson, Clifford Trafzer, and his administrative assistant, Eufemia Reyes Moore, for their administrative and moral support. No acknowledgment would be complete without mentioning the input and support from my dissertation committee, which included Ronald Chilcote, Carlos Cortes, and Ronald Loveridge. Lastly, I offer a thank you to UCR chancellor Raymond Orbach; to UCR vicechancellor James Erickson; to former UCR dean of humanities and social sciences Brian Copenhaver, now provost at UCLA; and to interim dean Carl Cranor for being constant sources of encouragement and support.

From left to right: PASO state chairperson Albert Fuentes, Young Republican state chairperson Kenneth Ferguson, U.S. senator John G. Tower, and chair of PASO's Texas A&I chapter Jose Angel Gutierrez. This photograph was taken in 1965 at a meeting in Kingsville, Texas, where these individuals happened to cross paths. *(All photos in this section are courtesy of Jose Angel Gutierrez.)*

MAYO spokesman Jose Angel Gutierrez *(left)* and Texas state senator Joe Bernal. This picture was taken in the summer of 1968 while Gutierrez worked for Bernal as his legislative assistant. Gutierrez had recently started work on a Ph.D. in goverment at the University of Texas, Austin.

Cuidadanos Unidos member Ramon Flores *(left)* and Ralph Guzman, a political scientist from the University of California, Santa Cruz. Guzman was addressing a Sunday meeting of Cuidadanos Unidos during the spring of 1970 at the Sociedad Funeraria Miguel Hidalgo in Crystal City.

Boycotting students performing their daily ritual of prayer and the Pledge of Allegiance during the Crystal City walkout of December 1969.

After having prayed and recited the Pledge of Allegiance, boycotting students marched from the Crystal City High School through the downtown barrios to their alternative school sites.

Severita Lara, boycotting students' leader; this photograph was taken ten years later in Crystal City in 1979 during a march commemorating the 1969 walkout. Behind Lara, in dark glasses, is Elva Castillo.

Pickets against Libby, McNiel, & Libby in Hartford, Wisconsin, in the summer of 1968. On the far left are MAYO members Arturo Gonzales and Rudolfo Palomo. Subsequently, both were elected to the Crystal City School District board under the aegis of the Raza Unida party. Addressing the protesters is Jesus Salas, also from Crystal City.

From left to right: Raza Unida party Crystal City mayor Francisco Benavides, Councilman Paulino Mata, Councilman Santos Nieto, City Manager Bill Richy, and City Attorney Jessie Gamez at a city council meeting in 1970.

A demonstration rally during the MAYO conference at La Lomita at Mission, Texas, in December 1969. Facing the crowd, from left to right: Mario Compean, Carlos Guerra, and, speaking, Ramon Tijerina, Reies Lopez Tijerina's brother.

Director of the Migrant Health Center Luz Gutierrez and United Farm Workers' president Cesar Chavez. This photo was taken in March 1971 during Chavez's visit to Crystal City in support of the RUP's efforts.

In the center of the photograph is RUP state chairperson Mario Compean addressing protesters prior to occupying the state capitol at Austin in 1972. The protest was in response to unfair funding of primarily Chicano school districts.

From right to left: RUP founder Jose Angel Gutierrez, unidentified individual, future RUP gubernatorial candidate Ramsey Muñiz, and Texas state representative Matt Garcia. This photograph was taken during the MAYO-RUP occupation of the office of Charles Purnell, chief of staff for Texas governor Dolph Briscoe.

At the center of the photograph is MAYO spokesperson and RUP founder
Jose Angel Gutierrez addressing an RUP rally in 1971 for Crystal City's
city council and school board elections. Student walkout leaders Diana
Serna is second from the left, and standing behind Gutierrez is Erasmo
Andrade.

RUP gubernatorial candidate Ramsey Muñiz addressing the RUP National
Convention held in El Paso in 1972.

Introduction. Paradigm for the Etiology of the Chicano Movement

Out of the vortex of discontent, the epoch of protest (1955–1972) gave rise to various social movements (SMs), all seeking to change this nation's institutions, laws, policies, and culture. Ours was a society caught up in a whirlwind of constant dialectical change. Seldom, if ever, has this nation witnessed so many movements, each seeking to advance its cause. None of these movements sought to prevent change or advocated a repressive change; they all propounded a form of change that was either reformist or revolutionary in scope and orientation. All these movements variously influenced or complemented one another in their attempts to change American society.

To understand the Mexican American Youth Organization (MAYO), then, it is important to understand the relationships among the divergent movements of the epoch of protest. As a political phenomenon, MAYO was the by-product of the Chicano movement (CM) and, later, of the Chicano Youth Movement (CYM); in turn, both of these movements resulted from internal and external antagonisms. The identification and analysis of these two types of antagonisms lie at the heart of my paradigm. To provide the reader with some information pertinent to this paradigm, I will analyze briefly the phenomenon of SMs and introduce some of the theories that purport to explain their origins.

Social Movements: Vehicles of Change

The literature on social movements contains a profusion of definitions, concepts, and theoretical approaches, many of which contradict one another. Nonetheless, any paradigm that attempts to explain the CM must first deal with SMs generally. Noted sociologist Herbert Blumer defined SMs as "collective enterprises oriented towards establishing a new order of life." He then divided them into three classes: general, specific, and expressive.[1] In his classic work, *Social Movements: An Introduction to Political Sociology*, Rudolf Heberle described an SM as aiming "to bring about fundamental changes in the social order, especially in the basic institutions of property and labor relationships." Heberle viewed SMs as a kind of "social collective."[2] More recently, scholars James Wood and Maurice Jackson defined SMs as "unconventional groups that have varying degrees of formal organization and that attempt to produce or prevent revolutionary or reformist types of change."[3]

SMs are inextricably linked to the phenomenon of dialectical change. John Wilson writes that SMs are inherent to the constant turmoil of dialectical change: "This turmoil relentlessly transfigures the pattern of relations between the various classes, ethnic groups, generations, and regional groups which make up society. . . . Society might always be seen, then, as constantly in the process of becoming something else."[4] Consequently, driven by an agenda for change, SMs are dynamic forces that spur one social order to evolve into another. Societies are not inert entities disturbed only occasionally by unrest. They are volatile wholes embracing discordant ideas, opposing interests, and competing groups. SMs are one way in which these various factions influence one another and the society that comprises them.

The lack of "definitional consensus" notwithstanding, I will use the following characterization based on various definitions found in the literature: An SM is a conscious, collective, and organized attempt to bring about or resist large-scale change within the existing social order using conventional and unconventional methods. Inherent to this definition are various other complementary characteristics. Most definitions of SMs stress that, besides being change oriented and involving a collective, they constitute an emerging and temporary form. In fact, when an SM becomes permanent, it ceases to be an SM. Movements are explicitly goal directed and are constantly either succeeding or failing to meet their objectives. SMs differ from more stable, routinized organizations in that they exist almost entirely through their activity rather than through a defined organizational structure.[5] Moreover, SMs are vehicles through which new ideas and practices enter the fabric of the social order. They can articulate either hope or despair. SMs are not sporadic or inconsequential upheavals. They have acted as the impetus or catalyst for social change throughout history. Thus, SMs have been the seedbeds of new political orders, as well as the caretakers of existing ones.[6]

Theories of SMs: An Overview

SMs do not arise unless there is a climate for change. Revolutionary or reformist movements are not products of spontaneity or haphazardness. Multifarious conditions must come together to create a climate of change. SMs spring from and are nurtured by human responses to changing political, cultural, social, and economic conditions.[7] There is a bonanza of literature in the social sciences on the etiology of SMs, especially those dealing with revolutionary change; the theories found therein identify various economic, psychological, political, and social preconditions. Theorists such as Marx, Tocqueville, Brinton, and others ascribe social change to economic factors. The Marxist theory of social change assumes an economic determinism predicated on dialectical materialism. Social change for Marx, Engels, and their apostles—Lenin, Trotsky, Mao Tse-tung, Guevara, Castro—is based on class struggle between the bourgeoisie and proletariat. Marx wrote, "If revolutions are the locomotives of history, class struggles are the locomotives of revolution."[8] For Marxists, revolutionary SMs emerge during times of progressively deteriorating economic conditions. In other words, Marx believed that a social revolution will take place when "productive forces" come into conflict with the "relations of production."[9] In this account, the proletariat is subjected to progressive and ultimately intolerable degradation, which causes it to revolt against the ruling class.

Countering the Marxist "misery theory" of social change is Tocqueville's "prosperity theory." Tocqueville wrote:

> Revolutions are not always brought about by a gradual decline from bad to worse. Nations that have endured patiently and almost unconsciously the most overwhelming oppression often burst into rebellion against the yoke the moment it begins to get lighter. The regime which is destroyed by revolution is almost always an improvement on its immediate predecessor. . . .
> Evils which are patiently endured when they seem inevitable become intolerable when once the idea of escape from them is suggested.[10]

He based his thesis on a long review of the economic and social conditions that preceded the French Revolution of 1789. France had gone through a period of economic decline in the seventeenth century followed by dynamic growth in the eighteenth. For Tocqueville, the climate is propitious for change when economic conditions have worsened and then dramatically improved.

Historian Crane Brinton, while studying the old regimes and revolutions of England, the United States, France, and Russia, echoed Tocqueville's prosperity theory of revolution. In writing on some of the uniformities of these revolutions, he wrote:

> These were all societies on the whole on the upgrade economically before the revolution came, and the revolutionary movements seem to originate in the discontents of not unprosperous people who feel restraint, cramp, annoyance, rather than downright oppression. Certainly these revolutions are not started by down-and-outers, by starving, miserable people. These revolutionists are not worms turning, not children of despair. These revolutions are born of hope, and their philosophies are formally optimistic.[11]

In other words, Brinton claims that it is not the poor and oppressed who create a climate of change; on the contrary, such a climate results from those who are achieving or have achieved some success (e.g., the intelligentsia) and who believe that their progress is impeded by existing conditions for which the current regime is responsible.

Most Western theorists of revolution have sided with Tocqueville. In his J-curve theory, however, James Davies combines a long-term Tocquevillian improvement followed by a short-term Marxist deterioration.[12] He postulates that revolutions are most likely to occur when a prolonged period of economic and social development is followed by a short period of reversal. Essentially, Davies argues that revolutions do not occur during periods of prolonged and increasing poverty. To the contrary, they occur when the bonds of oppression are loosened and some prosperity sets in, when the people's expectations continue to rise, only to be reversed by some socioeconomic development.[13] The widespread feelings of discontent, frustration, and anger that result predispose a society to pursue massive social change.

Some scholars studying the etiology of SMs have focused on a more psychological approach. For proponents of this approach, frustration and discontent are the by-products that generate social movements. In his book *Why Men Rebel*, Ted Robert Gurr uses a sociopsychological approach to the study of collective behavior. Predicating his account on Dollard's frustration-aggression theory,

Gurr develops the notion of "relative deprivation" to explain the etiology of revolution. He describes this concept as "people's perception of discrepancy between their value expectations (aspirations) and value capabilities (achievement)." Value expectations are the goods and conditions of life to which people believe they are rightfully entitled. Value capabilities are the goods and conditions people think they are capable of attaining or maintaining. Phrased differently, relative deprivation means the gap between what people have or expect to have and what they feel they are capable of having. However, whether relative deprivation explodes into actual violence is a function of two sets of intervening variables: (a) the scope and intensity of normative (historical, cultural, ideological) justifications for violence as well as men's perception of the effectiveness and utility of violence in solving social problems; and (b) the relative physical strength of the contending parties as well as their ability to provide institutionalized, peaceful alternatives to violent expression of discontent.[14]

The economic and psychological theories concur that pervasive discontent and frustration are essential preconditions to a climate for change. Eric Hoffer said, "For men to plunge headlong into an undertaking of vast change, they must be intensely discontented yet not destitute." Regarding frustration, he wrote, "To the frustrated a mass movement offers substitutes either for the whole self or for the elements which make life bearable and which they cannot evoke out of their individual resources."[15] Community organizing theories also incorporate discontent as an intrinsic variable of their frameworks. Saul Alinsky, in his two major works, *Reveille for Radicals* and *Rules for Radicals*, stressed the importance of discontent as a precondition for organizing communities. He declared that the organizer's role is to rub raw the sores of discontent.[16] Lee Staples complements Alinsky by saying that "the organizer doesn't simply assess dissatisfaction in the neutral fashion but helps maximize the existing anger."[17] Lyle Schaller, in *The Change Agent*, also elaborates on the paramount role discontent plays in community organizing. From Hoffer's macroanalysis of mass movements to Alinsky's more focused perspectives of community organizing, the message is the same: change comes not from people who are complacent, satisfied, and passive but from those who are frustrated, angry, and motivated by rising expectations.

The notion of social preconditions underlies numerous general theories on the etiology of SMs. Smelsor bases his theory of collective behavior on a social-structural approach, focusing on six social-structural conditions that lead to the development of SMs: structural conduciveness, structural strain, growth and spread of generalized belief, precipitating factors, mobilization of participants for action, and the weakening of social control.[18] The occurrence of all six simultaneously constitutes a sufficient or predicative condition for the rise of an SM. However, high levels of all six conditions must exist if an SM is to emerge.[19]

Chalmers Johnson's theory of change assumes a structural functionalist perspective, which deals with concepts of structure, process, function, role, status, and system.[20] Johnson's structural functionalism is basically Parsonian in its contention that the social system's vital functions consist of socialization, goal attainment, and integration. The social system itself is conceptualized as a self-sufficient, self-regulatory equilibrium.[21] Although Johnson's theory is complex, he simplifies it by identifying three ingredients necessary to produce a climate of change: power deflation, loss of authority, and an accelerator. Johnson argues that once the system reaches a period of "chronic disequilibrium," the stage is set for revolution. Power deflation occurs when the power holders can no longer rule and maintain order without using force. When the power holders cannot resynchronize the system by purposive public policy, they experience a loss of authority. Nonetheless, it is the accelerator that undermines the power holders' authority and constitutes the final and proximate cause for a revolution.[22]

The literature on the etiology of SMs is profuse, but regardless of their theoretical analysis, SMs are products of discontent. It is when people are dissatisfied with their circumstances and motivated by rising expectations that a society begins to produce a climate for change. In addition, it is not the poor and dispossessed who become the vanguard for change but rather the intelligentsia, those who feel that society is not meeting their expectations. SMs are conceived in the womb of discontent and nurtured by a climate for change that is rampant with frustration, anger, and hope.

Paradigm on the Etiology of the Chicano Movement

The literature on the CM is bountiful in description but lacking in theory. My paradigm combines both. I contend that the CM was a product of relative deprivation. The presence of unfulfilled expectations among Chicanos fostered a heightened level of frustration that in turn created the discontent that led to the CM. With U.S. society in a state of turmoil and conflict, the CM was nurtured by manifold contradictions that were produced by clashing antagonisms.

What are antagonisms? As previously explained, SMs are not conceived in isolation. Certain historical conditions and ingredients must be present before an SM can emerge. SMs develop only in social systems subject to dysfunctionality and disequilibrium. In *Revolutionary Change,* using a structural functionalist approach, Chalmers Johnson writes, "Since an equilibrium system is not a changing system, a changing system is one that is out of balance." Antagonisms are what produce the imbalance or dysfunctions within the social system. They come in varied forms: historical events, the passage of laws, increasing repression, the emergence of charismatic leaders, and so on. SMs never develop in social systems that are in balance.

Antagonisms can give rise to an SM. They can, either individually or in combination, produce pressure and conflict within the social system such that the demands placed on it by the SM are met. If they are not, the system faces the possibility of further dysfunctionality. Antagonisms can act as either "accelerators" or "precipitants" in giving rise to the conditions that create, impel, and organize an SM.[23] They help to create a climate for change necessary for an SM to emerge. Seldom if ever does a single antagonism generate enough discontent to create an SM. Only when they dialectically feed off one another do antagonisms yield the crop of chronic discontent that nourishes an SM.

The emergence of the CM and CYM and the formation of MAYO resulted from multiple antagonisms, both endogenous and exogenous. The endogenous antagonisms were historical phenomena that emanated within the Chicano community, whereas exogenous antagonisms originated outside it. Initially the CM was influenced more by exogenous than by the endogenous antagonisms, whereas with MAYO the opposite was true. I do not believe that the CM, CYM, or MAYO would have emerged or taken on such militant and radical postures if it had not been for the internal or external forces that permeated American society during this time. These entities, conceived out of an epoch of protest, challenged the contradictions of U.S. domestic and foreign policies.

The following chart illustrates and identifies what I feel were the most salient and important endogenous and exogenous antagonisms that gave rise to the CM, CYM, and MAYO.

Exogenous	*Endogenous*
Civil rights movement	History of Chicano resistance
New Left	Demographic growth
Antiwar movement	Changing socioeconomic profile
Black Power movement	Tijerina and the Alianza
Foreign movements	Chavez and the UFW
War on Poverty	Gonzales and the Crusade

An interdependency developed among these antagonisms. As historical forces, they influenced one another. In some cases one antagonism created another. In addition, the exogenous influenced the endogenous and vice versa. These changes occurred because of the internal contradictions inherent to each. Neither a Marxist nor a Hegelian analysis is needed to assert that these antagonisms were actuated by a dialectical historical process within the epoch of protest that generated changes in political ideas and strategies. For example, the *Brown vs. Board of Education* Supreme Court decision of 1954 contributed significantly to the rise and activism of the civil rights movement (CRM). In turn, the CRM gave impetus to the emergence of the New Left. As the war in Vietnam escalated, the New Left was instrumental in the development of the Vietnam antiwar movement. Finally, these multiple antagonisms gave form to the Black Power movement. Thus, with each antagonism in the epoch of protest there was a thesis, antithesis, and synthesis, with each successive antagonism constituting a higher form of radicalism.

1. The Chicano Movement: Impact of Endogenous Antagonisms

Chicanos became an intrinsic part of the mosaic of movements decorating the U.S. political landscape during the epoch of protest (1955–1972). Chicanos lashed out in an unprecedented fashion against what they perceived to be forces of oppression, exploitation, and racism—this nation's political and economic systems. The frustration, discontent, and anger that were rampant among Chicano activists can be understood in the context of the following observation: "The fortunes of the United States are closely tied in to the misfortunes of the Chicano."[1] Considered by some to be foreigners in their own land, Chicanos during the epoch of protest forged their own social movement—the Chicano movement (CM).

Never before in the political history of the Chicano community had such a movement existed. Although Chicano historians like Acuña describe the Chicano struggle since 1846 as one of resistance, the reality is that at no time were Chicanos as vociferous and resolute in their resistance as they were during the era of the CM. The old stereotypes of Chicanos as passive, docile, *mañana*-oriented, and incapable of organization were shattered by a renaissance of activism, militancy, and cultural pride. This renaissance of resistance oriented toward change and empowerment propelled the CM. During its brief existence, the CM spawned a great many organizations, leaders, and direct actions. In this chapter I provide an analysis and historical overview of the endogenous antagonisms that contributed to the CYM's and MAYO's emergence from the CM.

Chicano History: A Struggle of Resistance

The CM had deep roots in a history that was characterized by resistance to oppression and exploitation. With the exception of Native Americans, Puerto Ricans, and Hawaiians, no other ethnic group in American politics became a part of the United States through war and conquest. From the conclusion of the Mexican War (1846–1848) to the epoch of protest, Chicanos were subjected to a debilitating form of internal colonialism and suffered from poverty, powerlessness, destruction of culture, and racism. Numerous Chicano scholars, such as Rodolfo Acuña, Mario Barrera, Carlos Muñoz, and others, have posited such an analysis.[2] For these writers, the barrios of Aztlan were internal colonies. Acuña wrote, "The conquest of the Southwest created a colonial situation in the traditional sense— with the Mexican land and population being controlled by an imperialistic United States."[3]

Even though some would question the validity of internal colonialism as a conceptual framework for examining the "Chicano experience," Chicanos nevertheless have been victims of exploitation, oppression, and powerlessness since the conquest of Aztlan by the United States in 1848. While in theory the Treaty of Guadalupe Hidalgo was supposed to have protected and guaranteed the property and civil rights of Chicanos, in practice it became a treaty of broken promises. In the face of this heinous historical reality, Chicanos resisted their status using a variety of methods and forms. For purposes of analysis, I will divide Chicano history from 1848 to the epoch of protest into three different but interrelated and overlapping periods: (1) the epoch of resistance (1846–1915); (2) the epoch of accommodation (1916–1945); and (3) the epoch of social action (1946–1965). These three epochs are indicative of Chicano history's dialectical progression that led to the emergence of the CM.[4]

The Epoch of Resistance (1846–1915)

Chicanos during the epoch of resistance struggled for their property, civil, and religious rights using two antithetical weapons, armed self-defense and ballot-box politics. During these years Chicanos' lands were stolen, their rights were denied, and their language was suppressed; further, their opportunities for employment, education, and political representation were consistently thwarted. Some Chicanos resisted the conquest and the manifold inequities that followed using armed self-defense. As the literature on Chicano history points out, Chicano *guerrilleros* (guerrillas) like Joaquin Murrieta, Juan "Cheno" Cortina, and Tiburcio Vasquez, to name a few, violently resisted the conquest and occupation that followed. As historian David Weber said, some Chicanos "lashed out in angry violence."[5]

Other historians saw fit to describe the *guerrilleros* as bandits or outlaws. This interpretation fits British historian Eric J. Hobsbawm's model of a social bandit. For Hobsbawm, the social bandit was ideally a young, unmarried peasant who committed an act that the state regarded as criminal but that most of his peers regarded as justifiable or heroic. The social bandit might take the form of "the noble robber of Robin Hood, the primitive resistance fighter or guerrilla unit."[6] In studying Chicano armed resistance, Carey McWilliams complemented Hobsbawm by saying that "many of the outlaw bands, in fact, contained a hundred or more men and were organized for guerrilla fighting."[7] Leonard Pitt found that "10 to 20 percent of San Quentin inmates from 1854 to 1865 were Mexicans or Californians"; there was thus a much higher proportion of Chicanos in prison than in the statewide population.[8] Thus, from Murrieta in California to Cheno Cortina in Texas, some Chicanos responded to their inequities with the use of violent force.[9]

From the 1870s to 1915 Chicano social banditry declined. This did not mean, however, that Chicanos completely stopped resorting to armed self-defense. Weber writes, "Violent resistance to Anglo domination did not depend solely upon dynamic individuals such as Murrieta and Cortina. The entire Mexican American community took action when its vital interests were threatened." He alluded to the El Paso Salt War of 1877 and the emergence of Las Gorras Blancas (White Caps). Chicanos fought for their interests in both of these instances. In particular, Las Gorras Blancas used force in defense of their property. "They fought a guerrilla war in Moza, Santa Fe, and San Miguel counties that reached its peak in 1890."[10] In 1915 the use of armed resistance culminated in El Plan de San Diego. Although the plan was unsuccessful, it called for an armed insurrection by Chicanos in collaboration with African Americans and Native Americans that would result in a separate Chicano republic or the reintegration of the Southwest with Mexico.[11] All these historical examples suggest that Chicanos during this epoch were not passive or indolent and that from time to time they resorted to armed resistance against the system's inequities.

Concomitantly, Chicanos during the epoch of resistance used ballot-box politics to counter or deal with the many issues affecting them. Some Chicanos accommodated themselves pragmatically to the conquest. They adopted the new culture, worked within the system's institutions, and became politically involved. Some sought acculturation, while others opted for total assimilation. In the aftermath of the war with Mexico, some Chicanos became politically involved, especially in southern California, New Mexico, the Rio Grande Valley of Texas, and southern Arizona. In California, although Chicanos helped to draft the state's constitution and were involved in local politics, by the 1870s they were largely out of the political picture.[12] In South Texas the same situation essentially prevailed, whereas in Arizona some Chicanos were politically active in the Tucson area. A few Chicano elites participated in all these states, but most members of the Chicano community were nonparticipants in ballot-box politics.

The exception to this exclusion was New Mexico. Chicano *políticos* dominated the key elective office of territorial delegate from 1850 to 1911 and controlled the territorial legislature at least through the 1880s. Even in the ensuing years, Chicanos continued to be well represented until New Mexico became a state in 1912. Up to 1859 all sessions of the state legislature were held in Spanish. In addition, in 1897 Miguel Antonio Otero was elected governor, a position he held for nine years. Even as late as 1910, 35 of the 100 delegates to the constitutional convention were Chicanos. When New Mexico became a state in 1912, its constitution officially recognized both Spanish and English.[13] Thus, by 1915 Chicano resistance through ballot-box politics was essentially limited to New Mexico.

The Epoch of Accommodation (1915–1945)

The epoch of accommodation was an extension of the spirit of accommodation that to a large extent lay behind the use of ballot-box politics during the preceding epoch. A major difference in this epoch was that Chicano resistance relied not on armed self-defense or ballot-box politics but on organization as the main vehicle for adaptation, integration, and change. Chicanos during these years organized to improve their situations and to advance and protect their interests and rights. With increasing numbers emigrating from Mexico, the new immigrants and indigenous Chicanos engendered an unprecedented organizational buildup, the roots of which went back to the 1870s through the 1890s with the emergence of Chicano fraternal or mutual benefit societies, such as Club Recíproco in Texas (1880s) and La Alianza Hispana Americana in Arizona (1893).[14]

This organizational buildup culminated in the 1920s with the formation of other Chicano organizations. Fraternal organizations such as the Sociedad Progresista Mexicana in California, the Liga Protectora Latina in Arizona, the Liga Protectora Mexicana in Kansas, and others were particularly commonplace, especially among the newly arrived Mexican immigrants. It was during these years that Chicano civil rights– and reform-oriented organizations began to emerge. In 1921 La Orden de los Hijos de America (Order of the Sons of America) was formed, followed by its replacement in 1928 by the

League of United Latin American Citizens (LULAC). Both organizations sought to protect the rights of Chicanos by promoting the "virtues" of integration and assimilation.[15]

Unions were the third type of organization that became vehicles of Chicano resistance. From the early 1900s to the depression era, Chicanos became an integral part of the union struggle. According to Acuña, "The Great Depression of the 1930's only intensified the Chicano's struggle within the labor movement."[16] Facing increasing problems, Chicanos in 1938 formed the Mexican Congress in an attempt to strengthen their capabilities for change.

Politically, Chicanos other than those in New Mexico were still powerless during the epoch of accommodation. Juan Gomez-Quiñonez explains New Mexico's unique status:

> The Mexican political experience in New Mexico continued to be unique in comparison to other states. Because of the state's relatively large percentage of Mexican American population, Mexican politicians could wield significant political power at the state and federal levels of government. In New Mexico, Mexicans were actively courted by both parties because occasionally in the past they had provided a swing vote. Furthermore, leadership tended to be both continuous and stable. Voter turnout was enhanced by the greater percentage of adult citizens and local vote-delivering networks.[17]

No other state had produced the number of Chicano elected officials that New Mexico had. Dennis I. Chavez, for example, served in the state house of representatives during the 1920s. From 1930 to 1935 he served in the U.S. House of Representatives as one of New Mexico's two congressmen. He was then elected to the U.S. Senate in 1935 and served there until 1962. In 1942 Antonio Fernandez followed Chavez to the U.S. House of Representatives. Ceferino Quintana served as lieutenant governor from 1939 to 1942. Elsewhere, however, although by the early 1940s some Chicanos were beginning to be elected in such states as Texas, Arizona, and Colorado, the level of Chicano political representation was still insignificant. Texas, Arizona, and Colorado, although small in population, had more representatives than California.[18]

The Epoch of Social Action (1945–early 1960s)

The epoch of social action witnessed an intensification of change-oriented social action by Chicanos. While Chicanos continued to focus on organizational development and ballot-box politics, they became more adamant in their resistance to the system's inequities, especially to the use of de jure segregation. With the *Salvatierra* desegregation case in Del Rio, Texas, during the 1930s serving as a precedent, LULAC contributed to several schooling and antisegregation decisions, including *Mendez et al.* vs. *Westminster District* (1946) and *Delgado* vs. *Bastrop Independent School District* (1948).[19] These precedents influenced the *Brown* vs. *Board of Education* decision of 1954. Political scientist Ralph Guzman asserted that discrimination in education, housing, police protection, voter registration, and political representation kept the benefit levels for Chicanos well below those of the rest of society.[20] This wartime situation precipitated various attitudinal changes that affected both the Chicano community and American society in general. These changes were brought about by (1) veterans' wartime experiences; (2) greater job opportunities; (3) new educational opportunities (e.g., the GI Bill); (4) more possibilities for social mobility; (5) rising expectations for change; (6) acculturation; and (7) growing urbanization.[21] These factors created a climate for change that gave Chicanos more opportunities than ever before. Furthermore, they triggered Chicano advocacy and action against the issues and problems that had characterized the epochs preceding World War II.

These attitudinal changes created the second organizational awakening during the more activist-oriented epoch of social action. In California, by 1947 the Unity Leagues had been formed in southern California, followed by the formation of the Community Service Organization (CSO) that same year. Both organizations were advocacy- and participation-oriented. By 1959 Chicanos had formed the first statewide political action-oriented organization, the Mexican-American Political Association (MAPA). Its primary mission was to advance Chicano political representation and interests. The organizational awakening also influenced Texas, where it contributed to the formation of the GI Forum, a veterans' advocacy group, in 1948 and, in 1961, the Political Association of Spanish-speaking Organizations (PASO), the counterpart to California's MAPA. Meanwhile, older civil rights and fraternal organizations, such as LULAC and La Alianza Hispana Americana, also helped to promote increased Chicano activism.[22]

The epoch of social action witnessed increased political activity throughout Aztlan. New Mexico continued to lead the other states in ballot-box politics. For example, in 1957 Joseph Montoya won a special election held to fill Fernandez's former seat in the U.S. House of Representatives. Prior to being elected to Congress, he served in the state senate and as lieutenant governor. Meanwhile, Dennis

Table 1. *Spanish-Surnamed State Legislators*

Year	Arizona	California	Colorado	New Mexico	Texas
1950	0	0	0	20	0
1960	4	0	1	20	7
1965	6	0	1	22	6

Source: Figures were determined by consulting the *Book of the States,* Supplement I, *State Elected Officials and the Legislature* (Chicago: Council of State Governments, 1950, 1960, 1965). Figures for these years are approximate and involve the author's determination of Spanish-surnamed legislators by name.

Chavez continued to serve in the U.S. Senate until his death in 1962, at which time he ranked fourth in seniority. In 1964 Montoya was elected to the U.S. Senate. More important, according to Juan Gomez-Quiñonez, "he was the most active advocate for Mexican-Americans."[23]

In California, two years after an unsuccessful attempt in 1947, Edward Roybal was elected to the Los Angeles City Council with the assistance of the CSO. In 1954 he ran unsuccessfully for lieutenant governor. In 1962, however, he was elected as one of California's congressmen, the first Chicano to achieve this. Roybal's counterpart in Texas was Henry B. Gonzales, who was instrumental in forming an advocacy organization in 1947, the Pan American Progressive Association (PAPA). Gonzales was elected to the San Antonio City Council in 1953, ran successfully for the Texas State Senate in 1956, lost a race for the governorship in 1958, and in 1961 was elected to the U.S. House of Representatives.[24] Texans also elected another Chicano, Elizo (Kika) de la Garza, to Congress. Table 1 provides a breakdown of Chicano representation during the sixteen years of the epoch of social action.

Through their renewed use of ballot-box politics, Chicanos sought to influence the results of the 1960 presidential election. The candidacy of John F. Kennedy stimulated political activity among Chicanos, resulting in the formation of the Viva Kennedy clubs.[25] Originating in Texas, these ad hoc political groups spread throughout the Southwest like a prairie fire. Gonzales, Bexar County Commissioner Albert Peña, and his aide Albert Fuentes were the main organizing force behind the Viva Kennedy clubs in Texas. Carlos McCormick of La Alianza Hispana Americana headed the national drive. The clubs played a significant role both in mobilizing the Chicano vote for Kennedy and in forming PASO.[26] Adding to the political momentum created by the Viva Kennedy clubs was the 1964 constitutional amendment abolishing the poll tax. By the early 1960s Chicanos were beginning to experience a political renaissance. The number of Chicanos being elected gradually increased, which resulted in part from the group's rapid population growth, improved organizational capabilities, and growing politicization.

The Exodus: Changing Demographics

The Chicano population growth that preceded the epoch of protest became the second endogenous antagonism helping to form the CM. Carey McWilliams notes that at the conclusion of the Mexican War in 1848, there were perhaps 5,000 Mexicans in Texas, 60,000 in New Mexico, not more than 1,000 in Arizona, and perhaps 7,500 in California.[27] It is no wonder that Mexico lost 1 million square miles of territory to the United States. Without having a strong military and large populations to settle the vast Southwest, Mexico became an easy and vulnerable target for U.S. military aggression acting under the guise of Manifest Destiny. It was not until the late nineteenth century, when the railroad construction, mining, and agribusiness industries faced a labor shortage, that cheap Mexican labor was coveted and Mexican immigration to the United States began to increase. This started a trend that continued until well into the 1960s.

Immigration became the primary force driving the Chicanos' rapid population growth. Since its beginnings in the late 1880s, Mexican immigration to the United States has resulted from a number of push and pull factors that have produced what can be described as an exodus. The Porfiriato dictatorship (1876–1910), the Mexican Revolution of 1910, Mexico's postrevolutionary political instability (1917–1930), its chronic poverty (1880–1960s), and its well-developed railroads heading north were some of the cardinal push factors that helped produce the exodus. American business interests' insatiable hunger for cheap labor became the salient pull factor. The exodus, which brought millions of legal and illegal Mexican immigrants into the United States, occurred in three waves: 1880–1929, 1930–1941, and 1942–1960s.

First Wave (1880–1929)

During the era of the first wave, Mexicans went north to the United States to escape the increasing poverty and political repression stemming from the oppressive Porfiriato. Porfirio Díaz, a despot who governed Mexico from 1876 to 1910 "a pan o a palos" (with bread or with sticks), was the historical antagonism that gave rise to

Table 2. *U.S. Chicano/Mexicano Population*

State	1900	1910	1920	1930
Arizona	14,171	29,987	61,580	114,173
California	8,086	33,694	88,881	368,013
New Mexico	6,649	11,918	20,272	59,340
Texas	71,062	125,016	251,827	683,681

the exodus. Further, by 1908 Mexican railroad connections reached all forty-eight states, making immigration easier.[28] Carey McWilliams writes that "prior to 1900 there had been a trickle of Mexican immigration to the borderlands: Texas had an immigrant population of 71,062 in 1900; Arizona 14,172; California 8,086; New Mexico, 6,649."[29] The outbreak of the Mexican Revolution in 1910 further spurred the exodus. The Chinese Exclusion Act of 1882, coupled with the exclusion of the Japanese in 1907 and the decreasing numbers of European immigrants after World War I, created a powerful demand for cheap foreign labor. Mexico became the obvious source for that labor.

The data in Table 2 clearly show the immigration exodus during the first wave.[30] The U.S. Census Bureau first attempted to estimate the size of the Chicano population during the 1930 census. This census included Chicanos in the category of "Mexican," meaning all persons born in Mexico or having parents born in Mexico who were not definitely of European, African, Native American, or Japanese descent. The total Chicano population in 1930 was 1,422,533—the third largest "racial" group in the nation.[31] This figure includes Mexicans who immigrated to states outside the Southwest. Illinois reported 28,906 Chicanos, virtually all in Chicago. The Chicano population in Michigan was 13,336, with half residing in Detroit. In fact, the 1930 census underestimated the number of Chicanos. For example, it calculated the number of Chicanos in New Mexico at around 59,000, yet a school census put the figure at 202,709.[32] Thus, the Chicano population increased during the decade by 103 percent.[33]

Chicano history texts are full of illustrations of the nativist reaction to Mexican immigration. Acuña in particular traces the suffering and exploitation of the Mexican immigrant. He writes, "Newspapers at the time created an anti-Mexican environment by making Mexicans scapegoats during times of depression." He emphasizes that this pattern of repression would be repeated throughout the twentieth century.[34] During the era of the Mexican Revolution

(1910–1917), nativists responded with great concern to the so-called brown scare. The resurgence of nativism became more evident in restrictionist immigration policies, such as the Immigration Acts of 1917, 1921, and 1924. These acts, designed to stanch the flow of immigration, especially from southern and eastern Europe and Asia, precipitated a political battle between the nativists who wanted to keep the country "Anglo-American" and the business interests that set aside prejudices to obtain low-cost labor. With a quota system in place and a head tax of eight dollars in force, nativists continued to lobby against Mexican immigration.[35]

Congress reflected the nativists' influence in 1925 when it appropriated a million dollars for the formation of the U.S. Border Patrol. This was a significant move by the U.S. government to appease nativists. Prior to the patrol's formation, no force had existed to combat the widespread influx of illegal Mexican immigrants.[36] With increasing Mexican immigration into the country, the Border Patrol grew from 472 in 1926 to 781 in 1928. Nonetheless, in spite of the Border Patrol and restrictionist immigration laws, according to Moore and Pachon, "immigration continued quite steadily until 1929, prompted by an expanding demand in the United States for agricultural labor."[37]

Second Wave (1930–1941)

Instead of continuing the influx, the second wave was a reverse exodus from the United States to Mexico precipitated by a massive repatriation of Mexican immigrants. With the devastating depression that began in the United States in 1929, Mexican immigrants came under more intense attack by nativists. The depression's symptoms of severe unemployment and growing poverty made the Mexican immigrants convenient scapegoats for nativists. Hoffman wrote, "The Mexican workers were among the first to be dismissed from their jobs."[38] With millions of Americans unemployed, cheap domestic labor became available as the great migration from the Dust Bowl to the West began. Anglo urban workers competed vigorously for jobs on the farms and ranches. Thus, the economic pressures of the depression caused the stream of immigrants to dry to a trickle. According to Moore and Pachon, the drop in immigration also reflected massive efforts to send the Mexicans "home," where, it had always been assumed, they "belonged."[39]

During the depression no other ethnic group suffered such humiliating treatment. This was part of a double standard practiced by the federal government toward Mexican immigrants. Historically, when the demand for cheap labor was great, the federal government would cosmetically and rhetorically speak out against illegal immigration, yet it would not rigidly enforce its own restrictionist policies. The depression changed all this. With an unprecedented fervor, the U.S. Border Patrol took on an offensive posture in seeking out illegal immigrants. Meier and Rivera explain the negative effects of the depression on immigration: "From 1931 to 1940 inclusive only about 20,000 Mexicans legally immigrated to the United States, and the border was strictly patrolled to discourage illegal entrants. As a percentage of all immigration to the United States, Mexican immigration dropped from 20 percent in 1927 to about 3 percent in the mid-thirties."[40] Furthermore, Acuña states that whereas "the number of Mexicans entering the United States from 1925 to 1929 was 238,527, from 1930 to 1934 it fell to only 19,200. From 1935 to 1939 the number dropped even further to 8,737."[41] This decline did not soften the attacks of nativists. The depression gave them a platform from which to launch racist attacks against Mexicans throughout the thirties.

This nativist racism became even more apparent when the business interests that had supported Mexican immigration suddenly ceased to act on the immigrants' behalf. The trumpet of racism was heard loud and clear with the U.S. government's repatriation of thousands of Mexicans through both voluntary and involuntary methods. Between the years 1931 and 1934, thousands of Chicanos, many of them American citizens, were returned to Mexico in trains. According to Hoffman, some 400,000 Chicano men, women, and children were repatriated.[42] Some estimates, however, run as high as 600,000. In all, about one-third of the Chicanos who had been counted in the 1930 census were repatriated, about 60 percent of whom were children who had been born in the United States and thus were U.S. citizens.[43] Even the families of naturalized citizens were urged by the U.S. government to repatriate. Thus, the citizenship of U.S.-born children and naturalized citizens was often unrecognized or not taken into account by federal officials.

The repatriation transformed the barrios into communities under siege. No other ethnic or racial group in the United States was treated this way. Basically, the repatriated Chicanos fell into three categories: (1) those deported by the Border Patrol, (2) those who returned voluntarily, and (3) those who were threatened in various ways with deportation and left reluctantly.[44] Meier and Rivera suggest that the last group constituted the majority of Mexican repatriates. Texas had the most repatriates (132,000), California was second, and the Indiana-Illinois area was third. The siege mentality was further exacerbated by the introduction and passage of state and federal laws that complemented the federal government's repatriation efforts. In spite of the racism, bigotry, and discrimination leveled against Chicanos, however, World War II opened the way for another wave of Mexican immigration.

Third Wave (1942–1960s)

By late 1941 the need for cheap Mexican labor in the United States again became a powerful pull factor behind another exodus from Mexico. In 1942 the United States was in the midst of a serious labor shortage. Ernesto Galarza, in his classic *Merchants of Labor: The Mexican Bracero Story*, describes how the labor crisis was resolved through the Bracero Program,[45] which consisted of using Mexican seasonal workers to supply those areas of the economy where there were shortages of cheap labor, especially agriculture. The Bracero Program was developed in two phases. The first phase, which ran from 1942 to 1947, was initiated by a series of informal agreements between the United States and Mexico known as Public Law 45. The number of seasonal workers was relatively small, involving some 250,000 people. The second phase, from 1948 to 1965, comprised two subphases, 1948 to 1951 and 1952 to 1965. The passage of Public Law 78 in 1951 formalized the arrangement between the two nations.[46]

During the seventeen years of the second phase, some 4.5 million Mexicans came to work in the United States. A significant consequence of the Bracero Program was that it enhanced the exodus. Most of the braceros stayed, settling in the burgeoning barrios. After years of political pressure, the Bracero Program was terminated in December 1964. If the Bracero Program was meant to slow the exodus, it failed resoundingly. In 1965 Congress imposed a ceiling of 120,000 immigrants per year from all countries in the Western Hemisphere. The law became effective in 1968. With the passage of this immigration legislation the "close and friendly border" disappeared.[47]

The Bracero Program served as an endogenous antagonism to the growing exodus from Mexico into the United States. Millions of Mexican workers were induced to immigrate either directly or indirectly by the Bracero Program. Many braceros who returned to Mexico after their contract expired came back to permanently settle in the United States, either as legal immigrants or as undocumented workers. Moreover, braceros returning to Mexico with money in their pockets caused others to believe that things were much better economically in the United States than they were in Mexico. Mexico's poverty continued to be the major push propelling the exodus.

Millions of undocumented workers became part of the flow of humanity heading north during these years. In spite of the McCarran-Walter Act of 1952, the Immigration Act of 1965, and more stringent enforcement by the Border Patrol, the exodus continued to gain momentum as the push and pull factors became more acute. In 1949 immigration agencies started massive roundups of what they described as "wetbacks," or undocumented workers, culminating in 1953 with Operation Wetback. This quasi-military operation deported some 875,000 Mexicans in 1953 alone. The figure increased to 1,035,000 in 1954. By 1956, when Operation Wetback ended, the number of Mexicans deported dropped to 90,122.[48] (These roundups are characteristic of U.S. immigration agencies' actions. When the United States needs cheap labor, immigration enforcement becomes lax; conversely, when there is an economic downturn, the roundups are renewed.) Legal immigration from Mexico from 1951 to 1960 was approximately 300,000; from 1961 to 1965 the number declined to 220,000.[49] In 1971 some 350,000 undocumented workers were apprehended. The number increased in 1972 to 430,000.

High fertility rates also contributed to the rapid increase in the Chicano population. In 1970 the median age for Chicanos was 20.2 years; for U.S.-born Chicanos, only 15.8 years.[50] The average age for Chicanos was nine years younger than that of the U.S. population as a whole. Children younger than eighteen years made up 46 percent of the Chicano population; by contrast, only 33 percent of the Anglo population was less than eighteen years of age.[51] The result was a very high birth rate among Chicanos. By 1969 the birth rate among Chicanas was 40 percent higher than among Anglo women. In addition, Chicano families were larger than those of other groups. A typical Chicano family contained 4.5 persons, whereas the average Anglo family had 3.6 persons.

Thus, through immigration and a high birth rate, the Chicano population substantially increased during the epoch of protest. According to the 1960 U.S. census, Chicanos numbered approximately 4 million. By the early 1970s the Chicano population had increased to nearly 7 million.[52] Demographics suggested that there was at least another 1 million who had not been counted. In 1970 approximately 90 percent of the Chicano population lived in the Southwest. Out of that population, 84 percent resided in California and Texas. Each state had over 1 million Chicanos. Chicanos became the fastest growing segment of the Southwest's population. Between 1950 and 1970 the Spanish-surnamed population (the category used by the U.S. census) increased some 99 percent. "By contrast," Moore and Pachon write, "the Anglos increased only sixty-seven percent and Blacks sixty-one percent. In the single decade between 1960 and 1970, Chicanos increased thirty-two percent, the Anglos gaining twenty-five percent and the Blacks only seven percent."[53] By the 1960s the relative increase in the Chicano population was giving the group greater numerical significance in the population at large.

A Changing Socioeconomic Profile

With a dramatic increase in the size of the Chicano population, the community underwent a socioeconomic change. Although still plagued by poverty, Chicanos by 1970 were becoming more middle class, which was reflected in the change in poverty levels between 1960 and 1970. In 1960 the U.S. Census reported that 35 percent of Spanish-surnamed families, the great majority of which were Chicano, fell below the poverty line; this figure in 1970 was 24 percent. This change also acted as an antagonism toward the emergence of the CM. As the Chicano population increased during the epoch of protest, the issues affecting the Chicano community intensified. Poverty was still prevalent in the barrios. Twenty-four percent of the Chicano population lived below the poverty line. Few Chicanos were white-collar workers; the majority were blue-collar. In schools at all levels Chicanos suffered high "push-out" rates. On the average, in 1970 Chicanos over twenty-five years of age had received fewer than nine years of education; the comparable figure for Anglos was twelve years.[54] These factors served to create social problems such as unemployment, crime, drug and alcohol abuse, gang violence, and political disfranchisement, to name just a few. Culturally, the dramatic increase in Chicano population by 1970 served to reinforce the Chicano's culture, heritage, and retention of the Spanish language. The result was a deterioration of race and ethnic relations, particularly with segments of the Anglo community that were racist or nationalist. Nonetheless, for all the issues and problems that were commonplace to the barrios, Chicanos overall were better off during the epoch of protest than at any previous time in U.S. history.

Population growth coupled with the changing social, political, and economic profile of the Chicano community created a fertile ground for the emergence of the CM. The epoch of protest was as a whole an era of growing prosperity for the nation, but Chicanos became victims of relative deprivation. While the nation was progressing generally, many young Chicanos felt that the Chicano community was not. Their rising expectations gave Chicanos a greater appetite for change. This appetite was channeled through the emerging CM.

Reies Lopez Tijerina and the Alianza

During the epoch of protest Reies Lopez Tijerina and his Alianza Federal de Pueblos Libres emerged as a powerful endogenous antagonism for the CM. Tijerina became one of the major architects of the CM. In fact, historians Matt Meier and Feliciano Rivera group him with Cesar Chavez, Rodolfo "Corky" Gonzales, and Jose Angel Gutierrez, all four being leaders whose actions received national attention and whom Meier and Rivera describe as the sparks that ignited the CM's machinery and politics. Of the four, Tijerina took center stage during the CM's formative years (midsixties). Acuña went so far as to describe Tijerina as "el Tigre," the most charismatic of the CM leaders.[55]

Many writers have written detailed histories of Tijerina's exploits.[56] Tijerina was not an intellectual who influenced the formation of the CM through the power of his acumen or written works. Instead, he was a man of humble origins who was born on September 21, 1923, on a heap of cotton sacks in a one-room adobe shack outside Falls City, Texas.[57] While growing up he lived a marginal existence with his migrant family, which included eight children. With little formal schooling, he converted to a fundamentalist Protestant sect as a young man. Subsequently, after briefly attending a Bible school, he became a preacher. For years he wandered the Southwest, but in the 1950s he, along with seventeen families, established a commune named the Valley of Peace in the Arizona desert. In 1958 he arrived in northern New Mexico, where he assisted the Abique Corporation of Tierra Amarilla in its struggle for the restoration of land grants.[58] In 1960 he traveled to Mexico to study land grants and the Treaty of Guadalupe Hidalgo. He became totally immersed with the issue of land grants, believing that God ordained him to lead the fight for this cause.[59]

After years of research and preparation, Tijerina in 1962 formally unleashed a powerful populist movement of Chicanos in New Mexico under the name "Alianza Federal de Mercedes" (this movement was subsequently renamed several times, but I will refer to it here as the Alianza Federal de Pueblos Libres [AFPL]). The AFPL sought the return of some 1 million acres of land that had been lost through Anglo usurpation. Some of the grants to this land were made prior to the Mexican War of 1846. Initially, the land had been communally owned by Chicanos. Between 1848 and the early 1900s, however, the majority of Chicano land grants were lost to unscrupulous Anglos who relied on a variety of means, both legal (i.e., chicanery) and extralegal (intimidation, confiscation, violence, etc.), to gain control of the land. For years the various territorial governments had honored the land grants. During the twentieth century, however, much of this land became public domain and was turned over to the Forest Service. In turn, the Forest Service was authorized to lease the lands to private individuals and companies for the use and development of natural resources. The result was that "big money" interests benefited at the expense of impoverished Chicano small farmers. Tijerina accused the U.S. government of participating in fraud that deprived the people of the *ejido* (public lands).[60]

Tijerina's AFPL initially was not cast in the mold of militancy and protest. Instead, the AFPL developed from a moderate pressure group to an organization that embraced civil disobedience and eventually violence. When it was incorporated in 1963, the AFPL functioned more like a traditional interest group seeking to influence the federal and state governments to return land to the Chicanos. (Because of Tijerina's Pentecostal ministerial status and fiery oratory, some described the AFPL during its formative years [1963 to early 1965] as a nativist religious movement rather than a change-oriented organization.)[61] The strategy consisted of making legal claims, lobbying, and educating the public, especially Chicanos, on the particulars of the issue.

In 1965 Tijerina accelerated the AFPL's level of militancy, changing tactics and opting for more of a direct-action approach. Tony Castro writes, "The movement began with legal claims on the land grants, but Tijerina moved increasingly to confrontation style tactics in the face of government indifference."[62] In frustration, Tijerina organized marches on the state capitol but produced no real or positive results.

The change of strategy resulted in part from the AFPL's second convention, held in 1964. Before that time, the diverse activities of the AFPL had largely gone unnoticed by the media. Prior to the convention, Felix Martinez, a leader of the AFPL, had visited Watts after the riots and Cesar Chavez in Delano. He returned with the evaluation that Chavez's slow, nonviolent methods had not made the larger society aware of the problem as rapidly and forcefully as had the riots in Watts, adding that "revolution speeds up evolution."[63]

By 1966 Tijerina accelerated his use of unconventional protest tactics, transforming him into the Chicano community's most militant and radical leader. The organization's growing militancy was also due to the restiveness of its members. In 1963 the AFPL's ranks had grown to 20,000 members, with its strongest support coming from New Mexico's northwestern Rio Arriba region.[64] By 1966 frustration and anger began to set in.

On October 15, 1966, Tijerina and 350 members of the AFPL occupied the national forest campgrounds known as the Echo Amphitheater. With blaring oratory Tijerina promulgated the revival of *ejido* rights for the Pueblo de San Joaquin de Chama, whose 140 acres lay mainly within the Kit Carson National Forest. Acuña explains the incident that propelled Tijerina into the limelight: "In less than a week, state police, sheriff's deputies and Rangers began to move in. On October 22 *La Alianza* members took two Rangers into custody and tried them for trespassing and being a public nuisance. The court fined them and handed down a sentence of 11 months and [21] days in jail, then 'mercifully' suspended the sentence."[65] In an attempt to use the power of symbolic politics, the AFPL had also elected a governing board (*ayuntamiento*) and a mayor. In addition, during the occupation the AFPL declared itself to be the Republic of San Joaquin, giving it the trappings of a secessionist movement. Tijerina had sought to use the occupation to challenge openly, before the media, the U.S. Forest Service's jurisdiction over the land, consequently forcing the land-grant issue into the courts. Cognizant of the growing power of the media, Tijerina would orchestrate and manipulate events or say things that would catch the media's attention. An example of this was his remark that "Fidel Castro has what he has because he has guts. Castro put the *Gringos* off his island and we can do the same."[66]

In 1967 Tijerina accelerated his militantization with the Tierra Amarilla courthouse raid. This incident changed the strategy of the AFPL from civil disobedience to confrontational violence. Prior to the raid, tensions had been escalating on both sides. Anglo authorities and ranchers feared the possibilities of guerrilla warfare breaking out in northern New Mexico. Not since the days of Las Gorras Blancas (the White Caps) and La Mano Negra (the Black Hand) during the late nineteenth century had Chicanos succeeded in instilling so much fear and concern in the minds of the Anglo authorities. Concomitantly, even the traditionalist Hispanos led by U.S. Senator Joseph Montoya had become opposed to Tijerina's escalating militancy and radicalism. As Tijerina's militancy increased, he began to lose the support of many of his followers.[67]

On June 5, twenty Aliancistas, believing that Anglo authorities had violated their right of assembly, attempted to make a citizen's arrest of the area's district attorney, Alfonso Sanchez. Their action was in response to Sanchez's having declared an assembly in Coyote, northern New Mexico, unlawful, blocked the roads to town, and arrested other Aliancistas. Shooting ensued during the raid on the jail. Two deputies were wounded, and the incarcerated Aliancistas were freed. However, the Aliancistas were not successful in arresting Sanchez. As a result of the raid, Tijerina and the Aliancistas were forced into hiding in the neighboring forest.

The Tierra Amarilla courthouse raid gained Tijerina national and international attention. The incident provoked the direct military intervention of the New Mexico National Guard. The manhunt took on the trappings of a wartime operation. The National Guard, equipped with tanks and helicopters, joined with state and local law enforcement agencies; altogether, two thousand men participated in the pursuit of Tijerina and the Aliancistas.[68] After a two-day standoff, the governor of New Mexico assured their safety. Tijerina and his Aliancistas surrendered and were arrested. They and the AFPL members were charged with attempted murder, kidnapping, and other crimes, and Tijerina's trial in 1968 became a media event of defiance. With the assistance of two court-appointed attorneys, Tijerina conducted his own defense and was acquitted on all the charges stemming from the courthouse raid.[69]

Tijerina capitalized on his growing fame. In May and June 1968 he participated in the Poor People's Campaign. He became upset with civil rights movement leaders, charging them with failure to consult Chicanos regarding overall policies of the campaign's agenda. He felt that Chicanos were not treated as equals. Tijerina was given a role in the Poor People's March, but the experience left him bitter toward the civil rights movement leadership. Nevertheless, Tijerina used this trip to meet and lecture State Department officials on his interpretation of the Treaty of Guadalupe Hidalgo—in particular, as it related to land-grant guarantees.[70]

Later that year Tijerina ran unsuccessfully for governor of New Mexico on the People's Constitutional party ticket. Organized by the AFPL, this party became a precursor to the Raza Unida party in New Mexico, with the difference being that its populist platform appealed to a coalition of groups and individuals from different ethnic groups and with a variety of political views. Although his party garnered only 2 percent of the vote, Tijerina demonstrated his political acumen and determination by using the electoral arena as part of his battle plan to promote the land-grant issue.[71]

Tijerina's brief history as the CM's most militant recognized leader came to an end in 1969. In mid-February the Court of Appeals for the Tenth Circuit upheld the Amphitheater conviction, the sentence for which was two years in prison. On June 5, while appealing the decision, Tijerina and some of his followers attempted once again to occupy the Kit Carson National Forest at the Coyote campsite. Tijerina's wife and followers burned a few U.S. Forest Service signs. Two days later they were arrested, and Tijerina was charged with aiding and abetting the destruction of U.S. Forest Service property and assaulting and threatening a federal agent. Adding to his legal problems, on October 13 the Supreme Court refused to hear his appeal on the Amphitheater case, and Tijerina went to prison.[72] He served a two-year term at the federal prison hospital in Springfield, Missouri. Shortly after entering prison, Tijerina resigned as head of the AFPL. Santiago Tapia y Anaya was elected to take his place.[73] Chicano activists charged that Tijerina's imprisonment was part of a strategy by governmental entities to neutralize the AFPL by removing its prophet.[74]

Tijerina's absence did have such an effect. With the removal of its charismatic leader, the AFPL began to wither away quickly. Internal factionalism, harassment by law-enforcement agencies, declining membership, and an absence of resources further ensured its demise. The final blow to the AFPL came in 1971 with Tijerina's release from prison. Tijerina was placed on parole for five years with a stipulation that he could not hold an official leadership position in the AFPL. Equally devastating was his apparent change of attitude and demeanor. It appeared that the Tigre had been defanged. He was no longer willing to become involved in protests or radical forms of politics. He now spoke of brotherhood and love rather than of militant confrontational action.[75] This behavior was considered eccentric by some Chicano activists. They alleged that while in prison he had been subjected to some form of behavior modification. Tijerina had become very bitter toward some of the CM's leaders who he felt had not come to his aid during his incarceration. By 1972 Tijerina had ceased to play a major leadership role in the CM. Henceforth, without Tijerina, the AFPL became quiescent and no longer a major instrument of the CM.[76]

Tijerina and the AFPL left an important legacy to the CM. For some Chicanos, especially the youth, Tijerina was a prophet of the CM who preached a gospel that called for the return of Chicano lands. Lacking a clear ideology, he was like John the Baptist, with fiery, spellbinding oratory that infused minds with feelings of power, pride, and courage. Although he was not beheaded physically, imprisoning him was tantamount to beheading the AFPL. Through his actions and deeds he, along with the AFPL, became a powerful influence in the development and subsequent radicalization of the CM.

In particular, Tijerina became a symbol for Chicano self-determination. His confrontational style complemented that of the New Left, the antiwar movement, and the Black Power movement. His actions made him a role model for many young Chicanos in both the universities and barrios. While African Americans had Malcolm X, Martin Luther King, Jr., Stokely Carmichael, and others, young Chicanos had Tijerina as their movement leader and role model. Next to Chavez, Tijerina was the most nationally recognized Chicano leader of that time, whose daring escapades and oratory caught the attention of the media. Few, if any, other Chicano leaders could claim such importance.

Throughout the epoch of protest, Tijerina courted and nurtured the support of the CYM. He traveled extensively throughout the nation, especially the Southwest, planting the seeds of hope and activism. He made numerous appearances at universities, colleges, and communities. His presentations were those of a missionary seeking converts to his *causa*. Tijerina became one of the most effective politicizing agents for the CYM and CM in general. With his absence from the CM leadership ranks, a powerful endogenous antagonism was silenced. By 1972, with both the CM and the CYM in a state of decline, Tijerina's absence as a leader became more evident.

Cesar Chavez and the UFW

Like Tijerina, Cesar Chavez became a powerful endogenous antagonism of the CM. His constituency was the farm worker, regardless of ethnicity or race. Together with his union, the United Farm Workers (UFW), Chavez sought to represent and organize all farm workers. Because of the demographic realities, however, Chicanos constituted the majority of the UFW's membership. This was evident in the style, character, and symbolism Chavez and the UFW used in their strategy and tactics during the epoch of protest.

While the literature on the CM acknowledges Tijerina's valuable leadership contribution to the movement, Chavez is considered to be by far the most prominent Chicano leader that the CM produced. No other Chicano leader was as successful in developing a broad and diverse base of support that included both Chicanos and non-Chicanos. Rodolfo Acuña is one of many who acknowledge the profundity of Chavez's leadership contributions to the CM: "Cesar Chavez gave the Chicano Movement a national leader. In all probability Chavez was the only [Chicano] to be recognized by the mainstream civil rights and anti-war movements. Chavez and the farm workers were also supported by the center [Chicano] organizations along with the left."[77]

Like Tijerina, Chavez came from humble origins. Chavez was born in 1927 in a small town outside Yuma, Arizona, into a farm worker family of five children and grew up as part of the migrant stream that followed the crops from season to season. With only an eighth-grade education, he joined the navy for two years, and after getting married in 1950 he and his wife settled in the famous barrio of Sal Si Puedes in San Jose, California. There, Chavez met Father Donald McDonnell, who tutored him in *Rerum novarum,* Pope Leo XIII's encyclical that supports labor unions and social justice.[78] Father McDonnell introduced Chavez to Fred Ross, a community organizer who worked for Saul Alinsky's Industrial Areas Foundation and was organizing the Community Service Organization (CSO).[79] Ross was impressed with Chavez's potential for becoming an organizer and offered him a job organizing for the CSO.

From the beginning of his career with the CSO to his resignation in 1962, Chavez viewed the CSO as one route to organizing farm workers.[80] "His father," according to Acuña, "had belonged to farm labor unions and Chavez himself had been a member of the National Labor Union."[81] During his many discussions with Ross, Chavez inquired about the possibilities of the CSO organizing farm workers. After spending years traveling throughout California and Arizona organizing voter registration drives, citizenship training programs, and CSO chapters, Chavez became the CSO's national general director in 1958.

That same year Chavez approached the CSO board of directors with a general proposal to set up a full-scale farm worker–organizing campaign in Oxnard. They turned him down on the grounds that the CSO's focus had to remain on urban problems.[82] Contributing to this decision was the CSO's growing middle-class membership and heavy service and program orientation. During the next four years, Chavez unsuccessfully strove to convince the CSO leadership and membership of the importance of organizing farm workers. In 1962 Chavez once again introduced a proposal for organizing farm workers to the CSO board. When his proposal was again voted down, he resigned as the CSO's director.[83] After turning down several job offers, including one as Peace Corps director for Latin American countries, Chavez moved his family to Delano and began pursuing his dream of building a farm workers' union.

That same year Chavez began forming the precursors to the UFW. His effort began with the creation of the Farm Workers Association

(FWA), which evolved into the National Farm Workers Association (NFWA; to simplify the analysis, I will use "NFWA" to refer to both). These two organizations were the matrix from which the UFW emerged. During his first weeks in Delano, Chavez spent considerable time studying the history of past farm worker–organizing efforts, working in the fields of Delano, and organizing countless house meetings to hear the many grievances of farm workers. In addition, he versed himself in Mahatma Gandhi's teachings on the passive and nonviolent resistance known as satyagraha. Jean Maddern Pitrone explains Gandhi's influence on Chavez: "[Chavez had] the greatest of admiration for the Indian leader; [he] kept a Gandhi biography close at hand for study of the man's ascetic life—his refusal of earthly possessions and his insistence on wearing the simplest clothing . . . loincloth and shawl worn by the lowest of the Hindu castes, the Untouchable. Gandhi's own policy of *Kisma* (nonviolence) was to be Cesar's policy also."[84]

Chavez's use of passive resistance introduced a new organizing strategy to the CM. His avowal of nonviolence differentiated him from Tijerina, who used a more assertive, confrontational, and combative approach. The use of nonviolence coupled with Chavez's appeal to a broad base of support strengthened his movement. In addition, his strategy drew on three organizing traditions in which he had been schooled: (1) the multi-issue community organizing model of Saul Alinsky and Fred Ross, who formed the CSO; (2) the mutual self-help experience of Chicano fraternal organizations; and (3) the Roman Catholic Church, whose symbolism and influence had great importance to the farm worker community.

Assisting Chavez in the development of the NFWA were two loyal organizers, Dolores Huerta and Gil Padilla, with whom Chavez had worked in the CSO. In addition to developing organizing strategy throughout much of 1962, they spent countless hours holding meetings, identifying and developing the leadership, raising resources, dealing with farm worker issues, and in general developing the base for the formation of the NFWA. In September 1962 the NFWA held its first convention in an abandoned theater in Fresno. Some 150 delegates attended. In describing the results of the convention, Chavez said, "Besides adopting the flag, we voted to organize the farm workers, elected temporary officers, agreed to lobby for a minimum wage law covering farm workers, and adopted '*Viva La Causa*'—Long live the Cause—as our motto. We also voted to dues of $3.50 per month."[85]

The NFWA convention served to formulate the program of action for the next five years. The delegates emphasized building a credit union and offering members life insurance. Also approved were plans for establishing cooperatives, such as a gasoline station, drug store, grocery store, and medical clinic, as was the underlying goal of developing the capability of collective bargaining with the growers.

Over the next three years (1962–1965) the ranks of the NFWA increased. Chavez and his small cadre of organizers and volunteers continued to work patiently. He lived off donations, his brother's support, and a small salary. By 1964 the NFWA was self-supporting with some one thousand dues-paying members. Chavez deliberately maintained a low profile for the organization while building up the membership base and resources, later recalling, "Not once in that time did we get our name in the paper." Chavez felt that the time was not propitious for striking and that better progress could be made by working quietly and nearly unnoticed by the growers.[86] In essence, these organizing years were the calm before the storm, the formative years during which Chavez and the NFWA laid the organizational foundation for the struggle that would soon follow.

The storm clouds began to gather in 1965 with a number of events that seemed to propel Chavez's fledgling NFWA toward its destiny of becoming a union. First, the Bracero Program, a long-time obstacle to the organization of farm workers, expired in 1964. Second, the CM had continued to intensify its protests. Third, the New Left was beginning to form the embryonic antiwar movement. Throughout the nation there was an emerging spirit of activism and protest. Finally, the NFWA's membership base had grown to some 1,700 members. Thus, the historical stage was set for the precipitating event that would give birth to Chavez's true *causa*, the UFW—La Huelga [strike], the Delano strike.

The Delano strike became the organizing shot heard around the world. It was started by predominantly Filipino grape pickers, members of the AFL-CIO's fledgling Agricultural Workers Organizing Committee (AWOC), headed by Larry Itlong. AWOC in 1965 requested support from the NFWA. In September the NFWA decided to support AWOC. The famous Delano strike had begun. It was to become a long, drawn-out affair dominated by one man, Cesar Chavez,[87] and it catapulted him into the national limelight. Chavez's cleverness and foresight in embracing a strategy of broad inclusion (namely, of gaining support from a broad spectrum of sectors and groups from the civil rights movement, New Left, antiwar movement, unions, churches, and other organizations) helped him to take a quantum leap toward becoming by 1966 the most prominent Chicano labor leader in the country.[88]

Chavez's strategy of inclusion also produced additional resources for the Delano strike. Walter Reuther of the United Auto Workers (UAW) pledged $15,000 per month. Likewise, students from various universities agreed to support the strike. In particular, student activists from the University of California at Berkeley who had been involved in the Free Speech movement and civil rights organizations in Mississippi flocked to Delano in the summer of 1964. Chavez was also quick to recruit into his expanding cadre of organizers Marshall Ganz and Eugene Nelson, who had organizing experience from campus chapters of the Congress on Racial Equality (CORE), the Student Non-Violent Coordinating Committee (SNCC), and Students for a Democratic Society (SDS).[89] The Delano strike came at a time when white radicals were being pushed out of SNCC because of its developing Black Power orientation. Still others were leaving the SDS because of its shift from community organizing to resisting the Vietnam War. In spite of the controversy over their involvement, radical white students made up the administrative backbone of the NFWA and subsequently of the UFW, at least until the early 1970s.[90] Catholic priests and bishops and other individuals from the religious sector joined and supported Chavez. Even state and national politicians like California governor Edmund "Pat" Brown and U.S. senator Robert Kennedy became supporters of the strike. In emphasizing the importance of the timing, Acuña says, "The time allowed Chavez to make his movement into a crusade."[91]

By the end of 1965 the three-month-old strike had scarcely affected the growers, so Chavez called for a national boycott. Sixteen NFWA and AWOC organizers were sent to principal cities throughout the United States to set up boycott activities. Furthermore, Chavez decided in 1966 to march on the state capitol at Sacramento. This was a strategic move to involve politicians and dramatize the strike.[92] The three-hundred-mile, twenty-five-day march was utilized to bring attention and support to the fledgling Delano strike. At the end of the march, "El Plan de Delano" was proclaimed, stating the discontent of the farm workers and the aims of Chavez and the movement. It reminded society of the oppression Chicanos had endured: "The Mexican race has sacrificed itself for the last hundred years. Our sweat and our blood have fallen on this land to make other men rich."[93]

As a result of the pressure that the march created, grape growers Schenley and Christian Brothers signed an agreement with the NFWA-AWOC. Chavez next targeted the giant DiGiorgio Fruit Corporation. In response to DiGiorgio's use of the Teamsters, Chavez seized the opportunity to strengthen his power base by consolidating the NFWA and AWOC into the United Farm Workers Organizing

Committee (UFWOC, later shortened to UFW). Thus the UFW was born. After much conflict and protracted negotiations, DiGiorgio agreed to sign with the UFW.[94] In addition, the contentious struggle between the UFW and Teamsters was temporarily halted. An agreement was reached between the two unions that divided their spheres of organizing. The UFW secured the right to organize field workers, whereas the Teamsters focused on warehouse and cannery workers.[95]

By the end of 1967 the UFW had concluded some eleven contracts, largely with wine grape growers, including Gallo and Paul Masson.[96] That year the UFW also struck Giumarra Vineyards, one of California's largest table-grape growers. With the strike escalating, Chavez, fearing a loss of spirit and an increasingly violent mood among his followers, in February 1968 began a twenty-five-day fast to call attention to "the pain and suffering of the farm workers."[97] Chavez used this symbolic and powerful act also to rededicate the UFW to the principle of nonviolence. Even though Chavez successfully turned the fast into a massive national media event, the Delano strike with Giumarra as the target continued to escalate.

The UFW expanded its organizing efforts to other parts of Aztlan. In Texas Eugene Nelson, a former Chavez organizer, joined by Margil Sanchez and Lucio Galvan, founded the Independent Workers Association (IWA) in May 1966. In June the IWA voted to affiliate with Chavez's UFW. Sanchez and Galvan, resenting control by the UFW and the massive red-baiting against it, broke away and formed the Texas Independent Worker Association. After a series of marches, demonstrations, and farm worker arrests, Chavez realized that the organizing efforts in Texas were premature and in 1967 decided to pull back. He left Antonio Orendain in charge.[98] As a result, Orendain turned on Chavez and formed his own union. Concurrently, the UFW's Delano strike inspired many other farm worker organizing efforts in various parts of the Midwest.

While the UFW accelerated its national boycott–organizing activities, it continued to involve a wide spectrum of participation from divergent sectors. Using both conventional and unconventional protest methods, the UFW pushed its boycott of grapes nationally and internationally. In May 1969 the UFW initiated strikes on some eighty Coachella Valley growers. In June the strike was expanded to Arizona, where the UFW had been organizing workers for some time. During that year, however, negotiations with the growers broke down.[99] The UFW retaliated by increasing the pressure.

After nearly five years of arduous struggle, in 1970 Chavez and the UFW secured several contracts with grape growers, which became the crowning achievments of Chavez's organizing efforts. The impressive victories began when the Coachella Valley growers signed contracts with the UFW. Roberts Farms, which employed some five thousand workers and was one of the largest California citrus and nut growers, also signed a contract with the UFW. In June 1970 Giumarra and twenty-five other Delano grape growers who together produced about 50 percent of California's table grapes signed a three-year contract with the UFW.[100] These unprecedented victories vindicated the UFW's use of the boycott. Between 1966 and 1969 alone, the UFW sent about one hundred organizers to thirty-six major table-grape-selling cities throughout the continent, resulting in a one-third reduction of sales of grapes in those cities.[101] After these victories, the UFW in 1970 turned to organizing the lettuce workers in California.

In its efforts to organize the lettuce workers of the Salinas Valley, the UFW met stiff resistance and competition from its rival, the Teamsters. Using a divide-and-conquer tactic, the lettuce growers that summer signed sweetheart contracts with the Teamsters. By August some seven thousand lettuce workers had refused to abide by the Teamster contracts and walked out of the fields. Violence by the Teamsters ensued, and UFW attorney Jerry Cohen was savagely beaten. Chavez responded to the growing violence with another fast. In December he was jailed and held without bail in Monterey County for refusing to obey an injunction. The incarceration of Chavez gave further impetus to the lettuce boycott. Visited by the widows of Martin Luther King, Jr., and Senator Robert Kennedy, he was released twenty days later.[102] With the lettuce boycott intensifying in the spring of 1971, the Teamsters signed an agreement that gave the UFW sole jurisdiction in the lettuce fields and allowed arbitration to take place. The growers, however, refused to disqualify the Teamster contracts. The situation evolved into a stalemate.[103]

During the years of 1971 and 1972 the UFW continued its relentless boycott struggles. The UFW built on its gains, coordinated its administration of contracts, and expanded its boycott activities. Concurrently, however, the UFW became a target for destruction by a triad of adversaries—growers, Teamsters, and the Nixon administration. Death threats were made against Chavez during this time.[104] In expanding its organizing efforts to other states, the UFW continued to encounter resistance from this powerful triad.

Meanwhile, in California, the UFW succeeded in defeating Proposition 22. This proposition, which looked attractive because it gave workers the right to vote by secret ballot, in reality was detrimental to the UFW because it made the secondary boycott illegal. In the summer of 1972 Schenley again forced the UFW to strike. The UFW intensified its boycott activities to the degree that Chavez and Huerta were jailed. Both sides lost: Schenley Corporation lost about a million dollars, while the UFW lost a key contract.[105]

By 1972 the growers had garnered overt support from the Nixon administration. While traveling through California, U.S. Secretary of Agriculture Earl Butz condemned the UFW's White River Farms strike. He said, "Such actions should not be allowed. It is not fair for a farmer to work all year to produce a crop and then be wiped out by a two week strike."[106] The growers resorted to the National Labor Relations Act to block the UFW's boycott against wineries. The federal court ruled against the growers and nullified the legal action. The UFW's nemesis, the Teamsters, meanwhile drew closer to the Nixon administration. The Teamster's leaders openly campaigned for Nixon's reelection.[107] Since the Delano strike of 1965, the UFW had struggled, organized, and won against incredibly powerful forces. By 1972 the UFW was increasingly being put in a defensive posture, never having sufficient time to consolidate its victories, always struggling to keep La Causa, La Heulga, and "Si Se Puede [yes, we can]" alive.

Chavez and the UFW became one of the most powerful endogenous antagonisms of the CM. Their major contributions came in the areas of leadership, strategy, and tactics. Chavez became the most recognized, respected, and prominent of all the Chicano leaders during the epoch of protest, his reputation quickly being established with his entry into the Delano strike. His leadership was recognized nationally and internationally during those years. Nonetheless, Chavez never projected himself as being a leader of the CM. He perceived the UFW as nothing more than a union dedicated to improving the quality of the farm workers' lives. While concerned about the plight of urban Chicanos, he resisted any attempts to put himself into a leadership role on issues not directly related to the UFW's *causa*, the farm worker. This was very much the case in Chavez's hands-off position when it came to Jose Angel Gutierrez's and Rodolfo "Corky" Gonzales's efforts to form the Raza Unida party. For scores of Chicanos throughout the nation, however, Chavez was their most revered role model. He became the Chicano community's Martin Luther King, Jr.

Chavez's contribution to the CM became more evident with the contagion of activism he helped foster. Through his strategy of mass mobilization via boycotts, picketing, marches, hunger strikes, lobbying, and letter writing, the UFW stimulated Chicano activism. The UFW's manipulation of symbols—the black eagle on the UFW's red flag, the standard of Our Lady of Guadalupe, the Mexican and U.S. flags, and the invigorating rhetoric of La Causa, "Si Se Puede," and "Viva La Raza"—increased the numbers of Chicanos who responded to Chavez and the UFW movement. Such symbols and rhetoric were further exploited by the Teatro Campesino, led by Luis Valdez, and the UFW's newspaper, *El Malcriado*. Both became effective organizing instruments of politicization, communication, and proselytization. This spilled over into the universities, where many students and faculty perceived Chavez's *causa* to be synonymous with the CM. Posters, banners, and UFW flags decorated their offices. Chicano study courses at times accentuated the struggle of the farm workers as if no urban CM existed. Because of the Chavez mystique, few urban-based, CM-oriented organizations were as successful as the UFW in recruiting Chicano student support. The UFW's organizing contagion created a "hype" or "romanticism" of unprecedented proportion on university and college campuses. Consequently, students became a powerful base of support for the UFW's direct-action tactics. Chavez, Huerta, and numerous other UFW organizers frequently visited and spoke at collegiate conferences, symposiums, rallies, and student meetings. Chavez's charisma and mystique were clearly behind this phenomenon. Without a doubt, Chavez and the UFW were major trailblazers for the CM. Not a revolutionary but a reformer, Chavez by 1972 was by far the most revered and influential leader that the CM had produced.

Rodolfo "Corky" Gonzales and the Crusade

Rodolfo "Corky" Gonzales became an influential endogenous force in creating the CM and CYM. By forming the *movimiento*-oriented Crusade for Justice, Gonzales became a magnetic force instilling inspiration, pride, and courage in students and barrio youth. If Tijerina was an apostle for the return of Chicano lands, numbering in the thousands of acres in New Mexico, Gonzales was a prophet of cultural nationalism seeking the return of Aztlan—the formation of a Chicano nation.

Gonzales came from humble origins. He was born in Denver, Colorado, on June 18, 1928. Stan Steiner explains that Gonzales's "father was a coal miner in southern Colorado. As a boy Gonzales worked the sugar beet fields at the side of his father." He was both a city dweller and farm worker. During the fall to spring months he lived in the city, while during the summer he worked in the fields.[108] Life was not easy for or generous to him. He went to schools that did not educate. Acuña points out, "He came up the hard way—with his fists."[109] At the age of sixteen he worked in a slaughterhouse so he could finish high school. In his efforts to escape poverty he became a successful boxer who won the Golden Gloves Championship and subsequently became a featherweight contender. From 1947 to 1955 he won sixty-five of seventy-five pro fights. Explaining why he became a fighter, Gonzales said, "I became a fighter because it was the fastest way to get out of the slaughterhouse. So I thought."[110]

As a result of his boxing career, Gonzales became an influential leader in the barrios of Colorado. His influence grew in the late fifties and early sixties due to his involvement in Democratic party politics, his success in the bail bond and insurance business, and his subsequent involvement in administering War on Poverty programs. Befriended by the Anglo establishment at the age of twenty-nine, he became the first Chicano district captain of the Democratic party in Denver. In 1960 he was the Colorado coordinator of the Viva Kennedy campaign.[111]

By 1963 Gonzales had become very active in the community. That year he formed Los Voluntarios (the Volunteers), which demonstrated against police brutality. In 1965 Gonzales became director of Denver's War on Poverty youth programs, but his activist involvement in the Albuquerque Equal Employment Opportunity Commission (EEOC) and allegations of discrimination against non-Chicanos led him to resign from his position with the antipoverty agency in 1966. In protest, he utilized Los Voluntarios to picket the *Rocky Mountain News*, the paper that had printed negative stories about him. He followed up with an acrimonious letter of condemnation that he sent to Democratic party chairman Dayle R. Tooley. In the letter he wrote:

> The individual who makes his way through the political muck of today's world, and more so the minority representatives, suffers from such an immense loss of soul and dignity that the end results are as rewarding as a heart attack, castration or cancer. . . . You and your cohorts have been accomplices to the destruction of moral man in this society. I can only visualize your goal as complete emasculation of manhood, sterilization of human dignity, and that you not only consciously but purposely are creating a world of lackeys, political boot-lickers, and prostitutes.[112]

According to Acuña, poverty officials viewed Gonzales as too zealous in his defense of the Chicano community.[113] Conversely, Gonzales felt that the War on Poverty programs were designed to pacify the poor rather than help them improve their lives.

Disgusted with the constraints attached to funds from governmental agencies and private foundations, in 1966 Gonzales formed the Crusade for Justice. Gonzales's Crusade, like Tijerina's Alianza, did not appeal to traditional liberal or conservative Chicano organizations' agendas of assimilation and integration. By the late 1960s and early 1970s the community self-help organization that Gonzales committed himself to building had become part of the vanguard of the CM. Historian John Chavez provides a brief overview of the Crusade's grass-roots orientation: "Through their own fund raising efforts, the members established a *barrio* service center, providing such assistance as child care, legal aid, housing and employment counseling, health care, and other services especially needed in poor urban areas. The Crusade was . . . outspoken in its concern for Chicano civil and cultural rights."[114] The barrio service center housed a school, curio shop, bookstore, and social center. The school, named Tlatelolco, La Plaza de las Tres Culturas, enrolled about two hundred students from preschool to college and provided a curriculum that included socialist economics, Chicano history, and other subjects not common to other schools. Concurrently, the Crusade worked for community control of the public schools and was vigilant against police brutality.

Gonzales and the Crusade were one. Like Tijerina, Gonzales projected a strong, charismatic image of one who was not afraid to use unconventional methods to organize and mobilize Chicanos. In the Crusade for Justice, as in so many other movements, the leader *was* the organization. The presence of *personalismo*—the power of the charismatic personality—guided the formation and development of the Crusade. This meant that the Crusade's ideology, structure, strategy, and tactics were extensions of its leadership—*el Jefe* Corky. This becomes quite evident when one looks at the Crusade's adherence to direct-action tactics. During the epoch of protest Gonzales led the Crusade in numerous marches, demonstrations, and even violent confrontations with the police. Gonzales's commitment to a self-defense posture made the Crusade one of the most hated and persecuted by law-enforcement agencies.

One of Gonzales's major contributions to the CM was his espousal of cultural nationalism and self-determination.[115] Influenced by the Black Power movement, Gonzales became the CM's chief spokesperson for cultural nationalism. Although the CM never developed a consensus on ideology, Gonzales's cultural nationalism had the trappings of a quasi ideology—Chicanismo—that had elements of humanism and socialism. It categorically rebuked capitalism. While not Marxist, Gonzales's Chicanismo was influenced by socialist principles. He often spoke of the evils of capitalist materialism and imperialism. In addition, he raised the level of radicalism in the CM by openly and forcibly advocating Chicano separatism. Although he embraced the idea of returning Aztlan to Chicanos, however, he was never specific as to how this could be done.

For Gonzales, America's existing social order offered no hope for Chicanos. The only viable option available to Chicanos was to form their own nation. His epic poem, "Yo Soy Joaquin," was extremely critical of U.S. society. The poem dramatized the liberation of Chicanos from the materialism of Anglo society and expressed Gonzales's intellectual vision of a new cultural future for La Raza. The writings of José Vasconcelos, especially *La raza cósmica*, were a major cornerstone in Gonzales's Chicanismo. So committed was Gonzales to the notion of Aztlan that he made an unsuccessful appeal to the United Nations, where he requested a plebiscite to be held in Aztlan to decide whether Chicanos would prefer independence from the United States.[116] In terms of ideology, Gonzales, with his adherence to Chicanismo as a quasi ideology with Aztlan as its end, was far more radical then Tijerina or Chavez. In a symposium on Chicano liberation held in Hayward, California, in 1969, Gonzales explained the importance of nationalism to the CM:

What are the common denominators that unite the people? The key common denominator is nationalism. When I talk about nationalism, some people run around in their intellectual bags, and they say this is reverse racism. The reverse of a racist is a humanitarian. I specifically mentioned what I felt nationalism was. Nationalism becomes *la familia*. Nationalism comes and comes first out of the family, then into tribalism and then into alliances that are necessary to lift the burden of all suppressed humanity.[117]

Of all the Chicano leaders, none was as ideologically motivated and directed as was Gonzales. This was evident at the Hayward symposium with his call for the creation of a separate Chicano nation. He said, "We have to start to consider ourselves as a nation . . . a nation of Aztlan."[118]

Gonzales did not become a major leader of the CM until 1968, when a combination of historical antagonisms propelled him to major leadership status. That year, he joined Tijerina in leading a Chicano contingent to the Poor People's March on Washington. While there Gonzales issued his "Plan of the *Barrio*," which called for the following measures: "for housing that would meet Chicano cultural needs; for schooling, basically in Spanish; for *barrio* businesses that would be owned within the community; and for reforms in land-holding, with the restitution of community lands."[119] During their stay in Washington, Gonzales, Tijerina, and other Chicano leaders made their presence felt among government officials and civil rights leaders. State Department officials were confronted over violations of the provisions of the Treaty of Guadalupe Hidalgo. Moreover, the Mexican government was asked to intervene on behalf of Chicano grievances. The Southern Christian Leadership Conference (SCLC) was charged with being insufficiently attentive to Chicanos.[120] For Gonzales, the Poor People's March provided an opportunity to get national exposure and recognition as one of the main leaders of the growing CM.

The following year Gonzales continued climbing to major leadership status within the CM. With student and barrio youth groups surfacing all over, Gonzales focused on young people as his main constituency. His poem "Yo Soy Joaquin" and his advocacy activities made him a major catalyst within the formation of the CYM. Like Tijerina and Chavez, Gonzales spoke at numerous universities and colleges, which enabled him to influence the emerging CYM. In particular, in 1968 and 1969 the Crusade became involved with issues of police brutality and school walkouts in Denver. Gonzales also resorted to marches, picketing, and direct-action confrontational protest methods. This brought him notoriety and exposure nationwide.

Gonzales's stature as a leader of the CM took a giant leap with the Crusade's First Annual Chicano Youth Liberation Conference held in 1969 in Denver. Held in March, during the week of Palm Sunday, some two thousand Chicano representatives from more than one hundred different Chicano youth groups from throughout the nation gathered in a spirit of nationalism and proclaimed "El Plan Espiritual de Aztlán" (The spiritual plan of Aztlan). The conference was significant also because it brought together young people of all types—students, nonstudents, militant youths from the street gangs (*vatos locos*), ex-convicts (*pintos*)—to discuss pertinent community issues related to the CM.[121] The cultural nationalist underpinnings of the plan are evident in the following excerpt: "Conscious . . . of the brutal 'Gringo' invasion of our territories: We, the Chicano inhabitants and civilizers of the northern land of *Aztlan*, from whence came our forefathers, reclaiming the land of their birth . . . declare that the call of our blood is our power, our responsibility, and our inevitable destiny. . . . We do not recognize capricious frontiers on the Bronze Continent. . . . We Declare the Independence of our Mestizo Nation."[122] The plan further enhanced Gonzales's leadership

The Chicano Movement   41

stature and made him the leading theorist of the CM. Young Chicano activists returned to their campuses and barrios inspired by an energizing nationalism that the Crusade exemplified. Thus, the plan not only helped Gonzales but also served to stimulate further the wave of Chicano nationalism sweeping Aztlan. Political scientist Carlos Muñoz comments on the Crusade's growing organizational importance:

> Corky Gonzales and his followers . . . had developed the image of the Crusade for Justice as the "vanguard" of the rapidly growing Chicano Power movement. The Crusade, originally a multi-issue, broad-based civil rights organization oriented towards non-violence, came to symbolize Chicano self-determination and espoused a strong nationalist ideology that the youth found extremely attractive.[123]

By 1969 Gonzales and the Crusade had incorporated a position against the Vietnam War into their agenda. Although Chicanos were initially reluctant to support the antiwar movement, that year, as the movement intensified, so did Chicano support and involvement. Political scientist Ralph Guzman explains in part why the Crusade and other CM entities began speaking out against the war: "between January 1961 and February 1967, although the Chicano population officially numbered 10 to 12 percent of the total population of the Southwest, Chicanos comprised 19.4 percent of those from that area killed in Viet-Nam. From December 1967 to 1969, Chicanos suffered 19 percent of all casualties from the Southwest. Chicanos from Texas sustained 25.2 percent of the casualties of that state."[124] The disproportionate number of Chicano casualties acted as an antagonism in fostering antiwar protest activities, especially within the CYM. Ernesto Vigil of the Crusade for Justice; Rosalio Muñoz, former student body president of the University of California, Los Angeles (UCLA); Sal Baldenegro, a student at the University of Arizona; and many other young Chicanos refused induction.[125] Chicano activists began speaking out on the Vietnam War, and Gonzales and Tijerina took a position against it as early as 1967, but it did not become a priority issue for the Crusade until 1970.

In 1970 the Crusade held its Second Annual Chicano Youth Liberation Conference in Denver. At the conference Gonzales pushed for Chicanos to become more aggressively involved in the antiwar movement. The hundreds of young Chicano activists from throughout the nation attending the conference planned a score of local and national moratoriums. Subsequently, in August 1970, the Crusade's conference planning yielded the largest and most impressive Chicano demonstration against the war, the National Chicano Moratorium in Los Angeles. Organized by the National Chicano Moratorium Committee, the moratorium drew some 25,000 Chicanos from throughout the nation. Gonzales endorsed and attended the event and was scheduled to be one of the speakers, but the demonstration turned into a riot, and he was not able to speak. During the course of the riot, he and twenty-seven other Crusade members were arrested for robbery and for carrying concealed weapons. They were shortly released and later acquitted of the charges.

With the CM as a whole reaching its apogee in 1970, Gonzales struggled desperately to keep the Crusade alive. In Denver the Crusade became a target of increasing police harassment over the next two years. It continued to maintain its diversified programs and services, including the publication of its newspaper, *El Gallo*. Outside Colorado, with Tijerina incarcerated, Gonzales during these years sought to establish himself as the national leader of the CM. He continued to travel extensively throughout Aztlan, speaking at various universities, colleges, and barrios on a variety of issues. Overall, the Crusade struggled hard to maintain a proactive organizing thrust even though the CM was beginning to decline and to take on a more defensive posture.

During 1970 to 1972 Gonzales sought to consolidate his power base to become the CM's main leader. Instead of using the Crusade as the organizational vehicle for his drive for national power, however, he chose the Raza Unida party (RUP). He felt that he was entitled to it because the call for a Chicano political party first came out of "El Plan Espiritual de Aztlán."

In 1970, at the Second Youth Liberation Conference, Gonzales called for the formation of the RUP. Gonzales's recommendation called for the establishment of a party that would encompass Colorado, Aztlan, and the nation. In essence, Gonzales propounded the need for a national Chicano political party.[126] In addition, he advocated the formation of a Chicano congress that would comprise delegates from barrios throughout the nation. The congress would govern the party and handle all political questions concerning the nation of Aztlan.[127]

On March 16, 1970, the Crusade facilitated the formation of the RUP in Colorado by holding an organizing conference that drew some eight hundred people from throughout the state. The conference focused on various aspects of forming the party, such as selection of candidates, platform development, and legal requirements to get on the ballot. Instead of holding a statewide convention to nominate all candidates, a number of local RUP conventions were held to involve more people.[128] Without money, weak in organization, and with a pro-Chicano platform, RUP garnered few votes in the November elections. It never sought to form a broad-based coalitional effort. RUP's appeal was oriented exclusively toward the Chicano community. Garcia explains why the party chose this approach: "The Colorado Party . . . had a charismatic leader uninterested in what others had to say. This strategy hinged on arousing anger among Chicanos, not winning elections or even influencing elections. Gonzales had no desire to appear legitimate except to the vanguard of the Chicano Movement."[129] During the rest of 1972 Gonzales continued to pursue the role of the CM's most prominent leader. Increasingly, however, his pursuit was thwarted by the emergence of another Chicano leader, Jose Angel Gutierrez, who was concurrently building the RUP in Texas and elsewhere in the Southwest. This created a power struggle between the two leaders that in 1972 proved to be detrimental not only to both leaders but also to the CM (this issue will be dealt with in Chapter 7 and the Epilogue). By the end of 1972, while other CM organizations and leaders were beginning to disappear, Gonzales and the Crusade continued to preach their political gospel of Chicanismo and the dream of Aztlan.

Gonzales's contributions to the development of the CM were several. Like Tijerina and Chavez, he too became a major architect of the CM. Through his commitment to Chicanismo and Aztlan he became a powerful role model, especially for Chicano youth. His poem "Yo Soy Joaquin" did much to buttress Chicanismo as a quasi ideology. His Youth Liberation Conferences became powerful organizing vehicles infusing the CM with a sense of direction and strengthening its organizational capabilities. While the Crusade for Justice was ostensibly a Denver operation, without chapters or other structures in Aztlan, its influence within the *movimiento* was predicated on the magnetism of its leader, Gonzales. His ideas and ability to articulate them affected the development of the CM, including its radicalization.

Gonzales's influence became more apparent with the CM's progeny, the CYM. No other Chicano leader of the epoch of protest influenced Chicano youth as much as Gonzales did. Whereas Tijerina chose the poor of New Mexico and Chavez focused on the farm worker, Gonzales's main constituency was the Chicano youth. He was instrumental in politicizing the barrio youth, especially in Denver, and in giving them a *causa*. For college students he was a missionary preaching a gospel of Chicanismo and Aztlan. His courage, zeal, and commitment to his beliefs made him a target of law-enforcement entities. This was further compounded by his adherence to confrontational protest and even nonviolent forms of direct action. In fact, although Gonzales was never directly involved in violent confrontations with police, some of the Crusade's leaders and members were. Some Crusade members went to jail; others paid with their lives. After 1972, despite being very much a target of law-enforcement agencies, the Crusade continued espousing the politics of separatism. In the end, it will be remembered as a cardinal force in the development of the Chicano Youth Movement.

2. The Chicano Youth Movement: Catalyst for Change

Of the various elements that constituted the CM, its progeny, the CYM, made the most important contributions to the CM's growth and development. The CYM became a powerful force of activism, radicalism, and change. Some argue that the CYM was the vanguard of the CM; others disagree, asserting that its role, while significant, was not the whole story. Regardless of the profundity of its role, the CYM, like Tijerina, Gonzales, and Chavez, itself became an important endogenous antagonism that catalyzed social change. As the CYM became more militant and radicalized, so did the CM. In essence, the movements were inseparable and indistinguishable. While other sectors such as workers, *campesinos*, intellectuals, and clergy all participated and contributed to the CM, it was Chicano youths who joined with the other youths in the United States to produce the epoch of protest.

In this chapter I provide a historical analysis of the CYM's formation, briefly tracing the various historical antecedents that laid the foundation for the movement's emergence in 1967. In addition, I examine the Chicano student groups and Chicano barrio youth organizations that constituted the CYM from 1967 to 1972. A brief case study of each organizational type is presented. Finally, I examine the factors that led to the CYM's decline by 1972.

The Historical Roots of Chicano Student Activism

The rise of the CYM was one of the most important historical events in the United States during the 1960s.[1] Its historical roots are deeply imbedded in the Chicano experience of Aztlan. Chicano historians such as Acuña, Meier and Rivera, Chavez, Gomez-Quiñonez, and others point out that Chicanos fell victim to a process of conquest that relegated them to a powerless, impoverished, and subordinate status in American society. For 119 years, from the conclusion of the Mexican War until the emergence of the CYM, Chicanos had been poor, disfranchised, and victimized by discrimination that included an inferior education, among other forms. This historical reality, which is well documented in the literature on Chicano history, became in itself an endogenous antagonism that in the epoch of protest added fuel to the fires of Chicano discontent. For all these years Chicanos were deprived of education and kept at the bottom of the political, economic, and social ladder of U.S. society via de jure and, later, de facto segregation. African Americans were thus not the only targets of segregation-wrought bigotry, prejudice, and discrimination.

The architects of this country's educational systems from 1848 to the 1960s essentially used segregation to keep Chicanos ignorant and uneducated, a source of cheap labor. Chicano labor (and know-how) contributed substantially to the development of the Southwest—in particular, in agriculture, mining, railroads, and various forms of industry. Carlos Muñoz elucidates further: "like African-Americans, [Chicano] working class children able to attend school were placed in segregated schools. But in contrast, [Chicanos] never had access to even the sort of higher education provided by segregated institutions like Negro Colleges."[2] Unlike African Americans, Chicanos were never given the opportunity or support to establish their own Chicano colleges or universities. Even in the morass of their segregation, African Americans were allowed and encouraged to develop a black intelligentsia, whereas Chicanos were denied such racist compassion. This is confirmed by the fact that African Americans, by the time of the epoch of protest, had over one hundred colleges and universities of their own.[3]

It was not until the late twenties that the seed of the CYM was planted by the student activism of scholar and organizer Ernesto Galarza. In 1929 Galarza, then twenty-four years old, a first-year graduate student in history at Stanford University and its first Chicano graduate student, spoke out in defense of Mexican immigrant workers.[4] Galarza's defense of immigrants was one early recorded instance of student activism. From 1898 to the early 1930s there is no record of any Chicano student group. Galarza was instrumental in planting the seed of student activism by his involvement in issues confronting the Chicano community. The nonexistence of any group was basically attributable to the very limited number of Chicano college students. Access to institutions of higher learning was limited to a very small number of emerging Chicano middle-class students. In the 1920s, for example, during Galarza's undergraduate years at Occidental College, he knew of only five other Chicanos attending colleges or universities in southern California. While at Stanford, he remained the only Chicano student.[5] The overwhelming majority of Chicanos were shut out from higher education; even worse, few attended or even graduated from high school. Galarza, who did manage to get his Ph.D., subsequently became one of the Chicano community's intellectual giants, prolific scholars, and community leaders. Through the power of his scholarship and activism, he left Chicanos and others who care about social justice a legacy that will never be forgotten.

Perhaps Galarza's unique student activism can be understood in the context of his experience with the realities of segregation and the contradictory nature of America's educational system. Knowledge and understanding are powerful liberating forces. One can conjecture that Galarza's activism was a product of an educational system that lauded the virtues of democracy, the American way of life, and capitalism yet denied educational opportunities for the Chicano. This contradiction later became an antagonism that helped produce the CYM. A social order uses its educational systems to socialize, indoctrinate, and, in this case, Americanize the populace to its symbols, values, ideas, and beliefs.[6] Thus, education becomes a method of controlling the underclasses and legitimating the nation's dominant political culture. Instead of being a liberating force, education became in essence a controlling force. Chicanos during these years were subjected to a segregated mode of education that was designed to keep them in their impoverished and quasi-colonial controlled status.

During the depression other historical antecedents emerged that prepared the ground for the appearance of the CYM. The depression did not foster greater educational opportunities for Chicanos. Instead, Chicanos were faced with repatriation, growing discrimination, and a racism predicated on xenophobia. The literature on this era is full of illustrations. Nativists spoke with vitriolic rhetoric based on hatred and bigotry. Like Asian Americans, Chicanos were perceived as a peril and a threat to the social and cultural fabric of American society.[7] Public hearings conducted by House and Senate committees on Mexican immigration were used by nativist eugenicists and even organized labor to push for restrictionist immigration policies. At these hearings nativists argued that "Mexicans would create the most insidious and general mixture of White, Indian, and Negro blood streams ever produced in America."[8] Even more indicative of their ethnocentrism and hatred of Mexicans was their belief that Mexicans were inferior and unfit to be Americans. A professor of zoology at the University of California concluded: "[Mexicans are a] menace to public health, [a] serious burden upon our charities, . . . [of] low mentality, inherently criminal, and therefore a degenerate race that would afflict American society with an embarrassing race problem."[9] Racism and all its by-products (bigotry and discrimination) became an antagonism for the formation of the CYM. Even though some educational changes did materialize in the ensuing years, the stereotypes, myths, and negative perceptions of Chicanos continued to flourish in the thirties and beyond. With anti-Chicano racism rampant, Chicanos continued to live and suffer under the yoke of educational segregation.[10]

The Mexican-American Movement: Precursor to the CYM

In spite of the racism prevalent during the era, the depression produced some efforts to assist Chicano youth educationally. In addition, these years witnessed the formation of a few Chicano youth and student organizations that developed primarily from church, social welfare, and labor agencies. During the depression years the Catholic Church became more involved in assisting Chicano youth. Church authorities moved to diffuse a growing nationalism among Chicanos by conducting intensive drives to recruit Chicano youth to programs sponsored by the Catholic Youth Organization and the Catholic Settlement houses. Other entities, such as the Communist party and local unions, especially CIO locals, formed clubs of Chicano youth.[11]

The Young Men's Christian Association (YMCA) in California made a serious effort to service the barrios. In 1934 the Los Angeles YMCA branch received a gift of $30,000 to establish Boys' Clubs in the Chicano barrios of Watts. Its underlying goal was to convert Chicano youths, making them into good Americans and good Protestants.[12] Like the schools, the YMCA sought to socialize Chicanos and reinforce their acceptance of Christian and democratic values. One way the YMCA sought to do this was through conferences. The YMCA central branch in Los Angeles sponsored a number of youth conferences designed to improve its activities. The first one was held in San Pedro in 1934. Subsequently, these youth conferences were renamed the Mexican Youth Congress. The conferences did not always focus on educational issues; instead, their focus was often on recreational and sports activities. Nevertheless, these conferences were important because they sought to develop character, good citizenship, and desirable values among Chicano youth.

Beyond holding the conferences, the YMCA was instrumental in assisting Chicano admissions to colleges and universities.[13]

The YMCA conferences and activities created fertile ground for the establishment of the first Chicano student organization in the country, the Mexican-American Movement (MAM).[14] In 1938 a small, energetic group of mostly Protestant Chicano college and high school students was responsible for establishing MAM. Among some of the prominent student founders were Paul Coronel, Felix Gutierrez, Stephan Reyes, Juan Accevedo, and Rebecca Muñoz. MAM reflected the urban and rural Chicano activism and mobilizations that were taking place at the time, especially among labor and social change advocacy groups.[15]

The emergence of MAM was significant for many reasons. First, not only was MAM the first Chicano student group, but the name sent out a powerful message. The two key words used could be construed, considering the times, as bold and daring. The students' use of "Mexican-American" conveyed an acknowledgment of pride in their Mexican cultural roots. At the same time, it reminded an overtly racist society that Chicanos are Americans. Second, MAM's philosophy was to create Chicano leadership in education, social work, business, and other professions.[16] In 1939 MAM established a leadership institute and held its first regional conference at Santa Barbara. The following year, the Mexican-American Girls Conference, as well as the Mexican-American Teachers' Association and MAM, began to network with other similar groups. Third, MAM's commitment to education and Chicano youth was clear. From its inception, MAM worked continuously toward its goal of "Progress Through Education," for better schools and better family relations, as it fought discrimination and juvenile delinquency.[17] Finally, MAM was not a radical student group. It sought to promote change by working within the system without resorting to any sort of protest or militancy.

MAM developed the first Chicano student newspaper, the *Mexican Voice*. Headed by Felix Gutierrez, a student at the University of California, Los Angeles (UCLA), the mimeographed *Mexican Voice* publicized MAM's views and activities from 1938 to 1944. The newspaper stressed cultural symbols and identity but also projected negative identity problems.[18] This ambivalence was attributable to Gutierrez, who sometimes would urge Chicanos to take pride in themselves and other times would exhort Mexicans to identify as American first and Mexican second. Muñoz notes that at times the *Mexican Voice* even sided with those who contended that the root of the problems facing Chicanos in American society was a backward Mexican culture.[19] By 1945 the *Mexican Voice* became the *Forward* and its focus shifted essentially to reporting on MAM members in the armed forces.

Although MAM represented a valiant commitment by Chicano youth, members were few and faced a hostile environment.[20] In 1944 MAM held its first convention in Los Angeles. Attended by some one hundred members and prospective supporters, the convention sought to develop the resources and support needed to build and expand MAM's organizational base. Chapters were established in Los Angeles, Santa Barbara, San Bernardino, Anaheim, and Placentia, and plans had also been drawn for MAM's expansion into Colorado, Arizona, New Mexico, and Texas. This rapid development, coupled with MAM's liberal and civil rights orientation, fostered criticism and attack from right-wing groups and individuals who alleged that MAM was a "Communist organization." The FBI's investigation of MAM as a subversive organization further exacerbated popular suspicions.[21] Concerned about these allegations, MAM's leadership spent a great deal of time trying to convince the convention participants of the group's commitment to democratic principles.

More important, despite plans, meetings, and additional conferences, MAM was unable to overcome the disruption caused by World War II. MAM's membership and the participation of its constituents began to decline. Few of MAM's former members who had served in the armed forces resumed participation in the organization after their discharge. The new blood that was supposed to have materialized after the war never did. Furthermore, in 1942 MAM had incorporated as a nonprofit organization, yet it never succeeded in generating the financial resources necessary for its growth. Paul Coronel had absorbed many of the financial costs of MAM activities at a great personal sacrifice. MAM's demise came in 1950, by which time it had ceased to be a youth membership association.[22]

MAM's demise left a vacuum, for there was no other student or youth group to replace it. The GI Bill allowed some returning Chicano veterans to increase their level of education; of these, some went on to college or university. Most of these individuals were concerned primarily with individual success. Some youth, however, were involved with community organizational efforts, such as those of the quasi-political Community Service Organization (CSO) and LULAC in the late forties and fifties. Nonetheless, events in Chicano history during this period by and large followed a dialectical path. The activism of MAM met with student apathy and Chicano youths' preoccupation with the "agenda of the self." Gomez-Quiñonez describes post–World War II Chicano students as studious and largely self-oriented. However, he recognizes the crucial role they played in preparing the ground for the CYM's emergence.[23]

The Early Sixties: The Calm before the Storm of Activism

The CYM of the epoch of protest was an expression of the objective and subjective conditions of the times and the resurgent political mobilization that occurred in society as a whole and the Chicano community in particular.[24] For Chicanos by 1966, as the CM was picking up organizing steam, a multiplier contagion of activism was beginning to permeate Chicano communities throughout Aztlan. This contagion reached Chicano students in the universities and colleges by 1967. As the combined antagonisms became stronger, the few Chicano students on campuses became increasingly politicized and active. This new awareness among students in turn engendered feelings and attitudes of selective deprivation. Motivated by rising expectations they were quick to recognize the contradictions between their status and their goals. Thus, as the CM in general was a product of relative deprivation, so also was the CYM.

The growing frustration of Chicano youths from 1967 through 1972 was in part precipitated by their severe underrepresentation in the nation's universities and colleges. As previously mentioned, prior to the epoch of protest, Chicanos were essentially nonexistent in this country's institutions of higher learning. However, as Muñoz points out, Chicano student enrollment had begun to increase by the midsixties due to the political climate created by post–World War II changes and by the emerging civil rights movement. Prior to the emergence of the CYM, Chicano student activism had been largely nonexistent and limited to a few individuals who between 1963 and 1967 participated with such organizations as the Student Non-Violent Coordinating Committee (SNCC), Students for a Democratic Society (SDS), Southern Christian Leadership Conference (SCLC), and others.[25]

These few Chicano student activists were the precursors to the CYM and were indicative of a surge of Chicano student activism to come. According to Carlos Muñoz, Maria Varela became a key SNCC organizer in Oklahoma, where she established an adult literacy project. Originally from New Mexico, prior to joining SNCC she had been a member and co-founder of an SDS chapter at the University of Michigan. Another Chicana, Elizabeth Sutherland Martinez, also became involved with SNCC. She became the director of the New York SNCC office in 1964 and participated in SNCC organizing activities in Mississippi. Other Chicano students participated in the 1963 March on Washington organized by the SCLC. During this time, a handful of Chicano students from California State College, San Jose, participated in a protest involving an African American student who had been denied admission.[26]

At San Jose State, two Chicano student activists, Luis Valdez and Roberto Rubalcava, became involved with the Progressive Labor Party (PLP). Both traveled to Cuba as part of a PLP delegation. Inspired by the Cuban Revolution, they authored the first radical manifesto written by Chicano student activists. The manifesto drew parallels between the plight of Chicanos and that of Latin Americans: "The Mexican in the United States has been . . . no less a victim of American Imperialism than his impoverished brothers in Latin America . . . The history of the American Southwest provides a brutal panorama of nascent imperialism."[27] The manifesto also presented an acrimonious critique of the status quo–oriented Chicano community leadership: "Spanish-speaking leaders are not leaders at all; Americanized beyond recall, they neither understand nor care about the basic [Chicano] population, which has an identity of its own. . . . Having no leaders of our own, we accept Fidel Castro."[28]

At San Jose State College that same year, a few Chicano students became disenchanted with the lack of concern for Chicanos among the leadership of the civil rights movement. They were also concerned that the War on Poverty programs were not reaching the impoverished barrios of the Southwest. Led by Valdez, who had been a member of SDS and a supporter of SNCC, they organized the Student Initiative, the first student effort in the nation to bring attention to the needs of Chicanos and Chicano youth. Organized as a coalition of Chicano and Anglo students, the initiative sought to pressure the university administration into recruiting more Chicano students and establishing tutorial programs for Chicanos already enrolled.[29]

These examples of Chicano student activism at California State College were exceptions to the rule. Of the few Chicano students on campus, the majority were not involved organizationally during the early sixties. Off campus, some of the more traditional and middle-class organizations, such as the League of United Latin American Citizens (LULAC), the Association of Mexican-American Educators (AMAE), and the Mexican-American Political Association (MAPA), either directly recruited students or established youth programs. LULAC, for example, had a group called Junior LULAC for youths between the ages of fourteen and eighteen. The parent LULAC used Junior LULAC to implement its programs among teenagers. Moreover, it served as a training ground for youth leadership development. Since LULAC was a regional organization, Junior LULAC was established in various parts of the nation. Concurrently, in California, some Chicano youth continued to participate in the Catholic Youth Organization, Protestant YMCA, and city youth programs.

In Texas Chicano youth also began to get involved in the emerging CM. In Crystal City in 1963, Jose Angel Gutierrez, a student at a nearby community college, began his activist leadership development with his involvement with the unprecedented Chicano takeover of the Crystal City council. Under the auspices of the Political Association of Spanish-speaking Organizations (PASO), Gutierrez played a major role by giving speeches, registering people to vote, and mobilizing the vote on election day.[30] Like Gutierrez, other Chicano students in Texas were becoming more involved in politics through PASO. In 1964, at the PASO convention, students succeeded in lowering the age for membership eligibility from twenty-one to eighteen.[31] Subsequently, some PASO student chapters were formed in a few universities. Other traditional Chicano organizations, such as LULAC, demonstrated their concern for Chicano youth by providing a few scholarships and recreation-oriented programs. None of these groups, however, prioritized Chicano youth as a pivotal organizing constituency. Throughout much of the Southwest the early sixties were by and large politically quiescent for Chicano youth. These years were truly the calm before the firestorm of Chicano activism.

The Emergence of the Chicano Youth Movement

Beginning about 1967 a new sense of activism and ethnic pride manifested itself among Chicano youth. This activism and awareness were produced by the emerging CM. As the CM picked up momentum, Chicano youth became its most powerful sector. Inspired by a relentless desire for a rightful place for Chicanos in society, the CM provided new directions that "encouraged young Chicanos to become involved for the first time in an aggressive social movement whose prime objective was to force society to recognize members of La Raza as fellow human beings."[32] Chicano youths made an important contribution to the development of the CM by their commitment and activism in all its phases. There would have been no CM without their participation; Chicano youth became the movement's driving force. Yet as integral as they were to the CM, they went on to create the CYM, a submovement and progeny of the CM.

Impatient for change, driven by a new sense of ethnic self-worth, and optimistic about the future, by 1967 Chicano youth became in-

creasingly critical of what some Chicano scholars have designated
the "Mexican American generation."[33] The discontent was predicated in part on the youths' utter rejection of the Mexican American
generation's adherence to a more traditional, moderate, and work-
within-the-system approach. According to Gomez-Quiñonez, "the
student movement was directed not only against the status quo of
the dominant system but also at the status quo allied with domination within the [Chicano] community."[34] The epithets of *vendidos*
(sellouts) and "coconuts" (brown on the outside, white on the inside)
became popular and commonplace in the vocabulary of Chicano
youth activists. Many of them had little reverence for the traditional
Chicano organizations such as LULAC, GI Forum, CSO, MAPA,
PASO, and others. They rejected these groups and sought to form
their own leadership and organizational structures. What followed
was an organizational renaissance among both Chicano students and
barrio youth that produced a myriad of activist-oriented entities.

Conceptually, the CYM comprised two types of organizations:
Chicano student groups and Chicano barrio youth organizations.[35]
The two types emerged somewhat simultaneously. During the late
sixties the CYM flourished in most areas of the nation where Chicanos lived, and in many instances, either Chicano student groups
or barrio youth organizations resulted. Even though they both were
made up of Chicano youth, their constituencies were different in
socioeconomic status and interests. Chicano student groups were
university or college based; their constituency was students. Moreover, most student group members were essentially middle-class.
On the other hand, barrio youth organizations were barrio based,
and their members were not necessarily in school. Socioeconomically, they were essentially lower-class. Whereas the student group
agenda focused on matters relating to education, barrio youth organizations focused on a variety of community issues, including
education.

A wave of activism began to reach the universities and colleges in
1967, and student groups began forming simultaneously. According
to Gomez-Quiñonez, "to argue or assert which began first is moot."[36]
The student groups were not formed as part of a plan conceived by
a cadre of organizers. Instead, they resulted from exogenous and endogenous antagonisms.

In no other state did student groups flourish more than in California. Meier and Rivera wrote, "student organizations are most
strongly developed in California, which has taken an outstanding
leadership role in the Chicano Movement."[37] In January 1967 a
dozen students at East Los Angeles Community College formed the

Mexican American Student Association (MASA), which was perhaps the first student group in the Los Angeles area.[38] A few months later Chicano students met at Loyola University and founded the United Mexican-American Students (UMAS). In San Diego Chicano students formed the Mexican-American Youth Association (MAYA).

Concurrently, in northern California, the Student Initiative (SI), formed prior to 1967 at San Jose State College, changed its name to the Mexican-American Student Confederation (MASC). Chapters of MASC soon thereafter were established at Fresno, Hayward, and Sacramento state colleges. According to Gomez-Quiñonez, student groups in northern California initially were somewhat more advanced than their counterparts in the south. They had more carefully delineated goals, a much more coherent concept of the student role, and, not least of all, outstanding leadership. MASC organizers considered UMAS somewhat moderate, rather academic yet promising.[39]

The differences between the student groups of southern California and those of northern California were attributable to several factors. In southern California the barrios were overwhelmingly Chicano, whereas those in northern California, especially in the San Francisco area, were an admixture of Chicanos, Puerto Ricans, and other Latinos from Central and South America. This situation tended to create differences in goals and focus between both regional groups. In the south the size of the barrios tended to encourage students to focus more on community issues, whereas the northern groups concentrated more on university-related issues and became increasingly ideologically sectarian in their politics. Perhaps the growing radical New Left and antiwar movement politics of nearby UC Berkeley had spilled over into the other campuses. But whatever advantage the northern California student groups initially had proved to be transitory. During the ensuing five years, the groups of the south became the most active and numerous.

In 1967 the CYM spread like a prairie fire throughout Aztlan and beyond. In Texas the organizational renaissance was in full swing with the formation of the Mexican American Youth Organization (MAYO) and Mexican American Student Organization (MASO).[40] Comprising students and barrio youth, MAYO from 1967 to 1972 was the avant-garde of the CYM and CM in Texas. Not all campuses chose to go with MAYO. A few, like the University of Texas at Austin, established a MASO chapter, while others formed the National Organization of Mexican-American Students (NOMA). Next to California, Texas provided the most propitious climate for youth activism, especially with the relentless actions of MAYO.

As the CYM picked up momentum in California and Texas, it spread throughout Aztlan and even the Midwest. By 1968 Chicano students at the University of Colorado, Boulder, had formed a UMAS chapter. UMAS regional chapters were formed in numerous campuses throughout the Southwest.[41] Indeed, a UMAS chapter was formed in 1969 at the University of Notre Dame by Gilbert Cardenas, a first-year graduate student in sociology and former undergraduate member of UMAS in California, and several other groups were formed at various universities and colleges in the Midwest. From 1968 to 1972, wherever they were established, these groups provided a sizable portion of the cadre and troops at marches and demonstrations.[42] They became a powerful energizing force for the CYM.

UMAS: A Short Case Study

During the CYM's formative years UMAS became the most prominent of all Chicano student groups. In California the formation of UMAS was not spontaneous but dialectical. Beginning in 1967 Chicano students from UCLA began to meet to discuss their dissatisfaction with the university over a myriad of concerns. Topping the list of concerns was the small number of Chicanos enrolled at UCLA; during the spring of 1967 there were only sixty. As a result of the meetings, the students, led by Luis Ortiz and Jorge Aquiniga, formed a group. Unlike the older MASA students of East Los Angeles Community College, the Chicano students at UCLA were young, mostly in their late teens. They categorically rejected working with adult political groups such as MAPA and voiced a strong dislike for traditional politics. Their focus was on education and community involvement. In education they were reform oriented. They sought access to institutions of higher learning by calling for student recruitment and retention programs; the hiring of Chicano faculty, administrators, and staff; cultural programs; and so on. With a profound commitment to community involvement, they looked to Chavez and the UFW for their role models.

As Chicano student activism was increasing at UCLA and East Los Angeles Community College, during the spring of 1967 several students from Loyola, USC, California State College–Los Angeles, California State College–San Fernando Valley, UCLA, and East Los Angeles Community College formed a steering committee to organize a student conference. The conference was held on May 13 and was attended by some two hundred college and high school students. Although the conference addressed various issues, including racism, support for the UFW, and tutoring programs, the paramount result was the mandate to form a student group on each campus. The attendees voted to concentrate on the following areas: education reform (student access and retention programs); community involvement (mobilization issues); and social activity (cultural and recreation programs). Shortly thereafter, the issues of Mexican American studies programs and the Vietnam War were incorporated as priorities as well.[43]

During the ensuing months of 1967, UMAS activists held numerous organizational meetings. Several student organizing committees in the Los Angeles area converted to UMAS chapters. By late summer there were seven functional UMAS chapters that were part of a central coalitional coordinating structure comprising representatives from the various UMAS chapters and chaired by Alberto Juarez. During much of 1967 UMAS focused its organizing efforts on the Los Angeles area. In early 1968 UMAS central initiated recruitment drives in the San Diego, Riverside, San Bernardino, and Santa Barbara areas.

With the UFW intensifying its grape boycott, UMAS directed its community outreach efforts to support and assist the UFW. Some of the UMAS chapters became involved with community issues and projects. For purposes of enhancing their organizing and politicization efforts, UMAS chapters brought speakers such as Tijerina, Chavez, and Gonzales onto the campuses. These leaders provided a powerful organizing mechanism for Chicano students.

Ideologically, during its three-year existence, the essentially reformist UMAS never became the most militant Chicano student group. It was progressive in its awareness of the social, economic, and political ills affecting Chicanos but never became ideologically sectarian. Like other such groups of the time, UMAS was ostensibly ideologically heterogeneous. Its activist membership ranks included ardent cultural nationalists who were inspired by Chicanismo, traditional moderates who wanted change but sought it in a nonconfrontational way, and radical leftists who adhered to the notion of class struggle.

Nevertheless, UMAS, with its reform posture, was committed to liberating Chicanos from their second-class citizenship status by changing social institutions, especially education. UMAS sought to be an agent for change working within the existing framework but with the capability to exert pressure against those institutions that needed reform.[44] Although its rhetoric was embellished with progressive leftist jargon (*liberation, oppression, establishment*), by and large it sought the integration of Chicanos into American society. Even though it sought inclusion, however, it did not espouse assimilation. A UMAS newsletter circulated in 1968 clearly describes its commitment to a nascent cultural nationalist perspective.

> We have begun to recognize our role as an organizational agent through which Chicano students are able to recognize themselves as Mexicans and to take pride in it. We are the avantgarde of the young Mexican American liberation movement. We formulate a philosophy for our people and we provide the hope for the future of Mexicans of all generations. We recognize ourselves as a generation of doers as well as thinkers. . . . We are resolved to perpetuate an atmosphere of respect and dignity for our people. . . . We are the agents of progress and unity. We demand social justice for a people too long oppressed.[45]

Further suggesting its commitment to cultural nationalism, UMAS chapters widely circulated Gonzales's epic poem, "Yo Soy Joaquin."[46] At no particular point in its short history did UMAS advance any particular ideology. Beyond its social change and cultural nationalist perspective, it was ideologically heterogeneous and pragmatically open to any student who wanted to contribute to the betterment of the Chicano community.

UMAS's strategy as an agent for reform was not limited to changing the university. By 1968 UMAS had accelerated its involvement with community issues. During the 1968 presidential election UMAS chapters in Los Angeles, after much debate and controversy over whether to support Kennedy or McCarthy, decided not to endorse either one. They chose to endorse and actively work only for Chicano candidates who supported the UMAS platform. In the area of social justice UMAS chapters collaborated with and supported the Congress of Mexican American Unity, a coalition of advocacy organizations.[47] Integral to UMAS's community outreach were its efforts to encourage high school students to continue their education. Some UMAS chapters sought to bring the barrio to the university by encouraging community residents to participate in educational and cultural activities on campus.

On March 3, 1968, UMAS became involved in the massive Los Angeles school walkouts. That morning at Abraham Lincoln High School, a predominantly Chicano school in East Los Angeles, over a thousand students walked out of their classes, joined by teacher Sal Castro. Waiting for them outside the school were members of UMAS.[48] The high school students, angered by what they perceived to be racist school policies and teachers, used the walkout to call for freedom of speech, the hiring of Chicano teachers and administrators, and classes on Mexican history and culture. As high school students were joined by UMAS and other activists, the walkout spread to other campuses. By afternoon nine thousand more students from four other high schools—Roosevelt, Garfield, Wilson, and Belmont—had joined the walkout.[49] With shouts of "Viva la Raza," "Chicano Power," and "Viva la Revolución," the ten thousand students who had walked out succeeded in paralyzing the Los Angeles city school system, the largest in the nation. The boycott gained national media coverage. A *Los Angeles Times* reporter interpreted the walkout as "the birth of Brown Power."[50] The community, with the assistance of UMAS, formed the Educational Issues Coordinating Committee (EICC) to support the students' efforts and demands.

The walkouts, which ended a week and a half later, had both negative and positive ramifications. On the negative side, the demands essentially were not met. Moreover, the "L.A. 13," including teacher Sal Castro, UMAS leader Carlos Muñoz, and others from various activist groups, were indicted on misdemeanor conspiracy charges. After two years of appeal the court dismissed the charges on constitutional grounds.[51] On the positive side, the walkouts directed national attention to the Chicanos' plight in education. They also had a multiplier effect in that they encouraged other school boycotts throughout Aztlan and the Midwest. Within the next two months walkouts spread to Denver; San Antonio, Elsa, and Abilene, Texas; Phoenix; and Santa Clara and Delano, California.[52] "Overnight," according to Muñoz, "student activism reached levels of intensity never before witnessed."[53] In short, the Los Angeles school strike of 1968 went beyond the objectives of Sal Castro or UMAS. It was the first loud cry for Chicano Power and self-determination, serving to further the CYM, as well as the larger CM.

With the activism created by the Los Angeles school strike of 1968, UMAS accelerated its own activism. Besides holding several conferences in 1968 that drew both university and high school students, UMAS became more vigilant and aggressive in effecting educational change. At a UMAS statewide conference held in December 1968, along with discussing such topics as colonialism, international solidarity, organizational structure, and legal defense, the conferees directed much attention to the establishment of Chicano studies programs. Two months earlier UMAS had scored a victory at California State College–Los Angeles with the establishment of the first Chicano studies program. Acuña describes the ordeal that UMAS students had to go through to establish the program.

The first [Chicano] studies program in California began at Los Angeles State College in the fall of 1968. The administration made many promises but gave minimal assistance and support. It allowed hostile faculties to badger inexperienced students in pseudo-democratic faculty committees, and instructors in the program were rarely granted tenure. From the beginning the majority of the programs were set to fail. The frustration of dealing with petty and bullying administrators added to student disillusionment and increased their alienation from the system.[54]

In spite of numerous obstacles and problems, UMAS continued to struggle for Chicano studies programs, as well as for the hiring of Chicano faculty. Furthermore, UMAS pushed hard for more Chicano students, financial aid, and retention and support programs. Its growing cultural-nationalist thrust meant holding more conferences and special cultural events and bringing in CM speakers as part of its educational program going into 1969.

By early 1969 UMAS had developed more chapters in California and extended to other states in Aztlan and the Midwest. The formation of student groups like UMAS in some cases proved conducive to the formation of barrio youth organizations.

Chicano Barrio Youth Organizations: The Brown Berets

While the student groups were a powerful driving force of the CYM, Chicano barrio youth organizations likewise became important contributors. Instead of advancing change at the university, barrio youths focused on the deplorable social and economic conditions of the barrio. Due to the involvement of these groups, many barrios became hotbeds of Chicano youth activism. As exogenous and endogenous antagonisms heightened the expectations of the community, some barrio youth responded by forming action and advocacy organizations. Endogenously, the militant actions of Tijerina and Gonzales, coupled with the nonviolent direct action of Chavez, provided role models for both students and barrio youth.

As they emerged in the late sixties, barrio youth organizations were also influenced by exogenous antagonisms, especially the Black Power movement's radicalism and its adherence to black nationalism. With Stokely Carmichael, H. Rap Brown, and others shedding the garments of integration and nonviolence in 1966 and clothing themselves in the new ideological fashion of black nationalism and Black Power, Chicano youth, especially those in the barrio, also began adopting a similar perspective. Instead of Black Power, it was Chicano Power; in place of black nationalism was Chicanismo. Young Chicanos mimicked the symbolism, rhetoric, and even strategies and tactics of the Black Power movement. This became particularly clear in the case of organizations like the Black Berets and others that copied the Black Panther party's use of armed self-defense, a paramilitary posture, and quasi-revolutionary rhetoric and goals. This is not to say that all barrio youth organizations were carbon copies of Black Power groups. Each developed its own unique personality, but the influence of the Black Power movement was substantial.

Chicano youth barrio organizations were composed of Chicano youths from the barrios who in most cases were not students. Many were gang members who understood the value of organization. Gangs had been commonplace to many barrios since the 1930s, and gang turf wars had been fought for generations. The violence was primarily oriented inward. At times, however, the gangs also became embroiled in conflict with the police. The gangs offered Chicano youths a sense of family, community, power, identification, and security. For some poor youths who came from dysfunctional families, the gangs became their family. These factors explain why, as the CM began inundating the barrios, the CYM was able to recruit barrio youth. During the epoch of protest gang violence decreased and some gang members began joining various barrio youth organizations. CM leaders, including Gonzales, Tijerina, Gutierrez, and others, were instrumental in creating a politicized militia in the barrio that fostered a conversion of barrio youths, whether gang members or not, into the fold of the CYM.

Several barrio organizations formed during the epoch of protest. Gonzales's Crusade for Justice was one of the main CM-oriented groups that effectively organized and incorporated barrio youth as its primary constituency. In Chicago during the summer of 1966, as a response to the Puerto Rican riot, Chicanos formed the Latin American Defense Organization (LADO). Led by Obed Gomez, LADO sought physically to protect Chicanos of the community from any attack by other ethnic or racial groups.[55] In San Antonio the Mexican American Nationalist Organization (MANO) was formed. Led by Beto Martinez, a *pinto* (ex-convict) who had the title of minister of war, MANO was paramilitary and self-defense oriented. MANO functioned as a clandestine group in San Antonio and believed all Anglos were racists who should be driven out of the Southwest.[56] MANO was committed to curbing police brutality in San Antonio's west side barrios.

In New Mexico and in other areas the Black Berets also embraced a cultural-nationalist, paramilitary, and self-defense posture. Cognizant of the injustices and discriminatory, oppressive conditions suffered by La Raza, they were committed to the "Service, Education, and Defense" of the Chicano community. The Black Berets blamed local, state, and federal agencies for the Chicanos' plight. They sought to work against what they considered repressive agencies. Guided by a twelve-point program, the Black Berets preached a gospel of self-determination and liberation—in short, making Aztlan a reality. While not socialist, their nationalist perspective rejected capitalism. The twelve-point platform reflected their emphasis on armed self-defense: "We have to arm ourselves now to protect ourselves and the people from oppression perpetuated by the businessman, government, and police. When a government oppresses our people we have a right to abolish it and create a new one. El Chicano ha Despertado, Cuidate Chota [The Chicano has Awakened, Be Careful, Cop]."[57] In short, none of the organizations mentioned evolved to the point where they became prominent CM or CYM organizational leaders. However, they reflected the frustration and aggression that were rampant in the barrios. The one barrio organization, however, that did manage to become an endogenous antagonism was the Brown Berets.

The Brown Berets were the most prominent barrio youth organization to emerge during the epoch of protest. Formalized as a group in 1967 by David Sanchez, who dropped out of college to assume leadership of the organization, the Brown Berets became the most successful group in organizing barrio youths, some of whom were gang members, *pintos*, and alienated young, into a formidable paramilitary movement that was comparable in some aspects to the Black Panther party.[58] During the group's brief existence from 1967 to 1972, the Brown Berets developed numerous chapters, published a newspaper, *La Causa*, and eventually established a successful health clinic.[59]

The Brown Berets were conceived in the barrios of Los Angeles. As students in California gave impetus to the CYM, so did their barrio counterpart, the Brown Berets. Under the leadership of David Sanchez, the Brown Berets developed dialectically out of his involvement first in 1967 with the Young Citizens for Community Action, a community service club, and then with an "alert patrol" that set as its goal the defense of the barrio.[60] That year Sanchez was named outstanding high school student by the Los Angeles mayor's Advisory Youth Council. One of Sanchez's main projects became the formation of the Young Citizens for Community Action (later renamed the Young Chicanos for Community Action), which became involved in supporting the UFW by collecting food for striking UFW workers. After an abortive effort to set up a coffeehouse to provide recreation for barrio youth, Sanchez changed the name of the group to the Brown Berets.[61]

In 1967 David Sanchez dropped out of college to become the Brown Berets' prime minister. In the style of the Black Panthers, he coordinated the formation and development of Brown Beret chapters throughout Aztlan until the group's demise in 1972.[62] Carlos Montez, cofounder and minister of public relations, describes the Brown Berets' central organizing thrust: "Gang fights are going out. We're getting kids from all the different gangs into the Brown Berets. It's going to be one big *barrio*, one big gang. We try to teach our people not to fight with each other, and not to fight with our blood brothers from the south."[63]

The Brown Berets became the largest and most prominent Chicano barrio youth organization in the nation. At their high point the Brown Berets had some five thousand members and ninety chapters nationwide.[64] Most of the Brown Beret members were lower-class in origin, distrustful of Chicano professionals and businesspeople. They sought to include both genders and had some excellent women members.[65] Their membership and activity focus on barrio youth was an important contribution to both the CM and CYM, for they gave rebels La Causa (the cause).

The Brown Berets became the militant arm of the CM. Based in the barrios, the Brown Berets rejected establishment programs created out of the War on Poverty. Their open adherence to self-defense and zealous nationalistic ten-point program attracted the attention of law-enforcement authorities. In addition, their paramilitary posture of military garb, military formations, and self-defense training using weapons, coupled with their identification with the Mexican flag and revolutionary symbols, made the Brown Berets the focus of and target for harassment, infiltration, and repression by law-enforcement agencies. Acuña further elaborates on this point:

> The Brown Berets aroused a fear in Anglo-Americans that a Chicano group would counter U.S. aggression with its own violence. Law enforcement authorities believed that the Brown Berets were capable of inspiring violent action in other groups. . . . Police and sheriff's deputies raided the Berets, infiltrated them, libeled and slandered them, and encouraged counter groups to attack members.[66]

Law-enforcement entities vigorously sought to destroy the Brown Berets and to invalidate the membership in the eyes of both the Anglo and Chicano communities.[67]

The Brown Berets never developed a clear ideology of their own. Their initial ten-point program addressed issues of housing, culture, justice, employment, education, and so on. By 1972 they had adopted the "Brown Beret National Policies," which included sixteen articles defining various aspects of their action program.[68] Overall, the Brown Berets' quasi-ideological framework, although antithetical to capitalism, was predicated on cultural nationalism and not socialism or Marxism. Carlos Muñoz writes: "As cultural nationalists . . . they had more in common with US, the militant Black nationalist organization headed by Ron Karenga. They did not share the Marxist/Maoist ideology of the Black Panthers."[69] Yet the Brown Berets preached a form of secessionism. Besides being ardent proponents of Chicanismo, they supported the ideal of Aztlan— a separate Chicano nation. Gomez-Quiñonez described the Brown Berets as being the "ones who came closest to articulating an explicit call for self-determination."[70]

Impelled by a historical sense of mission, the Brown Berets participated in numerous protest and mobilization activities from 1968 to 1972. In 1968, along with UMAS, they were very much involved in a leadership role in the East Los Angeles school walkouts; in fact, David Sanchez was one of the "L.A. 13." The Brown Berets provided security during the marches, rallies, and picketing. In 1969 and 1970 the Brown Berets participated in the two Youth Liberation Conferences organized by Gonzales's Crusade, which means that they collaborated in the development of "El Plan Espiritual de Aztlán." In 1969 they became involved in the Biltmore Hotel incident. While Governor Ronald Reagan was speaking at the hotel, several fires broke out there. He was also interrupted several times with cries of "Viva La Raza" and the Chicano hand clap. Fourteen people were arrested, and charges were later brought against six, who became known as the Biltmore Six. Two of these Chicanos were Brown Beret members.[71]

By 1969, as the antiwar movement gained momentum, the Brown Berets began organizing and protesting against the Vietnam War. The Brown Berets that year joined Chicano student groups in forming the Chicano Moratorium Committee (CMC). The CMC held its first massive demonstration against the Vietnam War in December at Obregon Park in East Los Angeles. Some twenty-five hundred protesters participated. In January 1970 Rosalio Muñoz joined Sanchez in co-chairing the CMC. A second CMC-sponsored antiwar demonstration was held in February with some five thousand people participating. The leadership subsequently decided to hold a national Chicano demonstration against the war.

By the summer of 1970 the CMC had evolved into the National

Chicano Moratorium Committee (NCMC). With the antiwar movement continuing to intensify and following the lead of the NCMC,
the CM embraced the war issue. On August 29, with approximately
twenty-five thousand Chicanos participating, the NCMC held the
largest protest against the war in the history of the CM.[72] Initially a
creation of the Brown Berets, the NCMC became the avant-garde of
the CM's antiwar efforts.

The NCMC in January 1971 broadened its activism from the war
issue to police brutality, organizing a rally and march that drew
around fifteen thousand people to Belvedere Park in East Los Angeles. At the end of the rally, some five hundred people marched toward Whittier Boulevard. As the protesters entered the business
area, they were confronted by sheriff's deputies. According to Sanchez, "The deputies fired point blank at the crowd. Forty Chicanos
were hit by the gunfire." One person, a non-Chicano, died in the
confrontation.[73]

With the momentum of the CM declining, the Brown Berets in
1971 sought to reinvigorate themselves by organizing La Marcha
de la Reconquista (the March of the Reconquest). La Marcha was
designed to voice grievances. The one-thousand-mile journey com-
menced on May 5 in Calexico and ended three months later in
Sacramento. The marchers were mostly members of Brown Beret
chapters. La Marcha went through numerous Chicano communities, where the marchers stopped to hold rallies and talk to people.
Numerous CM groups and supporters provided the marchers with
food, water, and supplies. La Marcha concluded in Sacramento with
a rally in front of the state capitol, where the marchers raised the
Mexican flag. For the next five days the Brown Berets protested.
Their protests drew attention to several key issues, such as farm
worker rights, Chicano education, welfare rights, prison reform, and
the overreaction of capitol police;[74] nevertheless, La Marcha, which
was reminiscent of the freedom marches of the civil rights movement, never attracted a lot of participation or media exposure.

Despite La Marcha, the Brown Berets failed to inject the CM with
renewed activism. The year 1972 proved fatal for the Brown Berets.
After Brown Beret leader Sanchez toured different parts of the Southwest and Midwest in 1971 and 1972, the decision was made to in-
vade Catalina Island. Sanchez explains that the underlying rationale
for the invasion was to provide the CM with a symbol: the occupation of Catalina Island. Recognizing the urgency, he said: "We cannot wait . . . by next year it will be too late. Already the momentum
of the Chicano Movement is on the decline."[75] Referring to the invasion as Project Tecolote, the Brown Berets challenged the accepted
interpretation of the Treaty of Guadalupe Hidalgo's Article Five,

which according to them excluded Catalina Island. In their interpretation of the treaty the island still belonged to Mexico. The 1972 invasion ended peacefully and was the Brown Berets' last major activity. Sanchez that year held a press conference in Los Angeles and officially announced that the group had disbanded because of increasing power struggles, factionalism, and severe harassment by law-enforcement agencies.[76]

The National Chicano Youth Liberation Conference

UMAS and the Brown Berets are two organizations, one of students and the other of barrio youth, that became powerful organizing forces for the CYM. UMAS and the Brown Berets collaborated with each other, as did numerous other groups. Even though they had different organizing foci, uses and constituencies, their individual and collective actions also helped nurture the larger CM. One instance of this cooperation was the National Chicano Youth Liberation Conference held in March 1969 in Denver, Colorado. Hosted by Gonzales's Crusade for Justice, this conference made important contributions to the development of the CYM in particular and the CM in general. Some two thousand young activists representing one hundred groups from throughout the nation attended. Their mission was to develop more direction and organization for the CM. Elizabeth Sutherland Martinez and Enriqueta Longeaux y Vasquez, who attended the conference, describe its ambience in *Viva La Raza: The Struggle of the Mexican-American People*:

> Everywhere that you walked in the Crusade Building there were young people discussing politics, art, newspapers, theater, writing and many other topics. When the people were not in different workshops, they were gathering together in the large auditorium to see Chicano theater or listen to readings of Chicano poetry, Chicano music and Chicanos expressing their ideas. The theme song of the conference became "Bella Ciao," an Italian song rewritten by Che Guevara. The whole gathering was not so much a conference as a fiesta to celebrate the new spirit of Chicanismo. Our once secret whisper of "we are proud to be brown, we are beautiful," grew into a *grito*—a roar—that rocked the Crusade building and would . . . rock the nation.[77]

The conference's pinnacle of success was reached with the adoption of "El Plan Espiritual de Aztlán." After days of dialogue and the passage of numerous resolutions, "El Plan" became an evolutionary semi-ideological document influenced first by Gonzales's epic poem, "Yo Soy Joaquin," and second by two previous manifestos: "El Plan de Delano" and "El Plan de la Raza Unida." The former had been promulgated by the UFW in 1966 in the pursuit of social justice for farm workers. The latter was a product of various activist and traditional Chicano leaders who met in El Paso, Texas, in 1967. "El Plan" became the CM's most prominent manifesto written during the epoch of protest.

Brief in words but powerful in message, "El Plan Espiritual de Aztlán" was deeply grounded in cultural nationalism and the concept of Aztlan. It read in part:

> In the spirit of a new people that is conscious not only of its proud historical heritage, but also of the brutal "Gringo" invasion of our territories: We, the Chicano inhabitants and civilizers of the northern land of Aztlan, from whence came our forefathers, reclaiming the land of their birth and consecrating the determination of our people of the sun, declare that the call of our blood is our power, our responsibility, and our inevitable destiny.
>
> We are free and sovereign to determine those tasks which are justly called for by our house, our land, the sweat of our brows and by our hearts. Aztlan belongs to those who plant the seeds, water the fields, and gather the crops, and not to the foreign Europeans. We do not recognize capricious frontiers on the Bronze Continent.
>
> Brotherhood unites us and love for our brothers makes us a people whose time has come and who struggle against the foreigner "Gabacho," who exploits our riches and destroys our culture. With our heart in our hands and our hands in the soil, We Declare the Independence of our Mestizo Nation. We are a Bronze People with a Bronze Culture. Before the world, before all of North America, before all our Brothers in the Bronze Continent, We are a Nation, We are a union of free pueblos, We are Aztlan.[78]

"El Plan Espiritual de Aztlán" had a tremendous impact on the CYM and CM and became an endogenous antagonism. The plan was characterized by several notable aspects: first, the overt rejection of assimilation and an emphasis on the Chicano's Native American heritage; second, the strong adherence to cultural nationalism, or Chicanismo; third, the call for the formation of a Chicano political party; and fourth, a communalist orientation imbued with a spirit of equality and antidiscrimination. Mario Barrera, in his book *Beyond Aztlan*, wrote: "While the plan did not really make explicit whether it was calling for secession from the United States, it was very clear that it foresaw no possibility of ending oppression without Chicano control of the institutions that directly affected community life."[79]

The conference had a major impact on both Chicano student groups and Chicano barrio youth organizations, further accelerating the general radicalization of the CM. During the course of the conference Gonzales accentuated the need for students and barrio youths to play a revolutionary role in the CM.[80] In particular, Chicano youths from California came back from Denver very motivated, knowing that they had contributed significantly to the success of the conference. They had constituted the majority of the conference participants, reflecting the CYM's faster and more extensive maturation in California. Barrera further elucidates the impact of the conference on student groups:

> The plan had a special impact on those students and other Chicanos who had been brought up in the cities of the Southwest in the postwar era. It spoke of the value of Chicano and *Mexicano* culture to students who had grown up in a society that let them know in a thousand subtle and not so subtle ways that their culture was inferior. It stressed community and the solidarity of all Chicanos to a group that had been raised in an urban, acculturative milieu that often left profound doubts about that group's own cultural identity and created gaps between the generations. College students in particular felt cut off from their communities on campuses they experienced as alien institutions, far removed from the *barrios*, and where they were a small minority.[81]

The conference also affected Gonzales and the Crusade, which had organized it, acting as a powerful antagonism that helped catapult both Gonzales and the Crusade to more prominent leadership roles in the CM. Gonzales's emphasis on nationalism and self-determination helped both student groups and barrio youth organizations undergo a catharsis that stripped them of notions of assimilation and integration. Gonzales, via the conference and "El Plan," injected the CM with a stronger dose of Chicanismo.

MEChA: Product of the Plan of Santa Barbara

The increasing militantization of the CYM became apparent in 1969 with yet another conference. One month after the historic Denver Youth Liberation Conference, Chicano activists in California, motivated by "El Plan Espiritual de Aztlán," held a conference in Santa Barbara to deal with issues pertinent to Chicanos and higher education. The conference was organized by the Coordinating Council on Higher Education (CCHE), which comprised students, faculty, and staff from various universities and colleges in California. Held at the University of California at Santa Barbara, the conference was intended to develop a master plan of action for higher education that would include a more unified and common pedagogical philosophy, strategy, and curriculum for Chicano studies programs.[82] Moreover, it sought to unite politically and organizationally local programs and student groups in California and ultimately in the nation.[83]

This action program was entitled "El Plan de Santa Barbara" (The Santa Barbara plan). "El Plan de Santa Barbara" was less philosophical or ideological than "El Plan Espiritual," yet it subsumed many of its Chicano nationalist underpinnings. "El Plan de Santa Barbara" was much more action- and method-oriented. The plan provided Chicanos a blueprint for gaining further access to and reform of California's institutions of higher learning. Like its predecessor, it had a tremendous influence on the CYM and CM.

During the course of the conference students representing various groups sought to consolidate the student sector of the CYM. Inspired by the resurgence of Chicanismo, Chicano students opted for a name change for all student groups. Initially, the conference agenda did not call for a new student group but, motivated by "El Plan Espiritual de Aztlán," the conference, after much debate, agreed on strengthening the CYM by calling for all groups to drop their current names and become the Movimiento Estudiantil Chicano de Aztlán (MEChA)—the Chicano Student Movement of the Southwest. The rationale behind the name change was to consolidate, strengthen, and broaden the student sector of the CYM so that it could operate in both national and local politics. The birth of MEChA tended to kill off most other student groups, such as UMAS, MASC, and MAYA.[84]

Carlos Muñoz, himself a leader within UMAS, explains the significance of the name change in his *Youth, Identity, Power: The Chicano Movement*: "The adoption of the new name and acronym, MEChA, signaled a new level of political consciousness among student activists. It was the final stage in the transformation of what had been loosely organized, local student groups into a single, structured and unified student movement. A literal translation of the acronym MEChA was a 'match' or 'match stick.'"[85] Thus, in the minds of Chicano student activists the obvious symbol was fire, with all its connotations of militancy.

Beyond the creation of MEChA, of equal importance to the CYM was the call in "El Plan de Santa Barbara" for a comprehensive approach toward instituting major educational reforms in higher education. Borrowing extensively from "El Plan Espiritual de Aztlán," with its emphasis on Chicanismo, it took a strong antiassimilation orientation by stating: "Chicanismo reflects self-respect and pride in one's ethnic and cultural background . . . cultural nationalism is a means of total Chicano liberation."[86]

The Santa Barbara plan sought to shift the role and control of the institutions of higher learning, making them accessible to Chicanos. In drafting the plan, the conferees perceived these institutions to be controlled by and in service to the rich and powerful. They especially felt that these institutions served as mediums or agents of indoctrination and socialization. The conferees stressed that, in changing this, Chicano programs must not employ existing goals and structures of higher education as a frame of reference. To provide part of the answer, they wrote into the plan the importance of Chicano studies programs and the hiring of Chicano faculty, administrators, and staff.

The plan also emphasized the importance of cultural programs and close collaboration between the Chicano community and Chicanos in the universities and colleges. According to Gomez-Quiñonez, "in the midst of an increasingly militant rhetoric, emphasis was placed on educational reform in three areas: (1) administrative reforms K–12; (2) the promulgations of a bilingual-bicultural curriculum; and (3) access for student, faculty and staff in higher education."[87] The bottom line of "El Plan de Santa Barbara" was access to quality education for Chicanos. It too became an endogenous antagonism for the CM.

The Emergence of MEChA: The Cultural Renaissance

The CYM was tremendously affected by both "El Plan Espiritual de Aztlán" and "El Plan de Santa Barbara." A spirit of increasing Chicanismo and activism permeated both Chicano student groups and barrio youth organizations. Major mobilizations involving youth occurred in the ensuing two years. Like its parent movement, however, the CYM reached its pinnacle of activism in 1970. That year the student sector moved expeditiously to convert student groups to MEChA. After the Santa Barbara conference several groups in California changed their names. UMAS, the largest and most influential group in the state, all but disappeared. The use of "Mexican American" was out and "Chicano" was in. Hence, by 1972 MEChA was the dominant student group in California.

Outside California Chicano student groups developed somewhat differently. By 1971 few had converted to MEChA. In Texas MAYO continued to be the dominant student group until its demise in 1972. A MEChA chapter, however, was formed at the University of Texas at Austin. In other southwestern states, such as Colorado, Arizona, and New Mexico, few groups converted to MEChA; some of the UMAS chapters and other groups refused to convert and decided to retain their identity. In the Midwest, however, some groups did convert to MEChA. The reality was that even though "El Plan de Santa Barbara" sought to consolidate all Chicano student groups into a national unified movement, by 1972 it was but a dream. Muñoz attributes this to the uneven development of cultural, ethnic, and political consciousness among Chicano students.[88]

Nevertheless, during these two years of transition, Chicano student groups, at times supported by barrio youth organizations and other CM groups, were successful on numerous campuses in making operational the various educational reforms propounded by "El Plan de Santa Barbara." By 1970 in California alone, several universities, colleges, and community colleges enacted Chicano studies programs; hired Chicano faculty, administrators, and staff; and instituted Chicano recruitment and retention programs. These included California State College at San Fernando, California State College at Los Angeles, California State College at Fresno, University of California at Riverside, and Claremont Colleges, to name just a few. San Jose State College established both undergraduate and graduate Chicano studies departments. By the fall of 1970 a new Chicano-Indian University—D-QU (Deganiwidah-Quetzalcoatl University)—was established near the campus of UC Davis.[89] Inspired by the idealism of "El Plan Espiritual de Aztlán" and the action reforms of "El Plan de Santa Barbara," the student sector of the CYM had succeeded in making the universities and colleges more accessible and relevant to the Chicano students and community. These changes, however, were products of activism, struggle, and sacrifice on the part of students themselves.

The development of Chicano studies programs was motivated by a pervasive cultural renaissance among students. From 1967 to 1972 Chicano student groups became increasingly supportive of Chicanismo. This cultural rebirth was predicated on Chicanos reconnecting to their Mexican roots. Rejecting assimilation and embracing cultural pluralism, Chicano students found pride, self-worth, and greatness in their mestizo heritage. The spirit and symbolism of *indigenismo*, the Mexican Revolution, La Raza Cosmica, and Che Guevara were echoed in their rhetoric, standards, and protest activities. The students embellished their vocabulary with nationalist buzzwords, speaking of Maya, Toltecs, Aztecs, Pancho Villa, the Magon brothers, Zapata, *Tierra y Libertad,* and mestizos. Chicano studies programs were by-products of the cultural renaissance. This was manifested in numerous courses that made up the Chicano studies curricula. Offerings included courses dealing with past and present aspects of the Chicano experience, such as Chicano history, politics, sociology, and psychology.[90] During these years, because of a scarcity of Chicanos with doctorates, many of the courses that were offered were taught by persons with bachelor's and master's degrees.

This sense of cultural rebirth was especially evident in the various cultural and educational activities on and off campuses. These activities included conferences, symposia, concerts, dances, and Sixteenth of September and Cinco de Mayo celebrations. Some Chicano studies programs offered classes in ballet *folklórico,* mariachi, painting, and so on. Speakers were an important feature of the program in most of these events. Tijerina, Gonzales, Chavez, Bert Corona, David Sanchez, and, by 1970 to 1972, Jose Angel Gutierrez were brought in by student groups to politicize and raise the consciousness of the students and community people in attendance. Theater groups were particularly plentiful on the campuses. Luis Valdez's Teatro Campesino inspired the formation of student *teatros* that became positive mediums presenting issues pertinent to the Chicano experience and fostering cultural awareness and pride in Chicanismo. In sponsoring these events student groups sought to incorporate Chicanos from the barrios. The "bonding process" between Chicano students and barrio residents was an important dimension of the student groups' efforts to create one community.

On and off campuses the cultural renaissance inspired the emergence of what Meier and Rivera describe as "militant activist publications."[91] Cognizant of the important role newspapers have played in revolutionary movements, Chicano student groups, as well as some barrio youth organizations, developed their own newspapers. These heatedly polemical vehicles of protest would attack and criticize police, growers, government agencies, educational systems, politicians, and *tio tacos* ("Uncle Taco," or sellouts) of the Chicano community in a very subjective manner. Some of the more prominent were *Bronze, El Machete, La Raza, Con Safos, El Pocho Che, Regeneración, El Malcriado, La Voz Mexicana, El Gallo, La Verdad,*

El Tecolote, El Grito del Norte, Carta Editorial, El Papel, Basta Ya, Inside Eastside, Adelante, Inferno, Trucha, and *Que Tal.* Chicano prison inmates (*pintos*) also began to publish newspapers: *El Chino, La Voz del Chicano,* and *Aztlán.* A great number of newspapers were members of the Chicano Press Association, which was a network of community newspapers dedicated to promoting unity among Chicanos and the greater self-determination of La Raza.[92]

The cultural renaissance also included an intellectual and scholarly awakening. Limited in number, Chicano intellectuals from within and outside the university played a part in the cultural renaissance. Scholars such as Ernesto Galarza, Octavio Romano V., Rodolfo Acuña, Jesus Chavarria, and others influenced the CM. Outside the university milieu Ernesto Galarza became a prolific writer and labor organizer. To him, the university was a "cemetery of ideas," not a source of enlightenment, much less of radical or revolutionary change.[93] His scholarship and track record of activism made him a giant intellectual force in the CM.

The scholarly awakening was especially evident in the number of books on Chicanos written by both Chicanos and non-Chicanos during these five years. No longer were Chicanos the "forgotten people," "strangers in their own land," or "sleeping *peones* under the cactus." The void in literature on La Raza, although far from being filled, was at least reduced by a number of works that helped to foster the rediscovery of the Chicano. The CM wakened the nation to the presence of the Chicano. The increased scholarship in Chicano studies also resulted in the publication of several professional journals. By 1970 Chicano scholars had developed three journals: *El Grito: A Journal of Contemporary Mexican-American Thought,* edited by Romano V.; *Aztlan: Chicano Journal of the Social Sciences and the Arts,* edited by then-graduate student Juan Gomez-Quiñonez; and the *Journal of Mexican-American History,* edited by Jesus Chavarria.[94] Of the three journals, *Aztlan* was the most CM- and CYM-oriented.

Moreover, the awakening inspired the emergence of numerous Chicano writers, playwrights, journalists, novelists, poets, and artists. For many of these intellectuals, the university provided the ambience for and became the matrix of the awakening. Novelists Raymond Barrio and Richard Vasquez; short story writers Tomas Rivera, Daniel Garza, Enrique (Hank) Lopez, and Nick Vaca; poets Alurista, Miguel Ponce, Roberto Vasquez, and Jose Montoya; and playwright Luis Valdez, as well as many others, provided a literary explosion of intellectual endeavor. Chicano artists like Malaquias Montoya, Harry S. Israel, Ebel Villagomez, and others further contributed to the cultural renaissance through their paintings.[95] This awakening served as an instrument of cultural reinforcement and politicization.

The high point of activism for the CYM came in 1970. The conferences in Denver and Santa Barbara produced manifestos or plans that served to further invigorate the CYM. The antiwar activities of the NCMC, especially the August 29 mobilization, manifested Chicanos' growing discontent with the Vietnam War. The establishment of Chicano studies programs on numerous campuses by 1970 added to the overall CM momentum, as well as to that of the CYM. This was complemented by the involvement of both student groups and barrio youth organizations in dealing with a myriad of community issues. In some cases student groups catalyzed community activism to such an extent that some scholars (e.g., Meier and Rivera) considered students to have been the vanguard of the CM itself.

Chicano student leaders understood well that with the morass of social problems plaguing the barrios, the barrio community was a fertile ground for organizing, especially against the Catholic Church. Católicos por la Raza (CPLR), formed in November 1969 in Los Angeles, confronted one of the most powerful religious institutions in the world—the Roman Catholic Church. Led by a young law student from Loyola University named Ricardo Cruz, CPLR was organized in response to the Catholic Church's neglect of Chicanos. The catalyzing issue, however, was more specific, as Acuña explains:

> The organization's members were infuriated over the closing, allegedly because of lack of funds, of Our Lady Queen of Girls' High School, which was predominantly Mexican. Cardinal McIntyre had just spent $4 million to build St. Basil's in Los Angeles' exclusive Wilshire District. The members were incensed at the Church's refusal to involve itself in promoting social justice for Mexicans.[96]

On Christmas Eve, 1969, members of CPLR demonstrated in front of St. Basil's Church. Initially, CPLR simply picketed the mass, but the protest escalated and demonstrators entered the church. Sheriff's deputies intercepted the demonstrators, arresting twenty-one. Among those arrested were members of MEChA. David Gomez, in his work entitled *Somos Chicanos: Strangers in Our Own Land*, explains the issue's genesis and the role that Chicano students played:

> The open conflict began to develop in the Fall of that year when Chicano activists, many of them college and university stu-

dents and members of MEChA, raised the issue of the Church's flagrant neglect of its oldest, most faithful, and largest racial minority in the Southwest. "Any fool could see," said one Mechista, "that the Catholic Church has done nothing for our people."[97]

Twenty of those arrested stood trial for disturbing the peace and assaulting police officers. Ricardo Cruz was convicted of a misdemeanor and in 1972 began serving a 120-day sentence for his conviction. This incident was significant, for it showed that the CYM was so motivated by a passion for change that it had the audacity to challenge the institution that was the Chicano community's most sacred cow—the much-revered Catholic Church. The issue of the Church's treatment of Chicanos continued to be on the burner of activism throughout 1970 and 1971.

A second illustration of Chicano students providing leadership for community issues was the formation of the West End MAPA chapter (1968–1970) and its replacement, the San Bernardino/Riverside County Regional RUP (1970–1972). I was the organizer for both entities. At the time I was an undergraduate student at Claremont McKenna College, California, from 1968 to 1970 and a graduate student at the University of California, Riverside, from 1970 to 1974. Impressive and unprecedented victories were scored in the Chicano communities of the Inland Empire—San Bernardino, Riverside, and Ontario (the standard metropolitan statistical area).

In 1969, after one year of intensive grassroots organizing, the West End (Ontario, Upland, and Rancho Cucamonga) MAPA chapter orchestrated the first takeover of a school district in the history of California. Three Chicanos ran on a slate that displaced the Anglo-controlled school board of the Cucamonga school district. This electoral takeover preceded the Crystal City takeover of 1970. What followed was a major educational reformation, including bilingual/bicultural education; the hiring of a Chicano superintendent, principals, teachers, and staff; and the creation of several educational programs such as Saturday school and tutorial programs.

Numerous other projects were initiated from 1968 to 1970 under the aegis of the West End MAPA. Scholarships were provided, recreational youth programs were established, a barrio beautification program of cleaning lots and streets was implemented, and numerous cultural activities such as *posadas* at Christmas, celebrations of Cinco de Mayo and the Sixteenth of September, and dances were held. Constant political education, voter registration drives, and membership drives were part of West End MAPA's mobilization effort. All these activities were done without any government funding, and the programs were administrated by community volunteers. The chapter's success was ascribable to its grass-root and wide-base constituency of blue-collar workers, students, teachers, and businesspeople. At all times MEChA students from surrounding colleges and the Brown Berets participated in its diverse movement activities.

In November 1970 the West End MAPA leadership collaborated with MEChA and the Brown Berets, becoming the first groups to take steps to organize the Raza Unida party (RUP) in California. A number of preliminary planning and organizing meetings were held in late fall of 1970 at the University of California at Riverside (UCR) involving MEChA and other community groups. From within West End MAPA's structure, an RUP organizing committee was formed. The committee sponsored and organized the first statewide RUP conference at Chaffey College on April 17, 1970. With some five hundred activists in attendance, Jose Angel Gutierrez, founder of the RUP in Texas, was featured as the conference's keynote speaker. I presented a comprehensive plan of action delineating the RUP's program and strategy for California. With the same zeal for activism that had characterized the West End MAPA chapter, the RUP in San Bernardino and Riverside counties continued its social change organizing efforts.

In October 1970 some one thousand Chicano students walked out of five high schools of the Chaffey Union high school district (Ontario area). Precipitated by the beating of a Chicano student by Anglo football players, the walkout brought parents and students together into a formidable power bloc. With the walkout supported by MEChA and Brown Beret chapters from throughout the area, the all-Anglo school board capitulated and approved the RUP's demands after two weeks of protest activities that included marches, rallies, picketing, and alternative schools. The salient demands included the establishment of Chicano studies courses, cultural centers, and tutorial programs and the hiring of Chicano teachers, administration, and staff. The West End school walkouts became the only successful school walkout in California.

Concurrently, the RUP in this area had other successes in the political and socioeconomic arenas. Politically, the RUP in 1972 organized a grass-roots coalitional campaign that led to the successful election of Gustavo Ramos to Ontario's city council. With Chicanos constituting only 17 percent of the city's population, Ramos became the first Chicano ever elected to the city council. The election of Ramos became the only RUP electoral victory in California. Complementing the RUP's political empowerment agenda were its socioeconomic development corporations, whose formation was integral to my development of the trinity concept of community development, a holistic approach involving concurrent political, economic, and social changes. By 1972, under the RUP's profit corporation, Corporación Económica para el Desarrollo de Aztlán (CEDA—Southwest Economic Development Corporation), several low-income homes were built in the barrio of Cucamonga. All these developments were done without paid staff and, with the exception of the housing, without any government funds. They were done by students and community people becoming one community in unity and action guided by the power of organization.

The preceding two mini–case studies are indicative of the alliances for change that students and community people formed. It is important to note that in 1971 and 1972, while Chicano student groups and barrio youth organizations continued to deal with a variety of issues, student groups in particular became a pivotal organizing force for the RUP in California. Numerous conferences and meetings were held, and an RUP organizing committee formed. Students participated in signature-gathering efforts in an attempt to place the RUP on the California ballot by 1972. RUP candidates ran unsuccessfully in 1971 and 1972. In Los Angeles Raul Ruiz, a Chicano studies professor at California State University at Northridge, ran for the Forty-Eighth Assembly district in 1971, receiving 7.9 percent of the vote.[98] Ruiz again ran unsuccessfully in 1972 as an RUP candidate for the Fortieth district. Ruiz acted ostensibly as a spoiler in both races.[99] Elsewhere the RUP relied on both Chicano student groups and barrio youth organizations for support and troops. In Colorado the Crusade's RUP efforts involved both components of the CYM. MAYO was the organizing force behind the RUP's development in Texas. At the national RUP conference held in El Paso, Texas, in 1972, many of the delegates were youths. Thus, the CYM between 1970 and 1972 shifted toward a political empowerment agenda via the RUP.

With the CM reaching its apogee of activism in 1970, however, the CYM by 1971 began to decline. Both student groups and youth organizations experienced decreasing activism, increasing apathy, and factionalism. For instance, in explaining the decline of MEChA, whose experience is applicable to student groups in general, Muñoz says:

Despite its achievements—or perhaps partly because of them— student activism had declined dramatically by 1971. New student organizations emerged that were more career-oriented, emphasizing individual advancement. They were also extremely apolitical. Students in engineering and architecture programs formed their own organizations, as did those majoring in health, pre-law, education, and other areas. MEChA had to compete with these new organizations for influence among Chicano students. However, most incoming students lacked the experience of participating in political struggle that would have brought them closer to MEChA's ideological perspective. With protest and confrontation throughout the US on the downswing, mass demonstrations on behalf of Mexican American causes also declined. Most Chicano students no longer perceived MEChA as a viable organization for meeting their academic and social needs.[100]

Other scholars concur with Muñoz's analysis of MEChA's decline. Gomez-Quiñonez makes a more poignant analysis:

By 1971, many MEChA chapters had lost their militant stance, some membership becoming little more than debating and manipulated clubs. Others continued becoming decidedly influenced by Marxist ideas. Complacency and apathy were nonetheless pervading many student organizations. Some of the reasons for this decline included: (1) a loss of organizational direction and purpose, ironically caused by an inability to develop viable goals after achieving initial success in increasing the numbers of Mexican students and establishing Chicano studies programs; (2) the organizational inability to deal with the increasing heterogeneous class make-up of Mexican students; (3) ideological stagnation and cleavages; (4) increased institutional opposition to student political activity; (5) stronger and more varied political organization in the community.[101]

Thus, by the end of 1972 the CYM was beginning to stagnate. For student groups the decline was gradual, whereas for barrio youth organizations it was more precipitous. In 1972 student groups were still functional and active, although they became increasingly plagued by ideological cleavages and power struggles. Youth organizations like the Brown Berets were most affected by the decline. The Brown Berets became nonfunctional in 1972, a victim of factionalism, power struggles, and police harassment. The CYM between 1967 and 1972 was a principal force driving its parent, the CM, but by 1971 it had entered a transitional phase of decline.

The decline of the CYM was ascribable to the decline of its parent force, the CM. In turn, the CM declined precipitously at least partly because of a climate that was no longer actuated and dominated by the radical politics of the epoch of protest. Instead, a nascent but growing conservatism was ushering in a new epoch, one that witnessed the dramatic decline or disappearance of the civil rights, New Left, antiwar, and Black Power movements. As these movements declined, so did the CM and CYM. During the heyday of these two endogenous antagonisms, however, the Mexican American Youth Organization (MAYO) emerged as that epoch's most effective youth organization embracing both barrio youths and students.

3. MAYO: A Cadre Organization of Organizers

By 1967 a climate for change permeated the Chicano community. The growth of the Chicano Youth Movement (CYM) was given tremendous impetus by the formation of the Mexican American Youth Organization (MAYO). MAYO became the avant-garde of both the Chicano movement (CM) and the CYM in Texas from 1967 to 1972. No other CYM-oriented organization in Texas came close to matching its activism, militancy, and espousal of Chicanismo. Not since the turbulent years of Juan "Cheno" Cortina (1859–1870s) had a Chicano organization dared to confront what MAYO referred to as the *gringo* power structure of Texas in such a militant fashion.

The ensuing chapters examine the various aspects of MAYO's development from its inception in 1967 to its demise in 1972. Each chapter focuses on one pertinent aspect of MAYO's history and development. This chapter provides a comprehensive analysis of MAYO's history, quasi ideology, strategy and tactics, planning, structure, gender makeup and attitudes, and newspapers.

MAYO: Creation of Antagonisms

In 1967 the CM was gaining momentum throughout Aztlan. The Chicano organizational renaissance gave rise to numerous advocacy-oriented entities; one such organization was MAYO, which epitomized the militantization of the incipient CM. It was organized in San Antonio in March 1967 by five young Chicanos, Jose Angel Gutierrez, Mario Compean, Willie Velasquez, Ignacio Perez, and Juan Patlan, who were graduate and undergraduate students at Saint Mary's University, a small Catholic liberal arts college. Against the historical backdrop of the city of San Antonio, where Chicanos constituted over 40 percent of the population yet were powerless and impoverished, the group coalesced at the Fountain Room, a bar located several blocks from St. Mary's.[1] Gutierrez explains how the five young Chicano activists (Los Cinco) came together: "We all knew one another. By this, I mean all five of us did not know each other, but like I knew Nacho Perez, Nacho and Willie knew each other, Willie knew a little bit about me and so on. All five of us finally met at my invitation over a beer at a place called the Fountain Room."[2]

The issue that catalyzed the meeting of Los Cinco was their common interest in supporting the Texas farm worker movement. In addition, their discussions were permeated by a profound sense of urgency, frustration, and anger over the powerlessness and poverty of Chicanos in Texas. They realized that they had compatible interests and ideas and agreed that they needed to do more than just support the Texas farm worker movement.[3] With this in mind, they held discussions covering a range of topics and concerns. Gutierrez elaborates on their sense of urgency: "All of us were the products of the traditional Mexican American organizations. All of us were products of the changing mood in the community. All of us had spent some time in one issue or another. All of us were very frustrated at the lack of political efficacy, at the lack of any broad-based movement, and at the lack of expertise."[4]

Of major concern was the inefficiency of Chicano organizations in Texas. Although Los Cinco were cognizant of the contributions made by Chicano organizations such as the League of United Latin American Citizens (LULAC), the GI Forum, and the Political Association of Spanish-speaking Organizations (PASO), they were critical of their conservatism and saw them as not doing enough for Chicanos.[5] Moreover, Los Cinco saw these organizations as being incapable of resolving the manifold problems confronting Chicanos in Texas. In 1969, while on active duty with the Texas National Guard, Gutierrez wrote a position paper entitled "Notes from Jose Angel Gutierrez: Presently in Self-Imposed Exile." He explains why Los Cinco were critical of existing Chicano organizations:

> We feel that such groups as PASO, G.I. Forum, and LULAC are too traditional in their approach to problem solving. Their organizations are not as effective as they should be. They rely heavily on the passing of resolutions, signing of petitions, holding of conferences, voter registration and social activities. These tactics are ineffective and the results obtained through them are too meager.[6]

The more Los Cinco discussed, the more they realized that the main problem with traditional Chicano organizations was that their programs were not oriented toward helping or changing the barrios.[7] They felt that these organizations were neither committed to nor capable of providing advocacy for the Chicanos in the barrios.

Their discussions also focused on other concerns emanating from the deplorable and impoverished condition of the barrios. They felt that something needed to be done to improve the people's quality of life. Moreover, they were concerned about the educational status of Chicanos and the extermination of Chicano culture that they felt the Texas educational system was perpetrating.[8] According to Gutierrez, "Everything we stood for—*mariachi* music, speaking Spanish, *frijoles* (beans), and tortillas, or being Catholic—was wrong in the eyes of the system."[9] Another major concern was the Chicano's lack of job opportunities. They felt that Chicanos were relegated to low-paying jobs and that few Chicanos were professionals.

Their discussions brought them to the realization that they did not want to be part of the existing Chicano organizations. Instead, they wanted to create their own organization, which would be youth-oriented and committed to effecting social change for Chicanos. To deal with these concerns, they felt that Chicanos needed a new direction and a new approach to organizing. Gutierrez wrote, "Today we need to use yesterday's experience and apply today's methods. We need drastic change."[10]

Following the initial meetings at the Fountain Room they spent weeks discussing the type of organization they wanted to form. The five young Chicano activists felt that their backgrounds and experience provided the talent and leadership necessary to form a unique organization that would benefit La Raza. Gutierrez, a high school debate champion, became the group's spokesperson. The son of a Mexican physician, Angel Gutierrez Crespo, who served as a lieutenant colonel in Francisco Madero's revolutionary forces and settled in Crystal City, Texas, in 1928, Gutierrez had familial roots deeply embedded in Mexico's revolution of 1910. Gutierrez's activism began in 1963 with PASO's electoral revolt in Crystal City, which led to the election of five Chicano city councilmen. In 1967, after attending Southwest Junior College and Texas A & I University, Gutierrez enrolled at St. Mary's University in the graduate program in political science.

Friendship among Los Cinco helped them to divide the labor among themselves. Initially the rap sessions started with Gutierrez, Patlan, Velasquez, and Perez. Compean, whom Gutierrez recruited, was the last to join Los Cinco; with his involvement the leadership chemistry of Los Cinco jelled. Compean, who was well known for his activism in the barrios of San Antonio, became a field organizer and second in command to Gutierrez. Velasquez was a community activist from San Antonio who worked for the Catholic Bishops' Committee on the Spanish Speaking. His role became that of an administrator, since his forte had been administering programs, writing proposals, and raising funds. Perez, who had been working for the Texas chapter of the United Farm Workers Organizing Committee (UFWOC), became a field organizer. And Patlan, who was well known in South Texas for his activism, took on the role of recruiting talented youths.[11] Regardless of their specializations, Los Cinco were organizers above all, and according to Nacho Perez, they built MAYO on the premise that it was an "organization of organizers."[12]

Few activists within the CYM were as methodical and deliberate in building their organizations as were Los Cinco. MAYO was not built on spontaneity, nor was it formed as a response to a specific crisis. The planning sessions focused on developing a youth organization that would be different from Chicano student groups that were based exclusively in the university or Chicano barrio youth organizations that were anchored in the barrio. Exogenous and endogenous antagonisms affected their thinking on the kind of organization they were forming. Compean elucidates on their influence: "We talked a lot about what was going on with the Black Movement . . . the farm workers movement . . . Cesar Chavez in California, and other events. We discussed leaders like [Stokely] Carmichael, Martin Luther King, and others. We also discussed some of the recognized political leaders in the Chicano community in Texas and particularly San Antonio . . . and organizations such as LULAC and the American G.I. Forum."[13] The civil rights and Black Power movements significantly affected the thinking of Los Cinco. When questioned on the significance of exogenous antagonisms, the remaining four of Los Cinco (Willie Velasquez died in 1988) agreed that these were an influence on them, in particular the two previously mentioned. Juan Patlan recalled that "some of the ideas of the New Left were also topics of discussion."[14] Because of the Chicano community's initial strong support for U.S. involvement in the Vietnam War, the antiwar movement did not affect MAYO's Los Cinco until 1968.[15] Perez comments further:

Their impact was significant. There was a background: the Selma March in 1965, the Black Power movement, the Student Non-Violent Coordinating Committee. . . . We were interested in what they were doing. Here in Texas, we didn't see much of that here nor like there was in California, Midwest, and elsewhere.

Their activism was rather limited in Texas with the exception of
the University of Texas at Austin, which was a hotbed of political activism.[16]

During the spring months of 1967, besides studying other movements, Los Cinco developed a programmatic approach toward building MAYO. Prior to coming to their rap and study sessions, they read
voraciously on a variety of topics they felt were important to building the organization, such as electoral politics, revolutionary movements, biographies of political leaders, community organizing, and
parliamentary procedures. Gutierrez explains the kind of organization they wanted to build: "We wanted to be a group of active cru-
saders for social justice—Chicano style. This demanded [that the]
members be well-versed in one or more areas confronting the [Chi-
canos]; but more important it meant that the members . . . had to
experience the frustration of defeat; the joy of glory; the grind of day
to day work as learning to be real Chicanos. We wanted to begin
Aztlán."[17] Frustrated by the ineptitude and conservatism of existing
Texas-based Chicano organizations, they decided that the new organization was not to be based on mass membership. They opted for
an organization composed of talented, young Chicano organizers
who would be able to move into areas where they were needed. They
wanted a cadre organization of organizers.

To form an organization of well-versed organizers, Los Cinco read
and studied various topics but concentrated specifically on four:
(1) power structures; (2) for-profit corporations; (3) methods of organizing; and (4) existing Chicano and black organizations. The Anglo
power structure and business corporations were studied meticulously and with a definite purpose in mind. Los Cinco felt that
studying both the elitist and pluralist theories and knowing how
the Anglo power structure makes its decisions and how it governs
would facilitate their organizing efforts. Power as a concept was also
studied. Compean explains: "As we progressed in our discussions
we also came to realize a few things. For example, that you couldn't
change anything unless you have the means with which to change
it. What it has come to mean to us is power . . . if you don't have the
[power] in which to change anything, then you can't change anything."[18] Discussions often focused on the importance of understanding the intricacies of power relations for the simple purpose of
learning how to manipulate power and direct it against the Anglo
power structure.

Complementing their study of the power structure was their desire to learn how corporations were tied into the power structure

and how they functioned. Gutierrez explains why they studied for-profit corporations: "I remember we used to spend Sunday after Sunday poring over the business section of the newspaper. Studying who had moved up from one executive position to another and why and what were some of the things said good about them. So we could begin perceiving the power structure from that point of view."[19] In essence Los Cinco sought to ascertain who the power holders were and what made them tick. The principle of "know your enemy" thus guided their power structure research.

In their study and discussion sessions they also spent time on *Robert's Rules of Order* to learn the art of parliamentary procedure. This helped them to learn how the power structure operated and how it conducted its meetings and business. MAYO used the art of parliamentary procedure as a weapon against unresponsive Chicano and Anglo power holders.[20] Los Cinco felt that a thorough knowledge of parliamentary procedure could help them when confronting school boards and agencies or when participating in formal meetings with power holders by enabling MAYO organizers to use points of order, motions of sorts, and so on to disrupt meetings and beat the opposition with its own rules of the game.

Their sessions also dealt with various strategies and tactics of community organizing. Los Cinco read and discussed Saul Alinsky's *Reveille for Radicals*. Alinsky's use of issues as a means of organizing was studied and discussed thoroughly. During those spring months of 1967 they succeeded in bringing Alinsky to a symposium at Saint Mary's University. After the symposium Los Cinco had an opportunity to meet with him informally and discuss various aspects of community organizing. The influence of Alinsky's method of organizing subsequently became evident in MAYO's involvement in a multiplicity of issues.

Los Cinco rejected what they referred to as the "lone wolf approach" of the Mexican American old guard—writing letters, calling press conferences, using diplomacy, and raising substantive issues in an accommodating way.[21] Categorically rejecting this traditionalist approach, Los Cinco chose a more unconventional, eclectic strategy of protest influenced by Alinskyism, the Black Power movement, and the civil rights movement. Compean comments further on MAYO'S confrontational approach: "What we needed was an approach similar to what the Black Movement was using . . . demonstrating, marching in the streets. To which we incorporated a Saul Alinsky component of confrontation politics. And we said that was going to be the strategy . . . [the] use [of] confrontational politics based on information . . . well researched, but also forgoing the use of nice language."[22] In developing their eclectic approach, they based their integration of ideas, structures, and schemes on what worked. Emphasis was placed on pragmatism of application. According to Gutierrez, "We studied all we could from the structural side to try to determine how we could best organize ourselves and what techniques and strategies that worked were used or employed by other people."[23]

Furthermore, African American organizations from both the civil rights and Black Power movements were studied meticulously. Of special interest to Los Cinco were the Black Panther party and the Student Non-Violent Coordinating Committee (SNCC), which had evolved from a civil rights organization into a Black Power advocate. Los Cinco traveled, sometimes together, sometimes alone, into the southern part of the United States to talk to Carmichael and the organizers of Martin Luther King, Jr.'s, Southern Christian Leadership Conference, both of which influenced the organizational design being developed by Los Cinco.[24]

Los Cinco's pragmatic eclectic approach was also influenced by endogenous antagonisms within the emerging CM. They spent a considerable amount of time analyzing the strengths and weaknesses of CM entities and leaders. They read, studied, and met with the three most prominent leaders of the CM: Reies Lopez Tijerina, who headed the Alianza Federal de Mercedes (Federal Alliance of Land Grants) in New Mexico; Cesar Chavez, founder of the United Farm Workers Organizing Committee in California; and Rodolfo "Corky" Gonzales, founder and leader of the Crusade for Justice in Colorado. They listened attentively, took notes, and on their return reported to the others.

Tijerina was the CM leader who most influenced Los Cinco. Patlan explains why: "Tijerina was saying that this land is ours. That we didn't come here yesterday . . . that we've been here historically, that we were not outsiders and treated as outsiders. . . . We kind of associated our situation in South Texas to what Tijerina was saying. After all, we were here before the *gringo* came."[25]

Los Cinco admired Tijerina's courage, audacity, and fiery rhetoric in attacking the Anglo establishment in New Mexico. Along with others, Tijerina served not only as a role model for Los Cinco but as proof that they were not alone in their struggle.[26]

One important issue during the incipient organizing stage of MAYO (mid-1967) was what to call this organization of organizers. After some serious deliberating, Los Cinco named their new organization MAYO, but before selecting that name they considered several others: Liga de Estudiantes y Obreros Nacionales (LEON);

Partido Universitario Mexicano de Aztlan (PUMA); Sociedad de la Aguila y Serpiente (SAS); and La Raza Unida. LEON and PUMA were thrown out. Los Cinco narrowed the list to La Raza Unida, SAS, and MAYO. They felt that La Raza Unida worked better as a slogan than as a name for an organization, but it was to become a pervasive theme throughout their literature and rhetoric. Later it became the name of their political party. SAS was initially considered because, as Gutierrez explains, "we thought of ourselves as being very powerful in dealing death blows to the establishment—the ruling class."[27] It was rejected because they felt it sounded too much like a sinister backdoor organization where blood rites were practiced. MAYO, on the other hand, struck them as a fairly innocuous name and rather boy-scoutish. Furthermore, MAYO was the most American name they could think of. It was a safe name that did not conjure up any radical or revolutionary connotations. Gutierrez describes why they finally opted for MAYO: "It was going to keep people confused as to what this organization was all about for a while. It was going to be a name that people could identify with, similar to identifying with the Catholic Youth Organization (CYO) as with any kind of youth organization."[28] They preferred the use of *Mexican American* because the majority of La Raza in Texas did not identify with the term *Chicano.* To some, *Chicano* had a pejorative connotation. Terms such as *Mexican, Mexican American,* or *Latino* were more readily accepted by most Chicanos in Texas. The use of Mexican American and Latino was more prevalent among the Chicano middle class, whereas *Mexicano* was more commonly used among lower-class Chicanos. Gutierrez states that they "wanted to blend in and not stick out at that point."[29] MAYO struck them as not being threatening or provocative, at least in the incipient stage of their organizing, to either Chicanos or Anglos in Texas. The word *Youth* in MAYO was believed to be important as an appeal to the Chicano youth of both the barrios and universities.

Los Cinco decided to target South Texas for MAYO's organizing activities after considering the monolithic size of Texas, the concentration of Chicanos in South Texas, the volume of issues plaguing that region, and their very limited resources. For Gutierrez, the demographics of Chicanos and the numerous social problems in South Texas were the two cardinal reasons for choosing South Texas. "We picked South Texas because that is where our blood was found. Also, because South Texas so urgently needed change."[30] After numerous study sessions and discussions, MAYO was activated during the summer of 1967, ready to do battle with its archenemy, the gringo.

The Gringo: Archenemy of La Raza

In its struggle for social change and empowerment, MAYO identified the gringo as the archenemy of La Raza. A position paper entitled "Gringo," which Gutierrez wrote while he was on active duty in the Army National Guard, illustrates how MAYO used the term:

> The meaning of *Gringo* in South Texas is not any different from the rest of the Spanish-speaking nations to the South. A *Gringo* is one who has taken over the lands through violence, deceit, and intimidation. He is one who exploits our labors and talents. He denies us equal and full employment. A *Gringo* is indifferent to the poverty, illiteracy, vice and mortality rate of *La Raza*. A *Gringo* is one who talks of justice, liberty, freedom, democracy, equality and the Bill of Rights; yet, he systematically denies 12 million Spanish-speaking people in the USA meaningful participation in the affairs of this nation. A *Gringo* is one who discriminates against an individual because of his skin coloring, the spelling of his name, his manner of speech or his ethnic background. A *Gringo* is a racist and a bigot.[31]

MAYO made a distinction between the gringo and the Anglo. Unlike the gringo, who was categorized as harboring racist attitudes toward Chicanos, the Anglo was considered to be a person essentially of European stock who was understanding, sympathetic, and willing to help La Raza. An "Anglo," according to Gutierrez, "is someone who will stand up with us and fight regardless, because she or he sees the issues. Their posture of fighting is not in front of us in a paternalistic nature and not behind us in a self-adulating kind of posture, but right next to us taking blows and giving the blows as they come."[32] MAYO conceived of the gringo as being committed to oppressing Chicanos and the Anglo as willing to help Chicanos.

MAYO felt that to address the plight of Chicanos, gringos had to be confronted and exposed. MAYO felt that gringos did not want to do anything to improve the lives of Chicanos in Texas.[33] Gutierrez, in a position paper entitled "MAYO," expresses his hatred for gringos:

> The "good, kind-hearted" honkie—with his deceiving smile and blue eyes—has really socked it to us and royally. With his so called "educational" system he has us Chicanos believing we are inferior because we speak Spanish and eat tortillas and *frijoles con chile.* He tells us that our heroes of World War II and the "Korean Conflict" are not good enough to be mentioned in the

"American" history books by leaving them out completely. They had brown skin and brown eyes. Then he tells us that Chicanos are dumb by leaving us out of top jobs when promotion time comes around. He tells us we are incapable of governing ourselves by not voting for one of us . . . he tells us we cannot manage our own economic or financial affairs by refusing Chicanos a state charter for a Chicano-owned bank, and so on down the line.[34]

Gutierrez's comments are indicative of MAYO's distrust and animosity toward gringos. He further comments, "I don't believe white men are capable of having any kind of good faith and intentions. Not the white people I know. I've yet to travel and many people to meet and many years to go. So I am looking forward to that great revelation."[35] Throughout its existence MAYO ardently propounded an antigringo posture.

MAYO's organizing approach in part relied on attacking the gringo establishment with a degree of militancy unprecedented in Texas history. MAYO's rhetoric and action were directed at dispelling the gringo-perpetuated myth that the Chicano is apathetic, indolent, unsophisticated, and inferior to the European. MAYO sought to make Chicanos aware of the gringo's responsibility for their exploitation, oppression, and powerlessness. Furthermore, it wanted to prove that the gringo establishment was not omnipotent and could be beaten. Through its use of militant action and rhetoric, MAYO gave notice to the gringo that it was ready to defend the rights and interests of the Chicano community. Gutierrez illustrated this determination when he said: "We are going to tell the truth about conditions of the Chicano and we are going to develop our interest to carry out our programs using anything necessary to protect ourselves. . . . We would only hurt somebody when they tried to hurt us, out of self-defense."[36] By identifying the gringo as the archenemy of the Chicano, MAYO resorted to an Alinsky rule of organizing: always foster a polarization.

MAYO's Purposes, Goals, and Views

MAYO's first step was to organize the barrios of Texas to improve the overall quality of life there. It attempted to mobilize Chicanos in the barrios to address problems and to develop indigenous leadership. This orientation was evident in MAYO's constitution, which read as follows: "The purpose of the Mexican American Youth Organization is to establish a coordinated effort in the organization of groups interested in solving problems of the Chicano community and to develop leaders from within the communities. In order to accomplish this . . . MAYO is formed."[37] MAYO's constitution provided a framework through which the group sought to become involved in such areas as education, social welfare, and civil rights, as well as in lessening neighborhood tensions, eliminating discrimination, combating juvenile delinquency, and fostering political empowerment.

Under Texas law, MAYO's 1967 charter as a nonprofit, state tax-exempt corporation precluded the organization from attempting to influence specific legislation or participating directly in the political arena. It could engage mainly in charitable and educational activities.[38] In reality its activities were manifold—from politics to economics to social action programs to advocacy on issues. It functioned very much as a zealous interest group that was willing to use both conventional and unconventional methods to influence policies affecting Chicanos. This modification in its goals was evident in the literature that was published after its incorporation. For example, it propounded several goals in the areas of politics, economics, and education:

> *Politics:* We seek to form third parties or large membership organizations which will file [Chicano] candidates, draft Chicano programs of action and vote in mass as Chicanos for Chicanos. In short we seek control of local political units.
> *Economics:* We seek to make our organization self-sufficient by taking over *Gringo* businesses. We do this for ourselves and our community through boycotts, purchasing of franchises and strikes. Our goal is to transfer the ownership of those businesses whose market is a [Chicano] one from *Gringo* hands to Chicano hands. Furthermore, those businesses we will control in return will subsidize the various programs desired by the local community.
> *Education:* We seek to control local school districts or individual schools in order to make the institution adapt itself to the needs of the [Chicano] community rather than the present form of making the [Chicano] student adapt to the school. We seek to change the curriculum, quality of education, attitudes of administrators and teachers, method of financing the school, and method of instruction.[39]

Of these three goals, education reform received MAYO's heaviest involvement, which resulted primarily from the decision Los Cinco made in 1967 during their study and discussion sessions. They concurred that education was at that time the paramount concern of most Chicanos throughout Texas. Compean explains:

> For some reason education was top priority with just about every Chicano family in the state. This goes beyond Texas too. So that was the safest route for us to take, because if we could convince Chicanos, parents especially, that one of our major objectives was to help as many Chicanos as possible to get them a good education . . . then our [support] would increase. This is why from 1967 on to 1969 for almost three years even until the middle of 1970 MAYO concentrated almost totally on the educational area.[40]

Gutierrez further elaborates on how MAYO used education as a means of organizing: "people were concerned about education. Education has the rhetoric and the panacea that our people have been seeking all throughout our history. . . . People think about education. So when [MAYO] went into communities, education was the easiest thing to argue and discuss things about. . . . [Thus,] education was simply an issue that was acceptable to the community. So we worked it."[41] MAYO's accentuation of education was evident in the thirty-nine walkouts it was involved in between 1968 and 1970.

MAYO's purposes and goals were very much intertwined with its views on violence, action, and La Raza:

> *Violence:* MAYO seeks to pursue its goals in a peaceful and non-violent manner. Not once has any MAYO member been arrested, convicted or punished for any act of violence. In fact, no MAYO member has ever been charged with an act of violence. On the contrary, we've been harassed, arrested, and molested by police officers and *Gringos* for such nonsense as disturbing the peace, unlawful assembly, and parading without a permit. We are the victims of violence to the degree that we have to resort to self-defense measures. If we are attacked or abused, we will resist with equal force.
> *Action:* MAYO is organizationally minded. We provide the technical assistance for groups to petition for their rights. MAYO prefers to solve a problem by direct action through the use of marches, protests, boycotts, mass assemblies etc. . . . We do not believe in such ineffective measures as resolutions, petitions, or letters to officials.
> *La Raza:* We feel that we fall victim to seeds of division when we fight with one another. We need to spend less time fighting,

physically or verbally, other Mexicanos who are weak before the *Gringo* and to spend more time building a *Raza Unida* to combat the *Gringo* and his methods. We also stress pride and identification to our Mexican culture values. We cannot encourage anyone to assimilate or segregate himself from the rest of society until we know what we are giving up and until we rid the society of all racism and bigotry.[42]

These views exemplify MAYO's dissimilarity to other youth organizations. For example, none of the student groups propounded a self-defense posture or the willingness to use violence if necessary. Only a few barrio youth organizations such as the Brown Berets and Black Berets openly advocated such a position. Thus, MAYO, with its multifaceted purposes, goals, and views, was built on a pragmatist foundation.

MAYO's Pragmatist Quasi Ideology

MAYO as an organization did not have a definite ideology. Composed mainly of organizers, it was not ideologically dogmatic in its strategies or politics. From MAYO's inception, it was oriented toward pragmatic action rather than a rigid ideological framework. MAYO's pragmatism was predicated on the importance of getting the job done and on being resilient, adaptable to shifting political circumstances, and sensitive enough to the process of action and reaction to avoid being trapped by its own tactics and forced into circumstances not of its own choosing. MAYO never possessed any rigid dogmas propounding exclusive possession of the truth or, as Saul Alinsky wrote, "the keys to paradise."[43] Dogma was seen as being constraining in that it precludes freedom of action and choice. Gutierrez, when asked about MAYO's ideology, responded: "We . . . trained ourselves to be organizers with no set ideology."[44]

MAYO organizers generally perceived themselves as problem solvers or social engineers rather than dogmatic ideologues. MAYO organizers were also political relativists, persons who believe that truth is relative and changing.[45] Another idiosyncrasy of MAYO organizers was their political realism in their pursuit of change. Alinsky's words are apropos in depicting MAYO's political realist orientation:

The basic requirement for the understanding of the politics of change is to recognize the world as it is. We must work with it on its terms if we are to change it to the kind of world we would like it to be. We must first see the world as it is and not as we would like it to be. We must see the world as all political leaders have, in terms of "what men do and not what they ought to do," as Machiavelli and others have put it.

It is painful to accept fully the simple fact that one begins from where one is, that one must break free of the web of illusions one spins about life. Most of us view the world not as it is but as we would like it to be. The preferred world can be seen any evening on television in the succession of programs where the good always wins—that is, until the late evening newscast, when suddenly we are plunged into the world as it is.

Political realists see the world as it is: an arena of power politics moved primarily by perceived immediate self-interests, where morality is rhetorical rationale for expedient action and self-interest.[46]

MAYO's adherence to Alinsky's political realism was evident in that it was more interested in being a cadre than in being a mass-based youth organization. Carlos Guerra, who was elected MAYO's national chairperson in 1971, amplified this point: "MAYO was not an organization for everybody. It was an organization of organizers . . . [and] activists. We would flat out tell people, if you don't want to risk anything, don't get involved. There are safer groups to belong to. We started out telling people belonging to MAYO is a lifetime endeavor."[47]

MAYO was more interested in solving problems through action than in philosophizing on what had to be done. It confronted issues that were specific and immediate and proposed realizable solutions. Its propellant was action for the improvement of the Chicano's quality of life. MAYO's end was to change the conditions of La Raza through a variety of means. It understood well the needs for ends, but not at the price of sacrificing its freedom of choice of action. MAYO sought to have a degree of control over the flow of events.

Even though MAYO did not have a well-defined ideology, it was extremely critical of what it termed the gringo's institutions. During the late 1960s, pervasive to its rhetoric and literature were its acrimonious attacks alleging that American institutions were racist, hypocritical, and undemocratic. Gutierrez elucidates this attitude:

White America exemplifies this deep-rooted racism in her cherished institutions. Her educational system is represented by bigoted Americans who profess and espouse racist middle class values. Christianity in America is for the ignorant and the unchristian. The unchristian using Christianity to exploit the ignorant. The ignorant using Christianity as purpose for living. The political system has been organized, instituted and maintained by racists. Presently the democratic process is illegitimate and ineffective. Capitalism is an enterprise for White America only. Status in America is a reward given in contradictory order. . . . The institutions are sick because their makers and supporters are schizophrenic. White America deludes itself into lies, transforming hypocrisy into diplomacy, abuse into sacrifice, genocide into law and order, and exploitation into business.[48]

In a position paper entitled *"La Raza* and Political Action" Gutierrez further explains MAYO's negative perspective on American institutions: "The biggest factor preventing our participation is the fact that the political system was imposed on our people. We neither consented nor were consulted. We have viewed the entire government as the *Gringo's* government. We have accepted his policies without complaint. . . . We feel the system is neither ours nor for us. We are political prisoners neither allowed to participate nor able to participate."[49]

Besides being critical of American institutions, MAYO was also critical of capitalism, which it perceived as an exploitive and oppressive system that had relegated the Chicano to an economically powerless and subordinate status within the confines of the gringo's economic order and perpetuated the Chicano's poverty. Gutierrez, in discussing capitalism, mentioned that "any of us, given the chance, would not opt for a capitalist society."[50] Alberto Luera, who in 1971 became MAYO's state chairman, was equally critical of capitalism. He explained that "in our democratic system of government 100 percent of the wrongs within that democratic system stem from the capitalist system, where you can buy off politicians and sell them and have a very unresponsive government."[51] His words imply that even though MAYO did not have a well-defined ideology, it did have hints of an ideology or quasi ideology with leanings toward socialism.

Nonetheless, although MAYO overtly criticized capitalism, it never committed itself to any one ideology. Tenets such as Chicano self-determination, the inherent goodness of the Chicano community, redistribution of wealth, cultural nationalism, free medical services, and an adequate welfare system, among others, were expounded by MAYO.[52] Some of the principles adhered to by MAYO, such as redistribution of wealth and free medical services, are inherent to a collectivist type of political and economic system. Although it never openly advocated socialism, these views were popular and commonplace in MAYO's literature and rhetoric. Compean, for example, when asked what economic system would be more advantageous to the Chicano, replied: "The problems of the Chicano are such that right now the closest thing that comes to my mind is the socialist approach."[53] Luera concurred with Compean, but he espoused what he termed an eclectic ideological approach, predicated on a synthesis of political democracy and some form of economic socialism.[54] Gutierrez, who was instrumental in molding MAYO's quasi ideology, was critical of both capitalism and socialism. He explained that "there is always more than two sides to a story. There is a third side, where you don't have to play at all."[55]

MAYO's quasi ideology did resemble a hodgepodge. According to Guerra, MAYO's ideology was ostensibly inconsistent: "Not only was MAYO's ideology eclectic but internally inconsistent. On the one hand, we were talking about internationalism, then at the same time we were saying internationalism for Chicanos. . . . While we were pushing this ultra-nationalist line . . . we talked about universal equality, yet we sure didn't practice [it] most of the time."[56] All the numerous interviewees agreed that MAYO's ideology was a mixture of various ideas and beliefs. Daniel Bustamante, who served as statewide MAYO organizer, said, "Even though many attempts were made to portray MAYO as a leftist or communist organization, we weren't."[57]

MAYO's ideological eclecticism was covered by a thick veneer of Chicano cultural nationalism, or Chicanismo. Within the diverse student groups and barrio youth organizations that constituted the CYM, MAYO was the most zealous advocate of cultural nationalism. From the various discussion and planning sessions in 1967 to MAYO's demise in 1972, Chicanismo was a powerful force that energized its vehement rejection of assimilation. This was evident in the rhetoric of its leaders, literature, symbolism, and actions. On the issues of assimilation Gutierrez said, "We will not try to assimilate into this *Gringo* society in Texas nor will we encourage anybody else to do so."[58]

MAYO's cultural nationalism was pervasive at all levels of membership. When interviewed, MAYO's leaders, including Carlos Guerra, Alberto Luera, Lupe Youngblood, Rudy Rodriguez, Edgar Lozano, Daniel Bustamante, and others, as well as Los Cinco, all agreed that MAYO was an ardent advocate of Chicanismo. Unlike the individuals in some other Aztlan-based student groups, MAYO's leaders and members were "practicing" Chicanos or Mexicanos, bilingual and bicultural. They were articulate in both English and Spanish. This orientation was ascribable largely to the pervasive *Tejano* culture, which was grounded on its Mexicanness. Historically, the heavy concentration of Chicanos in South Texas and the border shared with Mexico helped to produce a culture that was much more Mexican than its counterparts in other states in Aztlan. MAYO's adherence to its Mexican cultural roots was evident in the usage and manipulation of Mexican symbols. MAYO's logo, for example, was the head of an Aztec warrior inside a circle. Moreover, this profound commitment by MAYO to its Mexican historical and cultural roots became obvious in its use of the Mexican flag in direct action activities, utilization of the Mexican Revolution's leaders and ideas, and the many pronouncements made in Spanish, particularly via MAYO's various newspapers. For MAYO, being a Chicano meant being proud of being Mexican. Consequently, MAYO used the terms *Chicano* and *Mexicano* interchangeably. Within the CYM, MAYO stood out in its adherence to Chicano nationalism. By 1969, when other student groups were jumping on the bandwagon of cultural nationalism, MAYO in Texas had a two-year history of acting as an endogenous antagonism for both the CM in general and the CYM in particular. MAYO's adherence to Chicanismo served to enhance its quasi-ideological, eclectic, and programmatic approach.

At the core of MAYO's quasi-ideological approach, however, was its adherence to pragmatism. Few Chicano organizations during the epoch of protest were as practical as was MAYO. Although the rhetoric of its leaders and spokespersons was embellished by Chicanismo, MAYO's leadership was directed by Alinsky's principle of using "what works." Many of MAYO's leaders were practitioners rather than ideologues. This is not to say, however, that MAYO did not have dogmatic ideologies within its membership ranks. MAYO organizer Daniel Bustamante recalled an incident when Gregory Salazar, a MAYO spokesperson from Houston who is now deceased, upon returning from a trip to Cuba in 1971 propounded that MAYO was "communist." The incident created a firestorm of protest from MAYO's leadership. MAYO's adversaries throughout the state used it to undermine the organization's credibility.[59]

MAYO's pragmatism was strongly influenced by the personality and leadership style of its main spokesperson, Jose Angel Gutierrez.[60] Intelligent, articulate, audacious, and very Machiavellian, Gutierrez was an organizer-turned-leader whose organizing style was reminiscent of Alinsky's. To Gutierrez, ideology inhibits creativity of action. He was neither a capitalist nor a socialist, although his rhetoric and actions stemmed from both. After all, it was Alinsky who said, "Dogma is the enemy of human freedom. Dogma must be watched for and apprehended at every turn and twist of the revolutionary movement."[61] In describing Gutierrez's Machiavellianism,

Guerra said, "Oddly enough, Jose Angel's political hero was a practical politician by the name of Lyndon B. Johnson."[62] The other MAYO leaders were also cast from the same pragmatic activist mold.

MAYO's Protest Strategy and Tactics

MAYO's pragmatic orientation was particularly evident in the organization's use of direct action tactics. This orientation was complemented by MAYO's adherence to a protest approach defined by Michael Lipsky: "Protest activity is defined in this study as a mode of political action oriented toward objection of one or more policies or conditions, characterized by showmanship or display of an unconventional nature, and undertaken to obtain rewards from political or economic systems while working within the systems."[63] Furthermore, according to Peter Eisinger, protest "is a device by which groups of people manipulate fear of disorder and violence while at the same time they protect themselves from paying the potentially extreme costs of acknowledging such a strategy."[64] Both Lipsky's and Eisinger's definitions of protest invoke direct action strategies and unconventional tactics. In the report entitled "The Politics of Protest," Jerome Skolnick, who headed the Task Force on Violent Aspects of Protest and Confrontation of the National Commission on the Causes and Prevention of Violence, describes the diversity of strategies and tactics employed in protest:

> Protest takes various forms: verbal criticism; written criticism; petitions; picketing; marches; nonviolent confrontation, e.g., obstruction; nonviolent lawbreaking, e.g., "sitting-in"; obscene language; rock-throwing; milling; wild running; looting; burning; guerrilla warfare. Some of these forms are violent, others are not, others are hard to classify. Some protests begin peacefully and, depending on the response, may end violently.[65]

MAYO was a great aficionado of unconventional protest methods. Many of what Lipsky, Eisinger, and Skolnick describe as protest tactics were practiced by MAYO (the exception being rock throwing, looting, guerrilla warfare, burning, etc.). With its cadre-oriented membership, MAYO relied on verbal and written criticism, petitions, picketing, marches, nonviolent confrontations, sit-ins, and the use of obscene language to create a contagion that ultimately mobilized large numbers of people. Although it often alluded to the possible use of violence and self-defense, such rhetoric was part of its bravado strategy of showing no fear to gringos and demonstrating courage to Chicanos. For all its tough talk, it never used violence. MAYO in theory was committed to meeting violence with violence, but in practice it was nonviolent and worked within the framework of the system's institutions.

For several months in 1967 MAYO experimented with a variety of organizing techniques in San Antonio's west-side barrios. The following illustrates MAYO's initial approach to organizing barrio youth:

> From this experience we have come up with some very effective skills. We developed strong, personal bonds with the *barrio* with no intention of "reforming" them or promising grandiose rewards for their loyalty and interest. We very simply talked about our troubles and our worries, about our future and our sons, about our people and our jobs. But we never rationalize or make excuses for our conditions, rather we explain to our blood how the *Gringo* has been and is responsible for a lot of our misery. Once we have won the trust of our blood we are guaranteed a line of communication to all members of that family. Usually we begin our organizing with the young Chicano who is out in the street. Sooner or later, word gets to the parents as to the new past-time [*sic*] activities of their young and we have an invitation to the home. A certain amount of "baby-sitting" goes into our organizing because this is the easiest way to capture the parents' curiosity. The son or daughter has a new phrase in their language— "*La Raza Unida*," "*Gringos*," "*Cultura* genocide"—and a new found source of dignity and pride. Parents, like all good Mexican parents, want to know what their sons are up to. Seldom do we engage in door-to-door organizing. The easiest and most profitable method of organizing Chicanos is through the pre-existing groups such as the gang, the extended family, the *compadrazgo* system, the *barrio* beer joint regulars, etc.[66]

MAYO did not organize simply to organize. In essence, it sought to assist the people in the barrios to organize themselves into effective groups to attain whatever change they deemed necessary. Concomitantly, it sought not to provide leadership but to develop the barrios' indigenous leadership by politicizing the people living there and providing leadership and encouragement via action.

Like its strategies, MAYO's organizing tactics were eclectic. MAYO was dramatically influenced by both Chicano and non-Chicano movement leaders and organizations. Concomitantly, it was the most "Alinskyist" of any of the CM entities to emerge during the epoch of protest. Attending to Alinsky's emphasis on issues as mediums for organizing, MAYO manipulated the issues that it felt would appeal to the self-interest of those segments of the Chicano community it was trying to organize. Because MAYO had limited resources, its tactics were often predicated on Alinsky's dictum that "tactics means doing what you can with what you have."[67] MAYO's tactics were designed to rub salt into the community's sores of discontent. It relied on the people's pain and frustration to effect social change. MAYO's eclectic protest approach often incorporated Alinsky's rules:

1. Power is not only what you have but what the enemy thinks you have.
2. Never go outside the experience of your people.
3. Whenever possible go outside of the experience of the enemy.
4. Ridicule is man's most potent weapon.
5. A good tactic is one that your people enjoy.
6. A tactic that drags on too long becomes a drag.
7. Keep the pressure on.
8. The threat is usually more terrifying than the thing itself.
9. Pick the target, freeze it, personalize it, and polarize it.[68]

MAYO was very much an organization oriented toward acquiring power.[69] MAYO understood well Alinsky's notion that power derives basically from two sources: money and organized people. Lacking money, MAYO relied overwhelmingly on its ability to mobilize people. Its adherence to Alinsky's first rule was apparent in its efforts to demonstrate to both the gringo and Chicano in Texas the group's capability to mobilize both students and people of the barrios. Its record of instigating thirty-nine walkouts between 1968 and 1970 plus other mass confrontations demonstrates the power and mobilization capability it developed during those years. As Gutierrez explains, MAYO learned the second rule the hard way, through experience: "When you organize, you organize around the issues that are important to the development of the community. You don't come in with your own agenda, we tried that. We tried coming in and telling the people to fight against imperialism, colonialism, and capitalism, that was like talking moon talk, whatever that is."[70]

Alinsky's third rule was one of MAYO's favorites. For example, in the Del Rio march of March 1969 MAYO protested the firing of some Chicano VISTA workers. The VISTA workers had been denied a parade permit, so MAYO decided to have a funeral for a dead rabbit it named "Justice." MAYO thus demonstrated its creativity and its sophistication in using symbolism—the dead rabbit—to circumvent obstacles and in doing the unexpected and the unthought of. In general, by going outside its adversaries' experience, MAYO sought to create fear and confusion among those that it considered to be its enemies.

The fourth rule, ridiculing the enemy, was a potent tactic in MAYO's arsenal. During the Del Rio march the governor of Texas ordered in the Texas Rangers, and many Chicanos were arrested. In the ensuing weeks MAYO members ridiculed the governor by throwing dead rabbits at his feet whenever he spoke in public. Obviously, MAYO members enjoyed this tactic, thus satisfying the fifth rule.

MAYO learned the sixth rule, like the second, through experience. In many of the school walkouts in which MAYO was involved, it found itself ultimately losing because the momentum of the issue was lost with weeks of protracted and futile negotiations, picketing, and demonstrations. At the beginning of the issue many people were usually involved; however, after a few weeks—and in some cases days—the protesting ranks gradually became smaller and smaller.

In the Crystal City school walkouts of 1969, however, the opposite was true. This was because, in organizing the walkout, Gutierrez followed Alinsky's seventh rule by using a "crescendo tactic"—the number of walkout participants gradually increased. It proved to be successful. MAYO understood well how to use pressure tactics to advance its change and empowerment agenda. Its pressure came in a variety of forms, from verbal denunciation of the system and politicians to demonstrations of various sorts.

The use of threat was one tactic that worked very effectively against MAYO's opposition. MAYO's self-defense posture coupled with its vehement and often belligerent rhetoric did much to engender fear and anger among its enemies. For example, Gutierrez in 1969 made his famous "Kill the Gringo" speech, which infuriated some and scared others. In that particular speech Gutierrez denigrated the gringos and called for their elimination by "killing them if all else fails."[71] This speech did much to enhance MAYO's militant image in Texas and throughout Aztlan. Gringo and Chicano establishment leaders reacted in adverse ways. For example, Henry B. Gonzalez, a congressman from Texas, called for a grand jury investigation of such organizations as MAYO, noting, "this is beyond one man's fight."[72] The speech fostered much controversy in Texas. It was unprecedented for a Chicano leader in Texas overtly to advocate the "elimination" or "killing" of a gringo.

Many Chicano activists perceived the speech as a victory because it demonstrated the audacity and fortitude required to speak out against and threaten the gringo. According to Rodolfo Acuña, "The speech had the effect of creating pride among many Chicanos who had always wanted to confront the oppressor, but who had feared doing so. It was a key to liberating many from fear."[73] Alinsky's rule about threats usually being more terrifying than the thing itself was one of the favorite and most frequently followed in MAYO's organizing efforts.

Alinsky's tactic of picking the target and then freezing, personalizing, and polarizing it was also very much used by MAYO. With its militant action, MAYO often alienated and polarized. Communities were frequently divided into two opposing camps—Chicano versus gringo—by its unconventional protest tactics. Sometimes the Chicano community itself became divided and polarized along ideological lines. This was especially true among those middle-class assimilationist Chicanos who were essentially moderate to conservative in their politics. MAYO's tactics were often designed to identify both its enemies and its friends; its emphasis on action and on getting results often created more of the former. Gutierrez elaborates on the problem MAYO had with its militant image:

> We failed in making friends. We were so bad we didn't care. We would rather be hated than liked. Pretty soon there were more people hating us than liking us. So our public relations was much to be desired. Our image was terrible . . . we went around looking for a fight. So pretty soon we had the image that we had a chip on our shoulders. Regrettably this was being seen by the Chicano community much more so than the *Gabacho* [white guy].[74]

In the eyes of MAYO's leaders there could be no innocent bystanders on the issues of civil rights and empowerment.[75] MAYO's attitude precipitated a designed and desired polarization that was evident even in its membership recruitment strategy. MAYO sought to attract idealistic youths and to alienate those who were moderate. MAYO's leadership sought true-believer types who would commit themselves to an ethnic political movement, which is what MAYO intended to be. Members were expected to put La Raza first and foremost.[76] These requirements were indicative of MAYO's commitment to developing a cadre of organizers who were zealous adherents of Chicanismo.

Thus, MAYO's tactics were essentially eclectic, amalgamating Alinsky's use of issues as a means of organizing with an unconventional protest approach that was common to a variety of organizations participating in the various movements during the epoch of protest. According to Compean MAYO's highest priority in 1967 was "to try to bring on the scene the tactics of the civil rights movement, which were picketing, demonstrating, and confrontation politics."[77] MAYO felt that Chicanos had seldom resorted to such tactics and that circumstances rendered it expedient to do so. The use of such unorthodox tactics was seen as conducive to dispelling myths of Chicano docility and servility to the gringo. Overall, MAYO's tactics were designed to mobilize Chicanos, especially the youth, into social and political action.

Furthermore, the group's eclectic tactics were designed to differentiate MAYO from other, accommodationist Chicano organizations in Texas. Its vehement rhetoric coupled with its protest politics orientation was directed at the gringo power holders. In confronting them MAYO sought to demonstrate their vulnerability. The idea that the gringo could be beaten was accentuated throughout MAYO's existence. The principal objective was to find the tactics that would actuate and mobilize the Chicano community. Throughout its years of activism MAYO constantly sought to play a "war of nerves" against those it labeled the opposition. An element of surprise kept the opposition off balance and unaware of MAYO's next moves. Its tactics had strategic psychological underpinnings—to instill in the minds of La Raza that the gringo power holder in Texas was not omnipotent and could be beaten.

By 1969 MAYO leaders began expounding on the need for MAYO to alter its image and tactics. The MAYO board minutes of October 10, 1969, read: "Jose Angel and Mario brought up the idea of facing reality and the real issues and leaving the romanticism behind."[78] By "romanticism" they meant manner of dress—long hair, beards, and berets. A lengthy discussion ensued on this topic. Those who supported Gutierrez and Compean explained why it was important for MAYO to change its image. They argued that MAYO had to have an acceptable image that would not "turn off" the community but rather win its confidence. Conversely, the opposition argued that manner of dress was irrelevant to the work being done and that it had nothing to do with MAYO's organizing. They further argued that discipline was what MAYO needed most. Even though the opposition won the debate, there was general agreement among the board members that MAYO's tactics had to be changed.[79]

MAYO's eclectic tactics were usually conceived in the planning sessions that were held prior to engaging any major issue. Planning was stressed from the beginning. It was used as a means not only for formulating strategy and tactics but also, and equally important, for engendering a collectivity of thought and action among the members. Compean amplifies: "Our planning for the first two years was within the group. Making sure we had a collective mind and a collective thought. Making sure that we knew all arguments, why we were doing what we were doing. Making sure we could answer people that would challenge us. Making sure we had the psychological frame of mind to confront people even though the odds were against us."[80] Compean further explains that "in most cases there was a lot of planning. There were a few cases where there was little if no planning and it showed in the results."[81] Such situations resulted in part from MAYO's organizational format. Although planning was constantly stressed, MAYO was sometimes encumbered by its loose and decentralized structure.

MAYO's Decentralized Structure

MAYO's structure was designed to give flexibility to its operation. From its beginning MAYO opted for a decentralized structure that would give it the latitude needed to improvise and experiment with various tactics and programs. Creativity of thought and action were sought. Section VII of its articles of incorporation describes its decentralized structure: "The board recognizes the autonomy of the different member organizations and does not see itself as a rigid control structure that can in any manner inhibit the programs or dictate policy to functioning organizations."[82] MAYO's decentralized structure called for a board of directors and individual chapters. There were no regional or district entities. Overall, its structure consisted of a board with little power and autonomous chapters with much power.

According to its bylaws, the governing board of directors was composed of Los Cinco and one representative from each chapter. Each chapter was also allowed to elect an alternate board member who would attend board meetings when its official elected delegate could not. The board met twice a year, on the last Saturday in January and on the last Saturday in June.[83] One meeting was devoted to planning; priorities and projects were selected for the year. The second meeting was usually held to evaluate the various programs and projects and to elect new officers. The board elected a chairman, a vice-chairman, a secretary, and a treasurer, each of whom held office for one year. All officers except the chairman were eligible for reelection. The chairman was allowed to appoint his own staff, which comprised two people, a secretary and an assistant. The chairman's primary responsibility was to ensure that the dictates or policies of the board were carried out. The following points in MAYO's articles of incorporation depict the policy orientation of the board of directors:

1. The board shall be unequivocally opposed to prejudice and discrimination in any form;
2. The board also recognizes that there are many groups interested in the betterment of the Chicano community and the board will seek to maintain active co-operation with other groups but feels that it should limit participation to groups directly involved in community development through organizations of problem solving groups. The participant groups will be bi-lingual and bi-cultural;
3. The board shall be bi-lingual and bi-cultural; and
4. The interest of the board is to foster co-operation and understanding among member organizations.[84]

MAYO's voting procedures were based on majority rule. Decisions on resolutions, motions, elections, or any other business were decided by simple majority. A two-thirds majority among members present, however, was required for any amendment to the bylaws. Also, an amendment to the bylaws required fifteen days' written notification to the membership. A voting quorum was simply the board members present. The voting and meetings were conducted utilizing parliamentary procedures as established in *Robert's Rules of Order*.[85]

In reality, however, MAYO's state structure, while always decentralized, changed over time. Lupe Youngblood, a MAYO state board member, described MAYO as evolving from a very loose structure in 1967 to a more formal one by 1969.[86] Even so, it never became markedly hierarchical and bureaucratic. Bustamante described MAYO's state board as a "cooperation or collective of people where group decisions were made."[87] To Patlan, the two yearly state meetings were more like conventions than board meetings.[88] In addition, according to Perez, "MAYO never had an elaborate system of committees."[89] In its effort to enhance what Youngblood described as "participatory democracy," by 1969 each MAYO chapter was allowed to have two representatives instead of one at MAYO's statewide board meetings.

MAYO's state structure was buttressed by a small administrative staff that operated out of San Antonio. This staff performed four major functions: (1) it followed up on the implementation of policies and decisions made at state board meetings; (2) it provided organizing assistance to MAYO chapters; (3) it maintained communications with other CM organizations throughout Aztlan; and (4) it organized MAYO's state conferences, press conferences, and so on.[90] MAYO's state officers would at times operate out of the San Antonio office, which was located in the barrios of San Antonio's west side. Because of the group's extremely limited resources, MAYO's small staff varied in size and was largely voluntary. Lupe Youngblood, who worked as a staff person, explained that they initially relied on a small grant from the Ford Foundation, contributions, and speakers' fees. However, resources were often so scarce that two or three staff members would live under one roof. This meant that one of the staff members would work full time so that they could pay for housing, utilities, and food. They did this on a rotating basis.[91] In comparison to other Chicano student groups, MAYO was unique in that it was able to maintain a statewide office and staff. At its administrative apogee, MAYO's staff numbered nine.

MAYO's Collective State Leadership

MAYO's leadership orientation was essentially collectivist. There was an emphasis on the group and not on the individual leader. Its criteria for membership included: "Owe allegiance to no man but to the idea of justice for all the *Raza*—no idols, saviors or super-Chicanos."[92] Power struggles were commonplace among both Chicano student groups and barrio youth organizations during the epoch of protest, but unlike many other Chicano organizations, MAYO was not plagued by power struggles within its leadership. At the state meetings emphasis was placed on reaching a high degree of consensus before making policy decisions. There was a sense of democratic centralism practiced in decision making. Policy issues were often hotly debated, but the leaders closed ranks once the decision was made. Personalism was mitigated through a no reelection clause for the chairman. The structure allowed for a circulation of leaders, which in turn permitted leadership mobility. Consequently, there existed an aura of trust and solidarity and a commonality of purpose and goals. Gutierrez elucidates on the prevalence of trust among MAYO's leaders:

> As organizers we were very critical of each other—[we were] very critical and honest with each other. . . . One of the things that kept us together and working is the respect that we each had for each other's talents and abilities . . . The implicit trust was always there . . . We always followed the assets of each other. We

recognized that the only way we were going to be viable was for [each of us to do our best].[93]

Another factor that contributed to this collectivist leadership orientation was the division of labor among MAYO's board members. When MAYO was being formed in 1967, members of Los Cinco recognized Gutierrez's public speaking ability. Consequently, the state board allowed him to continue to speak for MAYO even after he left the chair.

MAYO's Membership Base

MAYO's chapters were composed of youths from the barrios and colleges and its membership thrust was to bridge both segments. In the barrios it sought to transform gangs and *pachucos* into chapters and activists. Initially, in 1967, MAYO first focused on organizing barrio-based MAYO chapters. However, by 1968 MAYO chapters were also organized in the universities, colleges, and even high schools. The barrio chapters, however, remained the most numerous. They were composed predominantly of poor young men from the ages of thirteen to their early twenties. The ages varied according to each chapter's situation. At the university or college level, some members were poor, but in general they were middle-class.

Membership in MAYO was subject to the limitations set by the board of directors. MAYO's membership criteria were based on twelve requirements for new members (see Appendix 2 for all twelve). Those wishing to join had to adhere categorically to all twelve requisites, which were oriented toward sacrifice, dedication, knowledge, sincerity, courage, and discipline. The following two requisites illustrate MAYO's emphasis on courage and knowledge:

1. Courage to follow orders as well as to give them. When ordered to attack directly, must do so and he who gives orders must be ready to lead; and
2. A basic knowledge of what the movement is about. Romantic people and people out for kicks or publicity are not helping any. This movement is serious business, not a game.[94]

These two requisites reflect the cadre structure of its membership. The board sought to maintain MAYO as an organization of organizers. MAYO sought to recruit individuals who were compatible with its philosophy and goals. It sought those individuals who had the qualities of good organizers.

The actual size of MAYO's membership was never known. In fact, at the state level, membership rolls were not kept and dues were not collected.[95] MAYO did not require membership dues because, according to Compean, the records would have provided a convenient source of information for anyone from the gringo power structure of Texas and its law-enforcement agencies who infiltrated the organization.[96] To safeguard MAYO from infiltration, each MAYO chapter was responsible for maintaining records of its membership. To MAYO's leadership, the number of members was not important. What was important, however, was the quality and commitment of its members. Because of MAYO's emphasis on networking and involving others in the struggle, a few members properly organized and motivated could easily multiply themselves tenfold.[97] Intrinsic to MAYO's cadre orientation was the notion that change is always made by the few in the name of the many.

MAYO's chapter membership fluctuated as a function of the issues it confronted between 1967 and 1970, the years of its advocacy-oriented agenda. New members were recruited generally through two means, the use of issues and the dissemination of information.[98] MAYO's membership ranks increased with every issue the group confronted. The issue was utilized both as a means of organizing the barrios and as a medium for recruiting. Members were recruited also through the dissemination of information—speaking engagements and rap sessions in the barrios and the distribution of MAYO newspapers and pamphlets, buttons, and posters. Once a group of youths became interested in forming a MAYO chapter, it was required to follow at least four rules:

1. Practice La Raza Unida philosophy;
2. Increase communication and rigidly maintain it, with letters at least twice a month;
3. Maintain study sessions, learning process of all types, e.g., power structure studies; and
4. Application of service.[99]

These four rules, coupled with the twelve requisites, were stipulated as requirements for a MAYO chapter to be recognized by the board of directors. Once the chapters were recognized, they met at their discretion and established their own priorities.

Even though each individual chapter was initially permitted one and later two board members, individuals had to go through MAYO's three levels of membership before becoming part of the core group. In addition, a member had to progress through these three levels before he or she could assume a state leadership position. The three levels were as follows:

Level One: Those people interested in MAYO superficially, i.e., workers recruited through activity or issues, but did not believe or understand all of MAYO's position;

Level Two: After a time of being observed and of learning, people competent enough to make policy and provide leadership assistance—now they are MAYO; and

Level Three: People that are hard core to provide leadership, see direction; people with years of experience.[100]

The core group was constituted mostly of board members who were closely aligned with the original Los Cinco founders. The chair first went to Gutierrez, and then in 1969 it went to Compean.

Each chapter was sovereign in determining its own local priorities and agenda, providing these did not conflict with the board's general policies (the board seldom had a maverick chapter go against its policies and decisions). Consequently, the programs of action varied from chapter to chapter. Moreover, the level of organization also varied. Some were well organized, while others were loosely structured. Edgar Lozano, who was a spokesperson for one of the San Antonio chapters, described most MAYO chapters as loosely structured. He said: "None of them ran on *Robert's Rules of Order.* Their meetings were informal. You might have two guys who were elected chairperson or presidents or whatever, but they ran the organization very loose . . . because of the fluid membership you always had a core group of individuals who would hold the chapter together."[101] At the state level MAYO tended to be very deliberate in its organizing actions; some MAYO chapters, however, were the opposite, spontaneous and crisis-oriented. This sometimes violated MAYO's adherence to a theory of organization, similar to that of Lenin, of having a cadre of professional organizers ready for deployment when an emergency arose, ready to manipulate the issue or crisis to advance its own revolutionary agenda.[102]

Not all MAYO chapters were hotbeds of activism. Because of MAYO's barrio and university base, they sometimes differed in size, style of activism, age of members, and commitment to action. In general the university-based chapters were better organized and had more older members, but at times these members were cautious in their attitudes and actions. Barrio chapter members were younger but stronger in their commitment to dealing with controversial

Table 3. *MAYO Chapters in Texas*
according to Geographic Area and City

Central	
Austin	Waco
Tyler	San Marcos
Lockhart	Gonzales
Cuerso	
West	
Lubbock	El Paso
Midland	Pecos
San Angelo	Junction
North	
Dallas	Fort Worth
Denton	McKinney
Abilene	Wichita Falls
South	
San Antonio	Kingsville
Weslaco	Houston
San Juan	Harlingen
Laredo	Alamo
Pharr	Hondo
Falfurrias	Brownsville
Del Rio	Cotulla
Edcouch-Elsa	Eagle Pass
Crystal City	Carrizo Springs
Victoria	

issues. While *MAYOistas* in the universities were more cautious because of concerns about their careers, *MAYOistas* in the barrio had "no salida" (no way out). They were willing to take a risk.[103]

At its peak MAYO had a minimum of forty chapters. Like the total number of members, this number fluctuated according to the issues and personalities at center stage. Although the bylaws did not mandate the creation of regional structures, MAYO's chapters were concentrated in four main geographic areas. Table 3 identifies them geographically according to region and cities or towns.[104] South Texas by far had the most MAYO chapters, reflecting MAYO's early decision to concentrate its organizing activities in South Texas, where Chicanos were the majority in many counties. Moreover, Table 3 provides data only for MAYO chapters. In some communities no chapters were formed, but ad hoc MAYO support entities existed that were not required to follow MAYO's prescribed bylaws, structure, or policies. One obvious idiosyncrasy of MAYO's state and local structure stands out: while women were involved as members they were generally absent as leaders of the organization.

MAYO and the Gender Factor

MAYO's leadership was essentially male. All the interviewees attested to the involvement of women in MAYO's membership ranks; they also pointed out, however, that no women served in an official state leadership capacity. Among the remaining four of Los Cinco and other MAYO leaders interviewed there were differences of opinion as to the level and scope of the Chicana leadership involvement. Perez recalled that at the beginning of MAYO women were not directly involved.[105] In contrast, Gutierrez explained that women were always involved in MAYO's development. He said: "They were involved. I can remember having meetings at the home of Juan Patlan and at my home, Luz was there . . . collaborating, making comments, interjecting, . . . and voting."[106] Patlan echoed Gutierrez's comments by saying that Chicanas played a very strong role. They were always present and were always a part of MAYO's chapter-level activities and brainstorming.[107] While acknowledging that in MAYO's formative organizing stage there was not a focus on the role of Chicanas, Compean said, "Large numbers of women were involved, especially at the local level, in MAYO's activities. There was no formal definition of roles."[108]

Although agreeing with the founders of MAYO that women were involved with MAYO, other MAYO leaders disagreed with them as to their role. Carlos Guerra illustrates this point: "Actually, we are going through a very serious rewriting of history in dealing with the role of women in the movement. We would like to think that in the old days we were progressive about it, but we were not. We were pretty sexist. They were essentially second-class participants by and large."[109] Alberto Luera said that most of MAYO's leaders and spokespersons "were guys." Other MAYO leaders interviewed, such as Daniel Bustamante, Edgar Lozano, and Rudy Rodriguez, concurred with Guerra and Luera. Rodriguez commented that "in the beginning women had no role at all with MAYO. It was male dominated. . . . We really didn't go out and recruit women. It just happened that way."[110]

Chicanas were involved with MAYO and did play a significant role in its development, but they never occupied major positions of leadership. All the women interviewed on the gender issue agreed that women were involved, but not in major leadership positions. Luz Gutierrez explained, "Women were not necessarily in a leadership capacity because at the time we really didn't demand to be recognized as leaders as we do now. We were just partners in the whole development of MAYO."[111] Choco Meza, who was active with MAYO, explained the Chicanas' lack of power within MAYO by saying, "There were no women in leadership roles in MAYO . . . because the male gender has always built a very strong network among themselves and have limited themselves to being in control. . . . I think males generally see themselves as ones who can out-strategize and out-think females . . . able to gain respect for their ideas better than females . . . unfortunately that's not true."[112] Other Chicanas, such as Rosie Castro, Juanita Bustamante, and Viviana Santiago, were generally in agreement with Luz Gutierrez's and Choco Meza's analysis of the gender factor.

In essence, Chicanas played a vital supportive role in MAYO. Juanita Bustamante explained, "We were involved in different roles. We were in the picket lines. We provided support for the publication of MAYO's newspaper, either writing articles, typing, mailing, among other things."[113] Viviana Santiago describes her work as "supporting," doing a lot of the legwork.[114] Rosie Castro commented that it wasn't until Raza Unida that they saw a lot of leadership by women. Unlike Raza Unida, MAYO didn't have visible female leadership.[115] Luz Gutierrez concluded, "As always the women are the ones that do most of the work and the men get all the credit."[116]

The reasons for the absence of women in leadership roles are manifold. First, MAYO initially sought to organize the barrio youth who were members of gangs. Luz Gutierrez explained that this was perceived as men's work since they were organizing male gang members.[117] Second, the prevalence of a strong Chicano/Mexicano culture in Texas rendered the leadership involvement of women problematic. In addressing this concern, Choco Meza stated that because MAYO's image was extremely radical, parents were concerned about their daughters getting involved with MAYO.[118] Third, *machismo* was a factor. Juanita Bustamante said, "Decia mi papa que eran un bonche de machos who took advantage of women, que andaban en esa onda [My father would say they were a bunch of strong males . . . who were involved in that activity]."[119] Finally, there was a sense of partnership among MAYO women members. Luz explains why the Chicanas involved never really pushed the issue of leadership inclusion: "We tended to feel that we didn't want the feminist issue to divide us. So we tended to want to be united for *la causa* as a family and not divided. We wanted to go forward together."[120]

The pervasiveness of the Mexican culture in Texas coupled with MAYO's strong adherence to cultural nationalism was the paramount obstacle to women playing a major role in MAYO. Rosie Castro reaffirmed this position: "Even in my own development when I would go out to the barrios and try to get women to register to vote they wouldn't without the men's permission. . . . It was told to women do not get involved in politics. That was a carryover from the Mexican [culture]."[121] Viviana Santiago also agreed. The emphasis on cultural nationalism was evident in her response. She said, "From my point of view, our unified goal was to keep the family intact. By doing that we had to also boost the Chicano man, who had been emasculated by the system."[122] Even the males interviewed agreed that the Chicanos' conservative culture in Texas was a major factor impeding the inclusion of women in MAYO's leadership ranks.

It was not until the transition from MAYO to the RUP that women began to play a leadership role. Even prior to the transition in 1971, Chicanas, particularly in the universities, were beginning to exercize leadership. All the women interviewed graduated from college. Armed with increased knowledge and somewhat free from their parents' direct influence, these Chicanas became MAYO spokespersons for various issues and were involved in various activities. Rosie Castro, for example, was an active member of the Young Democrats prior to working with MAYO. Juanita Bustamante, while attending Morehead State College in Minnesota in 1968, assisted in organizing a MAYO chapter there. In 1971 Choco Meza was a major spokesperson for a MAYO-sponsored school walkout at Eagle Pass High School. And Viviana Santiago played a major organizing role in 1971 and 1972 as a staff person in the transition from MAYO to the RUP.

At the local level there were numerous other women who played significant spokesperson roles in MAYO. There was Severita Lara, who led the Crystal City walkout in San Antonio; Evi Chapa in Fort Worth; Rebecca Flores in West Texas; Yolanda Birdwell in Houston; Alma Canales, who in 1972 ran for lieutenant governor under the RUP; and others. These women were indicative of how some women did take on a spokesperson leadership role. According to Compean, however, "It has to be qualified; it was not strongly defined that women would be allowed equal roles."[123]

Newspapers: Vehicles of Organizing

Starting in 1968 MAYO began developing its own newspapers, which, according to Carlos Guerra, were used for communication, propaganda, agitation, recruiting, and organizing.[124] As propaganda vehicles they articulated MAYO's programs and views. They were used to agitate chapters, supporters, and communities into action. By encouraging action they also enhanced MAYO's overall recruitment and organizing efforts. Their paramount role was to influence the unorganized Chicano population of Texas and engender unity and action among MAYO's chapters. Lenin describes the importance of newspapers: "Without a political organ, a political movement deserving that name is impossible. . . . Unless we have . . . a paper, we shall be absolutely unable to fulfill our task . . . of enriching the revolutionary movement of the proletariat."[125] MAYO's leaders, cognizant of the role of newspapers sought to use them to enhance MAYO's status throughout the Chicano-populated areas of Texas.

By 1969 MAYO had four newspapers operating in Texas: *El Degüello*, from San Antonio; *Hoy*, published in the Rio Grande Valley; *El Azteca*, printed in Kingsville; and *La Revolución*, from Uvalde.[126] In general, the four newspapers served to promote MAYO's pro-CM orientation. For example, *El Degüello* took its title from an ancient bugle call signifying no quarter and battle to the death; General Santa Anna used it in the battle for the Alamo. An editorial explained why the newspaper was named after the bugle call: "Just as the bugle rang out that quiet morning, so, too, must it ring in every Chicano's ears. As Chicanos we have given the *Gringo* pleas, requests, and even demands. The *Gringo* still refuses to hear our voices just like Travis did. Obviously, *Gringos* didn't learn much in 120 years. So *El Deguello* must again shout out its war cry to tell all Chicanos that we must rise up against the *Gringo* again. He has had his last chance."[127] In another editorial, *Hoy* dedicated itself to the unity of the Chicano and to the downfall of all the forces that exploit the Chicano community. The above phrases and commentaries were commonplace among MAYO's four publications. According to the *San Antonio News*, they were underground newspapers of "cheap printing and crude illustrations," but they packed a wallop. Because of their content they increasingly came under political attack by Congressman Henry B. Gonzalez and others. Gonzalez called them "hate sheets." He remarked: "These sheets reflect the language of Castro and incorporate language that is alien to our area of the country."[128] The tone of the articles in the four newspapers paralleled that of the antigringo statements made in public by Gutierrez and other MAYO leaders.

As was expressed in a MAYO position paper, there were five general goals common to all four MAYO newspapers:

1. an end to white supremacy . . . ;
2. an end to economic exploitation of the minority groups and unequal distribution of the economy;
3. realization by all Chicanos that we cannot fit into the *Gringo* society and that we must not try;
4. exposure of all those individuals who oppose *La Raza;* and
5. a lot less asking and a lot more demanding.[129]

The four newspapers were usually published on a monthly basis. Their audience was primarily the young segment of the Chicano community. Funds for printing the papers came from a variety of sources, from donations to ad sales. Their circulation was limited because of their limited finances; they were always plentiful, however, whenever MAYO was involved with issues.

Without the required resources, the four newspapers proved to be transitory and by 1969 began to go out of circulation. Other sources of financial and labor support, such as the Mexican-American Unity Council, VISTA programs, and the Mexican American Legal Defense and Education Fund, began to dry up. Because of their affiliation with MAYO, these organizations came under severe scrutiny and criticism from politicians and government officials and were compelled to sever their relationship. Therefore, in the absence of its newspapers, MAYO relied on the periodic distribution of newsletters to its chapters and communities.

In addition, MAYO relied on manipulating the traditional electronic and print media for disseminating its views and advancing its *causa.* Often its tactic was to whet the media's appetite by using strategies and tactics that were controversial, polarizing, and loaded with the potential for conflict. MAYO understood well what was newsworthy; Jose Angel Gutierrez's "Kill the Gringo" statement (which will be elaborated on in ensuing chapters) was an example. MAYO's militant actions and image provided the hooks that were needed to gain media attention and credibility, particularly in the organization's role as the Chicano community's leading proponent for educational change in Texas.

4. MAYO: Protagonist for Educational Change

The goal of MAYO's advocacy efforts was to bring about social reform for Chicanos throughout the state of Texas. With a relentless drive MAYO confronted a multiplicity of issues and developed programs for their resolution. Of the numerous issues it dealt with, educational reform became its priority during 1968 and 1969. MAYO joined several Chicano student groups throughout Aztlan in challenging the many educational inequities plaguing the Chicano community. None of the student groups, however, was as resolute, aggressive, or militant in its pursuit of educational change as was MAYO. Until its demise in 1972, no other Chicano organization in Aztlan could equal its track record of direct action in the arena of education reform.

This chapter presents a comprehensive historical analysis of MAYO's educational reform efforts from 1968 to 1970. After examining MAYO's perspective on educational reform, I provide case studies of MAYO's three most important school boycotts: Edcouch-Elsa, Kingsville, and Crystal City. Of the thirty-nine walkouts that MAYO was involved with during those three years, these three did the most to propell MAYO into its avant-garde educational role.

MAYO's Education Reform Agenda

From the onset educational reform was MAYO's paramount priority in Texas. Most of its efforts to effect educational reform occurred in the heavily Chicano populated area of South Texas. Many of La Raza in the barrios were motivated to act as a result of the protest activity that pervaded the growing Chicano movement. Chicanos young and old became infused with an unprecedented zeal and desire to ameliorate their inferior and subordinate educational status. The grim reality facing MAYO was that Chicanos were in the midst of a devastating educational crisis driven by generations of de jure and de facto segregation. Chicanos throughout Aztlan were badly educated and ill-prepared to participate effectively in American society. In 1960 Chicanos in the United States had attained a median of 7.1 years of education, significantly less than the 12.1 years for Anglos and 9.0 years for nonwhites.[1]

For Chicanos in Texas de facto segregation translated to a deficient education. The median level of education for Chicanos was 4.8 years. Chicanos were victims of an inferior education at all levels, which contributed to their numerous social problems. Most schools were poor and lacked adequate facilities. Barrio schools received three hundred dollars less per pupil than the predominantly Anglo schools.[2] In addition, their faculties were less qualified. In San Antonio, for example, 98 percent of the teachers without degrees were concentrated in the barrio schools. Finally, Chicano teachers, faculty, and administrators were largely nonexistent. Compounding these problems were pervasive racism and its by-products of prejudice and bigotry leveled against Chicanos. Some gringos were determined to keep Chicanos under their control by denying them educational opportunities and upward mobility.

With Chicanos in Texas at the bottom of the educational ladder, MAYO's first order of business was to take on Texas's educational system. Compean explains why MAYO's top priority was education:

> From 1967 on . . . for almost three years, even till the middle of 1970, we concentrated almost totally in the educational area. This was attacking the public school system for things such as the cultural extermination that was going on in the Chicano community; the deficiency in the curriculum; and the deficiency . . . in the teachers that were being used to teach our children. . . . We attacked those problems even to the extreme that we organized boycotts of classes by the students at all levels of schools and different parts of the state.[3]

When MAYO made the decision in 1967 to challenge the Texas educational system, instead of resorting to the traditional approach of quiet diplomacy and litigation used by other Chicano organizations, it opted for unconventional direct action. This meant that MAYO relied heavily on the school boycott, or walkout (these terms will be used interchangeably). MAYO's leaders perceived the boycott to be the most powerful weapon in their arsenal of direct action, because the school districts received state funding based on how many days the children attended school during the year. The more student absenteeism, the less money.[4] The use of the boycott was buttressed with other confrontational direct action tactics such as marches, picketing, and sit-ins.

Beyond furthering their intent to effect education reform, MAYO used the school boycott to enhance its activist and militant image, to facilitate its organizational growth, and to act as a catalyst for change. Los Cinco, MAYO board members, and staff acted as facilitators, advisers, and sometimes as leaders of boycotts. On many occasions MAYO leaders from outside a community would assist nascent MAYO chapters with the mechanics of organizing boycotts, such as setting up press conferences, writing demands, and troubleshooting the community mobilizations. MAYO's cadre of organizers was ready to be deployed if invited. Sometimes the organizers needed no invitation but would voluntarily help to create the circumstances that led to the people's mobilization. In other words, MAYO took a more proactive than reactive organizing position.

No student group in the CYM came close to matching MAYO's track record of school boycotts. Between 1967 and 1970 MAYO was involved in thirty-nine school boycotts. Though most of the school walkouts ended in failure (meaning that MAYO's demands were not met), MAYO's militant and activist reputation grew by leaps and bounds. Through these mobilizations MAYO was instrumental in furthering the organizational leadership, activist, and cultural renaissance that characterized much of the CM. Thousands of Chicanos in Texas and other parts of Aztlan, especially youths, became involved in the CM and CYM. The boycotts themselves became effective instruments in the formation of MAYO chapters. With its dual orientation of being both a Chicano student group and a Chicano barrio youth organization, MAYO bridged two constituencies and made them one.

MAYO's educational agenda was reformist, yet MAYO never formulated a comprehensive agenda that sought a massive transformation of the structures and policies of the Texas educational system. MAYO's reform agenda sought merely the inclusion of Chicanos into the educational system: equal educational opportunity and respect for the Chicanos' heritage, language, and culture. It wanted an end to the de facto segregation that was inhibiting the Chicano community's progress. MAYO was determined to direct a serious blow against the forces of racism, prejudice, and bigotry.

MAYO's educational reform agenda was flexible and fluid; it was tailored to the institutions and circumstances. This agenda generally called for the hiring of Chicano teachers, administrators, counselors, and staff; the establishment of Chicano studies programs or Chicano courses; the formation of special educational programs;

and the elimination of the "no Spanish" rule forbidding the use of the Spanish language on the school grounds.[5] In the case of colleges and universities, MAYO's agenda called for the recruitment and retention of Chicano students.

With such a change agenda MAYO was able to become active on college campuses and in many of the high schools of the barrios of Texas. MAYO's aggressive educational reform offensive began in 1968. Numerous school boycotts were initiated from Lubbock in West Texas to the Rio Grande Valley and San Antonio in the south.[6] MAYO's leadership was eager to use the boycott to flex MAYO's developing mobilization muscle. In addition, MAYO was determined to create its own mark of leadership by becoming itself an endogenous antagonism for the CM. MAYO's leadership perceived itself as being ahead of its counterparts in other states. Former MAYO state president Alberto Luera explained, "MAYO was not influenced by the East Los Angeles walkout. In many ways, MAYO was far ahead of everyone else in the use of the boycott."[7]

It is not within the scope of this study to examine all the school boycotts in which MAYO was involved. The various MAYO leaders interviewed concurred that the Edcouch-Elsa, Kingsville, and Crystal City boycotts had the greatest effect on MAYO's image and growth. Nonetheless, it is important to note that these three walkouts were not the first ones initiated by MAYO.

MAYO's first involvement in a school confrontation occurred in early 1968 in San Antonio at Sidney Lanier High School. Weeks of organizing under the auspices of the Students for Better Education finally paid off when the administration agreed to nine of the ten demands. MAYO itself never took the leadership—Mario Compean and Nacho Perez were involved only as advisors—yet in the end MAYO took some credit for the Lanier victory.[8] Shortly thereafter the Edgewood High School and Lanier High School walkouts occurred. Arturo Ignacio Garcia describes this confrontation as being successful in that subsequent media investigation supported most of MAYO's charges.[9] The Lanier and Edgewood successes acted as a catalyst for the Edcouch-Elsa school boycott.

The Edcouch-Elsa Boycott (1968)

The Edcouch-Elsa walkout was MAYO's first major boycott in 1968. It was also the first boycott to occur in the predominantly Chicano Hidalgo County of the Rio Grande Valley of South Texas. With this boycott MAYO made its debut and successfully gained a foothold in the Rio Grande Valley. Its involvement in the boycott helped to establish footholds in adjacent communities as well: San Juan, Pharr, La Valla, Weslaco, Mercedes, and Mission.[10] MAYO's chapter at the Pan American University acted as the catalyst and was responsible for MAYO's expansion into the other communities.

In the early days of November 1968 a handful of MAYO organizers from the Pan American University began to organize the high school students of the Edcouch-Elsa Independent School District. MAYO's organizing strategy was to fan the fires of discontent by charging the Edcouch-Elsa Independent School District with blatantly racist policies perpetrated against Chicano students. MAYO leaders felt that the district had a long history of practicing a form of educational genocide on the powerless Chicano community. To them, this was a flagrant violation of the tenets of the Treaty of Guadalupe Hidalgo, which protected Chicanos' property, civil rights, language, and religion. More specifically, they felt that the gringo sought to eradicate the Spanish language and diffuse Chicano culture by deliberately imposing what MAYO leaders called the "gringo culture."

To MAYO the Edcouch-Elsa Independent School District manifested a racist mentality. Indicative of this mentality was the use of the "no Spanish" rule, which prohibited Chicanos from speaking Spanish in school. As one reporter for the *Valley Monitor* wrote: "Every Chicano this reporter talked to agreed that the issue at heart of the current controversy was the school rule against any use of Spanish on a campus located in the heart of bilingual Texas."[11] Alma Canales, who wrote an article on MAYO in the Edinburg *Daily Review*, amplifies MAYO's concern over efforts by schools to suppress the use of Spanish: "The Chicano college student thinks back to the time when he was slapped across the back of the hand for knowing and speaking . . . Spanish. With his college education he has regained a pride in being bi-lingual and works to make his little brother or sister proud of bi-lingual talents."[12]

Some Chicano parents perceived the "no Spanish" rule as a way of demeaning and degrading the Chicano community of Edcouch. Other allegations made by the parents included the prevalence of racist teachers and favoritism practiced by the district toward Anglo students. These allegations produced a rather precarious and volatile situation that in turn facilitated MAYO's organizing efforts. From the beginning MAYO was at the forefront, directing and mobilizing the youth and parents into action.

With MAYO in place, it waited for the right moment to strike. The moment came in the last week of October 1968 when two Chicano students were expelled from high school for failing to get haircuts. A group of local high school students, along with two MAYO members from the Pan American University, met with the Anglo superintendent concerning the expulsion. According to a local newspaper, "at that time they also complained about alleged favoritism shown to Anglos in the schools."[13] The meeting ended with nothing resolved. The students began meeting to plan a school walkout.

Edcouch-Elsa school officials met on November 4. Their agenda focused on developing ways to head off a confrontation with the Chicano community. The precipitating element was a letter that outlined a new board policy: expulsion for the term and loss of credits for any student engaging in activities, such as demonstrations and walkouts or becoming a member of any organization bent on disrupting school.[14] The letter concluded: "This action by the administration and school board is taken to prevent mostly outside agitators from disrupting the education of your child."[15] The superintendent commented to the press that the outside agitators were from the Pan American University and that they had moved in secretly to work and meet with the high school students.[16]

The high school students organized by MAYO held a meeting on November 11 to present formally their first list of demands. At this meeting the students drafted fifteen demands and two recommendations, charging, among many things, "blatant discrimination." Three of the more salient demands were (1) that Chicano students be allowed to speak Spanish on school grounds, (2) that history courses demonstrate the many contributions of Chicanos to Texas history, and (3) that courses on Chicano culture be developed and taught.

Those present at the meeting, including some two hundred parents, listened to the five-member student committee's explanation of the demands and request for parent support. State Senator Joe Bernal and Richard Avena, a member of the U.S. Civil Rights Commission, both from San Antonio, headed a list of speakers exhorting the parents to stand behind the student demands. Bernal mentioned at the meeting that he had been asked to come down by the Chicano community, whereas the Texas Rangers had been invited by members of the gringo community. His reference was to old Chicano complaints involving Rangers who had assisted Starr County authorities in suppressing Chavez's United Farm Workers Organizing Committee (UFWOC) labor-organizing efforts in the area.[17] The result of the meeting was a request for a special school board meeting for Wednesday, November 13, for the purpose of formally presenting the demands. The request was denied by the school board.

When the school board refused to hear the list of fifteen demands and two recommendations, MAYO reacted by initiating a boycott of classes on Thursday, November 14. Some 140 students participated in the walkout. The Chicano demonstrators congregated across the road from the campus while MAYO student leaders met with the principal of the high school. Several students carried placards. A large banner entreating the students to "boycott classes" was especially apparent. During the course of the demonstration one student hoisted the red-and-black strike flag of the UFWOC. The demonstration was well organized and orderly. There was no intervention by the police; consequently, no arrests were made.

That afternoon the principal met with student leaders and emphatically said, "We will not yield one iota as long as I am principal. The students will not dictate the policy."[18] The principal further warned the students that "any student not in school would automatically come under the board's policy and would be expelled for the semester."[19] The student leaders responded by demanding a meeting with either the superintendent or the school board. After contacting the superintendent, the principal informed the student leaders that a meeting would be held on the following Monday at 8:00 P.M. and at that time the full school board would meet to listen to the complaints. One student leader told the principal, "The school belongs to the parents and students. The school is supposed to meet every emergency. This is an emergency. Get the board here."[20] Their request for an immediate meeting with the superintendent or board was rejected. The principal responded by expelling all 150 students who had walked out. He sought permanent expulsion under the policy that had been unanimously adopted earlier by the board.

In the following days students continued to march up and down in front of the high school, chanting and clapping. Teachers stood in the doorway busily writing down the names of those students they recognized. The boycotting students circled the flagpole, pledged allegiance to the U.S. flag, and sang "The Star-Spangled Banner."[21] This was a popular tactic used by MAYO to dispel allegations of its being a communist or radical organization. Above all, however, the boycott hit the school where it hurt—in its bank account. By cutting down on the daily average attendance, it reduced the school's available funds.

Integral to MAYO's strategy was to involve other Chicano organizations in the boycott. One such organization was the Mexican-American Unity Council, a creation of MAYO from San Antonio. Its representative was MAYO cofounder Juan Patlan. Other organizations that buttressed the boycott were the Political Association of Spanish-speaking Organizations (PASO), the Mexican American Legal Defense and Education Fund (MALDEF), and representatives from Volunteers in Service to America (VISTA). Hector Garcia, founder of GI Forum, was also invited as an observer for the U.S. Commission on Civil Rights. The students were also able to get support from migrant ministry representatives of the Texas Council of Churches. In addition to receiving the legal assistance of MALDEF, the students secured legal council from Bob Sanchez, an attorney from McAllen, Texas.[22]

On November 15 Hidalgo County sheriff's deputies arrested 5 of the estimated 150 student demonstrators. The students were arraigned before the justice of the peace on misdemeanor charges of loitering on the school premises. The complaint was filed by the principal. During the hearing the small office was jammed, and hundreds stood around outside. The students were hauled in on trucks and later departed on trucks.[23] Earlier the principal had met with officials from the Department of Public Safety, as well as the Hidalgo County sheriff's office, and he had also conferred with a major from the National Guard. An adviser from the U.S. Civil Rights Commission charged that the major and the Department of Public Safety officials were using tactics of intimidation against the students.[24] The five students were found guilty; bond was set at five hundred dollars apiece, and the students were taken to the county jail in Edinburg (conviction on this charge called for a maximum penalty of twenty-five dollars). MAYO reacted to the incarceration of the students by organizing a vigil. A crowd of some three hundred people stood outside the jail until the students were released.

On Monday, November 18, the school board voted to suspend the boycotting students, pending conferences between the school administration and the pupils. Even though the student population of the school district was 96 percent Chicano, the school board was made up of three Anglos and two Chicanos. All three Anglos voted to suspend the students. The two Chicano board members split— one voted for the action while the other abstained. The school administration was also Anglo-controlled. Both the superintendent and principal of the high school were Anglos. The board's action affected the 150 students who had initiated the boycott.

Prior to the passage of the measure, attorney Bob Sanchez, representing the students, pleaded that the boycotting students be allowed to return to classes. Furthermore, he asked that the question of punitive action be dealt with later. He also recommended the formation of an eighteen-member committee of students, teachers, parents, and board members to look into the charges. The board rejected the former recommendation and ignored the latter two.

During the course of the meeting Sanchez also formally presented the fifteen student demands to the board. He further stated that "the loitering charges were questionable in constitutionality" and added that he felt students were being persecuted instead of prosecuted. In defense of the student boycott he argued: "Our forefathers gave us some civil rights, which the poor, down-trodden Chicano students just now are awakening to and thank God they are."[25] The board rejected the demands. Those attending left the meeting and congregated outside, where they listened to various speakers deprecate the actions taken by the board.

The mood of the board and administration throughout the boycott varied from indifference to apprehension and fear. The board's indifference was expressly demonstrated in its inability to compromise and meet the demands at least halfway. Its posture was one of intransigence rather than conciliation or empathy. The apprehension stemmed from the belief that local high school students were being instigated by outside agitators bent on propagating similar protests throughout South Texas. This fear was amplified by the Corpus Christi *Caller,* which alluded to the prevalence of this outsider-agitator phobia among school districts in the Rio Grande Valley when it reported, "officials continued their planning to meet with full force of law the spread of the student revolt. Prospects for further revolt depend to a large extent on developments at Edcouch-Elsa."[26] The press did much to publicize the charges of the involvement of outside agitators. Fear of Chicano students usurping the administration's power was evident. The superintendent reflected that fear when he said in a public meeting: "What it boils down to, is simply this . . . who shall control and operate the school system. Shall the board or shall the students?"[27]

The demonstrations came to an end over the ensuing two weeks. Edcouch board members and administrators conducted student hearings to decide whether the boycotting students would be expelled for the semester and lose all credits for participation in the walkout. In the first week over one hundred students requested board hearings and readmission;[28] none of them were MAYO leaders of the boycott. Most of the students who requested hearings were given them. Out of seventy-eight students, thirty-one were expelled while forty-seven were readmitted on probation. Ninety-four students had yet to request hearings by the end of that week.

More hearings were subsequently scheduled by school officials. The results of the hearings were not positive for the students. Some sixty additional students were suspended for the remainder of the semester. The mandatory-hearing-before-expulsion policy was ordered by a federal judge who ruled that the board should have given hearings to all the students who walked out before they were expelled and not after.[29] The court hearing resulted from a request by five of the expelled students for a temporary restraining order enjoining the district from excluding them from school. The action taken by U.S. District Judge Reynaldo Garza compelled the board to hold hearings on the remaining ninety-four students before any expulsions could be initiated.

Concurrently, five suspended students filed suit for $50,000 in alleged damages in the U.S. District Court of Brownsville. The suit was filed against the school district, the superintendent, the principal, and the five board members. Three of the five arrested were among the plaintiffs in the suit. The suit alleged that the five students were deprived of their public education without due process in violation of their constitutional rights.[30] Bob Sanchez, the attorney who had represented and assisted the students throughout the boycott, was the attorney for the five students. Sanchez was assisted by attorneys from MALDEF.

On December 19, 1968, Judge Garza ruled that the Edcouch-Elsa board's policy of prohibiting demonstrations and boycotts was unconstitutional. A defense attorney contended that the school board's restrictions were unconstitutional because they involved the legal principle of prior restraint. When the superintendent was questioned about the criteria used in enforcing the expulsion policy, he replied that they took into consideration the pupil's attitude toward the school and how the pupil felt he or she had been treated by the school. Judge Garza replied: "In other words, if they kow-towed to you and said you were a nice principal, they got back in?"[31] The superintendent admitted that there were no written criteria. As a result of the suit the district agreed to readmit the students, expunge expulsions from student records, and pay nominal damages.[32] Thus, by January 1969 most of the students who had been expelled returned to school.

The Edcouch-Elsa school walkout was basically unsuccessful. The school district neither approved MAYO's demands nor implemented its recommendations. MAYO, however, managed to salvage a victory through MALDEF's successful damage suit against the district and demonstrated that educational reform could be accomplished through the judiciary. The fact that the courts sided with Chicanos was construed as a significant victory in itself.

Moreover, the court's favorable decision meant that MAYO could begin utilizing the power of the courts to promote educational reform. MAYO also triumphed in demonstrating its ability to mobilize students and parents into political action. During the boycott school officials throughout the Rio Grande Valley were apprehensive about MAYO spreading boycotts to other districts. In fact, the boycott did precipitate more walkouts in Texas. Thus, MAYO's involvement in the Edcouch-Elsa boycott did much to enhance the group's political action image, catapulting it into the vanguard of protest politics in Texas.

The Kingsville Walkout (1969)

Motivated by the Edcouch-Elsa boycott, MAYO accelerated its educational reform struggle in 1969. That year MAYO initiated several school boycotts throughout Texas, including one that did much to enhance its image and stature, the Kingsville walkout. MAYO's presence was pervasive during this boycott. MAYO chapters from all over Texas came to Kingsville to participate and support the local MAYO chapter. This walkout exemplified MAYO's ability to rapidly deploy its organizing efforts. Unlike the Edcouch-Elsa boycott, this one involved the direct participation of the state MAYO leadership. Especially active were Jose Angel Gutierrez, Mario Compean, and Carlos Guerra, an emerging MAYO leader. The boycott was begun on April 14, 1969, by the local MAYO chapter; John S. Gillet Junior High was the target.

The Kingsville boycott started when school officials refused to call for a special meeting to deal with Chicano student demands. The seven demands were reproduced in a MAYO document:

1. no punishment for students who demonstrated for a better education;
2. no punishment for speaking Spanish;
3. books about the Chicano heritage in school libraries;
4. more bilingual and bicultural programs;
5. teachers to stop taking political sides and preaching them to their students;
6. an end to the racist literature that erased the contributions of the Chicano from the pages of history; and
7. more Chicano teachers, administrators, and especially counselors.[33]

After the demands were largely ignored by school officials, some seventy-five students initiated the school boycott. Chicanos constituted approximately 80 percent of the junior high's student population. By afternoon the number of Chicano students demonstrating had increased to over two hundred. Several of the boycotting students carried signs saying "Who cares? Kingsville teachers should." MAYO passed out leaflets. Scrawled on the leaflets in ink and pencil was the phrase "Chicano Liberation Day. Please do not attend classes."[34]

The demonstration, which was held in front of the junior high school, was orderly and without incident. The boycotting students and parents met that night to determine what was to be done next. On Tuesday the boycott continued, with over one hundred students demonstrating in front of the school. A candlelight vigil was held that evening at the junior high. As a result of the vigil, city fire units were called on what appeared to be a false fire alarm. That same evening the Kingsville school board issued a statement giving boycotting students until the following Thursday to return to classes or face the possibility of suspension or expulsion from school.[35]

Upon the initiation of the boycott the Kingsville MAYO chapter put out a general call for action and support from MAYO chapters throughout Texas. Ignacio Perez, in a letter sent to all MAYO chapters in support of the Kingsville boycott, wrote: "Our MAYO brothers there have once again shown that Chicanos will not let injustices go by unnoticed and without speaking out against them."[36] It was commonplace for MAYO chapters to request assistance and support from other chapters. From MAYO's inception its organizers emphasized the need for collective action to produce social change.

By Wednesday, April 16, the boycott had intensified. Students were now boycotting three schools: Gillett Junior High, Memorial Junior High, and King High School. Forty demonstrators picketed at Gillett, thirty at Memorial, and forty-five at King High School.[37] That afternoon the demonstrating students consolidated their numbers and demonstrated in front of the administration office.

After picketing the office the students proceeded to Memorial Junior High. On their way there they marched ten to fifteen abreast down the middle of the street through the central business district. They never made it to their destination. Instead, they were stopped in the heart of the city by the city's chief of police and about a dozen local police officers. They were told that they were under arrest for unlawful assembly and disturbing the peace. The students were given the option of being placed in police cars for the trip to jail or peacefully walking to the police station. They chose the latter, and no violence occurred. Later that afternoon another twenty students were arrested in front of the police station. They were charged with unlawful assembly, disturbing the peace, and failure to comply with the lawful order of a police officer. Some of these students were members of the PASO chapter at Texas A & T University.

With the incarceration of the students, sympathizers began gathering outside the jail, boosting the morale of those who had been locked up. Signs were hurriedly printed with such slogans as "Justice Is a Virtue," "We have waited too long," "Viva la Raza," "Peace," "Kingsville: Learn or Burn," and others.[38] The protest, however, did not end with the incarceration of the students. Inside the jail yells of "Viva la Raza," "Viva MAYO," "Abajo con los perros" [down with the dogs], and "Racist cops" were commonplace. A letter sent by the MAYO board of directors to its chapters explained what occurred inside the jail:

> No one was given a chance to call home until nine o'clock P.M. The young *carnales* [brothers] outside brought food through the windows to the jailed. Candy, cokes, and cigarettes were also brought. . . . The cops forgot about bringing food to the jailed until ten o'clock. The Chicanos accepted the food, but threw it right back in their faces. No cop was admitted into the jail cells, due to the fact that the guys were armed with cups full of water. They wasted the jail—throwing paper, water and cigarette butts on the hallway.[39]

Press coverage of the event seemed to concur with the content of MAYO's letter. The San Antonio *Express* described the situation as follows: "At the jail, some of the demonstrators beat on the bars and chanted the same slogans and hurled cans of water from their cells. Later, while being fed, they tossed the food onto the floor of a passageway opposite the cells, refusing to eat."[40]

Late that afternoon, parents and other sympathetic adults joined the students picketing in support of the incarcerated students. A MAYO document describes the precarious situation that ensued:

> Some five hundred parents gathered outside the jail. The cops were scared as hell. They quickly armed themselves with shotguns and mace. The students held back the crowd of angry parents promising them that the Mexican American Legal Defense Fund (MALDEF) was coming to their rescue. Sure enough MALDEF came to the rescue. The guys were photographed, finger printed and given an angry look and released.[41]

By six o'clock that Wednesday evening all the juveniles had been released to their parents. Only adults remained in jail awaiting the arrival of MALDEF representatives from San Antonio. Those arrested included fifty-six juveniles and fifty-four persons who were over seventeen years of age. Out of the fifty-four young adults, twelve were released on fifty-dollar cash bonds, while the remaining forty-two were released on personal recognizance. Carlos Guerra requested assistance from MALDEF. In a statement that he made as the arrested youths were being released, Guerra said, "All people arrested have been released. In this sphere we have been successful. As for the demands which we have made on the school system, they have not been met or even adequately answered. Chicano youth have shown their commitment to the cause of the betterment of the Mexican American in education and elsewhere."[42] Later that evening school officials told the boycotting students that any student returning to school the next day would not face disciplinary action.

Most of the students returned to classes the next day, Thursday, April 18, without any incident. Only six students failed to comply; consequently, they were expelled. Expected demonstrations never materialized. Nonetheless, the local police force of twenty-eight men had been reinforced with fourteen state highway patrolmen. The Kingsville chief of police described the situation: "Everything is real quiet. Of course, I don't know how long that will last." He further said that MAYO was "planning some type of demonstration for the future."[43] Thursday was peaceful, free from demonstrations. That evening a small rally and a subsequent meeting were held at local MAYO headquarters, where plans were formulated for the next few days. As a result of the meeting, a parent-student committee was organized to meet with school officials. The committee was to request a special board meeting for the following Saturday to consider and take action on MAYO's demands.

The parent-student committee presented the demands to school and city officials on Friday. School officials refused to negotiate with the parent-student committee on the demands. Officials felt that the special meeting requested by the committee was out of the question. After some discussion, however, school officials agreed to meet the attorneys representing the protesting students to set up a meeting. That afternoon the committee met with a special city commission to no avail. MAYO members and parents walked out of the meeting after a MAYO spokesman was not permitted to speak. The purpose of the meeting supposedly had been to open lines of communication between the protesting students and the city commission. Students also met with Hector Garcia, a field representative of the U.S. Civil Rights Commission. Garcia came to Kingsville to investigate alleged violations of students' civil rights.

Meanwhile, the PASO chapter at Texas A&T University organized a rally in support of MAYO's demands. The many meetings increased tensions. The *Kingsville Record* wrote: "Tensions mounted during the day Friday as principals in the drama moved from one meeting to the next. . . . An unconfirmed report Friday morning held that two city officials had received threats on their lives."[44] By Friday evening MAYO members from Del Rio, San Antonio, and the Rio Grande Valley began to arrive for rallies scheduled for Saturday and Sunday. MAYO's rally on Saturday night drew some two hundred people. Most of the participants were students. Union speakers dealt with the theme that MAYO and the young people would no longer wait in their pursuit for justice. Narciso Aleman, a MAYO organizer, told the crowd, "The youth who walked out don't want to wait until tomorrow."[45] A five-part skit was staged by MAYO members depicting various themes. The local MAYO chapter announced at the rally that a press conference and another rally were to be held on Sunday.

MAYO's rally on Sunday drew more than five hundred people. The rally and press conference attracted the support and participation of MAYO's state leadership. State MAYO chairman Jose Angel Gutierrez addressed the rally and spoke of MAYO's determination to change the system, using violence if necessary. Other speakers on the program included Bexar County commissioner Albert Peña; state representative Joe Salem of Corpus Christi; Texas A&T University PASO chapter chairman Carlos Guerra; and Rene Trevino, one of the local MAYO organizers.[46] During the course of the rally, police were alerted that a bomb had been set to go off during the rally. Gutierrez elaborates on how MAYO used the bomb threat to further galvanize support among the rally participants.

It was a Sunday afternoon, we were by the MAYO headquarters . . . and we were speaking from a flatbed truck. All of a sudden while I was in the middle of the speech all the police and fire trucks . . . converged on the crowd. Then this guy came running right up to me and motioned for me to stop, which I did. Then he told me that he was a detective and there was a bomb threat. . . . I didn't believe there was really a bomb. I thought they were trying to get us to disperse and wanted to search our building to see what they could plant inside the building. So I refused to let them have the PA system. I informed the crowd that this pig was trying to break us up and scare us and that . . . bomb threats or no bomb threats we were not going to be dispersed or intimidated. . . . I proceeded to turn around saying we are going to have a countdown since

Chicanos can't go to the moon, we might just qualify this time. So let's begin our countdown.[47]

The bomb did not go off, but the countdown was an effective means of "turning on" the crowd. Very few people left the rally. The crowd's spirits and enthusiasm increased with Gutierrez's defiance of the bomb threat.

Sunday's rally reaffirmed MAYO's efforts in Kingsville. Peña, speaking in defense of MAYO's actions and demands, said: "This is their crusade and this is a crusade of young people and we ought to stick with them." Carlos Guerra, in response to a question asked by the news media on the probability of violence occurring, replied that force would be used by the group only in self-defense and only in an amount equal to the force applied by the offensive group.[48] All the speakers spoke on behalf of MAYO's demands. Petitions were also circulated in support of the demands.

The second week of MAYO's confrontation involved more meetings among student leaders, parents, and school officials. On Monday, April 21, MAYO members gathered in front of the school administration office, waiting for the school board to arrive for a meeting that MAYO had scheduled. The meeting never took place, because the board failed to show up. In retaliation MAYO members raised MAYO's red-and-black flag on the school administration's flagpole and a minirally ensued. At the end of the rally the MAYO flag was lowered, and the students adjourned to MAYO's local headquarters for a planning meeting. A statement was prepared and released to the press. It read: "This controversy can now be placed only on the officials of the school system who have once again refused to face the problems of the Mexican-American people."[49] On Tuesday fifty-five youths who had been arrested during the demonstration pleaded not guilty before the court. The judge scheduled trial dates. That evening the school board met to consider demands. The board took the demands under advisement.[50] MAYO interpreted the school board's procrastination as a whitewash. Questions asked by MAYO representatives were largely ignored or evaded.[51] The school board's procrastination prompted MAYO to renew the boycott of classes on Wednesday.

The next major event, a protest march, occurred on Sunday, April 27. The protest march was the culmination of the two-week-old Kingsville school strike. The march drew more than three hundred people. During the march a scuffle broke out between young MAYO demonstrators and a deputy sheriff who attempted to keep the youths from raising MAYO's flag on the Kleberg County courthouse's flagpole. Earlier during the march demonstrators had posted lists of demands at city hall and at the school district's administrative building without incident. A parade permit had been issued to Carlos Guerra earlier that week. The march concluded with no arrests or injuries.

Like many Chicano school boycotts throughout Aztlan, the Kingsville walkouts concluded in failure. Alberto Luera summarized the results of the strike: "Negotiations were held and were continued for two more weeks. School ended and meetings were supposed to be held during the summer. Committees were set up, thus the whole thing went into committees . . . the whole thing died, it stayed in committees."[52] One result of the strike was that a student was hired by the school board to develop a Chicano studies program, but only one course was subsequently developed. There were two primary reasons that the MAYO demands died in committee: most of the students who had led the walkout graduated that May, and with students out of school for summer vacation, it was virtually impossible to maintain the boycott's momentum.

A series of errors contributed to the failure of the Kingsville boycott. Foremost among them was MAYO's failure to win over the parents and other adults in the Chicano community. According to Gutierrez, the students had forgotten the basic requirement in organizing a successful walkout: to secure the support and participation of their parents. He describes the negative reaction of Chicano parents to the boycott: "The parents, of course, thought that all of this was evil. Outside agitators came in and promoted . . . the violence and the division in the community."[53] For example, in one of many meetings held, a local Chicano teacher challenged the validity of MAYO's demands and then proceeded to admonish the MAYO organizers to quit using the students to accomplish their militant goals.[54] The city and school officials and the negative press coverage MAYO received did much to polarize and divide the Chicano community. MAYO was constantly depicted as being militant and out to use Kingsville as a target city to test its power and mobilization capability. Fears of violence were prevalent among both the Anglo and Chicano communities.

MAYO encountered many other problems as it organized the Kingsville boycott. First, the constant presence of law-enforcement agencies helped foster fear, intimidation, and acute polarization. Second, the students failed to recognize the coercive capability of law-enforcement agencies. Third, most of the local MAYO members were relatively young and inexperienced. In reference to this, Gutierrez said, "Our constituency of supporters were junior high kids, ten and eleven years old. The leadership was comprised of over-grown kids . . . of twenty year olds, who were young and inexperienced."[55] Fourth, although MAYO gained support from some Chicano elected officials, it failed to secure support and participation from traditional Chicano organizations.

The support that MAYO was able to galvanize came from several CM-oriented organizations. The support, however, was essentially in word and not in numbers or money. Corky Gonzalez, chairman of the Crusade for Justice in Colorado, sent a telegram of support. It read:

> The Chicano Movement across the nation is keeping close watch on the walkout of Gillette. The Crusade for Justice of Denver, Colorado, fully supports honorable demands of students and expects for them to be met. The causes for such student actions are not isolated to Kingsville, but affect all of us across the Southwest. Therefore we give our brothers full backing in their courageous and inspiring stand.[56]

MASO in Texas and UMAS of California sent telegrams of support. One telegram sent by Saacedra Teatro Chicano Armas read: "We support your demand to end oppression of our people by an insensitive, racist system. Nuestra cosa es la liberación de nuestro pueblo suroeste" [Our thing is the liberation of our people in the Southwest]. Valdez's Teatro Campesino wrote: "Keep up the struggles in schools. Que viva nuestra Raza hasta la victoria siempre" [Long live our people until victory forever]. The newly formed MALDEF also supported MAYO's educational efforts in Kingsville.

The Kingsville walkouts did much to enhance MAYO's image, reputation, and organizing endeavors. The walkouts amplified MAYO's "multiplier effect" put into play by the Edcouch-Elsa walkouts; in other words, the Kingsville walkouts helped to instigate more walkouts throughout the barrios of Texas. The contagion of activism these boycotts created helped to set the stage for MAYO's most successful school protest, the Crystal City boycott.

The Crystal City Boycott

The Edcouch-Elsa, Kingsville, and other boycotts MAYO launched in 1969 prepared the ground for the Crystal City school boycott. The architect of this boycott was Jose Angel Gutierrez. The boycott was a product of the Winter Garden Project (WGP), which was approved by MAYO at a state conference held in May 1969 (the WGP, which will be dealt with subsequently, sought to create political and economic empowerment for Chicanos within the targeted Winter Garden area). The primary focus of the conference's agenda was to plan MAYO's direction and priorities for the coming year. In addition, Gutierrez stepped down as MAYO state chairperson and was replaced by Mario Compean. Gutierrez commented on his tenure of leadership: "It was a very good year and we were very successful in our educational projects. We proved our point. We showed we could be organized, that there were civil practices in the schools, and that we were able to make changes."[57]

In April 1969 Gutierrez found Chicano students in Crystal City in the midst of organizing themselves against the city's schools. Chicano high school students, disenchanted with the discriminatory practices used in selecting cheerleaders, decided to do something about the situation. For many years cheerleaders had been elected by the student body. However, as the Chicano student population began to increase, making the Anglo students a minority, the system was altered so that a committee of teachers, appointed by the principal, selected the cheerleaders. Up to 1969 the teachers' committee used a simple, unofficial formula—three Anglo girls to one Chicana. John Shockley explains, "Because the Anglos could afford to send their daughters to cheerleader training schools, judgement on the basis of competence always meant the Anglos were selected."[58] The Anglos of the community saw the Anglo cheerleaders as a symbol of their control over the high school, even though the Chicanos were in the majority.[59]

That April, the teachers' committee was in the process of selecting the cheerleaders for the next school year. The same unofficial three-to-one formula was being utilized. A few Chicano students, aware of the discriminatory selection process, decided to do something to change the policy. Shockley further explains the incident that induced the Chicano protest:

> In the Spring of 1969 the normal routine practice again occurred. This time, however, two of the Anglo cheerleaders had graduated leaving vacancies, and a [Chicana], Diana Palacios, was considered by the student body to be as good as any of the Anglos trying out. The [Chicanas], however, already had their "quota" in Diana Perez, so the faculty judges again chose two Anglos to fill the vacancies.[60]

The faculty judges' decision added to the discontent. A climate of change began to form that was conducive to a mobilization of

Chicano students. Chicano high school students were familiar with MAYO's educational reform efforts. They felt that the time was propitious to organize. From the earliest stage of the Crystal City boycott to its conclusion, two high school students, Severita Lara and Armando Trevino, played a very significant leadership role. Once the committee made its selection, the two student leaders presented a petition to the principal, John B. Lair, complaining about the disproportionate number of Anglo cheerleaders. He rejected the complaint. The students then went over his head to the school superintendent, John Billings, concomitantly increasing their demands to include other issues. The petition presented to him contained some 350 student signatures and seven demands.[61] They were:

1. no punishment for students who demonstrate for better education;
2. teachers to stop taking political sides and preaching them to their students;
3. twirlers should be elected by band members;
4. students should elect the most beautiful girl, most handsome boy, most representative boy and girl and the cheerleaders;
5. the school should have bilingual and bicultural education;
6. paving of the school parking lot; and
7. new band uniforms.

While meeting with school officials the students began to spread the rumor of a possible boycott. In retaliation school officials persuaded some parents to come and sit in classes, hoping to discourage a boycott.[62] The students' reactions were mixed. Most of them were pleased that school officials were meeting and speaking with them. The changes on which school officials and students agreed were based on the 1896 *Plessy* v. *Ferguson* decision of separate but equal education. Shockley summarizes the concessions made by Billings: "He . . . agreed to adopt an explicit quota system for cheerleader selection: three Anglos and three Chicanas. The other demands, concerning the election of twirlers, high school favorites, and the establishment of bilingual/bicultural education, were met either with more quota systems or with a commitment to 'check' what other communities in the area were doing."[63]

The Chicano students' acceptance of the concessions was ascribable to Gutierrez's influence and pragmatism. During his occasional reconnoitering trips to the area in preparation for his permanent return during the summer of 1969, Gutierrez advised the students that it was too late in the semester to push for major educational change. He felt that the students needed more time for planning and organizing the confrontation. Understanding the difficulty, if not impossibility, of sustaining a boycott during the summer vacation months, Gutierrez suggested to the students that they table the confrontation until they returned from vacation in late August. The students agreed with him and accepted the superintendent's concessions.

These concessions to the students, however, were nullified by the Anglo-dominated school board in June. As Shockley explains, the board "feared that by pandering to the hot-headed students, Billings might be opening a pandora's box."[64] Accompanying their nullification of the concessions was a resolution that dealt sternly with student unrest. With the schools closed and many of the students and their families on the migrant trail, nothing was done by the remaining students to protest the board's reversal of the superintendent's policy.[65]

Some of the students who remained began to work during the summer months with Gutierrez's WGP. The board's action on the concessions coupled with its new student protest policy provided Gutierrez and the student leaders with an issue that helped them to sell the objectives of the WGP. The school board was depicted as being utterly racist and insensitive to Chicano students. Their rejection of the demands served to intensify the Chicano students' frustrations and discontent, aiding Gutierrez's proselytizing efforts. In his numerous rap sessions with both parents and students, the inevitability of another confrontation with the board permeated the discussions. It was agreed that some time during the fall months a major "school blowout" would occur.[66]

Conditions auspicious for initiating the confrontation, however, did not emerge until October 1969, when the Crystal City School Ex-Student Association decided to have its own queen and court at the annual homecoming football game. The association announced plans to choose a homecoming queen to be elected by the alumni from among high school girls who had at least one parent who had graduated from the local high school. The eligibility requirement meant that few Chicanas would be eligible. Out of the twenty-six eligible girls, only five were Chicanas.[67] Gutierrez considered their eligibility clause to be comparable to a "grandfather clause." Superintendent Billings and the school board approved the Ex-Student Association's plan of holding the coronation at the homecoming football game. Their decision provided Gutierrez and the students with the issue they needed to begin mobilizing the Chicano community. The board and superintendent had fallen unwittingly into Gutierrez's web. They gave him the spark needed to ignite the boycott.

Thus, by October the stage was set for the school boycott to begin.

After months of planning and organizing, students were ready to boycott the schools. Parents, especially the women, angered over the board's insensitivity and racism, were equally ready. Gutierrez felt that the months of organizing both adults and students had rendered the time propitious to strike. Consequently, the pressure against the school board was gradually intensified. Student leader Severita Lara published a leaflet protesting the grandfather clause. She was suspended from school for three days for doing so. The next day many students came to school wearing brown arm bands in response to Lara's suspension. Gutierrez then called on MALDEF for assistance. A MALDEF attorney from San Antonio, Gerald Lopez, intervened. With increased pressure exerted by MALDEF and the community, school officials permitted Lara to return to school after two days' suspension.[68]

By November the students working closely with Gutierrez were ready to renew their confrontation with the board and school officials. On November 3 the students and their parents attended a school board meeting to protest the grandfather clause. They also presented a petition that included fourteen demands; speaking for the group were Gutierrez and Jessie Gamez, an attorney from San Antonio.[69] Some 450 people attended the contentious board meeting. The meeting was so crowded that scores of people congregated outside the office, and those in the room sat surrounding the school board members. The students suggested that the meeting be moved to the school auditorium because of the crowded conditions. The school board rejected the students' request. Gutierrez describes what transpired during the first few minutes.

> The first ten minutes they were in control because they called the meeting to order and they just ruled people out of order and accepted the minutes. Then it started getting hairy and ugly . . . pretty soon all the stereotypes started playing against them in their minds. A lot of the Chicanos had beer breath. Some were talking in Spanish—hechando madres (using expletives). . . . Somebody in the back would be cursing. . . . This sounded familiar to them and they started getting punchy and scared.[70]

Throughout the meeting the board was attacked vociferously by both parents and students. Both Gutierrez and Gamez requested that the crowning of the Ex-Student Association homecoming queen not take place on school property because the method of selecting the queen was discriminatory.[71] After the first few precarious minutes of the meeting the students presented the petition. During the course of the meeting board members were reminded that if the crowning of the queen took place, students would disrupt it. Under intense pressure by an increasingly organized Chicano community, the school board reluctantly voted to deny the Ex-Student Association the right to use school property for its coronation. The petition's demands were taken under advisement, and the board agreed to review them at the next school board meeting in December. The granting of the one demand by no means took the momentum out of the protest. By forcing the board to reverse itself, the Chicano community demonstrated its growing power.

The November 3 meeting was successful because of the preparation and organization that went into mobilizing the people. By November the students were ready to initiate the confrontation. When the meeting occurred they were prepared for it. The students were especially successful in gaining the support and participation of their mothers. Getting support from their fathers and men of the community, however, took some maneuvering and persuasion. Since the beginning of the school issue the men generally had been reluctant to participate. Prior to the November 3 meeting Gutierrez and a few others contrived a strategy for getting them involved. The strategy played on their machismo. Gutierrez elaborates how they succeeded in tricking some of the men into attending the meeting:

> We got them together through trick and mix because we used alcohol very effectively. We went into beer joints early in the afternoon right after work and talked about the latest developments, where they threw out the kids a month ago and now they were throwing out the women. . . . Then we came back after eleven o'clock when people were drunk. By that time there were no noncommittals. . . . They were saying hell yes, I am going to go down there and if . . . I had known they had thrown out my wife I would have beaten the crap out of those son of a bitches right there and then.[72]

By the time Gutierrez left the beer joint many of the men were ready for action. By keying in on their machismo he had maneuvered many of the men, in the presence of their *compadres*, into committing themselves to attend the meeting. The next day they were reminded in the presence of others about their commitments. Gutierrez explains what followed: "We didn't take them at the beginning of the afternoon or at the beginning of the meeting. We waited until 8:30 or 9:00 when they had a couple of beers under their belt."[73]

Another trick he contrived was to have the women and students sit toward the rear of the boardroom and the men in the front. It was always the students and women who did most of the talking at the meetings; thus, the trick was to surround the board members with the men, who were intoxicated. Because the board refused to move the meeting place to a larger place the setting was perfect for the trick. The women and students arrived early to the meeting and sat at the rear of the office. Consequently, when the men started arriving, they had no choice but to sit in the front. With the chairs taken up, the men, some of whom were drunk and armed with knives, began crowding around the board members. When the board began to procrastinate on the homecoming queen issue, the men began to use profanity and shouted threats at the board. The Alinsky-inspired trick proved successful, for it created fear and intimidation among the board members.[74] The board capitulated to the Chicanos' demand to bar the coronation from the school grounds.

The Ex-Student Association's coronation was subsequently held in a vegetable shed located on the periphery of the community.[75] Its action further infuriated many in the Chicano community. It also polarized the community—gringo versus Chicano. Some of the gringos of the community began criticizing the board for being too soft or selling out. While the gringo segment of the community began to experience disunity, Chicanos demonstrated a strong spirit of solidarity.

The students continued their preparations for the eventual confrontation with the board. Some Chicanos construed the board's action as a great moral victory. According to Gutierrez, people got a sense of victory in defeating the board. "They felt empowered—that they had the ability to do many things. They began understanding the notions of mass movements and confrontational politics. They were no longer afraid. They began to see group solidarity as a strength. People were now ready for another confrontation."[76] Gutierrez and the students, anticipating the board's rejection of their demands in December, began preparing for a possible school boycott. Meetings and rallies became commonplace over the next few weeks. Ciudadanos Unidos (CU), the newly formed adult organization, met at the Campestre, a local dance hall, for planning purposes. Throughout this time students held several meetings, rallies, and discussion sessions.[77] Concurrently, the students, in conjunction with Gutierrez, began adding to the original demands submitted earlier in April.

During the process of organizing the boycott, the students would come to Gutierrez and ask him what should be done next. His role, however, was essentially one of an adviser. For example, the formulation of the demands became a collective endeavor. He would ask them questions: Are we being discriminated against? Why? What percentage of the teachers are Chicanos?[78] The questions were many and varied, and they were instrumental in guiding the students' formulation of their demands. Gutierrez stated: "I never wrote a word. I never put anything into their heads in terms of saying make these demands number ten or etc. But I did explain to them the need for Chicano studies . . . and counseling. I made them see all the relationships to all these different problems."[79] By December the demands that had been presented in November were increased to eighteen (see Appendix 3 for all eighteen demands). The students felt that increasing the demands would ensure that the school board would reject them, consequently giving the students a reason to call for a boycott.

In December the students and parents began pushing for a showdown with the board over the eighteen demands. They requested a special meeting for the purpose of discussing the demands. The board denied their request. This action only exacerbated the polarization. The Chicano community, now more angered, began increasing the pressure until the board agreed to meet. On December 8 the school board held a meeting with the parents to discuss the demands. The students recognized the board's strategy—the parents could be persuaded or intimidated into halting the students' protest activities.

To the surprise of the board members, the meeting was attended by both students and parents. The meeting became bogged down in rulings on parliamentary procedure.[80] After a few minutes the board passed a motion by a three-to-one vote (three board members were absent) that, after a careful study of the petition, no instance of discrimination had been found and that because many of these matters were administrative, the board would take no action.[81] Trevino and Lara, the two student leaders, warned the board that it could "not deny responsibility for the consequences of negating the petition."[82] The board's rejection of the demands was the action needed by the students to justify their decision to call for a boycott the very next day. That same night the students began preparing for the boycott. Gutierrez describes what transpired that evening: "All during that night, between say 10:00 at night and 7:30 the next morning, the students went house-to-house and recruited other students. They planned the strategy for the first day. We chose the one hundred kids that would go out of school. We chose them according to the parents that were more strong."[83] The idea was to involve the students whose parents would give them support throughout the boycott. The size of the extended family was also an important factor in the selection of the boycotting students.

The strategy that was formulated could be described as having a crescendo effect. Gutierrez had learned from previous MAYO boycotts that, usually, during the first few days of a walkout many students would participate. For a multitude of reasons, however, such as opposition of parents, after two or three days the protesters' numbers would decrease, often dramatically. Indeed, the number would dwindle to only a handful. Consequently, the school officials needed only to wait out the boycott, and it would fade away. Gutierrez's crescendo strategy, however, was to gradually increase the number of participants. He explained, "All that was done was simply reverse the order."[84] The strategy thus involved using only a small number of students for the first day of the boycott and gradually increasing the numbers every subsequent day.

The next morning some 200 students assembled in front of the high school. Some of the students carried placards that read: "We want our rights now," "Chicanos want to be heard," "We are not afraid to fight for our rights," and so on. By the afternoon their ranks had swelled to about 550 students; the boycott had spread to the district junior high school. Gerald R. Lopez, staff attorney for MALDEF, was on hand to see that the students did not get into any legal trouble.[85] John Lair, the high school principal, responded to the boycott by pointing out that each student would be penalized according to school regulations, which specified that each day of unexcused absence would result in two points off the student's grade.

The next day, December 10, the students decided to march through the downtown area. According to George Sanchez, the students, who had a police permit, marched around the school and then headed downtown chanting "Sock it to 'em, chile power; sock it to 'em, chile power."[86] School officials reported that absences reached around 710 for all grades, with normal enrollment being about 2,200. That evening student walkout leaders met with Superintendent Billings to try to work out an agreement for ending the boycott. The meeting concluded at an impasse, and the student leaders vowed to continue the walkout. Earlier during the day school officials had contacted the administrative service division of the Texas Education Agency and requested that a team of troubleshooters come to Crystal City to investigate the causes of the walkout and to try to bring about a settlement.

Over the next four days the students began gradually to intensify the boycott using Gutierrez's crescendo strategy. On Thursday, December 11, they continued to focus on the high school and junior high. School officials again reported some seven hundred absences. On Friday, December 12, the school board offered to meet with a group of parents in an attempt to negotiate an end to the boycott. They stipulated that the meeting would occur only if the students returned to class the following Monday. The board made it clear that it did not wish to negotiate with the students. Shockley describes the students' reaction: "This angered the students, who felt that they should be the ones to discuss the matter with the board. They also realized that their parents would be more vulnerable to the board, because of lack of education and fear of [losing] jobs."[87] The students made it clear to school officials that any meaningful negotiations would be with them and not with their parents. The parents stood fast with their children and refused to attend the meeting, and conditions remained at a precarious impasse.[88] The school absentee figures for Friday remained at over seven hundred, while the number of students picketing remained around six hundred.

The school boycott took on another dimension on Saturday, December 13, when participants began an economic boycott of Spears Mini-Max, one of the biggest Anglo-owned grocery stores in the community. Two students who worked part-time at the store were fired for participating in the march through the downtown area on December 10. Gutierrez describes the owner of the store as a local bigot, well versed in the classic methods of intimidating Chicanos.[89] The firing did much to intensify the school boycott, since it further infuriated the Chicano community. In the ensuing days other businesses that were unsympathetic to the school boycott became victims of the students' economic boycott. The hope was that if the gringo power holders were hurt in their pocket books, they would then exhort school officials to negotiate with Chicano students.

On Sunday, December 14, the students held a mass rally at the local park. Over one thousand people attended the rally and listened to a host of speakers: Bexar County commissioner and PASO state chairman Albert Peña; Reverend Henry Casso, an activist priest; and Gutierrez. Sanchez describes the significance of the rally: "The walkout of four days now took on the features of a common cause with other [Chicanos] in the state who shared their complaints against persistent forms of discrimination and racism."[90] After the rally a parade was held through the downtown section. This event demonstrated the students' growing support from Chicanos within and outside the Winter Garden area.

During the first four days of the school boycott some efforts were made by the local clergy to bring about dialogue between boycott leaders and the school board and school officials. The church committee, comprising Catholic, Methodist, and Baptist clergy and laypeople, was unable to bring the two groups together, its failure being due to polarization and the resentment of the school board and administrators toward the boycotters' purpose.[91] The antagonisms between the two groups increased, hampering negotiations. The increased tensions, however, had the positive effect of fostering greater unity among Chicanos. Even some of the more moderate Chicanos of the community who worked for Anglo businessmen or farmers refused their employers' suggestions to go against the boycott. As a result, the local Chicano community was more united than probably at any other time in its history.[92]

Subsequently, the students increased the momentum of the school boycott. The student boycott spread from the high school and junior high school to the elementary schools of the district. On Monday, December 15, there were about four hundred students absent from the district's elementary schools. This action resulted from a meeting held by some three hundred parents of elementary school children, who voted to keep their children out of school in support of the students' demands.[93] By Tuesday, December 16, absences from the district school reached over thirteen hundred.

Meanwhile, some four hundred students picketed the district's schools. School officials justified the high absentee rates by saying that parents of some of the missing children had kept their children home to avoid trouble.[94] On Thursday, December 18, out of 2,850 students in the district's schools, over 1,700 students had boycotted classes. On Friday, December 19, the last day before Christmas vacation, the absentees still numbered 1,700 students. According to Sanchez, however, the majority of the absentees were students from the elementary and junior high schools, with about 400 out of 670 absent from the senior high school.[95]

Throughout the week the local police, state police, and Texas Rangers were out in force, making sure no violence occurred. There was some intimidation and harassment by police against the student protesters. The police ensured that the students were on the sidewalks and off school property and had parade permits.[96]

The second week of the boycott saw an increase not only in the number of supporters but also in the boycott's intensity. Early in the week Gutierrez announced an impending trip by student boycott leaders to Washington, D.C., to meet on the boycott issue with concerned U.S. senators and other government officials. He stated that senators Ralph Yarborough, Democrat; John Tower, Republican; and George McGovern, Democrat had all expressed an interest in the school controversy. Later that week student leaders Severita Lara, Diana Serna, and Mario Trevino met with Yarborough, Senator Edward Kennedy, and HEW officials in Washington. Expenses for the trip were met by the students themselves, their local supporters, and Yarborough's office.[97]

During this time, TEAM (Texans for the Educational Advancement of Mexican Americans) announced its plans for a "tutor-in" during the Christmas holiday period, including two weeks of special classes to make up the time students lost during the boycott. Educators from high schools and colleges from all over South Texas conducted special classes for students. Attendance was strictly on a voluntary basis.

Concomitantly, state senator Joe Bernal sent a telegram to student leader Severita Lara. He expressed concern and said he planned to ask state authorities to accompany him to Crystal City to see what could be done to resolve the boycott.[98] On Friday, December 19, a fact-finding team headed by Carlos Vela, state coordinator of HEW's regional office for civil rights in Dallas, announced its plans for a federal investigation of the Crystal City crisis, claiming that this was the first time so many children and parents of all age groups had supported such a school protest.[99] During the week rumors of the boycott spreading to nearby Cotulla became prevalent.

With schools closed for Christmas vacation, the protesters focused their energies, with the assistance of TEAM, on setting up "liberation schools." Instruction was given at a variety of places: private homes, city parks, Sacred Heart Catholic Church, the Mexican Chamber of Commerce building, Salon Campestre, and Hidalgo Hall. School officials permitted students to pick up their books from the high school. Part of the curriculum of the liberation schools was oriented toward assisting students to catch up on the studies they had missed since the boycott began. The other part, however, was courses geared toward the Chicano experience—culture, history, literature, and politics. The courses were taught by some fifty members of TEAM, most of whom were certified teachers and liberal Anglos. The teachers would come in on different days. Others stayed in town throughout the Christmas vacation. During the two weeks of their instruction, over five hundred students participated in the liberation schools.

After class hours students conducted voter registration drives throughout the Winter Garden area as part of their civic training. Gutierrez elaborates: "The protesting Chicano students went out . . . and registered Chicanos who were eligible to vote. 'Registration, *registración'* was the word uttered daily by young Chicanos.

As a result all-time voter registration records were set in all three counties."[100]

Integral to the students' instruction was a sustained effort of political education of both students and parents. The voter registration drives were intended to lay part of the political foundation for subsequent political action that would give Chicanos eventual control of the local schools. Throughout the two next weeks rallies, meetings, and solidarity marches were also held. The spirit of Christmas coupled with the people's enthusiasm for the boycott did much to create the community's first Christmas celebration.[101] Parents, students, businesspeople and people across the political spectrum expressed a solidarity seldom enjoyed by the Chicano community. It was a struggle predicated on the many and not the few. The unity of the Chicano community in conjunction with the voter registration drives helped to maintain the boycott's political thrust.

The boycott was concluded on Tuesday, January 6, after three lengthy sessions including school board members and a Chicano negotiating committee comprising five parents and five students. Two representatives from the community relations service of the U.S. Department of Justice acted as mediators. That evening the agreement was presented for approval by the boycotting students and parents. It was approved overwhelmingly, and the students were back in class the next day. The most successful Chicano walkout in the history of Aztlan had ended. The agreement basically approved most of the students' eighteen demands. Shockley provides a summary of the agreement:

> No disciplinary procedures were taken against the striking students and they did not receive unexcused absences resulting in grade penalties. The board agreed to pursue the establishment of bilingual and bicultural programs in the school system, agreed to try to find new means of testing pre-school youngsters, and consented to cheerleaders and nearly all school favorites being elected by the student body. Dress codes and the censoring of the student papers were to be reviewed. The board . . . consented to the establishment of an assembly period on September 16th, the Mexican holiday.[102]

With the exception of a few points, such as the election of twirlers by outside people, it appeared that the students had scored a stunning victory.

The reaction to the settlement of the walkout varied: student leaders termed the negotiations "successful," but the people of the community had mixed emotions about them. Student boycott leader Trevino stated: "We got what we wanted and we are satisfied with the outcome." However, he added a word of caution: "We are just hoping that the school board will keep its word, but if they don't I guess they will suffer the consequences."[103] Gutierrez reacted with mixed feelings. He termed the negotiations "victories," but he also said, "There are a lot of things in there that don't mean a damn thing. It doesn't look like they're going to do much of anything."[104] Besides voicing this note of cynicism, he said he hoped that the gringos had learned a lesson. He added: "I think they have learned their lesson very well," alluding to the gringo myth about Chicanos being disunited and not organizable. This was Gutierrez's meaning of victory.

The gringo community's reaction was vehemently negative. One gringo citizen commented, "You give them everything they ask for and they just ask for more." Another, equally bitter, said, "They're [Chicanos] not capable of handling the education they are getting. They don't need more."[105] Some Anglos were convinced that Gutierrez had "riled up" the students, encouraged them in their walkout, and given them financial assistance to go to Washington. Some felt that Gutierrez had been trained in communist Cuba and was receiving financial support from communist sources. Moreover, many in the gringo community felt that, by approving the students' demands, the board had enhanced the possibilities of more walkouts as soon as other demands were thought up. These reactions increased the probability of violence against people in the CM, especially Gutierrez. Few Anglos came forward in support of the Chicano students' demands. In general, the reaction from the gringo community was one of anger, fear, despair, and resentment.[106]

Conversely, the Chicano community generally felt satisfied with the results. One Chicano's letter to the editor of the local newspaper epitomized the indignation over some of the Anglo reaction to the walkouts: "When this *peon* cries out in indignation over whipping you immediately you want to ship him back to his motherland as if he were a bought slave."[107] The general reaction was one of joy, courage, hope, and determination for a better tomorrow. Throughout the boycott Chicanos had been politically united, active, and intransigent as a community in their unwillingness to maintain any more of the status quo.

The Crystal City boycott, unlike the many others that failed, succeeded for several reasons. First, the students' efforts were not spontaneous; they were calculated and well planned. They began in May, and by November, through the organizing leadership efforts of Gutierrez, the majority of the Chicano community, both parents and students, was organized and ready for action. A plan of action was contrived during the fall and ready for implementation in November. Gutierrez succeeded in drawing leadership from both students and parents. Hence, when the time came to strike, the Chicano community moved with the efficiency of a well-built and lubricated machine. Second, the majority of the Chicano community was psychologically prepared for the strike. Throughout the boycott there existed a strong feeling of unity and community. Parents and students were united in purpose and action. The boycott succeeded in pointing out that the real enemy of La Raza was the gringo. The Chicano community, conscious of its plight in education, struck with relentless persistence in its struggle to effect educational reform. Finally, the boycott's success was also ascribable to the crescendo strategy of steadily increasing the boycott's pressure and student and community mobilization, which destroyed the board's hope of waiting out the boycott. It also altered the board's perception of the Chicano community as unorganizable and disunited.

Furthermore, the Chicano students used a variety of tactics that contributed to the boycott's success. One was Alinsky's tactic of confrontation as a means of engendering group solidarity. A second was Lipsky's tactic of involving third parties in the protest. Involving influential U.S. senators like Yarborough, Kennedy, McGovern, and others accomplished the following: (1) it pitted Democrat against Republican; (2) it created more publicity for the boycott; (3) it produced apprehension in the gringo community; (4) it enhanced Gutierrez's leadership image among both Chicanos and gringos; and (5) it demonstrated to both Chicanos and gringos alike what Chicanos could do when organized and united.

In addition, these tactics worked equally well in bringing into the school imbroglio various federal and state agencies, which in the end benefited the Chicano community. Officials from the HEW, Welfare's Civil Rights Office, and the Department of Justice agreed that students had won a victory but later questioned how much of one. Thus, Gutierrez understood well Michael Lipsky's proposition that in protest activity, the powerless must persuade third parties to enter the implicit or explicit bargaining areas in ways favorable to the protesters.[108]

To dispel negative media publicity such as allegations that the boycott was organized by communists and radicals, every morning, prior to doing any picketing, the students would first have a "patriotic ritual." In the presence of the press and government officials, the students would congregate every morning in front of the high school flagpole, where they would raise the American flag and then say the Pledge of Allegiance and a prayer. This action helped to dispel and neutralize allegations that the boycott was communist inspired or organized, suggesting that, on the contrary, it was as American as baseball and apple pie. The tactic in fact convinced some members of the press, government officials, and the Chicano community that the boycott was not radical. In order to avoid violent confrontations, parents would either join the picketing or stand across the street from the school and make sure no violence occurred.[109]

A major tactical weapon that demonstrated the consumer power of the Chicano was the economic boycott, which proved to be effective in augmenting the pressure against the school officials. The boycott's first target was a Mini-Max owner who had said that Chicanos should be grateful for the opportunity to attend schools with Anglos and the right to sit next to them. The owner further stated that if Chicanos did not like the kind of education they were receiving, they should shut up or return to Mexico. Gutierrez describes the result of the boycott: "The owner [of the Mini-Max] usually sold some three hundred pounds of ground beef per weekend. Within a few days, it was down to ten pounds." The students also had persuaded Chicano bread distributors to boycott the market. Not a single loaf of name-brand bread was sold. The store was off-limits.[110]

Other businesses also became targets of the economic boycott. A Lone Star Beer distributor was boycotted because his sister-in-law, who was a local school teacher, publicly made a racist statement. Two other businesses were also boycotted, a dry cleaner's and a drive-in grocery.[111]

Throughout the boycott Gutierrez kept MAYO's involvement at a very low profile. This was part of a tactical decision he made. Even though Gutierrez was still very much a MAYO spokesperson, some local student leaders were MAYO members, and the boycott had been part of the organizing strategy of the WGP, MAYO was seldom mentioned throughout the boycott. The protesters played down MAYO's input to accentuate that the Chicano community had instigated the boycott, not MAYO. For example, the students were organized under a tricounty body called YA ("now" in Spanish). After the boycott, however, YA became MAYO.

In their efforts to increase the pressure on the school board, some of the students periodically visited nearby communities such as Cotulla, Uvalde, and Carrizo Springs. This tactic was designed to increase the local gringo power holders' apprehension of the boycott spreading to their schools. Gutierrez explained how it worked: "the students would drive up with banners and buttons and whatever to the gas stations that had the most pick-ups with rifle racks. They would stop and ask for directions to the nearest high school. . . . That's all that was needed to be done."[112] The attendants would inform local gringo power holders of the students' presence. Fearful of the boycott spreading to their communities, they would call school officials in Crystal City, angrily demanding that they do something to end the boycott.[113] This tactic worked well in pressuring the school board and school officials to expeditiously end the boycott.

The Crystal City school walkout became a high point in MAYO's struggle for educational change. It was the culmination of numerous MAYO-induced school boycotts. This walkout, in conjunction with the Edcouch-Elsa and Kingsville boycotts, helped to spread a contagion of activism among Chicanos in Texas. There was more to MAYO, however, than just education. MAYO's relentless pursuit of educational reform was an integral part of its broader role as advocate for social change.

5. MAYO: Advocate for Social Change

Along with being a protagonist for educational change, MAYO was an ardent advocate for other forms of social change. It sought to foster change by addressing a diversity of issues and providing needed social services to the impoverished barrios of Texas, especially South Texas. MAYO's social action or advocacy efforts were designed to mobilize the youth of both the barrios and educational institutions into confronting the many social problems plaguing the Chicano communities of Texas. From 1967 to 1970, armed with the weapons of protest, MAYO took on the politicians, institutions, and bureaucrats who were perceived to be racist and unresponsive to meeting the various needs of the Chicano community.

In this chapter I provide a historical analysis of MAYO's struggle for social change beyond the issue of education. This chapter does not examine all the issues and inequities that MAYO dealt with, however, nor does it delineate all MAYO's programs and efforts to acquire resources. It does, however, analyze some of the issues, programs, organizations, and events illustrative of MAYO's social change agenda.

MAYO's First Social Action Endeavors: 1967–1968

On its formation in 1967 MAYO began to tackle issues. Even while it continued its efforts to solidify its structure and programs, MAYO began to involve itself in social action issues. In July 1967 it conducted its first demonstration, protesting the Independence Day celebration held in San Antonio. The three MAYO leaders who initiated and led the demonstration were Jose Angel Gutierrez, Mario Compean, and Nacho Perez. The MAYO protesters, armed with placards, made a symbolic declaration of Chicano independence. Compean explains: "It was really something to see all three of us there with suits and ties and picket signs calling for Chicano Independence." The real purpose of the demonstration, however, was to begin exposing MAYO to the public. In the words of Compean, the intent of the picket was "to tell certain audiences that we were in the scene and we had arrived." The demonstration provoked an incident. Several people threatened to attack the demonstrators physically. This proved to be the demonstration's success, for the threats caught the curiosity of the news media covering the event.[1] As a result, the demonstration's objective was accomplished: it exposed MAYO to the public and media.

To enhance its organizing efforts MAYO that year established an office in one of the barrios of San Antonio. Willie Velasquez secured the office rent free. MAYO initially used the office, which was on the top floor of a west-side drugstore, to coordinate its organizing in the barrios of San Antonio. Subsequently, it was also utilized to coordinate MAYO's statewide activities. Even though Los Cinco were attending university, the barrio youths of San Antonio became their first organizing target. Once Los Cinco began to win their confidence and support, the youths would congregate at the office. Numerous rap sessions were held dealing with a variety of topics, from Chicanismo to how Chicanos were being pushed out of the schools. Books and articles that dealt with Mexican and Chicano history, culture, and leaders were used to complement the topics discussed. A major concern of Los Cinco was to find ways of mitigating gang violence, which was prevalent in the barrios of San Antonio. MAYO's message to the barrio youths was to refrain from taking out their frustration and anger at each other; instead, it should be directed at the gringo who was responsible for their plight. Moreover, MAYO emphasized the importance of pride, self-confidence, and unity among themselves.[2]

MAYO's organizing approach when working with barrio youths was predicated on staying within their experience. This was an Alinsky principle of community organizing. Alinsky also mentions that the acceptance of "an organizer depends on his success in convincing key people—and many others—first, that he is on their side, and second, that he has ideas, and knows how to fight to change things; that he's not one of those guys 'doing his thing,' that he's a winner."[3] MAYO's organizers adhered to Alinsky's three organizing techniques. Luz Gutierrez describes the use of these three techniques by MAYO organizers:

> They would get the leaders of gangs like Richard . . . they'd take
> him and they would tell him, "Trayte tus camaradas" [bring your
> friends], we're going to meet at such and such a place and such

and such a time. So Richard would get his five leaders. They were the ones who controlled the whole thing. All they did was get this one guy and he would control the rest. So se sentaban y hablaban [they would get together and talk]. They would get tired of just bull-shitting and they would start talking about the real meat of the whole thing. . . . What was MAYO?[4]

Once the rap sessions focused on MAYO, then the organizers proceeded to sell them on MAYO's objectives, programs, and viewpoints. Denunciations of the gringo and the glorification of the CM were common. Within a few months MAYO began transforming some of the belligerent and contentious gangs into *movimiento* groups ready to confront issues of social injustices. Like the Brown Berets and other Chicano barrio youth organizations, MAYO sought to give the pachuco, or gang member, a cause that would displace gang rivalry and violence.

With its organizers working and living in the barrios and using organizing techniques that complemented the life-style of the youth, MAYO succeeded in winning over some of the gangs.This organizing project in San Antonio typified many similar social action projects that other MAYO chapters implemented throughout the barrios of Texas.

MAYO's Conference Activities: 1967–1968

During the latter part of 1967 MAYO became involved in various conferences. Conferences were important to MAYO's development in three ways: (1) as educational vehicles for the membership; (2) as opportunities for MAYO leaders and members to make valuable contacts with other movement-oriented organizations and leaders; and (3) as a forum for MAYO to market itself and become well known. The first major conference MAYO was involved in was the Raza Unida Conference, held in El Paso, Texas, in October 1967.

This conference resulted from opposition by various Chicano activist organizations throughout Aztlan to President Lyndon B. Johnson's Inter-Agency Hearings. The purpose of the Inter-Agency Hearings was to educate Johnson's cabinet members on the problems of the Chicano.[5] The Johnson administration, however, invited only the more moderate and conservative Chicano leaders; activist leaders and organizations were excluded. One week prior to the El Paso cabinet conference Reies Lopez Tijerina held a conference in Albuquerque that attracted Chicano student groups and barrio youth organizations, including MAYO. It was at Tijerina's conference that the idea of having the first Raza Unida conference in El Paso came about. Compean, who participated in planning the conference, elaborates on how it was conceived:

> What we did there was do the groundwork for some of the events that were supposed to occur a week later in El Paso. Number one, in talking about La Raza Unida, we talked about the concept. We talked about what was needed to be done. . . . It took us three sleepless nights to get a commitment from the people there . . . to go to El Paso. They had previously wanted to boycott the conference. From there in Albuquerque emanated the idea of having our own conference right in El Paso.[6]

One week later in El Paso, MAYO and a host of other CM-oriented organizations held the Raza Unida Conference in protest to the Inter-Agency Hearings concurrently being held there. The conference convened at a church hall in El Segundo, one of the city's poorest barrios. Armando Rendon describes the barrio of El Segundo: "It is infested by *presidios* (tenements), clusters of one-room apartments that look down into inner courtyards where refuse and human waste collect in standing pools of slimy water, while at one end open toilets reek of a heavy, lingering stench."[7]

One major result of the conference was to popularize the theme of La Raza Unida among CM-oriented groups. Rendon further amplifies on the significance of the conference: "After El Paso, a new phase of organization and aggressiveness developed that Chicanos had not known before. From La Raza Unida Conference there developed lines of communication between . . . groups all over the country; an increased group awareness and a sense of national purpose touched everyone that was present."[8]

The concept of La Raza Unida became the theme to a follow-up conference held in San Antonio in January 1968. Compean expounds on the importance of this particular conference to MAYO: "That conference was very important to us in that people were able to see what MAYO was capable of doing organizationally in bringing some 300 people to a conference from all walks of life . . . whereas previously people said that if you get Chicanos in one room you begin fighting immediately. So they thought it couldn't be done."[9] The conference was a success. The MAYO leadership was so inspired that it held another Raza Unida Conference in Laredo in March 1968.

During the early months of 1968 MAYO began holding conferences throughout Texas with four objectives in mind: (1) recruitment of new members, (2) legitimation of its program, (3) activation of Chicano power holders, and (4) publicity to enhance its organizing efforts. To promote its legitimacy MAYO brought people with political credentials such as state senator Ernesto Bernal to its conferences. By including reputable and influential Chicanos MAYO sought to neutralize criticism of being too militant or communist or just a bunch of brats.[10]

In addition to attending Chicano-oriented conferences in 1968, MAYO at times attended African American meetings and events. During the first half of 1968 it supported and participated in two major African American events: a conference held by the Southern Christian Leadership Conference (SCLC) and the Poor People's March on Washington, D.C. In February 1968 MAYO members from San Antonio attended the SCLC conference. Compean explained that MAYO members attended the conference to network and to learn more about Martin Luther King, Jr.'s, operation. Of special interest was the opportunity to examine for themselves the workings of the Student Non-Violent Coordinating Committee (SNCC). After the conference MAYO members stayed an additional three days in Washington and met with SNCC officials.[11] The conference was also attended by Rodolfo Gonzales and Reies Lopez Tijerina. The purpose of the conference was to begin planning the Poor People's March. In May 1968 MAYO collaborated with the SCLC, and several MAYO chapters participated in the march. MAYO formed one element of the Tijerina Chicano contingent.

In 1969 MAYO members attended Gonzales's National Chicano Youth Liberation Conference in Denver. The conference served to reinforce MAYO's commitment to Chicanismo. Subsequently, however, MAYO had very limited participation in other conferences outside Texas.

MAYO's Struggle for Resources

MAYO's social action efforts during the first half of 1968 were complemented by its efforts to develop resources. MAYO developed resources by involving itself in programs targeting the barrios. These service programs helped to meet four objectives: (1) entry into the barrios; (2) provision of services to the barrio poor; (3) resources development; and (4) salary subsidies for those MAYO organizers who worked as paid program personnel. MAYO basically relied on four entities for accomplishing the above objectives: the VISTA Minority Mobilization Program (VISTA MMP), the Mexican-American Unity Council (MAUC), the Mexican American Legal Defense Fund

(MALDEF), and the Texas Institute for Educational Development (TIED).

VISTA and the MMP were both products of the Office of Economic Opportunity (OEO). VISTA, otherwise known as Volunteers in Service to America, was a domestic Peace Corps type of operation designed to assist poor people to help themselves. The objective of the MMP was to train local people to work with VISTA workers.[12] The MMP was an integral part of the overall VISTA program whose essential goal was to organize the poor using locally recruited volunteers. This differentiated it from the more general VISTA program, which recruited its volunteers nationally, that is, outside the targeted project area rather than locally. Compean further elaborates on the rationale of the two VISTA programs: "VISTA wanted to fund a minority project for VISTA volunteers, because it had a lot of bad experiences especially in San Antonio with VISTA volunteers, because they were all do-gooders, who didn't understand much about Chicanos. They came screwing around. They were loose in their morals. They ended up being thrown out of the communities."[13]

Cognizant of the above situation, MAYO maneuvered to control the VISTA MMP, especially in South Texas, primarily in three ways: (1) pressure politics, (2) negotiations, and (3) infiltration. Pressure politics was used to force VISTA MMP officials to negotiate with MAYO. During negotiations MAYO accentuated the importance of having Chicanos organize Chicanos. Through its infiltration of the VISTA MMP's infrastructure, MAYO was able to maintain a continuity of pressure. It succeeded in obtaining the directorship of the VISTA MMP in Austin for Jose Uriegas, a friend of Gutierrez and a supporter of MAYO. The directorship was used to bring MAYO organizers onto the payroll of the VISTA MMP. According to Luz Gutierrez: "[MAYO] had a lot of people in VISTA. We had a control because MAYO was the Chicano organization in Texas."[14] MAYO's multifaceted efforts proved to be lucrative. The VISTA MMP project was funded in June 1968 and provided for some two hundred paid personnel. MAYO gained control of many of the allocations. It also placed MAYO members in supervisory and administrative positions. Compean was hired as a recruiter and trainer for the program. Compean explains how MAYO benefited from the VISTA MMP: "MAYO had two hundred people employed. We had a budget. We had salaries for people. We had transportation. We had telephones. We had travel monies. Consequently that really allowed MAYO to expand. We knew that it was only a one-shot deal. So we used it to the maximum."[15] MAYO skillfully and adroitly infiltrated the VISTA MMP and used it quite effectively to advance its own organizing and advocacy agenda. Gutierrez explains how this was done:

The last part of April 1968 . . . we began taking over the VISTA program. We began to infiltrate VISTA. . . . We always had some VISTA volunteers and supervisors from MAYO in VISTA. After the action in Del Rio, we massively began putting in our people, so we could have access to the maximum amount of money. We knew we were a terminal project. So we tried to get as much mileage out of it as we could. We succeeded very well.[16]

Through the VISTA MMP, MAYO extended its sphere of operations and influence throughout different parts of Texas. There were five primary target areas: Laredo, San Antonio, the Rio Grande Valley, El Paso, and Del Rio. The Chicano population was substantial in all five target sites. This program allowed MAYO's capability to foster social change to increase tremendously. Furthermore, MAYO's leadership used the VISTA MMP to organize and develop MAYO into a statewide operation. Many MAYO chapters were subsequently formed. From 1968 to 1969 MAYO continued to utilize the VISTA MMP apparatus to enhance its organizing and social action programs.

The Mexican-American Unity Council (MAUC) was MAYO's second source for resources. MAYO began forming MAUC during the early summer months of 1968. By August 1968 MAUC was chartered as a tax-exempt, nonprofit economic development corporation. Its chief architects were Gutierrez and Willie Velasquez. MAYO's rationale for organizing MAUC was to augment its financial resources and to promote economic development in and provide services to the Chicano barrios of San Antonio. Luz Gutierrez elaborates on why MAUC was organized: "We were thinking about setting up funds so we could . . . have something to work from. In other words, we had to have an organization to provide jobs for people that were going to do organizing. So this is why we organized the MAUC."[17] Velasquez, one of the MAYO incorporators of MAUC, stated that MAYO's role was to equip and train Chicano groups to solve their own problems.[18] This was done through barrio sessions with the residents. These sessions were designed to involve the people in discussing whatever problems they had, from lack of police protection to the need for better services, and allowed MAYO via MAUC to organize specifically in the barrios of San Antonio.

At MAUC's helm was Willie Velasquez. Very much an expert on proposal writing and fund raising in general, Velasquez wrote a proposal to the newly formed Southwest Council of La Raza (SCLR). This was an important regional Chicano organization that had emerged out of the Raza Unida Conference held in El Paso in 1967. As previously mentioned, MAYO played a significant role in the formation of the SCLR, which was a major Chicano nonprofit corporation whose goals were to fund other Chicano groups, to provide them with technical assistance, and to carry out the development of its own programs, largely in the area of economic development.[19] In February 1968 the SCLR obtained a $630,000 Ford Foundation grant to serve the barrios of Aztlan. MAYO's leaders were cognizant of the SCLR's ability to fund groups such as MAUC. In submitting the proposal for MAUC, Velasquez and Gutierrez contacted Dr. Julian Zamora and Dr. Ernesto Galarza, both associated with the SCLR, for their support of the proposal. MAYO's lobbying efforts proved to be successful. In September 1968 MAUC received a grant of $110,000 from the SCLR for a five-year operation. Velasquez mentioned that MAUC planned to be self-sustaining after five years.[20]

During the latter part of 1968 MAUC opened up an office in one of the barrios of San Antonio. The office was initially operated by volunteer help. The first director was Jose Angel Gutierrez. In November, however, Gutierrez left for six months' active duty in the army reserve. As a consequence, Velasquez became the director, and Patlan, the assistant director. These two MAYO members were largely responsible for getting MAUC off the ground.[21]

Under the auspices of MAUC, a confederation that sought to upgrade the quality of life for Chicanos in the barrios of San Antonio by developing a program and service capability to complement MAYO's organizing efforts, MAYO was able to initiate and support various projects in the barrios of San Antonio, including the Edgewood District Concerned Parents, the Cassiano Park Neighborhood Council, La Universidad de los Barrios, Barrios Unidos, and the Committee on Voter Registration.[22] The Edgewood District Concerned Parents sought improved school facilities and curriculum for Chicano students of the Edgewood Independent School District. The Cassiano Park Neighborhood Council was a group of Chicano residents of the Cassiano housing project in San Antonio that sought better police protection and participation in the management of the project. La Universidad de los Barrios was a youth center in San Antonio where young people congregated to discuss problems related to the barrios. Barrios Unidos was an organization comprising diverse groups. Its main objective was to acquire and disseminate information on the Model Cities Program. The Committee on Voter Registration was a group oriented toward conducting voter registration drives.

A major activity of MAUC was funding other Chicano groups. Initially, MAUC provided outreach services to the poor and funded groups that helped young drug addicts find ways to deal with their addictions and problems and that sought better police protection in the barrio. In addition, MAUC expanded its activities to include the financial support of small businesses and job-training programs for young Chicanos and Chicanas in the private sector. It subsequently also became involved with other issues, such as health. It received funding to train health and other professionals for social work. In all cases education was MAUC's paramount concern.[23] Within four years MAUC became one of Texas's most successful and largest economic development agencies.[24]

MAUC was MAYO's creation. MAYO's organizing purpose in creating MAUC was to give it access to people and resources. Through MAUC, MAYO in 1968 secured a grant of $10,000 from the Ford Foundation. The funding allowed MAYO to hire one staff member. MAUC provided MAYO a means to maintain day-to-day contact with the people. Through the provision of services, MAYO felt that it could influence the people's political education and mobilization and that the people would begin to develop a sense of loyalty to MAYO's social change agenda. MAYO was cognizant of how the political machines and even guerrilla movements relied on material inducements to organize and maintain the loyalty and support of the people.

Besides working with the VISTA MMP and MAUC, MAYO worked closely with the newly formed Mexican American Legal Defense Education Fund (MALDEF). MALDEF was organized in Texas in 1968 primarily to provide legal assistance to Chicanos in civil rights cases. The idea to form an organization comparable to the National Association for the Advancement of Colored People (NAACP) was discussed as early as 1961 by George I. Sanchez of the University of Texas and Pete Tijerina, an attorney who was long associated with the legal battles of LULAC and had handled a discrimination case for the NAACP. It was not until 1968, however, that the advocacy agency became a reality. MALDEF was funded by the Ford Foundation for approximately $2.2 million to be spread over a five-year period.[25] The headquarters in San Antonio had a full-time staff of ten attorneys, six legal secretaries, and one field-worker who traveled around Texas gathering information on cases of discrimination against Chicanos. In addition, a small office staffed by one attorney and one secretary was opened in Los Angeles. There were eighty-seven attorneys throughout five states—Texas, California, New Mexico, Arizona, and Colorado—who could receive fees for any cases in which they represented MALDEF. Pete Tijerina became MALDEF's first executive director.[26]

MALDEF's paramount mission was to seek out and assist in what the organization deemed to be the most important cases involving alleged discrimination against Chicanos. For activists, this meant that finally the weapons of the CM had been broadened to include litigation. The courts were now to be a major battleground in the struggle for Chicano civil rights. Instead of relying only on confrontational protest politics, through MALDEF the CM could use the courts as vehicles of redress and remedy via class action suits involving civil rights issues. MALDEF made it clear that its purpose was not to deal with criminal cases or provide legal aid services. Instead, MALDEF's primary role was to be a legal advocate for Chicano rights. Because of this focus and the fact that the organization was based in San Antonio, Texas, MALDEF was well received by MAYO.

To MAYO, MALDEF was a potentially powerful organizing and social change resource that needed to be tapped. Between 1968 and 1969 MALDEF handled some two hundred cases and complaints. Commenting on MALDEF's civil rights role, Tijerina stated that before MALDEF was formed, Chicano attorneys did not have the money or time to take on civil rights cases, which impeded the development of their expertise in the arena of civil rights law.[27]

MALDEF's resources were also directed at providing scholarships for Chicanos interested in going to law school. Integral to this was disseminating information to the colleges and universities on the availability of scholarships and on the prospects of Chicano students pursuing a law career. MALDEF's intent was to produce a large pool of Chicano attorneys and to encourage more Chicano attorneys to return to their barrios and assist in the struggle for Chicano civil rights.

From its inception MALDEF was instrumental in providing MAYO with needed legal assistance. Through the efforts of Gutierrez MAYO and MALDEF developed a close working relationship. Gutierrez was hired by MALDEF in 1969 as a field researcher or troubleshooter. Through his efforts MAYO and MALDEF worked together on a variety of issues, from the Edcouch-Elsa walkout in 1968 to the VISTA issue at Del Rio in 1969. Indicative of the close collaboration between the two entities was a letter sent to Gutierrez, then chairman of MAYO, by MALDEF's director, Pete Tijerina. It read in part:

> Since the MAYO objectives emphasize the need for social changes and to provide equal opportunities for Chicanos in employment, education, and the administration of justice, please be assured that MALDEF's legal staff will be available to provide legal defense in all those cases arising from arrest as a result of confrontations on the issues . . . which involve violations of civil rights.[28]

In a memorandum also sent to Gutierrez, Tijerina was more specific about the type of situation in which MALDEF would provide legal assistance: demonstrations, marches, picketing, civil disobedience, allegations of civil rights violations, and setting up corporate charters. Besides providing legal assistance for these situations, it committed itself to MAYO in four other areas: (1) postconviction legal services; (2) the provision of a full-time social worker for rehabilitation assistance; (3) assistance in securing bail money; and (4) assistance in public relations. MALDEF assigned one full-time attorney to fulfill these commitments and also to conduct a legal education program for *MAYOistas* and non-*MAYOistas* alike.[29] Throughout 1968 and the first half of 1969 MALDEF collaborated with MAYO on numerous issues. MALDEF's support of MAYO was especially felt in the area of educational change.

In 1969 MAYO's access to resources was further increased with the formation of the Texas Institute for Educational Development (TIED). Nacho Perez, who headed the organizing efforts of TIED, secured both federal and state funds to provide health care to farm workers and other disadvantaged groups. Through TIED free clinics and other health agencies directed by Chicanos began to appear in South Texas. Several years later the agency turned its attention to health education rather than to direct services.[30] Like MAUC and the VISTA MMP, TIED was used to employ MAYO members as well as to help MAYO with its organizing efforts.[31] Unlike the preceding entities, TIED did not become a priority target of MAYO's adversaries.

Thus, in 1968 and 1969 MAYO succeeded in developing resources by which it could sustain its advocacy efforts. Through infiltration, formation of front agencies, and the utilization of other advocacy entities such as MALDEF, MAYO began taking on the image of David, ready to battle the gringo Goliath. These actions allowed MAYO to tap state and federal funding sources indirectly while at the same time claiming that it would not receive or accept money directly from government sources. By doing this MAYO was able to place its cadre of organizers in positions where they were earning a wage while organizing for MAYO.

Nevertheless, this success in using other entities' resources became an Achilles heel for MAYO. A movement-oriented organization must possess sufficient resources of its own to develop a capability for mobilization and to carry out its organizing and advocacy activities. Such was not the case with MAYO. It never became financially self-sufficient. The result was that MAYO was caught in the web of financial dependency on other bodies: VISTA, the MMP, MAUC, and TIED. Exacerbating this "dependency syndrome" was that all four entities themselves were dependent on funding from external sources.

This dependency syndrome added to the precariousness of MAYO's development. When MAYO became embroiled in controversial educational and social issues, there were serious ramifications for its four primary funding and support entities. MAYO's adversaries saw fit to come after these groups politically for their relationships to MAYO. All four entities came under fire in 1969, and MAYO's financial and material resources were substantially reduced by 1970. Without access to such resources in 1970 and 1971, MAYO's overall social change efforts began to decline. Unlike other Chicano student groups and barrio youth organizations, during its formative years MAYO was successful in part because of its ability to place its organizers in full-time organizing positions with front or collaborative groups that were supported by resources such as office equipment and phones. The issue that precipitated the reduction of MAYO's resources was the Del Rio incident.

The Del Rio Incident

The simmering unrest in Del Rio began to boil into public view by February 1969, when the Val Verde county commissioners formally requested that the local Community Action Agency (CAA) discontinue the VISTA MMP.[32] The county commissioners' decision to terminate it compelled MAYO to take a counteraction to save the program. MAYO chapters throughout the state became embroiled in protesting the termination. The city of Del Rio had been one of the five targeted sites picked when the MMPs were funded by the OEO in 1968. MAYO had successfully infiltrated and used the VISTA MMP in Del Rio to carry out its organizing efforts. Involved in the VISTA MMP programs were twenty paid workers, including two MMP supervisors and eighteen staff personnel.

At the crux of the controversy were charges that VISTA workers had violated federal guidelines by becoming involved in political activities. More specifically, three VISTA workers were charged with taking part in MAYO-sponsored activities.[33] The Val Verde county commissioners had concluded that VISTA was doing more harm than good. A Chicano attorney who spearheaded the drive to terminate the two programs contended that someone had misled members of MAYO by teaching them to hate gringos.[34]

In their efforts to save the program, the Val Verde CAA board of directors, which was responsible for their supervision, conducted its own investigation into the allegations. The investigation led to the dismissal of one VISTA worker and two MMP workers based on their involvement in MAYO organizing activities. They were accused of participating in a MAYO-sponsored demonstration held in January 1969 at the federal courthouse in Del Rio. The demonstration was organized by MAYO to protest a grand jury's "no bill" in a case in which a highway patrolman had been accused of beating a Uvalde Chicano couple.[35]

In an emotion-packed five-and-a-half-hour meeting, the three VISTA MMP workers were released by the CAA. On March 10, in retaliation for the CAA's action, the county commissioners voted unanimously to request Governor Preston Smith to terminate the two programs. Governor Smith complied with this request and, acceding to a motion from the Val Verde county commissioners, on March 13 asked the OEO to remove the MMP and national VISTA programs from the county. In rebuking MAYO's alleged militant activities in Val Verde County, the governor commented: "The abdication of respect for law and order, disruption of the democratic process and the provocation of disunity among our citizens will not be tolerated by this office."[36] Governor Smith further requested that funds earmarked for VISTA in Val Verde county be reallocated to other poverty programs in the area. The governor's rationale for supporting the commissioners' request was based on the State and Federal Relations Act, which was discretionary and not mandatory. It read: "The Governor of such state agency established for such purpose shall take whatever action . . . he deems necessary or appropriate to meet the needs of such city, county, school district, hospital district or other political subdivision."[37]

Fermin Calderon, chairman of the CAA's board, rejected the governor's decision. He asserted that the Val Verde county commissioners had lied. He alleged that the three commissioners who had led the VISTA termination movement represented only 6 to 7 percent of the population of Val Verde County. He further criticized the governor for being undemocratic in not bothering to investigate the other side of the argument.[38]

Following the governor's decision to uphold the commissioners' request, MAYO initiated its protest activities in Del Rio. On Saturday, March 14, MAYO organized a peaceful demonstration in Del Rio to protest the governor's decision to abolish the VISTA MMP in Val Verde County. Two weeks prior to the demonstration the city council passed an ordinance requiring permits for parades or demonstrations, but MAYO decided to have the demonstration anyway. Since the ordinance did not require a permit for funerals, MAYO decided to stage a funeral procession, thus circumventing the restriction.

The demonstration took the form of a funeral procession for a

dead rabbit named "Justice." The dead rabbit symbolized the absence of justice for Chicanos in Del Rio.[39] MAYO used a hearselike
vehicle to carry the dead rabbit, and hundreds of Chicanos marched
behind the hearse through the streets of the barrio of San Felipe in
Del Rio. The funeral procession was halted by local, county, and
state law officers. Thirty-four demonstrators were arrested for vio-
lating the newly passed city ordinance. That evening MAYO demonstrators congregated in front of the Del Rio police station. No
incidents or violence occurred that evening, but local police, reinforced by state highway patrol units, were placed on alert that evening and the next day, Sunday.[40]

Anticipating arrests, MAYO had requested the legal support of
MALDEF prior to the demonstration. Understanding the gravity of
the situation, MALDEF responded by sending attorneys to provide
legal assistance. In fact, they were present when the thirty-two defendants were arrested. Bond for the defendants was set at twenty-
five dollars each by the corporation court judge. Through Calderon
and MALDEF attorneys, those arrested were released on bond that
Saturday evening. Trials were subsequently set to commence on
March 20.

The next day MAYO held a meeting in Del Rio to formulate its
strategy against the governor's action to terminate the VISTA MMP.
The meeting was held at the local American GI Forum building.
Some four hundred people attended the meeting. It was decided that
a massive procession would be held again to protest the governor's
decision.[41] Calderon, who was present, mentioned that the procession was also being organized because of the plight of the Chicano
in what he perceived to be a police state.[42] To bring attention to the
issue, it was decided that Chicanos from all over the nation should
be invited. During the next two weeks several meetings and press
conferences were held to formulate strategy and secure exposure for
the Del Rio incident.

MAYO went on the offensive and began soliciting support from
prominent Chicanos outside Del Rio. Bexar county commissioner
Albert Peña, in a press conference held on March 22, told reporters
about the procession, which was to be held on Palm Sunday. MAYO
again activated influential power holders to buttress its cause. At
the press conference Peña came out unequivocally in support of the
procession. In reference to the procession he said: "[If] we're not to
have a parade, [then] we're going to have a procession. We're not
there to protest a phony law. We're there to demonstrate for a
cause."[43] Alluding to the VISTA issue, he stated that the problem
was no longer limited to Del Rio but was an insult and an affront

to all Chicanos throughout the nation. He reiterated Calderon's charges that the governor had been utterly arbitrary and undemocratic in his decision to abolish the VISTA programs. Peña also announced that a manifesto was being written. He described the manifesto as "El Plan de Del Rio" (see Appendix 4 for the full text of the manifesto). The "Plan de Del Rio" calls for a Chicano bill of rights, a Chicano declaration of independence, and full restoration of the dignity and identity of the Chicano.[44]

On March 24 a seminar was held specifically for the purpose of writing the manifesto. By the following week Jorge Lara, a MAYO member who initiated the writing of the document, had completed a rough draft. Later that week Lara and several other MAYO members and supporters met at the Holiday Inn in Del Rio to finalize the manifesto. The document was extremely critical of what MAYO described as the gringo-controlled establishment. Ten criticisms were leveled against the Gringo power establishment:

1. It is they who built a multi-million dollar school for their children, then built barracks for ours.
2. It is they who stole our land, then sold it back to us bit by bit, crumb by crumb.
3. It is they who speak one language and resent us for speaking two.
4. It is they who preach brotherhood and practice racism.
5. It is they who make much ado about equal opportunity but reserve it to themselves or their replicas.
6. It is they who proclaim concern for the poor through a welfare system calculated to keep our people in perpetual dependency.
7. It is their police system that harasses and over-polices our sons and daughters.
8. It is their educational system that violates the innocence of our children with required literature like *The Texas Story*, a book that caricatures our ancestors.
9. It is their double standard of justice—minimum penalty for gringo and maximum for Chicano—that makes criminals of our young men.
10. It is they who denounce our militancy but think nothing of the legal violence they inflict on us mentally, culturally, spiritually and physically.[45]

While the manifesto was being written, MAYO's overall strategy relied on the use of various forms of pressure. MAYO leaders Gutierrez and Nacho Perez met with the governor on March 18 in reference to the VISTA issue. The meeting was arranged by members of the state legislature but concluded with nothing resolved or agreed upon. During the course of the meeting the two MAYO leaders "told the governor to go to hell."[46] That same day MAYO issued a press release that was sent on behalf of Gutierrez; Perez; state representative Carlos Truan; state senator Joe Bernal; Henry Muñoz, representative of the AFL-CIO; Jose Uriegas, director of the VISTA MMP; and Merle Smith, assistant director of the VISTA MMP. The press release was directed at the governor and was written in a vitriolic style: "[Governor Smith's] 'legal' trickery has been what is provoking the Chicanos in this state. Should he wish political action—we are ready to meet head on with him on March 30, 1969 in Del Rio, Texas. We ask him to send the symbol of *Gringo* injustice, Ranger Captain A. Y. Allee to stop us."[47] The meetings, press conferences, and press releases, coupled with the support received from Chicano influentials and politicians, were all interim tactics used by MAYO as part of its strategy of gradually intensifying the pressure.

Prior to the Palm Sunday procession MAYO made a strategic decision to escalate the mobilization statewide. A number of support demonstrations were held in various communities in South Texas. These minidemonstrations were used as premobilizing vehicles for the Palm Sunday procession. In addition, they illustrate another aspect of MAYO's crescendo strategy, which was to create multiple pressure points. These demonstrations also served to enhance MAYO's image.

In Laredo on Sunday, March 23, MAYO organized a protest demonstration against the governor, who happened to be in the city's Hamilton Hotel that day addressing a women's organization, the Pan American Round Table. The governor was speaking on the VISTA issue. MAYO greeted him in front of the hotel with a picket involving some 250 MAYO and VISTA supporters. The demonstration was so well organized that the governor was unable to enter the hotel through the front door and was compelled to use the rear entrance. During the demonstration one of the assistants to the governor met with a seven-member MAYO committee. In a news article entitled "Protestors in Laredo Detour Governor Smith," reporter Odie Arambula explained what happened after the MAYO committee requested a meeting with the governor: "Minutes later, [the governor's] aide let it be known [that] Smith had no intention of confronting the leaders of the crowd outdoors. The aide accepted a rabbit, named 'justice,' on behalf of the Governor, and the MAYO representatives told him another rabbit bearing the same name had been buried several days earlier, signifying that the VISTA termination meant justice was dead."[48] The dead rabbit given to the aide wore a bright red ribbon on its neck. Several protesters in the demonstration also carried dead rabbits. The speakers during the demonstration sought to galvanize support for the upcoming Palm Sunday procession. The demonstration concluded without any arrests.

A few days prior to the Palm Sunday procession, thirty-two demonstrators who had been arrested at the demonstration of March 14 were exonerated of charges of parading without a permit. Corporation judge Watt Murrah ruled that the city had not properly advertised the ordinance and consequently dismissed the charges.[49] The mayor of Del Rio, Alfredo Gutierrez, publicly repudiated and criticized MAYO's involvement in the VISTA issue. He headed a city council that comprised five Chicanos and two Anglos. Speaking at a press conference on March 28, the mayor declared that the city of Del Rio would not permit a handful of local dissenters to bring in disunity and militancy.[50]

At the press conference Del Rio's attorney, Arturo Gonzalez, commented that the city government did not object to the VISTA MMP. The city's criticism stemmed from the political activities of some of the VISTA personnel and their alliance with MAYO. Calderon, who had been active in supporting the retention of the VISTA MMP, joined city officials in denouncing MAYO for making allegedly irresponsible statements. Consequently, he disassociated himself entirely from MAYO.

That week the governor, in meeting with Calderon, reiterated his decision to terminate the program. He made it clear that he would reconsider his decision only if the Val Verde county commissioners changed their minds.[51] Meanwhile, prior to the procession, the city council, led by Mayor Alfredo Gutierrez, unanimously voted to support the county commissioners' decision to ask the governor to remove the VISTA MMP program from both Del Rio and Val Verde County. The decision, made by the Chicano-majority city council led by a Chicano mayor, made the situation difficult for MAYO, since it appeared that Chicanos were fighting Chicanos.

These actions taken by MAYO's adversaries were used by MAYO to foment more support and participation for the upcoming Palm Sunday procession. Days prior to the procession Chicanos began to arrive in large numbers from throughout Texas and elsewhere in the nation. Some three thousand persons participated in the procession, making it the biggest protest demonstration in the history of the CM in Texas. The participants generally were of three types: (1) recognized Chicano politicians, (2) spokespersons and members of various Chicano organizations, and (3) MAYO members from throughout Texas. MAYO also succeeded in drawing support from several Chicano leaders and organizations outside Texas, from California to Michigan.

In its efforts to draw people to the procession, MAYO accentuated the importance of "Raza solidarity." During the course of the procession shouts of "Viva La Raza" and "Chicano power" were common. The processional route was around three miles long and moved through the main thoroughfare of the dusty city. Shouting demonstrators stopped at the Val Verde County courthouse, where Gutierrez read MAYO's manifesto, "El Plan de Del Rio," and then posted it on the courthouse door.

Prior to Gutierrez's pronouncement MAYO members hoisted the red-and-black MAYO flag on the courthouse flagpole amid yells of "Brown Power" and "Viva la Raza."[52] The presence of MAYO was obvious throughout the procession. One newspaper observed the following about MAYO's involvement in the procession: "MAYO members were prominent in the group, with their flowing Zapata style mustaches, beards, sarapes, combat boots, brown berets, and rolled blankets slung diagonally across their chest and back campaign style."[53]

Gutierrez delivered a blistering speech denouncing and challenging what he called "the *Gringo* oppressor." He stated: "We have been oppressed for too long and we will tangle with the *Gringo* anywhere he wants."[54] He made it clear that MAYO did not expect the help of the poor people in its struggle. He asserted that MAYO itself would "tackle the *Gringo*."[55]

Other speakers less belligerent in tone spoke on various related themes. Bexar County commissioner Albert Peña expounded on the significance of the procession. He told the crowd: "We have raised the cactus curtain." Peña further read a supportive telegram from U.S. senator Edward Kennedy. It read: "My strong conviction is that the nation should listen to what is being said in Del Rio." Reverend Henry Casso, a speaker representing the San Antonio archdiocese, concluded by saying, "Ya basta," and then translated it: "We're fed up." State senator Joe Bernal spoke on the disproportionately high numbers of Chicanos who were being killed in Vietnam. Hector Garcia, founder of the GI Forum, reinforced Bernal's speech on the Chicano's valuable contribution to the defense of the United States. Some of the speakers directed hostile comments against Congressman Henry B. Gonzalez for not supporting the retention of the VISTA MMP.[56]

The procession also attracted the interest of the Republican party.

Celso Moreno, an assistant to the National Republican Chairman in charge of Spanish Affairs, was in Del Rio during the procession as an observer. He set up a hospitality room with beer and hard liquor to entertain the procession participants. A few days after the procession Governor Preston Smith declared: "Apparently the Republicans are there with money, marbles and tequila." As a result of his activities, Moreno lost his position at the recommendation of the state Republican officials. One Republican official stated: "The Republican party takes no part and will have no part of these militant revolutionaries and it will continue vigorously to oppose them."[57] (Earlier in the week, however, U. S. Senator Tower, a Republican, had sent a telegram in support of the VISTA MMP.)

MAYO's efforts to halt the termination of the VISTA MMP ended in failure. The governor and the Val Verde county commissioners remained intransigent in their decision to abolish the program, and in the end, it was terminated.

For MAYO, the VISTA issue in Del Rio had both positive and negative ramifications. On the positive side, the VISTA issue was instrumental in increasing MAYO's visibility and membership. The Del Rio VISTA issue, coupled with MAYO's concurrent involvement with various school walkouts, helped MAYO to propagate activism throughout Texas and beyond. Consequently, many Chicanos, especially youth, became involved in promoting social change. Second, the VISTA issue served to catapult MAYO's stature and image to a higher level of recognition within the CM and CYM. The fact that Chicanos from throughout the nation participated in the Del Rio procession was indicative of MAYO's power-mobilizing capability. Numerous CM-oriented newspapers carried story after story on the VISTA issue at Del Rio, making MAYO a household word. No other Chicano organization at the time was able to manipulate the media better than MAYO could. Consequently, the Del Rio VISTA issue put MAYO into the driver's seat of the CM's avant garde in Texas. MAYO was becoming the CYM's leading protagonist for change by 1969.

The VISTA issue at Del Rio also created serious negative ramifications for MAYO. Foremost was its loss of control and influence over some of the VISTA MMP programs throughout Texas. In addition, MAYO's success in demonstrating its power-mobilizing capability activated and reenergized its adversaries. The presence of three thousand Chicanos created a fear factor for MAYO. Politicians, government officials, and members of the press produced a fire storm of attacks on MAYO and especially on its main spokesperson, Gutierrez. This brought MAYO's activities and collaborative programs under harsh and meticulous scrutiny. The mobilizing success of Del Rio led to the evaporation of resources and staff that MAYO relied on for carrying out its organizing activities.

MAYO Comes under Attack

The Del Rio VISTA issue created a window of opportunity for MAYO's adversaries to neutralize MAYO's growing power mobilization capability by going after MAYO's Achilles heel—its dependency on MAUC, VISTA MMP, and MALDEF for its organizational support and resources. By the spring of 1969 these three entities came under fire from establishment politicians and bureaucrats for their association and collaboration with MAYO.

Texas congressman Henry B. Gonzalez became MAYO's most vociferous, implacable, and deadly adversary. Considered a liberal mainstream Mexican American politician, Gonzalez reacted to MAYO's Del Rio VISTA activities with a personal vengeance. He ferociously denounced MAYO for propagating antigringo literature, accusing the organization of having been infiltrated by Cuban-trained revolutionaries from California. He described MAYO's literature as "hate sheets" that reflected the rhetoric of Castro and incorporated language alien to the United States.[58]

During the first few days of April 1969 Gonzalez escalated his crusade against MAYO. On April 14 he lashed out at MAYO in a speech before the U.S. House of Representatives. The speech, which was entered into the *Congressional Record*, accused MAYO of propagating inflammatory hate literature. The following is an excerpt:

> MAYO styles itself the embodiment of Good and the Anglo-American as the incarnation of evil. That is not merely ridiculous, it is drawing fire from the deepest wellsprings of hate. The San Antonio leader of MAYO, Jose Angel Gutierrez, may think himself something of a hero, but he is, in fact, only a benighted soul if he believes that in the espousal of hatred he will find love. He is simply deluded if he believes that the wearing of fatigues . . . makes his followers revolutionaries. . . . One cannot fan the flames of bigotry one moment and expect them to disappear the next.[59]

For three days Gonzalez acrimoniously attacked MAYO from the floor of the House of Representatives. His attacks were not just on MAYO's leadership but on what he called the older radicals such as Bernal and Peña, whom he criticized for lending their support to

Gutierrez and Compean, whom he in turn categorized as orators of racism and hate.[60]

On April 5, 1969, Gonzalez stated to the press that a MAYO leader had exhorted some MAYO members to wreck the computer system at Kelly Air Force Base. Furthermore, he stated that his office had obtained proof that pro-Castro individuals had infiltrated MAYO and that a participant of the Del Rio Palm Sunday procession had openly advocated a Castro-type uprising. By April 8, 1969, Gonzalez began directing his rhetoric at those agencies and entities with which MAYO had some association. From then on MAYO and its resource entities were under constant attack from Gonzalez.

Gonzalez's rhetorical assaults on MAYO and its resource and support entities proved to be detrimental. By the latter part of 1969 MAYO had lost most of its resources. For example, the VISTA MMP in Del Rio was terminated. Although not directly responsible for its termination, Gonzalez took an active part in effecting it. He publicly accused VISTA workers of assisting MAYO members in distributing hate sheets at the Palm Sunday procession.[61] He charged the OEO—the funding agency of VISTA MMP—with permitting "war profiteering" among the War on Poverty programs. He was critical of the OEO for its way of contracting out some of its programs to private agencies. Foremost among the targets of his criticism were the lack of supervision of some of the contracting firms and their poor training facilities. He proposed that legislation be passed to preclude the issuance of such contracts.[62] In his efforts to amass proof against the VISTA programs, he compiled statements and tapes from disenchanted local VISTA workers. In applying pressure to the OEO he referred to its director as a "wheeler-dealer." The attacks proved to be detrimental. By the latter part of 1969 many MAYO members were purged from the VISTA MMP. This was a major setback for MAYO. The loss of these resources greatly reduced the number of MAYO's full-time paid organizers, making it less able to propagate activism.

Congressman Gonzalez's attacks were also directed at MAUC. After the VISTA issue at Del Rio, MAUC also came under heavy fire from Gonzalez because of its association with MAYO. He blasted it for being "irresponsible and inefficient in local administration." These allegations were specifically directed at Willie Velasquez, director of MAUC. The congressman said that Velasquez had astounded people by turning over fistfuls of money to controversial projects such as La Universidad de los Barrios and MAYO. The Universidad was criticized by Gonzalez as being an ill-defined project. He contended that it had become a center for drunken rebels whom police were often called to quell. He further attacked MAUC for funding MAYO. He said: "This is money that has been underwritten and paid for by the circularization and printing and general dissemination of hate literature and the clearly calculated activities intended to arouse public passion and civil disorder."[63]

The bottom line to Gonzalez's criticism of MAUC was directed at its source of funding, the Ford Foundation. Throughout much of 1969 and into 1970 Gonzalez was relentless in his efforts to block MAYO's access to resources, especially the Ford Foundation. At his request, a study was conducted on the effects of Ford Foundation-supported programs in his district. The study concluded that the projects that the foundation had funded had proven to be divisive and inflammatory despite good intentions. Gonzalez blamed this result on the lack of supervision from the foundation's upper echelons.[64] He further alleged that the grants had not created jobs or skills for struggling Chicanos but had stirred racism and unrest and fostered fragmentation and frustration, resulting in greater tensions and dangers to the community as a whole.[65] During April 1969 Gonzalez requested that the Bexar County grand jury investigate the activities of MAYO and other activist groups that he alleged were spreading hate in the community. Throughout the spring months of 1969 Gonzalez increased the intensity of his attacks on the Ford Foundation, alleging that it was not creating new leadership but merely financing the ambitions of greedy, ruthless, and irresponsible men.[66]

Officials at the Ford Foundation responded to Gonzalez's allegations with concern. Investigators were sent to San Antonio to check out MAYO's activities, and their report was not at all flattering. In June 1969 they summoned Willie Velasquez, Jose Angel Gutierrez, Albert Peña, and others involved with MAYO and MAUC. A Ford Foundation official bluntly announced to the group that no more money would be allocated to MAYO. At that point, Peña angrily told the official what he could do with all three billion dollars of the foundation's assets. Velasquez, outraged, accused the foundation of capitulating to Gonzalez's pressure out of political expediency. Ford Foundation officials responded that Gonzalez had nothing to do with it and that it was clear that MAYO had misused foundation funds by getting "overtly involved" in the San Antonio city elections of April 1969 and by campaigning openly for its candidates.

In an effort to prevent similar situations from occurring, the foundation imposed strict new rules on MAUC and its subsidiaries, thus limiting its action. MAUC survived the attacks and subsequently prospered. Juan Patlan replaced Velasquez as its director and moved the organization away from politics and MAYO's control. Thus, by the summer of 1969 Gonzalez and other politicians had begun to dry up the two major sources of MAYO's resources—the VISTA MMP and MAUC.

Gonzalez subsequently redirected his energies at MALDEF for its strong ties to MAYO. As was MAUC, MALDEF was funded by the Ford Foundation; consequently, it too came under fire from the congressman for its involvement with MAYO. When MALDEF was formed in 1968, MAYO and others hoped that, because it was funded through nongovernment sources, it would have a great deal of latitude to litigate in the area of civil rights and social justice. The reverse was true. The reality was that MALDEF was utterly dependent on outside funding sources and capitulated to political pressure. Rodolfo Acuña elaborates on why it became a victim of political pressure:

> In Los Angeles the MALDEF board of directors dismissed militant lawyer Oscar Acosta; his defense of clients was too aggressive. Congressman Henry B. Gonzalez was upset because money had been given to MAYO. Gonzalez applied pressure on the Ford Foundation to curtail grants to the Southwest Council of La Raza which was the funding through which the Ford Foundation went. Gonzalez charged that they were funding subversive organizations. Pressure was also applied to limit the scope of MALDEF's cases. As a consequence, the headquarters of MALDEF was moved out of San Antonio.[67]

MALDEF representatives explained to the press that their organization was compelled to move its headquarters from San Antonio because of its involvement in controversy and politics.[68] The Ford Foundation had threatened to cut off funds unless it moved its headquarters from San Antonio. MALDEF acquiesced and shortly thereafter moved its headquarters to San Francisco, leaving MAYO without a strong legal weapon. Gutierrez, who had been on staff for MALDEF, was fired right after the Del Rio march. Again, Gonzalez's crusade against MAYO and its leaders had proven to be successful. Adding fuel to the fires of Gonzalez's anti-MAYO crusade was Gutierrez's famous (or perhaps infamous) "Kill the Gringo" speech.

Jose Angel's "Kill the Gringo" Speech

Gonzalez's mordant attacks on the VISTA MMP, MAUC, MALDEF, and especially the Ford Foundation were further motivated by Gutierrez's "Kill the Gringo" speech. Gutierrez gave speeches that were controversial and provocative during the whole VISTA affair. After the Palm Sunday procession of Del Rio, however, during a press conference in San Antonio on April 10, Gutierrez argued that unless there was social change for Chicanos in the barrios, if worse came to worst it might become necessary to eliminate gringos by killing them.[69] Joining Gutierrez at the press conference were Mario Compean, then vice-chairman of MAYO, MALDEF attorney Juan Rocha, and Reverend Henry Casso, who taped the session as a precautionary move. In an obvious jab at Congressman Gonzalez, Gutierrez stated: "MAYO will not engage in controversy with fellow [Chicanos] regardless of how unfounded and vindictive their accusations [might] be. We realize that the effects of cultural genocide take many forms—some Chicanos . . . become psychologically castrated, others . . . become demagogues and gringos as well. And others . . . come together, resist, and eliminate the gringo. [MAYO] will be with the latter."[70]

Gutierrez was asked at the press conference how MAYO intended to eliminate the gringo. He responded by saying: "You can eliminate an individual in various ways. You can certainly kill him but that is not our intent at this moment. You can remove the base of support that he operates from, be it economic, political or social. That is what we intend to do."[71] What made Guiterrez's statement so controversial, however, was his use of the phrase "killing them [gringos] if all else fails." During the press conference, reporters asked a variety of questions dealing with diverse topics—from the role of the Church to MAYO's objectives in economics. In responding to other questions, Gutierrez denounced the Catholic Church for not being an instrument of social justice. He explained that the church had been used by the impoverished Chicanos as a crutch. He also expressed no confidence in the court system of Texas. Whatever justice the Chicano gets, he asserted, comes essentially from the federal courts. He was asked whether he had heard of Fidel Castro or whether he had an opinion on the Cuban Revolution. He replied that he knew little about Castro or his revolution.

Compean went on to explain briefly the educational and leadership aims of MAYO. Rocha elaborated on MAYO's effectiveness in disseminating public information. One reporter asked Gutierrez whether he hated gringos; Gutierrez replied, "Yes, I do."[72] He further said, "Gringos are a bunch of animals." When asked to name a few, he mentioned Mayor McAllister from San Antonio.[73] The mayor was particularly singled out because of his efforts at pressuring the Ford Foundation to stop funding MAYO. Because of the various controversial issues that were discussed, both Gutierrez and MAYO gained much national notoriety.

Gutierrez's decision to make the "Kill the Gringo" speech was motivated essentially by two considerations: his anger at the way things were going for MAYO everywhere, and strategic and tactical reasons. According to Luz Gutierrez, when Jose Angel gave the speech "he was angry and mad." He was angry at the way the VISTA issue at Del Rio had turned out. He was angry at the way some MAYO members had handled MAYO's campaign in the San Antonio city council elections that April. In general, she said, "He was angry at the world."[74]

Strategically and tactically, by 1969 Gutierrez had maneuvered himself into a major leadership role not only within the CYM but in the broader CM as well. He achieved this by orchestrating events and manipulating the media, using the gringo as the focus of attack. He felt that the time was right to serve notice on both gringos and Chicanos alike that MAYO was resolute in its struggle to effect social change. His cardinal tactical consideration was to send a clear message to those whom MAYO considered to be gringos that MAYO was willing and unafraid to take them on utilizing a diversity of means—including violence, if necessary. In defining the gringo, Gutierrez went on to say that a gringo is a person or institution that identifies with a certain policy, program, or attitude that reflects bigotry, racism, discord, prejudice, and violence, whereas an Anglo is a white person who is considered a friend, enlightened and caring about helping Chicanos.[75]

Tactically, Gutierrez used the speech as a psychological weapon to instill fear of and respect for MAYO. It was directed at both gringos and those Chicanos whom MAYO considered *vendidos* (sellouts). During the press conferences, in referring to the role of Chicanos, Gutierrez explained that he would not hesitate, if he felt it was necessary, to identify and attack vociferously those Chicanos who he felt were traitors to La Causa and had aligned themselves with the gringo power structure. He made it clear in subsequent media pronouncements that MAYO was prepared to denounce all those who resisted MAYO's change and empowerment efforts.[76]

For those Chicanos who wanted change, MAYO worked to instill in them courage, confidence, and determination. MAYO sought to debunk the stereotype of the Mexican as passive, fearful, and resigned to subordination and powerlessness. Gutierrez played on the Chicanos' emotions, anger, and machismo. After all, Gutierrez was aware that not since the turbulent years of *guerrillero* Juan "Cheno" Cortina (1859–1875) had Chicanos in Texas been willing to challenge the gringo power structure with such fervor by publicly calling for its elimination—if necessary, by the use of violence.

The audacity of Gutierrez in making the "Kill the Gringo" statement had mixed results for both him and MAYO in general. The media tuned in on his "Kill the Gringo" statement out of the numerous topics covered in the press conference. This had the positive effect of catapulting him to national prominence. Regardless of the slant given to the statement, he gained tremendous name identification, especially among Chicanos, not just in Texas but nationally. Television, radio, newspapers, and magazines began carrying stories on Gutierrez and MAYO as an organization. The CM press depicted both Gutierrez and MAYO as courageous and militant in their struggle to bring change and empowerment to Chicanos in Texas. Very few other Chicano leaders of the epoch of protest knew how to work and manipulate the media to advance their agendas as well as Gutierrez did. He was a master of media manipulation. This in particular drew attention and praise from Chicano student groups within the growing CYM, which, impressed with MAYO's militancy and daring, began monitoring the organization and, in some cases, following its lead.

On the negative side, the controversial "Kill the Gringo" statement further infuriated MAYO's increasingly numerous adversaries. Congressman Gonzalez became relentless in his crusade to neutralize MAYO as an organization, its leadership, and its resource and support entities. The media created a furor by emphasizing the words "Kill the Gringo." Gutierrez responded to the growing tempest by qualifying and later retracting some of the militancy of his words, but to no avail; MAYO lost in the public debate. Congressman Gonzalez labeled MAYO leaders as "Brown Bilbos" (a reference to Theodore Bilbo, a segregationalist senator from Mississippi) for being practitioners of a new racism. Furthermore, the statement opened the floodgates for more scathing criticisms of MAYO from both gringos and Mexican Americans.[77] Ultimately, the statement proved to be the straw that broke the camel's back—in other words, an end to MAYO's manipulation of external resources and support from some entities.

MAYO's Struggle for Change Intensifies

In spite of the Del Rio VISTA issue, the "Kill the Gringo" controversy, and numerous attacks by its adversaries, MAYO in 1969 continued to intensify its social change efforts. In May 1969 the MAYO chapter in Hidalgo County became involved in protesting against the social inequities in the county's welfare system. That month at a meeting with court officials at Edinburg, MAYO representatives presented a list of demands oriented toward overhauling Hidalgo County's welfare system. Some of the demands were:

1. That copies of all regulations, written and unwritten, be published regularly in local newspapers or on the local radio stations so that the recipients of welfare food commodities may know the regulations that determine eligibility.
2. That material announcing the existence of the welfare rights organization be distributed, and that welfare recipients can join this national organization to protest for their rights.
3. That the mistreatment and the intimidation of welfare recipients cease and desist immediately, and that welfare recipients, especially ladies, be treated with proper respect.[78]

The county judge who presided at the meeting angrily denied every one of MAYO's demands. At the meeting, the MAYO representative who presented the demands was arrested for failing to identify himself to the judge. Consequently the judge charged him with contempt of court and jailed him for twenty-four hours.[79]

In retaliation MAYO held a demonstration two days later at Edinburg. It applied for a parade permit that would allow it to demonstrate in front of the courthouse. The chief of police rejected MAYO's parade permit request. However, MAYO was told that it could demonstrate as long as it did not block the streets or sidewalks or walk on the courthouse lawn. The demonstration was attended by some 150 demonstrators, who marched in file around the courthouse chanting "Viva La Revolucion" and carrying pickets denouncing the judge's decision.

The demonstration then moved on to the Edinburg city park. While on route to the park, the marchers chanted in unison, "Gringo, matenlo, matenlo—gringo, kill him, gringo kill him."[80] Once the demonstrators reached the park, a rally was held and numerous speeches were given. The MAYO spokesman who earlier had been arrested reiterated MAYO's demands, including one for the formation of a committee of poor people to initiate changes and formulate policy. A priest from the Brownsville Catholic diocese praised what he called MAYO's "love of poor people."[81]

The demonstrators were nearly matched in number by a corps of newsmen, sheriff's deputies, city police, and Texas Rangers. The demonstration was orderly, however, and ended with no violence and no arrests. In the end, MAYO's demands for welfare reform in

Hidalgo County were rejected, but the issue exemplified its commitment to and tenacity in creating social change for the poor Chicano.

By late 1969 MAYO began to get involved in organizing mass demonstrations against the war in Vietnam. During November 1969 MAYO held an antidraft protest demonstration in McAllen. Some 150 MAYO demonstrators took to the streets to protest both the Vietnam War and the inequities of the draft system. Most of the MAYO speakers claimed that draft boards in the lower Rio Grande Valley called a disproportionately large number of Chicanos.[82] Efrain Fernandez, one of the MAYO spokesmen for the demonstration, had mentioned in an earlier press conference that statistics published in the *Congressional Record* indicated that Chicanos made up 14.8 percent of Texas's population, yet 24.4 percent of the state's war dead in Vietnam during a six-month period had been Chicanos. Fernandez went on to say: "Why don't some of these flag waving, patriotic white Anglo-Saxon farmers send their boys to fight in Viet Nam instead of sending them off to college?"[83]

MAYO, however, never made the antiwar movement a major priority. Those chapters that did participate in antiwar activities were essentially college-based. Gutierrez explains that if MAYO had joined the white radicals in their antiwar movement, it would have had negative ramifications in the barrios, where the war was not an important issue. To the contrary, many Chicanos supported the war. Thus, MAYO felt that it would be a strategic mistake for it to oppose the war because of the pervasive patriotism among Chicanos in Texas.[84] This contributed to MAYO's merely lukewarm support for the antiwar movement.

MAYO's social change agenda also included supporting striking workers in Austin. In November 1969 MAYO initiated a demonstration in support of the workers striking against Austin's Economy Furniture Company. MAYO demanded that the company accede to the workers' demands for better wages and working conditions. Prior to the demonstration MAYO had requested a parade permit from Austin's city council. The council refused to grant the permit, but its action did not deter MAYO from having a parade. MAYO circumvented the council's decision by having demonstrators walk on the sidewalks four and five abreast. The demonstrators numbered over six hundred and stretched for more than two city blocks. Placards and banners were carried throughout the march. Shouts of "Viva La Raza Unida" and "Viva La Huelga" were frequent, and the flag of Mexico was briefly hoisted on the pole at the state capitol's main entrance. The march went from the state capitol through downtown Austin, then by the governor's mansion and back to the capitol. The march concluded without any major incidents.[85]

Prior to the march, however, a rally was held in front of the state capitol. Several speakers addressed the more than six hundred people. Bexar County commissioner Albert Peña was one of the main speakers. He reasserted his support of MAYO's efforts for social change. He declared: "The people of Texas better realize we are united, because 1970 is the year of the Chicano. If my brothers need me in Del Rio, Corpus Christi, or Austin, I will go there. I am here to do anything you want me to do."[86] Speaking against the Austin City Council's decision not to grant a parade permit to MAYO, Peña said that it was shameless to restrict the demonstration. He further stated:

> This is our land . . . our nation. We were here before Columbus or Cortez. It was our land when the Alamo was built . . . it is still our land, and we will reclaim it in 1970. . . . Ya basta. We have had it. We are going to march and demonstrate whether they give us the right to do it or not. We are going to march and protest until we can say . . . I am free. Thank thee, Lord at last I am free![87]

Peña and other speakers went on to attack Governor Preston Smith and Lieutenant Governor Ben Barnes as enemies of the Chicano community. Rally speakers were loudly cheered and given the clenched-fist salute.

Throughout the rally and especially the march, law-enforcement officers from the Texas Department of Public Safety and local police were deployed; some of the law officers were equipped with riot control equipment. Other officers, meanwhile, directed traffic during the approximately fourteen-block march. The march was indicative of MAYO's ability to use any issue as a means of bringing attention to La Raza's problems and inequities.

By late December 1969 MAYO had expanded its scope of protest activities by attacking the Catholic Church's reactionary role. Its first major encounter with the church came on the closing days of December 1969, when MAYO held a national conference in the Rio Grande Valley town of Mission, Texas. The conference was held at the Oblate Missionary Seminary south of Mission and featured panel discussions and workshops on various topics. The conference had several goals: (1) to inform Chicano youth about MAYO's programs; (2) to select new programs; (3) to increase coordination among MAYO chapters across the state; and (4) to link up and coordinate with the growing CM. The conference was attended by scores of MAYO delegates from throughout Texas and youth representatives from as far away as California, Arizona, Minnesota, Illinois, and Colorado. Politicians, government officials, and heads of various organizations also attended the conference.

An incident occurred at the conference that caught the attention of the media. At a special mass on Sunday, December 28, protesting MAYO delegates painted the statue of Our Lady of the Immaculate Conception the color bronze. The press, in particular, interpreted MAYO's action as flagrantly offensive, if not outrageous, and a direct challenge to the policies of the Catholic Church. Leroy F. Arons, a reporter for the *Washington Post,* describes the painting of the statue:

> Festive in berets, brightly colored ponchos and serapes, MAYO delegates climbed the five foot high pedestal one by one to take a turn at spraying the life size gray stone statue. On the sidelines, two guitarists and three singers provided an accompaniment of revolutionary songs . . . *"Viva La Raza!"* The crowd cried when the *Virgen* was bronzed from head to toe, *"Viva la Causa."* [88]

A red-and-black *huelga* flag was draped across the shoulders of the statue. This incident was precipitated largely by two factors: (1) the refusal of the Oblate fathers to turn over the unused seminary to MAYO for the establishment of a Chicano college and (2) MAYO's criticism of the Catholic Church for its unresponsiveness to the manifold needs of the Chicano community.

This symbolic protest was perceived by some MAYO members as an act of affirmation and challenge. Arons wrote: "MAYO members . . . saw themselves as affirming their pride in their brownness and as throwing down the gauntlet against the Catholic Church, which in their eyes stood guilty of neglect and exploitation." [89] It was a daring political move on MAYO's part, for no institution stands higher in the esteem of La Raza than the Catholic Church. MAYO leaders felt it was a warning of things to come. In addition, MAYO used the protest to enunciate its call for the establishment of a Chicano college in Texas. After some deliberation, they voted to establish Jacinto Trevino College and asked that the Oblate priests turn over the abandoned mission to MAYO so that the Jacinto Trevino College could be established there. The mission, abandoned by the Oblate order, was badly in need of repairs. It was leased to the Colorado Migrant Ministry, which in turn permitted MAYO to use it for its national conference. MAYO requested that the mission be turned over with the provision that MAYO would rehabilitate it.

Integral to the request was a declaration that the Oblate mission belonged to the people.[90] One Oblate father complained that the mission had been desecrated, alleging that the protest was the work of communists.[91] "These accusations of communism," according to Alberto Luera, "prevented MAYO from getting the Oblate Mission for the college site."[92]

The national MAYO conference marked an important turning point in MAYO's history and development. Since its inception in 1967 it had been a staunch advocate of unconventional tactics of protest politics. No institution, personality, or issue was off-limits or too sacred for MAYO to take on in its struggle for social change. Its tactics exhibited a militancy seldom espoused or practiced by Chicano organizations in Texas. Between 1967 and 1969 it attacked and confronted vigorously those it considered oppressors and exploiters of La Raza. Its confrontations, picketing, demonstrating, and school strikes were geared toward mobilizing and politicizing La Raza, especially the youth.

MAYO by 1969 had reached its pinnacle of activism. That year it had over forty chapters throughout Texas. Its involvement in the VISTA affair at Del Rio, the Kingsville and Crystal City walkouts, and the San Antonio city council elections were but a few of the salient incidents illustrative of its militant activism. It began to change its program of action, however, beginning with the MAYO state meeting held in May 1969 and followed by the MAYO national conference held in December of the same year. Luera explains MAYO's change of focus: "The tactics such as the attacks on officials, boycotts, and picketing were getting us nowhere. It was like hitting ourselves against the wall. We were not moving. We took out everything we could have with those tactics. The people we were going to affect had been affected already. We were not going to move much more."[93] The discussions that occurred at the national conference were indicative of a change of attitude that MAYO's leadership was beginning to undergo. Gutierrez further elaborated on this: "By 1969 the name of MAYO had become some kind of a joke. Because we were certainly not the good old boy scouts everybody thought the name implied. People were terrified. We were associating more and more with *Chicanismo* and some of the more radical movements of the time."[94]

MAYO's national conference had an important effect in changing its priorities. As a result of this conference MAYO began to take on a more programmatic orientation.[95] For example, besides possessing an advocacy capability, some MAYO chapters, such as the one from San Antonio, in 1970 became involved in providing relief to Chicanos in Corpus Cristi who had been victimized by a devastating hurricane. Other MAYO chapters followed suit. Specific projects such as the establishment of Jacinto Trevino College and the formation of a Chicano political party were its top priorities for 1970.

MAYO's role as an agent of social change continued well into 1970. In September of that year MAYO, along with other groups from the barrios of San Antonio, initiated what became known as the San Antonio Savings Association (SASA) boycott. This came about because of what MAYO state chairperson Alberto Luera and others construed as condescending and racist comments made by the then-mayor of San Antonio, W. W. McAllister. As Luera explains, "McAllister had been interviewed by one of the national television networks in response to the National Chicano Moratorium riots that occurred in Los Angeles, California on August 29. He said something to the effect that in San Antonio Mexicans had not rioted or been troubled by such unrest because they were fun loving and easy going, that they loved flowers, parties, dancing, and were a content people."[96]

McAllister's comments stirred up a hornet's nest of outrage among many of the Chicano activists of San Antonio, including those in MAYO. Initially, however, the response to the comments came from non-MAYO activists; MAYO's role was one of collaboration and support. The leadership for the SASA boycott came from several individuals: George Velasquez, a local MAYO activist; Albert Peña, commissioner for Bexar County's first precinct; and MAYO state leaders Ignacio Perez and Alberto Luera. These leaders and their followers felt insulted by Mayor McAllister's comments and resorted to direct action. For several days thirty to forty people picketed the McAllister-owned SASA.

The SASA boycott culminated in the arrest of thirty Chicano protesters. Ignacio Perez explains the circumstances that precipitated the confrontation between the police and Chicano protesters:[97]

It all began with an Anglo sheriff or bailiff, I am not sure what he was, who was wearing plain clothes [and who] provoked a confrontation with us. As he left the SASA building, he cursed at us and pushed George Velasquez's girlfriend. George became aware of the incident and proceeded to follow him to another bank a block away now known as Lubby's. We followed George into the building and cornered the guy on the elevator. From everywhere the police came out in full force. We didn't allow the police to get him out. We weren't going to let him out, we wanted assurances from the police that he was going to be charged for assault and battery.

The imbroglio escalated into violence. As the police entered the building with the intent of rescuing the officer from the protesters, shouting and pushing erupted between the two groups. An altercation ensued when a police officer pushed and manhandled Perez's six-month-old daughter, Xochi, who was being held by her mother, Orvilia Perez.[98] Luera witnessed this incident and confronted the officer. According to Luera, "This angered me. We got into it verbally, then the fists started." The scuffle between Luera and police officers was recorded by a photographer from the San Antonio *Express*, and on the next day photographs of it accompanied an article that reported the arrest of thirty protesters on charges of unlawful assembly. Among those arrested were Commissioner Peña, Perez, Luera, Gonzales, and Frank Tejada (now a U.S. congressman), as well as others. To Luera, the melee was "nothing less than a setup, an ambush by the police to provoke us into a confrontation."[99]

Even in jail, tensions continued to mount between those arrested and the police. "While [we were] in jail," Perez explains, "the police were so angry at us that threats of bodily harm were made. But, fortunately, cooler heads prevailed."[100] Within a few hours the Chicano protesters were released on fifty-dollar bonds. A few weeks later the charges against them were dropped on grounds of insufficient evidence.

The general response of the Chicano community in San Antonio and throughout Texas was favorable. The SASA boycott demonstrated MAYO's zealous commitment to militant direct action, that when push came to shove, MAYO's leaders were willing to take control and provide direction. The SASA boycott and the accompanying incidents thus served to enhance MAYO's social change image. Even though there were other groups involved, MAYO's leadership received most of the exposure.

By the end of 1970 MAYO's militant orientation toward social change gave way to the pursuit of political empowerment through the formation of the Raza Unida party. This is not to say that all MAYO chapters had abandoned advocacy at the local level. Many of them continued to address a variety of issues such as the Vietnam War, the establishment of Chicano studies, and so on, but it was politics that constituted the focus of much of MAYO's activities.

6. MAYO: Precursor to the Raza Unida Party

No other CM-oriented organization in Texas during the years 1967 to 1972 developed as quickly, gained such notoriety, and was as committed to bringing about social justice for Chicanos as MAYO. MAYO focused primarily on educational and social issues during its first two years. Electoral politics took a backseat to MAYO's social change agenda. By as early as 1968, however, MAYO began broadening its focus to include political empowerment. Because of its nonprofit status, MAYO's bylaws prohibited it from becoming directly involved in politics. Since its inception, however, Los Cinco had discussed and planned for MAYO's eventual entry, in some form or another, into the arena of Texas local and state politics. With the approval of the Winter Garden Project (WGP), the stage was set for its entry through the formation of the Raza Unida party (RUP).

This chapter examines MAYO's political empowerment agenda from 1969 to 1970. More specifically, it analyzes the various circumstances, activities, and events that were instrumental in nurturing the climate for change necessary to give rise to the RUP. Inherent to the analysis is a two-part thesis: MAYO, as an organization, was the precursor to the RUP in Texas, and the formation of the RUP precipitated the demise of MAYO by 1972.

MAYO's Emerging Political Agenda

MAYO's political involvement began in 1968. In March of that year MAYO representatives attended the Texas Conference on New Politics held in Austin. The paramount concern of the Anglo activists responsible for the meeting's organization was the Vietnam War. Compean relates what transpired at the conference: "We hadn't been there half an hour when the whole discussion was concerned with the antiwar movement. So we told them [off] and we left."[1] The reasons that MAYO refused to participate in the conference and was subsequently reluctant to participate in antiwar activities are further explained by Compean:

> MAYO . . . [was] always criticized for not being more active in the antiwar movement. MAYO took . . . flack from everybody on that. Most of it came from the Young Socialist Alliance and Socialists Workers' party saying that in some cases MAYO was reactionary for refusing to support the antiwar movement. Simply it had not been good politics for MAYO . . . it hadn't been practical. If MAYO would have spoken out against the war in the barrios it would have been run out immediately.[2]

The conference proved to be a bad political experience for MAYO in dealing with Anglo activists of the antiwar movement. They expected MAYO's support against the war, but MAYO's response was one of rancor and distrust. Beyond perceiving that to embrace the antiwar issue would have been detrimental to its overall organizing efforts in the barrios, MAYO simply did not like or trust the Anglo activists. This was ascribable to MAYO's profound apprehension not just of gringos but of Anglos as well, whether radicals or not. It was a distrust predicated on a fear of being used. According to MAYO, Anglo activists were paternalistic and condescending and cared more about advancing their own agendas than the Chicanos.[3] MAYO's cultural nationalist posture also helped to prevent its entrance into coalitions with radical Anglo groups.

During April 1968 MAYO members from the San Antonio area got involved for the first time with the Democratic party primaries. Mario Compean and Juan Patlan worked in Albert Peña's campaign for Bexar County commissioner. They became actively involved, working in the predominantly Chicano precincts of San Antonio. After weeks of intense political organizing, their efforts paid off. They succeeded in delivering the vote in key Chicano precincts. In May, during the primaries, MAYO's leaders were approached by the Democratic Women of Bexar County to work on behalf of liberal Democratic candidates on election day. MAYO requested three hundred dollars to get the vote out in key precincts on election day, a request that was subsequently rejected.

MAYO's political agenda in 1968 was not well defined. Its political organizing efforts were more probing actions than anything else. During the primary months of April through June, MAYO also became involved in the campaign of Jose Uriegas, a Democrat who ran for state representative in the Uvalde area of South Texas. Prior to his campaign for state representative, Uriegas had been appointed

by the Anglo-controlled Uvalde City Council to serve out the term
of an Anglo city councilman who had died. Luz Gutierrez, who with
her husband was active in Uriegas's campaign, explains why they
got involved:

> He was a token. . . . [Uriegas] was an upcoming Chicano and the
> [Anglos] wanted to move him up into their ranks. So he was ap-
> pointed to the city council . . . so we said, "Vamos a pescarlo an-
> tes que se haga bien vendido [Let us bring him into our ranks be-
> fore he becomes a sellout]." Before he forgets. . . . Este [This] guy
> was in the city council just for two months and he decided to run
> for state representative without even thinking about building up
> a reputation in the city council. He had a beautiful opportunity
> but instead queria mas [he wanted more]. So he decided to run . . .
> so we ran him for state representative.[4]

Jose Angel Gutierrez became the campaign manager for Uriegas.
He and Luz would go to Uvalde every weekend to work on the
campaign. Precincts were canvassed, literature distributed, meetings held, and social functions organized throughout the campaign.
MAYO's objectives in the Uriegas campaign were primarily two: to
get Uriegas elected to the state assembly and to get MAYO organized
in Uvalde. To achieve both objectives Gutierrez called on MAYO
members from other communities of South Texas for assistance.
Luz explained that many MAYO members came with one thing in
mind: "Que donde nos esten chingando [wherever they are oppressing us], let's all go in and help."[5] VISTA volunteers also came to
Uvalde to assist MAYO in the campaign. For weeks MAYO and
VISTA members worked diligently in Uriegas's campaign, but to no
avail. He lost the election.

The Germination of a Chicano Party

With the inception of MAYO in 1967, the idea of forming a Chicano
political party began to germinate. The idea was planted during the
many discussion sessions held by Los Cinco, during which they discussed the dynamics of American politics. There was a sense of
unanimity when they analyzed the two-party system. They felt that
neither the Democratic nor Republican party was responsive or sensitive to the needs of Chicanos. In particular, Gutierrez was adamant in his position that Chicanos could not realize empowerment
through either party. He felt Chicanos could not effectively compete
in the political arena since they did not have the money and were

perceived by both parties as being unqualified.⁶ The pervasive attitude among Los Cinco was that both parties were antipoor and anti-Chicano. Even though there was a definite anti-two-party bias among Los Cinco, the idea of forming a Chicano party was merely discussed in 1967 and not acted on.

It was not until 1968, just prior to going on active duty with the army reserve, that Gutierrez began to research the legal aspects of forming a political party in Texas. He spent a considerable amount of time at the law library at Saint Mary's University reading about the legal particulars.⁷ After completing the research, he drafted a report and mailed it to various MAYO leaders and members to get their input on the party idea. The overall response was poor. He stated, "No one really wanted to do it. That hurt me a little bit, that people thought it was not a very good idea."⁸ The next time that he proceeded to make a formal presentation on his party idea was at MAYO's state executive committee meeting. The reaction again was negative. Gutierrez explains, "They thought I was crazy and that it would never happen."⁹ Instead of making an issue about having his proposal denied, he decided not to push his party scheme just then and to wait for a more auspicious time for its reintroduction.

It was not until his active duty tour that Gutierrez was better able to conceptualize his Chicano party scheme. During this time Gutierrez continued his research and began to develop a plan of action for the formation of a Chicano political party. His research also focused on third-party movements, such as Wallace's American Independent party. He was impressed with the similarity of conditions but not with the American Independents' rhetoric or ideology.¹⁰ Eager to expand on MAYO's activities, Gutierrez began writing position papers on various topics. The paper that dealt with a pro-Chicano party was entitled "La Raza and Political Action." This position paper focused on the various problems that he felt had impeded La Raza's political empowerment—from fear, distrust, and ignorance of the existing political system to the pervasive parochialism among Chicanos. In the position paper he provided a partial solution to these political problems. He wrote:

> A partial solution to our current dilemma in the political area
> lies in our developing parties for the promotion and protection
> of our interests. Bloc voting must become a reality. Our *barrios*
> must begin to hold conventions regularly to deal with local prob-
> lems and to establish political structures. Our programs must
> be determined by our needs and not their acceptability to the
> white man. *La Raza* should begin to control the local councils

of government and begin bargaining directly with presidential candidates and aspirants. There are no reasons why we should not be masters of our destiny. All we have to do is look around us and within us to see why we must.[11]

Prior to Gutierrez's release from active duty in early 1969, his idea of forming a Chicano political party had been largely an abstraction: "It was like dreaming. It was like knowing what you want to do, but you don't know how to get there." The idea of trying to form an independent power base and a political party was only a vague idea that he was trying to get MAYO to support.[12] Between the time he concluded his research on the party in 1968 to his release from the army in 1969, he became resolute and emphatic about the feasibility of the idea. He explained his persistence by saying: "I always kept it in the back of my mind that . . . it was the same old problem that when you want something done you might as well do it yourself. So I waited for another opportunity."[13] The opportunity to begin testing his party scheme came during the San Antonio City Council elections of April 1969. It was in this election that MAYO experimented with the strategy of bloc voting.

San Antonio City Council Elections

In December 1968 MAYO decided to test the feasibility of organizing a Chicano political party. While Gutierrez was doing his military service, Mario Compean and other MAYO leaders met with him to discuss the possibility of having MAYO back candidates for the San Antonio city elections scheduled for April 1969. During this meeting Gutierrez warned them that conditions were not propitious for running candidates. They disagreed. They felt that nearly three years of intense MAYO organizing efforts in the city's various barrios had rendered San Antonio's political climate conducive to change. Therefore, MAYO's San Antonio leadership decided to experiment with some of the aspects of Gutierrez's Chicano political party scheme. Once the decision was made, Gutierrez supported it wholeheartedly.

Specifically, MAYO's interest was in testing the strategy of bloc voting, which was central to Gutierrez's party model. MAYO believed that if the strategy worked in San Antonio, it could also be utilized elsewhere, especially South Texas. With this in mind, in the early months of 1969 MAYO decided to sponsor three candidates under a front entity named the Committee for *Barrio* Betterment (CBB). Mario Compean, who ran for mayor under the CBB label, elaborated on the importance of the city council elections to MAYO's politics:

We wanted to test the model to be sure. But also we wanted to tear down some of the myths that were carried out against Chicanos. One common myth was that the Chicano was not interested in getting involved politically . . . didn't want to be sophisticated enough to be able to run campaigns or candidates and win . . . and we were just plain apathetic which was not the case. We said no to these myths.[14]

MAYO's strategy emphasized the importance of educating Chicanos about the workings and realities of the political system. Moreover, if MAYO's candidates could win or at least do well, that would project a positive image of Chicanos on the road to empowerment.[15]

The CBB's entry into San Antonio's political arena seemed difficult, and a win appeared almost impossible. After all, the opposition was a powerful political machine, the Good Government League (GGL), which had dominated San Antonio politics for more than two decades. Beyond dealing with this David-and-Goliath scenario, the CBB had to overcome numerous other factors: candidates running for the city council had to run at large; the mayor was not elected by the people but appointed by the city council; and the incumbent mayor of eight years, Walter McAllister, was one of the most powerful and affluent men in San Antonio. Some Chicanos perceived Compean's candidacy in a negative context. He states, "Everybody said you are really crazy to file against the guy [referring to Mayor McAllister]—he is the hardest to defeat."[16] Compean maintained that McAllister was the most vulnerable candidate running and that he could be beaten.

The CBB's candidate platform was predicated on a "Chicano power" strategy that sought community control of the city's political institutions. The underlying message of the platform was self-determination: the idea that Chicanos must have a voice in governing themselves. Gutierrez's tactic of bloc voting was incorporated into the campaign strategy. From the outset CBB candidates concentrated all their political efforts and limited resources on the heavily populated Chicano and poor precincts of the city. CBB candidates, in their attempts to appeal exclusively to Chicano and poor voters, dressed and spoke according to their targets' mode of dress and vernacular. They never wore suits or formal wear. According to Gutierrez, they "didn't dress and look like other candidates."[17] Their speeches were laced with phrases in the vernacular of the barrio. In other words, they spoke to the people in words and terms they could understand.

Their oratory struck hard at the unresponsiveness of the GGL in meeting the needs of the people. They also stressed the many issues endemic to the barrios—from the devastating effects of poverty, such as dilapidated housing, unemployment, and crime, to the people's political powerlessness. In theory, the campaign's strategy was to take on the tenor of a poor people's campaign oriented toward wresting power away from the GGL political machine. In practice, however, MAYO's CBB strategy did not push coalitional politics. While using and including all the poor in its campaign rhetoric, in actuality little was done to embrace non-Chicano groups.

The reality was that the CBB candidates seldom, if ever, ventured out of the targeted barrios of San Antonio. According to Compean:

> No effort was made to tie in the black community . . . or the white-liberal Anglo. Only twice did I venture out of the west side to campaign. It was just barely on the borderline. So that was downtown . . . speaking at meet-the-candidate rallies. . . . For the most part we stuck to our side of town. We stuck to that strategy. We went to [the] streets for bloc work. What little money we had we spent on signs and on the Spanish-speaking media.[18]

The CBB purposely disregarded the possibilities of forming coalitions with either African American or Anglo liberal elements and decided to run an aggressive campaign that appealed only to Chicanos in the barrios of the west side of San Antonio.

Chicanismo very much drove the campaign. Chicanismo meant talking to people about the many virtues of the Chicano culture. It meant instilling in the people a profound sense of pride as to who they were and where they came from. The campaign offered an opportunity not just to politicize the people but to awaken them culturally. The CBB candidates alluded in their speeches and literature to the greatness of Chicano heritage and the importance of preserving the language and culture. They vehemently rejected assimilation and integration. They also attacked the gringo-dominated political system for being oppressive, exploitive, and racist.[19] MAYO's cultural nationalist zeal was evident throughout the campaign.

The CBB's effort toward the closing days of the campaign were largely directed by Gutierrez. While the CBB's campaign manager of three months, Mariano Aguilar, continued to work the nuts and bolts of the campaign, Gutierrez was brought in as a consultant specifically to direct the CBB's get-out-the-vote drive. Prior to Gutierrez's arrival, Aguilar was successful in structuring the CBB into a loose alliance of "old guard" Chicano liberal activists like Peña and "new guard" CM activists like Compean. Moreover, each of the three CBB candidates brought to the alliance his own networks and support mechanisms. When Gutierrez arrived he found a grassroots network in place that was ready for the final push. Luz Gutierrez explained that in one week Jose Angel succeeded in consolidating the various campaign mechanisms, which translated into securing hundreds of volunteers to get out the vote.[20]

In this case, the Goliath of the GGL triumphed over the David of the CBB. Considering MAYO's ethnic sectarian strategy and practically nonexistent finances, however, the CBB candidates did extremely well against the well-financed and powerful GGL machine. Compean, who directed his campaign chiefly at the GGL's most powerful candidate, Mayor McAllister, received 11,838 votes and ran third in a six-person race. Compean came very close to forcing the incumbent mayor into a runoff, lacking only another 362 votes to do so. After the results of the election were in, Compean stated: "If I'd have stuck to traditional politics—that is, if I would have appealed to a broader base—I would have beaten McAllister easily."[21] The CBB's other two candidates, for city council, although they lost, also did very well. C. H. Candy Alejo received 13,787 votes and ran second in a three-person race. Dario Chapa did even better than Compean and Alejo, polling 17,877 votes. He also ran second in a three-person race. The CBB candidates received between 30 to 35 percent of the vote. They surprised the gringo power structure by the number of votes all three candidates received. James McCrory, a reporter for the San Antonio *Express*, commenting on the results of the campaign, wrote: "Perhaps the greatest surprise of the election was the number of votes received by the three candidates fielded by the Committee for *Barrio* Betterment."[22]

The results of the San Antonio City Council election served to buttress MAYO's strategic use of bloc voting. The CBB carried every precinct in the west-side barrio after conducting a very thorough voter registration drive that augmented the number of Chicano registered voters by 26 percent. Utilizing a grassroots, get-out-the-vote drive, the CBB increased the Chicano voter turnout by 11 percent.[23] Its efforts to appeal primarily to Chicano voters worked well. MAYO felt a powerful message had been sent to the gringo power structures in Texas that Chicanos were no longer going to take a backseat politically. The election proved that Chicanos could vote as a bloc if organized. Furthermore, it added impetus to Gutierrez's efforts to form a Chicano political party.

In spite of insufficient financial resources, MAYO's leaders felt a major victory had been achieved. With very little funding, MAYO, through the CBB, had demonstrated its political organizing powers and prowess. Because of the CBB's concentration on Chicano precincts, the few dollars that were raised came from the people who resided in the barrios. The CBB, however, failed to galvanize financial support from the Chicano middle- and upper-middle-class strata of San Antonio. They perceived MAYO to be too radical and militant and not representative of their interests. Consequently, the three CBB candidates raised only modest amounts for their campaigns: Compean, $1,200; Alejo, $2,000; and Chapa, $2,700. In reference to the problem of finances, Compean contended that "in retrospect, just a little bit more resources would have done the trick."[24]

The problem of finances was further compounded by the fact that MAYO's leadership was overextended. In other words, MAYO was not able to use all its human resources because of its involvement with other issues. During the month of March MAYO became embroiled in the VISTA issue at Del Rio. Gutierrez, Compean, and other MAYO members from San Antonio became involved in both the campaign and the VISTA issue. Consequently, the VISTA issue hurt the campaign by taking valuable time and resources away from it. The day prior to the election Gutierrez was in Del Rio leading the Palm Sunday demonstration. Immediately after the procession he returned to San Antonio to coordinate the CBB's get-out-the-vote drive. Most of the other problems were ascribable to the bloc-voting strategy of the campaign. By running a "Chicano power" campaign the CBB lost potential votes among blacks, Anglo liberals, and some middle-class Chicanos. The GGL boldly attacked the CBB candidates for propounding a kind of reverse racism. MAYO's entry into the campaign activated other adversaries as well, such as Congressman Gonzalez, who attacked MAYO for overtly participating in the election.

Although none of the CBB candidates won, the results demonstrated the potential of the bloc-voting strategy, which, to Gutierrez, enhanced the feasibility of the party scheme. The elections proved the inherent strength of bloc voting. Gutierrez more than ever was convinced that a Chicano political party in South Texas could mean the beginning of a new political era for Chicanos, an epoch where the Chicano was not the powerless but the powerful. His next opportunity to propose the party idea to MAYO came in May 1969, at a MAYO statewide meeting where the Winter Garden Project was approved.

The Winter Garden Project (WGP)

Following MAYO's political quasi-success in San Antonio, Gutierrez's idea of forming a Chicano political party was given further impetus during a MAYO statewide board meeting held in Uvalde during the month of May. The agenda essentially focused on two major items: election of new officers and a determination of MAYO's projects and activities for the ensuing months. First, Compean was elected MAYO state chairperson, replacing Gutierrez. The second item, the WGP, consumed a great deal of dialogue and debate. Intrinsic to this part of the agenda were two major concerns: the formation of a Chicano political party and the selection of a geographical area for the implementation of an empowerment and community control organization.

Gutierrez re-introduced his proposal for a Chicano political party. Equipped with maps and handouts, he presented a comprehensive strategy as to how it could be organized. Unfortunately, with the exception of Compean, the MAYO leaders gave his party idea a lukewarm response. They felt that MAYO could not undertake the project at that time. Some went so far as to consider it ludicrous.[25] In describing their negative response, Gutierrez explains, "It's just one of those things that when it's new, it demands a lot of work and people don't want to get into it."[26]

Instead, there was a pervasive feeling among the MAYO leaders that MAYO needed to change the focus of its organizing strategy. After two years of taking on numerous educational and social issues, they felt that MAYO needed to give top priority to efforts designed to win control of those political, educational, and economic institutions that govern the lives of Chicanos.[27] Gutierrez further amplifies on MAYO's reasons to consolidate its previous projects into one:

> What we ended up doing was voting and trying to consolidate the whole affair of MAYO's previous activities into one project. We had done school walkouts. We had done police brutality cases. We had done political campaigns. But all were single shot issues. We never tried to comprehensively cover all the fronts. Never tried to do a complete working of a community. . . . Second we had some very definite objectives. We wanted to change the institutions and work within the institutions to see how far we could go. Third, we wanted to present at least alternative models for other people to follow and emulate.[28]

In essence, the board members expressed reservations about focusing exclusively on the use of direct-action methods of protest. They wanted to become more political but in a nonpartisan way. This allowed them to have electoral designs without considering the need for a new party.[29] Instead of supporting Gutierrez's idea, MAYO's

Table 4. *Population of Winter Garden Counties*

County	Population	African American	%	White	%	Chicano	%
Zavala	11,370	38	.334	2,075	18.1	9,275	81.5
Dimmit	9,039	112	1.2	1,546	17.1	7,781	81.6
Uvalde	18,093	10	.005	1,736	9.6	16,347	90.3
Maverick	2,006	121	6.3	437	21.7	1,448	72.1
Val Verde	5,014	9	.17	1,074	21.4	3,931	78.4
Kinney	17,348	309	1.7	8,237	47.4	8,802	50.7
La Salle	27,471	763	2.7	11,159	40.6	15,549	56.6

Source: U.S. Census, 1970.

leadership decided to back an empowerment and community control program designed to win Chicano control of a particular area in rural Texas.

Of great importance to MAYO's new focused strategy of empowerment and community control was the selection of a targeted geographical area where such a project would be implemented and developed. Four areas with large concentrations of Chicanos were considered: the Winter Garden area (a seven-county area in South Texas that included Crystal City); the Plainview/Lubbock area (located in West Texas); the Kingsville area (where Texas A&I University was located); and the Rio Grande Valley area, located along the border in South Texas.[30] For each of these areas, MAYO either had done some organizing in it or had key persons from it within its leadership and membership ranks. To Gutierrez, these four areas "were all monsters controlled by racist gringos with their capitalist structures everywhere."[31] After serious deliberation, the Winter Garden area was finally selected, and the project was designated the Winter Garden Project (WGP).

In making their decision MAYO's leaders took into consideration factors such as location and demographics. Winter Garden included the following seven counties: Zavala, Dimmit, La Salle, Uvalde, Maverick, Val Verde, and Kinney. These counties are located to the south of San Antonio and to the west of Laredo, and they touch the Mexican border. The decision was made to target only three of the seven counties: Zavala, Dimmit, and La Salle. The Chicano population of the area was a major factor in MAYO's decision. Table 4 clearly illustrates the importance of MAYO's choice: Chicanos made up 73.1 percent of the area's population, totaling some 62,733.[32]

Beyond the heavy concentration of Chicanos, political strategy also helped to determine the selection of the Winter Garden area. MAYO leaders agreed on the promising political possibilities of the area. It was felt that, if organized, the Chicano majority could take power away from the gringo minority. If MAYO were to win control of local government and school institutions, it would unleash a domino effect throughout Texas and even beyond, translating to major policy changes vis-à-vis issues affecting Chicanos. MAYO leaders were also cognizant of Crystal City's political revolt that led to Chicano community control of the city council in 1963.[33] Because of this historical precedent, they felt that the people in the area would be more sympathetic and supportive of MAYO's Winter Garden Project empowerment goals.

There were other, more practical considerations that entered into the decision. First, Gutierrez was a native of Crystal City and was returning there with his family to live. Second, Juan Patlan, one of Los Cinco, was from Dimmit County. Third, Compean was well known in La Salle County, particularly in Cotulla, and MAYO had a strong chapter there.[34] However, it was Gutierrez's return to the area that became the paramount factor leading to the selection of the Winter Garden area. Virginia Musquiz, who subsequently became a Crystal City community leader, said, "When Jose Angel was gone from the community, the people would ask for him. The people waited for his return."[35] Prior to the state meeting Gutierrez had indicated to Compean that he and his family were going to return to Crystal City and begin organizing.

On a larger scale, there were also educational, political, and economic considerations that factored into the decision to select the Winter Garden area. In the realm of education, the primary goal of MAYO's Winter Garden Project was to effect major educational reform through political action by gaining community control of the three targeted counties' several school districts. The educational statistics clearly pointed out the devastating educational crisis afflicting Chicanos. Up to 1969 over 70 percent of the students dropped out of high school in Crystal City. In the seven-county Winter Garden area the "push-out" rate was over 80 percent. The median education of Chicanos twenty-five years and older in Zavala County in 1960 was 2.3 years. The median for the previous decade was 1.8.[36] Conversely, the median for Anglos was well over nine years in 1950 and eleven in 1960.[37] The boards of education, administrators, teachers, and directors of school curriculum and programs were all Anglos throughout the various school districts of the area, yet the overwhelming majority of students were Chicano. De facto segregation still existed in the Winter Garden area. The goal of the project was to take over the schools to provide a liberating instead of oppressive educational experience.[38]

The second goal of the WGP was to bring democracy to the powerless majority of the area. MAYO sought political empowerment for the Chicano communities. For MAYO, the political realities of South Texas were similar to those of South Africa, where the minority population controlled the majority. Political apartheid was a reality for Chicanos. The difference was that, in theory, Chicanos could politically compete for the power; in practice, however, Chicanos historically had been denied access to political power through a variety of repressive means such as the poll tax, white primary elections, literacy tests, residency laws, limited registration hours, and physical intimidation. The bottom line was that Chicanos had been socialized to believe that they lived in a democracy; in actuality, however, the power rested with the small gringo minority and not with the overwhelming Chicano majority. To MAYO, the Chicanos of the area, as well as the rest of South Texas, were controlled through what Robert Blauner and other scholars have described as "external administration," an aspect that was inherent to their internal colonial status.[39]

MAYO's third goal was to organize the local Chicanos to begin to extricate them from their colonized status.[40] To accomplish this, MAYO sought to expose, confront, and eliminate the gringo's power in the WGP by polarizing the communities of the Winter Garden area—Chicano versus gringo—utilizing a variety of issues. This goal was to expose what MAYO termed the gringo attitude of racial superiority, paternalism, divine right, xenophobia, bigotry, and animalism.[41] MAYO set out to prove that gringos could be beaten, that they were not omnipotent, and that the time had come for the gringo minority to surrender both political and economic power to the Chicano majority. MAYO sought to stop the gringos' attempts to destroy the indigenous Chicano culture through their racist practices and control of the area's political, educational, and economic institutions.

MAYO's fourth goal for the WGP was to promote economic development among Chicanos of the three-county area. MAYO postulated that it could begin altering the Chicano's subordinate and dependent status through economic development. Gutierrez explains that MAYO's economic development program sought to replace the existing gringos who performed managerial functions with Chicanos and to transfer economic power from gringos to Chicanos. To MAYO, the economic empowerment of La Raza was requisite for true change. The empowerment of the Chicano community could

Table 5. *Family Income by Ethnic Composition in Winter Garden Area*

County	Median income		Total below poverty line	Percentage below poverty line	
	Anglo	Chicano		Chicano	Total
Zavala	$8,076	$3,984	4,981	52.7	43.1
Dimmit	5,771	3,527	4,062	62.2	50.9
Uvalde	6,907	3,887	5,612	45.8	28.9
Maverick	8,214	3,906	4,510	51.2	44.2
Val Verde	8,037	4,859	6,472	39.8	24.5
Kinney	5,204	3,088	3,905	63.9	44.2
La Salle	6,560	3,000	4,056	65.2	47.9

Source: U.S. Census, 1970.

never be complete without improving its economic status. In essence, the economic agenda of the WGP was to have La Raza eventually control the area's agribusiness and oil and gas industries and displace the modern-day land and cattle barons.[42]

The Chicanos of the Winter Garden area lived under a heavy yoke of poverty. Chicanos were nothing more than a source of cheap labor living at the mercy of powerful gringo agribusiness. In 1967 the agribusiness in the Winter Garden area grossed about $31 million. In 1960 the median gross income of Chicano families in Texas was $2,913. The median income for Anglo families was nearly double ($5,626) that of Chicano families. In Crystal City in 1968 there were 359 families that earned less than $1,000 per year. There were also 764 families that had yearly incomes of $1,000 to $2,990. The average size of a Chicano family was 5.6 persons.[43] The poverty figures for the three counties were equally depressing. In Zavala County 52.7 percent of the Chicano families' incomes were no higher than $3,984 per year. Table 5 on family income by ethnic composition provides a statistical overview of the total seven-county Winter Garden area.[44]

The effects of poverty on Chicanos were especially evident within the three targeted counties of Dimmit, La Salle, and Zavala. The 1970 U.S. Bureau of the Census figures showed that in Dimmit County, 62.2 percent of Chicanos lived below the poverty line with an annual income of $3,527. La Salle County was the worst, with 65.2 percent living below the poverty line and an annual income of $3,000. Zavala County was second-best of the seven counties, with

Table 6. *Employment Status of Familes in Winter Garden Area*

County	Labor force	Employed	Unemployed	Unemploy- ment rate
Zavala	2,965	2,620	345	11.6
Dimmit	1,065	940	125	11.6
Uvalde	2,455	2,150	305	12.4
Maverick	8,725	7,370	1,355	15.5
Val Verde	7,005	6,560	445	6.4
Kinney	9,640	8,925	715	7.4
La Salle	5,055	4,420	635	12.6

Source: U.S. Census, 1970.

Table 7. *Landholdings over 300 Acres, by Ethnicity of Owner, in Winter Garden Area*

County	Chicano		Anglo	
	Number	%	Number	%
Zavala	1	.03	310	99.7
Dimmit	2	.09	219	99.1
Uvalde	22	.03	547	99.7
Maverick	0	0.00	162	100.0
Val Verde	3	.01	204	99.9
Kinney	2	.01	302	99.9
La Salle	6	.05	100	99.5

Source: County tax rolls, 1972.

52.7 percent of Chicanos living below the poverty line and a yearly income of $3,984.

Chicanos also suffered from very high levels of unemployment. Table 6 provides a statistical analysis of the labor force and unemployment rates for the Winter Garden area.[45] These figures do not reflect the "labor reality": a large number of the Chicanos were very much a part of the seasonal migrant stream. Because of scarcity of yearlong employment, many workers and their families were compelled to travel annually to work in the fields in different states.

The "gringo colonialism" whose existence MAYO asserted was particularly evident in the Winter Garden area Chicanos' virtual landlessness. The data in Table 7 support this claim.[46] The concentration of wealth in the hands of a few gringo landowners was thus part of the economic reality of the area. For example, in Zavala County ten gringo landholders owned 46 percent of the land. Furthermore, seven out of ten landowners in the Winter Garden area were absentee landholders.[47]

In short, the WGP was well researched and carefully calculated before MAYO made its selection. MAYO's leaders at the May 1969 board meeting felt that the WGP, if successful, would dramatically alter the educational, political, and economic power relationships of the Winter Garden area, South Texas, or wherever Chicanos resided in significant numbers. MAYO also felt that the WGP would deal a mortal blow to the colonialist syndrome of political, economic, and social powerlessness to which the Chicano had been historically relegated.

The Implementation of the Winter Garden Project

With the Winter Garden area selected as MAYO's target area, MAYO's new state chairperson, Mario Compean, selected Gutierrez to implement the WGP. Compean, however, did not make the decision until Gutierrez and his family had returned from a trip to New Mexico and Colorado in June 1969. Gutierrez had met with CM leader Reies Tijerina in New Mexico and Rodolfo "Corky" Gonzales in Colorado to get a feeling for the type of organizing they were doing and to network and position himself as an emerging CM leader. Gutierrez and his family returned to Crystal City in June. He explained, "We came back to Crystal City in June of 1969 because it was a matter of economics."[48] There was a second reason for his return to his hometown. He felt a profound sense of commitment to return to Crystal City and change the Chicanos' powerlessness and poverty there. In his diary, he explains:

> Our young Chicanos must learn and accept the fact that to not return to your hometown and organize for La Raza means that we're no better than the guy who says he's not Chicano. We are in effect saying: My people and my town are not worth going back to help. I wonder how our young educated and bright Chicanos can think of joining VISTA or the Peace Corps or the Army and not see the struggle is where they come from.[49]

By returning to his hometown to organize, Gutierrez felt he was setting an example for others. "If more Chicanos did this, then the CM would become a much greater movement."[50] Shortly after Gutierrez's return to Crystal City, Compean informed him that he had been selected to implement the WGP. Although there was a title to the position, there were no financial resources to go with it. Gutierrez willingly accepted the appointment knowing that he would have to raise the money to begin activating the WGP. This meant that to survive, both he and his wife had to find employment.

In June both Gutierrez and his wife, Luz, applied for teaching positions in several school districts within the targeted three-county area. Both were more than qualified: Gutierrez had a master's degree in government while Luz had a bachelor's degree and a teaching credential. Denied employment everywhere they applied, they extended their employment search to the whole seven-county Winter Garden area. No one wanted to hire them. Luz explains why: "They said to us they didn't have any teaching positions. It was their way of keeping us out of the area. They had already heard that Jose was coming back. The rumors had started . . . he was known as the activist, the troublemaker, the mean Mexican."[51] The truth of the matter was that most of the districts within the Winter Garden area were clamoring for Chicano teachers, but not for these two. To Gutierrez and his wife, it was all part of the gringo power holders' way of making it difficult for them to stay in the area.[52]

Gutierrez and his family managed to persevere financially. During the summer months of 1969 Gutierrez received severance checks from the Mexican American Legal Defence and Education Fund (MALDEF). Prior to his active duty tour in the army reserve, he had been hired by MALDEF as a research investigator. Because of the pressure exerted by Congressman Gonzalez, the Ford Foundation, and others antagonistic to MAYO and its resource and support entities, however, MALDEF was forced to fire Gutierrez. He contested MALDEF's decision, writing later about the incident: "I got plenty [mad] and told him [Pete Tijerina, MALDEF's director] how gutless he was for bending to Ford."[53] MALDEF acquiesced and agreed to pay him his salary until his contract expired that fall. His MALDEF salary was complemented by donations of food from Victoriano "Nano" Serna, a local Chicano in the convenience store business.

While looking for a job Gutierrez began his WGP organizing efforts. One of his top priorities that June was to secure organizing staff for the three-county area. Prior to his return to the area, he had met with Bill Richy and his wife, Linda, who were both VISTA volunteers, and discussed the possibility of their coming down from Austin to assist him and his wife, Luz, in organizing the area. The two families had been close friends since 1967, when Gutierrez and Bill were students at Texas A&I University.[54] In spite of the political heat and scrutiny being directed at MAYO by Congressman Gonzalez, Gutierrez was still able to have the Richys assigned to Cotulla.

After receiving some training through VISTA, they were scheduled to arrive in Cotulla in August.

Meanwhile, without full-time staff support, Gutierrez and his wife began conducting power structure research during the months of June and July. The intent was to identify the influential people and leaders of the area. Their power structure research was based on two approaches: the reputation method and the extended family method of organizing. Each method complemented the other. The reputation method simply consists of identifying community leaders by asking people in a systematic manner to state who in their opinion the leaders of the community are. Those that were identified by Gutierrez's respondents became the ones he targeted to meet with to secure their support for and participation in the WGP. Even though he was a native of Crystal City and knew many of the people, Gutierrez proceeded with caution in identifying both the Chicano and gringo power holders through the use of the reputation method. Although he did not meet with many influential gringos, he was able to meet with some of the Chicanos who worked for them. They were helpful in providing him with the names necessary to understand the gringo community's power structure.

Furthermore, as Gutierrez identified the power holders, he also identified those with the largest extended families. His extended family method of organizing was based on the idea that if he could win over a key individual of some prominence, members of both the nuclear family and extended family would be supportive as well. The converted person would function in a sense like a disciple. Once a few members of the family were converted, they in turn would proselytize others. The whole approach was based on using the cohesion and strength of the Chicano culture in such a way that a multiplier effect would be created within the extended families of the targeted individuals.[55] Gutierrez rejected the notion that the Chicano family was an impediment to organizing. To him, the Chicano family facilitated organizing. Gutierrez describes the two basic advantages of his extended family approach: "The extended family makes it easier for two things to take place. One is that a natural organization develops on kinship lines. Second, it makes the organizer's job easier."[56] Using this approach, he contended, not only expedited his organizing but lowered the number of organizers needed to implement the WGP.

After a few weeks of identifying key Chicano extended families and conducting his power structure analysis, Gutierrez began meeting with those Chicano leaders who he felt would support both MAYO's WGP and his own Chicano party scheme. Nano Serna, owner of the Oasis Drive-In, became his first convert. In his diary

Gutierrez recorded the following about a session he had with Serna: "We talked of getting together later on with a group of influential elders and discussing some ideas. Nano is very helpful . . . he has provided his place for meetings and refreshments. He is a good man and I believe he will turn out to be a very good ally."[57]

During the following weeks he continued to meet with community leaders and other power holders to discuss various topics, such as economic development schemes, related to the WGP. Throughout the numerous discussions he sought to learn the people's interests, ambitions, and agendas and how they perceived the various issues and problems of the community.[58] Instead of focusing on politics, Gutierrez focused on issues and topics related to their self-interest; he stressed the Chicano's lack of economic power. To some, the idea of doing something about their economic powerlessness became increasingly enticing.

In some instances, however, the people's reaction to his presence was mixed. Gutierrez realized that Emmett Sevilla, manager of the local White Auto Store, was suspicious about Gutierrez's real motives for being in town. Gutierrez further elaborated on this type of reaction: "He asked a question that has repeatedly followed me: Why are you here? What are you planning on doing here? You certainly don't expect to work here do you? I am not at a loss for words usually, but these questions have been the most difficult to answer."[59] Thus, Gutierrez initially had to earn the people's trust and confidence. He was viewed with suspicion by some Chicanos. They were not sure why he had come back to the area. Was it to establish his own political empire? Consequently, at times even his sincerity and capacity for leadership were questioned.[60] Gutierrez states some of their apprehensions: "Some people didn't like my big ears. Some people didn't like the fact that I was *güero* [light-complexioned]. Some people didn't like my glasses. Some people didn't like the way I explained things. Some people didn't like a million things."[61] But these feelings of distrust, although ever present, never seriously thwarted his organizing efforts.

Another challenge confronting Gutierrez was the difficulty that some people had in understanding the breadth of the WGP and what Gutierrez meant by organizing. They would listen but not fully understand the totality of the WGP. With tenacity, patience, and understanding he continually explained the various aspects of the WGP while simultaneously pursuing his efforts to dispel doubts and win support from other influential Chicanos of the community. With Serna already ardently supporting him, Gutierrez next focused on Julian Salaz, Zavala County justice of the peace.

Salaz was elected justice of the peace in 1968, but the gringo power holders who controlled Zavala County never permitted him to exercise his functions. They denied him cases to try; prevented his access to the courthouse; and refused him a telephone, supplies, and even an office. Essentially he was elected, sworn in, and then forgotten. During discussions with Gutierrez, Salaz was perplexed as to what could be done to change his situation. Gutierrez recognized the man's influence and the potential of using Salaz's powerless status as a means of convincing others about the exploitive nature of the local gringo power holders. As Gutierrez explained Salaz's predicament, "He didn't know what to do. He needed some support. Of course, nobody could support him because nobody knew what to do. So here was a man that a community saw as a symbol of an elected official who was powerless."[62] In return for Salaz's support, Gutierrez pledged to resolve the matter through the intervention of MALDEF. Salaz's backing of and confidence and participation in the WGP in turn enhanced Gutierrez's credibility in his efforts to proselytize others.

Gutierrez continued to expand his contacts, cataloging different problems with which people identified. Describing his discussions, Gutierrez observed that "our middle-class Chicanos do feel superior to the lower-class Chicanos, but all of us feel inferior to the gringo."[63] In acknowledging the pervasiveness of this attitude, he said, "It's amazing how institutionalized this gringo superiority is, for even a gringo truck driver or gas station attendant is higher on the social ladder than a Chicano manager or professional."[64]

With the help of Serna, Salaz, and others, by July Gutierrez had expanded his number of converts by initiating "beer talks," which were simply group discussions with plenty of beer and food. At these meetings Gutierrez led discussions that often lasted well into the late hours of the night. He had to resort to a variety of methods to stay half-sober:

> It was almost every night that I drank beer. I started developing . . . an ability to consume great amounts of beer and not get drunk . . . I used to trick people. I used to go home and eat four to five slices of heavily buttered bread . . . or I would drink sometimes a tablespoon of olive oil . . . I couldn't get drunk because it would coat my stomach and the alcohol would just pass through.[65]

At the beer talks Gutierrez was repeatedly questioned by apprehensive individuals who wanted to test his intelligence, leadership, and commitment. Questions were diverse: Some individuals would ask him who the greatest president of Mexico was and why. Others would ask him questions on geography or science.[66] He passed the tests with great success, and this group of men that Serna invited to the beer talks became the core of the WGP organizing leadership through the formation of Ciudadanos Unidos (CU). The following formed the initial nucleus: Nano Serna, Julian Salaz, Hector Trevino, Albino Santos, Pete Galvan, Pablo Puente, Joe Serna, and Natividad Granados. After establishing this leadership base, Gutierrez sought subsequently to create a strong community grassroots advocacy organization that would be in place by the fall of 1969 in preparation for the upcoming school confrontation in Crystal City.[67]

During the course of his power structure research, Gutierrez had identified not only influential individuals with large extended families but also several Chicano *clicas* (cliques) to which some of the influential Chicano elites also belonged. Serna's clique was perhaps the most political. Once Serna endorsed the WGP, other members of his clique followed, even contributing financially. Gutierrez also succeeded in convincing a clique of Chicano businessmen about the potential and financial promise of forming Chicano corporations for economic development. The idea of the Chicano wresting economic power away from the gringo power holder whet their self-interest appetite.

One particular clique that operated out of the Hide-A-Way Cafe, however, was utterly pessimistic toward the WGP and was categorically antipolitical. Gutierrez describes their negative attitude toward the project by saying: "The Hide-A-Way . . . clique . . . was antipolitical. Not only antipolitical, but they believed the anti-Chicano social science fiction that Chicanos were innately inferior . . . that Chicanos were doomed by destiny to always be subservient."[68] He goes on to say that they "had very cynical and ugly scars from being castrated psychologically. They did not think anything could be done."[69]

This kind of cynicism and fatalism was ascribable in part to the political fiasco of Crystal City's first Chicano electoral revolt in 1963. The successful Chicano takeover in 1963 had become a political disaster in 1965 essentially for two reasons: infighting among the five elected Chicano councilmen, which led to the discrediting of the council itself, and doubt among La Raza of the community in the Chicano's ability to administer city problems responsibly and effectively.[70] The political scars left by the takeover impeded Gutierrez's WGP organizing efforts. In his words: "The defeat . . . in 1965 caused a cynicism and pessimism to develop. It was very vicious because people would say things to me like you are crazy trying to do it again. We already did it once and it didn't work. We are just incapable of self-governing."[71] Furthermore, every time Gutierrez brought up the possibility of once again gaining control of Crystal City's city council, many of the people would concur on such an objective in principle but would give "ten thousand reasons why it was not going to work."[72] Their fatalism, especially toward politics, was a function of other factors as well, such as the colonialist syndrome of poverty; low levels of education; political and economic powerlessness; the use of coercion and repression by gringo power holders to maintain their control of the area's political, economic, and social institutions; and the absence of political organization and leadership built on a base of community support.

Gutierrez's efforts to neutralize some of the people's fatalistic attitudes were essentially based on Alinsky's principles. His approach was simply to introduce ideas, get the poor infused with hope and a desire for change, and then convince them of his qualification to help them achieve their desires and aspirations. This was complemented by his ability to convince key people that as an organizer he was on their side, that he had a workable and practical plan of action to engender change, and that he was a winning organizer.[73] By July he was on his way to accomplishing all these things.

While working to convince people of the WGP's merits, Gutierrez also began to expound on the virtues of his Chicano party scheme. To him the WGP and the Chicano party idea were one and the same. He conceived the party as the political vehicle needed to realize the goals of the WGP. As he convinced people of the viability of the WGP objectives, he also sold them on the idea of forming a Chicano political party.

While working to consolidate his power base in Zavala County, by July Gutierrez had expanded his organizing efforts to the other two targeted counties. At a meeting in Carrizo Springs he discussed the merits of Chicanos having their own political party. Present at the meeting were Juan Patlan and David Ojeda, who was the WGP's new staff member in Carrizo Springs. In his diary Gutierrez described his difficulty in convincing the people of his Chicano party idea: "I think Juan is as sold on it as I am, but I find it difficult to sell it to our people because of their traditional orientations toward the Democratic Party."[74] After much discussion and persuasion by Gutierrez, the people began slowly to buy into his party plan.

Encouraged by the response in Carrizo Springs, Gutierrez began to meet with interested individuals and groups throughout the area. At the same time he tried to persuade Juan Patlan and his wife to stay and work to organize the party. According to Gutierrez, "They chickened out at the last moment."[75] While strengthening his base in Carrizo Springs, he also began holding meetings with groups in Asherton and Cotulla.

In August Gutierrez was able to get organizing support from some old friends, the Richys, who arrived as VISTA volunteers in Cotulla that month. One of Bill Richy's first assignments was to assist interested individuals of the area in formulating economic development schemes. In concert with the WGP's objective of transferring wealth from the gringo to the Chicano, Gutierrez convinced several businessmen of the potential of organizing profit and nonprofit economic development entities. Bill Richy was designated by Gutierrez to head the project's economic development program. Gutierrez wrote in his diary: "Richy has now taken over the economic development program in the Winter Garden Project. He'll put together our proposal to PEDCO for the housing corporation, *Industrias Mexicanas* (our franchise holding company) and our family corporation."[76]

Gutierrez had now begun to organize Industrias Mexicanas, a nonprofit corporation. The idea of economic clout was a powerful inducement in convincing people of the merits of the project, especially his core group. In addition, Richy was assigned the task of coordinating the continued power structure research for the entire three-county Winter Garden Area.

At a meeting in Asherton in August Gutierrez addressed a group of local Chicanos on the mechanisms and strategy for organizing a political party. He stressed the arguments for the party scheme: "Less expenditure, complete domination by Chicanos of the party, not as regimented and certainly more open for participants due to its convention approach; and solve the problem of illiteracy by voting straight ticket."[77] The reaction, however, was lukewarm. He wrote: "It is difficult to make people see how it can work."[78] Subsequently, in a discussion with a new staff member, Ignacio Lozano, it was decided to have his party research examined by an attorney.

August was an important month in Gutierrez's efforts to develop the resources needed for additional staff. During the summer months, in conjunction with the Mexican-American Unity Council (MAUC), he began to put together a new funding structure, the Texas Institute for Educational Development (TIED). Gutierrez was appointed its interim director and promptly began looking for sources of funding. After meeting with various foundations, such as the Norman Fund, the Field Foundation, and the Inter-Faith Organization, he succeeded in securing $7,000 for TIED.[79] The money was to be utilized for hiring additional staff and for the project's administration and operation, but it was not actually received until the latter part of 1969. Gutierrez was also able to secure a commitment from the Colorado Migrant Council for the establishment of Headstart centers to serve the migrant families of the area.

That same month a representative from the migrant council toured Crystal City and promised to fund a Headstart center there and in Asherton. Both Gutierrez and his wife were subsequently hired to run the centers. TIED's money and the Colorado Migrant Council's centers were both instrumental in increasing the resources of the Headstart project; they also served to enhance the organizing efforts of the WGP. Gutierrez was employing the old MAYO tactic of using organizations as fronts, utilizing their resources to advance his agenda. This time Gutierrez's agenda was to organize not only the WGP but also a Chicano political party.

From the time of his arrival in June, Gutierrez realized that he would need a newspaper to expedite the organizing process. He could not rely on the local newspaper, the *Sentinel*, for it was owned and operated by a gringo power holder. By August Serna and Natividad Granados recommended that a newspaper be started.[80] The new paper would fulfill three functions. It would provide a medium for organizing, a channel for a point of view different from that of the gringo-oriented *Sentinel*, and a means of politicizing and raising the consciousness of La Raza of the area. Gutierrez recognized that incumbent to the growth of any movement organization was having a newspaper or other means of communicating with the masses of Chicanos. Lenin, in his treatise *What Is to Be Done?*, wrote about the role of a newspaper in a revolutionary movement: "The role of a paper is not confined solely to the spreading of ideas, to political education and to procuring political allies. A paper is not merely a collective propagandist and collective agitator, it is also a collective organizer."[81] Gutierrez, well versed in the study of revolutionary movements, concurred with Lenin's perspective on the role of newspapers. He felt that CU needed a very subjective and biased political organ to begin getting through to the unorganized majority of La Raza.

By late August Gutierrez had begun moving on the idea of a Chicano newspaper. By early September he had secured the assistance of Ignacio Lozano. He and Ignacio wrote most of the articles, and Luz Gutierrez typed them.[82] The paper was laid out in Crystal City but printed in San Antonio. The first issue of the paper, which was temporarily entitled *El Papel* (the paper), came out on September 16 and focused on the history of the Mexican Revolution of 1910. Editorials also stressed the paper's purpose. Subsequently, a contest was held to find a permanent name for the paper. The contest was held to induce the people to participate and to bring the paper to their attention.[83] The name selected was *La Verdad* (the truth). It was decided that it would be published biweekly from September to May, because by May many of the migrant families left the area and did not return until late August or September.

By October some of the students with whom Gutierrez and Luz had worked during the summer began assisting in the operation of *La Verdad*. Students who helped to put out the paper were given political education through rap sessions where numerous topics were discussed. Sometimes the quality of the students' work was questionable—the students were simply too immature, unsophisticated, and unskilled—but nevertheless, they tried.[84]

During the ensuing months *La Verdad* was distributed throughout the Winter Garden area. Meanwhile, in Cotulla, the Richys also sought to start a newspaper but were unable to secure funding. Consequently, *La Verdad* became the movement newspaper for the entire area. Luz explained that the Richys would come to Crystal City for the paper, or people from Crystal City would go to Cotulla and the other areas to deliver *La Verdad*. Lozano likewise arranged to have *La Verdad* distributed in Asherton by the local MAYO chapter. By the fall of 1969 *La Verdad* was effectively disseminating and propagating the ideas and objectives of the WGP throughout the three-county target area.

In no time *La Verdad* increased its circulation and became relatively self-sustaining. It depended on two sources of financing: contributions and the sale of advertising. In the first few months of operation Serna, for example, contributed some seventy dollars per month.[85] Granados, who operated the local bus depot, also saw that the paper was delivered free from San Antonio, where it was printed, to Crystal City. Lozano mentioned that "sometimes we barely made it. Sometimes we were financially short and we had to get contributions for it."[86] The sale of ads became the main source of funding for *La Verdad*. They normally sold enough advertising to print at least three thousand copies of *La Verdad* at a cost of ninety dollars. They would try to sell it for ten cents a copy, but most of the time the paper was given away. The sale of advertising and contributions made it possible to distribute the paper to people who could not afford it.

After months of organizing, by November 1969 Gutierrez had established the organizational leadership and the financial foundation needed to take on the gringo power holders. Up to that time he had succeeded in forming a powerful support base from both key individuals and diverse cliques through his extended family method of organizing. *La Verdad* gave him access to the people, and he had become a powerful source of political education. With additional resources from such entities as TIED, the Colorado Migrant Council's Headstart, and other programs, Gutierrez had succeeded in stabilizing the WGP's organizing efforts throughout the area. With the majority of Chicanos still unorganized, in order to advance WGP objectives as well as his Chicano party scheme, he decided to create an areawide mass mobilization via an emotional and polarizing issue—the Crystal City walkouts.

Prior to his arrival to Crystal City in June, Gutierrez had been involved in an advisory capacity with the abortive student protest in May. Anticipating MAYO's approval of the project and his selection as its implementor, he had begun making frequent trips into the area to initiate his power structure research. He met with student leaders over the impending issue and advised and encouraged them to table their confrontation for a more auspicious time, such as sometime during the fall months. He warned them repeatedly that for a school walkout to be successful, conditions had to be right. Consequently, throughout the summer and part of the fall months, Gutierrez held innumerable rap and planning sessions with student protest leaders.

Once school was back in session, the student leaders began organizing the student body for the forthcoming confrontation. Gutierrez states: "The beginning of the fall of 1969, the younger students, the freshmen and sophomores, who were the ones who spearheaded the effort in spring of 1969, began to organize."[87] He advised them initially to organize just a few students and form them into a cohesive nucleus. Their responsibility was to organize the migrant students returning in September.[88] By October the students were organizationally ready to resume their struggle for educational reform, as was Gutierrez.

Thus, by November, the political stage was set wherein the diverse elements of the community would coalesce to strike a major blow for educational reform. More important, the blow provided the conditions and circumstances that allowed Gutierrez's party scheme and the WGP to be realized. Since his arrival in June Gutierrez had convinced some students to assist him as staff volunteers. This meant that by November his WGP staff included his wife, Luz, Ignacio Lozano, Severita Lara, Beatrice Mendoza in Crystal City, David Ojeda in Carrizo Springs, and Bill and Linda Richy in Cotulla.[89] Gutierrez was also able to secure attorney Warren Barnett as legal council for the impending Chicano political party effort.[90]

During December 1969 Gutierrez was preoccupied with the Crystal City walkouts, a truly unprecedented mobilization involving both parents and students. The walkout had been programmed by Gutierrez as the catalyzing issue needed to mobilize the support behind the WGP and give birth to the Chicano political party. After months of holding meetings, forming informal groups, and consolidating the needed community leadership, Gutierrez moved to transform CU from a nucleus of Chicano community influentials into a mass-based political-action and advocacy organization. CU became the foundation on which the WGP goals of community control and empowerment would be realized. In addition, it gave impetus to the formation of the RUP. During the course of the numerous walkout meetings, rallies, and picketing, Gutierrez and others exhorted the people to join CU. Specifically, CU was meant to give Chicanos the capability of exercising political leadership and openly advocating the defense of their political, social, and economic interests.[91] The paramount objective of CU was to promote change, unity, and empowerment within the Chicano community.[92]

On December 17 Gutierrez held the first official CU townhall meeting in Crystal City. The following individuals were elected as officers: Armando Trevino, president; Pablo Puente, vice president; Jose Serna, secretary; Julian Salaz, treasurer; Ramon Lomas, sergeant at arms; Arturo Gonzalez, parliamentarian; and Jose Angel Gutierrez, legal counsel.[93] During the preceding five months, the CU core group had been chaired by Julian Salaz and later Pablo Puente.

During the course of the CU elections Gutierrez was nominated for several official positions. He was first nominated for president, but he declined. He was then nominated for the remaining officer positions—from vice president to secretary—but declined every nomination. He explains why: "All this time I had been saying to all of them that I was just an organizer and nothing more . . . I didn't want anything. So I refused."[94]

At the meeting in which CU's membership criteria were formulated, it was reaffirmed that only trusted members who believed in the organization's objectives would be admitted. CU's membership admission process was to be selective. Gutierrez explains the reasons for such rigid membership procedures:

> Membership into CU was by invitation only. It was kind of . . . a fraternity. Someone would be nominated at a prior meeting, then at the subsequent meeting, after some discussion, a vote was taken and with unanimous approval of the existing members the new ones were brought in. In most cases the new member was another family member or close friend of one of the existing members.[95]

CU was fully functional by December and took a strong proactive position in support of the students throughout the entire school boycott issue. CU became the primary mobilization vehicle in galvanizing the necessary community support for the students. Through CU's efforts the students received strong backing from the parents and other adults of the Chicano community. This became a key to the success of the Crystal City school boycott.

In December 1969 Gutierrez reintroduced his Chicano party scheme to a national MAYO conference held December 27 through 30 at Mission, Texas. Alberto Luera, MAYO state chairperson for 1971, explains the significance of the conference to both the WGP and the party scheme: "The outcome was that we brought all kinds of people together—*todas las palomitas*. We had workshops on various themes. The outcome was a plan of action. One major conclusion reached was that we had to begin to establish our own institutions, for Chicanos and with Chicanos. Control was to be in three areas—political, economic, and social institutions."[96] The emphasis of the conference was on the need for MAYO to develop a more programmatic approach. MAYO also selected four specific institutions it would attack or confront in the coming year: the Democratic and Republican parties, organized labor, and the Catholic Church. A MAYO press release issued on December 31, 1969, read: "There is no order of priority because all four are equally corrupt and all four serve as the epitome of hypocrisy and *Gringo* racism."[97]

The delegates by the end of the conference designated two projects as MAYO priorities for 1970: the formation of a Chicano political party and the establishment of an all-Chicano college. At the conference Gutierrez reintroduced his party idea and reported on the WGP. He spoke out vehemently against both the Democratic and Republican parties. The following words characterize the thrust of his discourse:

> Democrats and the Republicans are all alike. They are all *Gringos* . . . neither party has ever delivered for the Chicano . . . both parties have promised a hell of a lot, but neither had delivered. Now, we as Chicanos are calling their bluff. Baby, you pay up for your mortal sins, otherwise we as Chicanos will collect at twice the interest rate. As far as we in MAYO are concerned, the only viable alternative is to look into the political strategies which will yield maximum benefits for *La Raza*.[98]

For Gutierrez and MAYO the alternative to the two-party system was the formation of a Chicano party that would be used to wrest power from the Democrats in South Texas.

This time the reaction to his party scheme was favorable. There was some squabbling among the delegates, however, over which project should be MAYO's highest priority—a Chicano college or a Chicano party. Luz Gutierrez describes this issue: "There was a lot of squabbling going on at the meeting. The thing was, can we take on both ideas or should we just take up one idea . . . some said we could do both. We all agreed with both ideas, but what had been done up to that time in setting up a Chicano college—nothing. What had been done as far as setting up the party—a lot."[99] Gutierrez's arguments for the party were predicated on MAYO's not having enough money and people to do both. He felt that initiating both projects concurrently would drain MAYO's meager resources. Gutierrez also predicted during the discussions that when the time came to implement both projects, the number of people willing to work would be few. Narciso Aleman was the leading advocate for undertaking both projects simultaneously. However, Luera recalls that Aleman was in charge of organizing and developing the idea of a Chicano college. After some lengthy discussions, the delegates voted to support both the party and college projects.

His Chicano party scheme having been approved, Gutierrez requested volunteers to assist him with the WGP and with getting the party off the ground. Out of some six hundred delegates present at the conference, only three volunteered: Viviana Santiago, Alberto Luera, and Ruben Barrera. Viviana and Ruben returned to Crystal City with Jose Angel and Luz.[100] Alberto followed two weeks later. Gutierrez returned to the Winter Garden area more determined than ever to make his WGP and his party idea operational. He felt confident that the boycott had made the conditions and timing ripe for the implementation of both the WGP and his party plan. As early as November he felt it was "go" on both projects. In reference to the WGP he wrote: "Today I made time to write because so many things have happened, and our famed Winter Garden Project is off the ground and moving along so well it's almost miraculous."[101] The party scheme was further enhanced by the voter registration drives that were conducted during the winter and, equally important, by the solidarity of the Chicano community during the boycott. Once the boycotters' demands were accepted by the school board, Gutierrez, with the support of CU, shifted the momentum toward organizing the Chicano political party and running candidates for local office.

It is important to note that the boycott became an endogenous antagonism for the implementation of both projects because of its success in five areas. First, to Chicanos and Anglos alike, it demonstrated the political power of the Chicano community. Second, it made local Chicanos conscious of their economic power through the use of the economic boycott. Third, it engendered solidarity and unity among the majority of the Chicano community. Fourth, it mitigated some of the people's fatalism and feelings of inferiority. And finally, it was instrumental in politicizing, mobilizing, and organizing the Chicano community to an extent that it never before had been. Thus, with the conclusion of the boycott, the historical stage was set for the emergence of the RUP and for the decline and demise of MAYO.

7. MAYO: Decline and Demise

Most of the movements that colored the American political landscape during the epoch of protest reached their pinnacle of activism and radicalism in 1970. The Chicano movement (CM) and its progeny, the Chicano Youth Movement (CYM) were no different. All these movements began to decline in 1971, and MAYO was not exempt from this decline. From 1967 to 1970 MAYO was the avantgarde organization of social change and empowerment for Chicanos in Texas. Its decline, however, was precipitated by its success in 1970 through 1972 in realizing the Winter Garden Project (WGP) goals of community control and empowerment and the emergence of the Raza Unida Party (RUP).

This chapter analyzes the historical forces that led to MAYO's decline by 1972. Specifically, however, emphasis is directed at topics related to the development of both the RUP and WGP. Integral to this analysis is the thesis that MAYO's decline was a dialectical result of its success in implementing both projects. The decline was also ascribable to the growing debilitation of both exogenous and endogenous antagonisms, which by the early seventies had lost much of their capability to mobilize power.

The Genesis of the Raza Unida Party

The Crystal City boycott of 1970 became the instrument that Jose Angel Gutierrez needed to implement both the WGP and his Chicano party scheme. The success of the boycott set the stage for two achievements historically unprecedented for Chicanos: the emergence of a Chicano third party, the RUP, and a peaceful political revolution in the Winter Garden area that would send ripples of rising expectations for empowerment to Chicano communities throughout Aztlan. The boycott energized, politicized, and encouraged Chicanos throughout Aztlan to organize themselves politically. Originally known as the spinach capital of the world, Crystal City made the political map as the point from which the matrix of the Chicano struggle for empowerment radiated. In particular, Jose Angel Gutierrez was catapulted to a prominent leadership position within the CM. It was in 1970 that Gutierrez joined the CM's core leadership of Reies Lopez Tijerina, Cesar Chavez, and Rodolfo "Corky" Gonzales.

With Chicanos in Texas having tasted the fruit of success (i.e., the approval of the boycott's demands), Gutierrez did not allow the dynamism and momentum of the boycott to dissipate. Since his return to Crystal City in 1969, he had in a very calculated and systematic way combined both the WGP and the party project. Instead of pushing for a nonpartisan advocacy organization at the vanguard of the struggle for Chicano empowerment, Gutierrez opted for RUP to fulfill that role. He recognized, however, the important role that a nonpartisan advocacy-oriented organization could play on a daily basis in giving life to the RUP. This is why Gutierrez, prior to formally establishing the RUP, organized Ciudadanos Unidos (CU). Throughout the boycott Gutierrez appeared at numerous meetings, rallies, pickets, and marches to speak on behalf of both projects. The voter registration drives were also used to prepare the ground for advancing both projects. MAYO's approval of his party scheme in December 1969 further served to legitimize his ongoing "crescendo strategy" of graduated intensity and conflict.

Gutierrez used Alinsky's tactic of rubbing the people's sores of discontent. He acknowledged the boycott's importance and accomplishment, but instead of glorifying the victory, he sought to create an insatiable hunger for more change. Throughout the boycott the people were well prepared to continue the quest for power and reform. After the boycott Gutierrez worked to convince them that they had not really won a victory and that the real victories were still ahead. He explained this tactic: "I wanted for us not to win totally on all of our demands . . . so that as soon as we sobered up we would realize that we hadn't won that much. Then it would spill over into the election."[1] Many of the students and parents realized after the school board met their demands that their victory had been a shallow one. Students began complaining that some teachers were still harassing them or that school officials were procrastinating on the question of amnesty.

Meanwhile, CU members were eager to flex their developing political muscles. Throughout January 1970 Gutierrez continued to fan the fires of discontent. He met with numerous Chicano leaders and people from the communities of the area and reiterated his position that the real victory would be in winning control of the school board and city council in the upcoming April elections. At the same time, he explained that a Chicano political party was necessary to achieve such a victory. In this way Gutierrez, always the organizer, prepared the people for the next battle. In his mind the boycott victory had been merely a skirmish with the real battle still ahead. Gutierrez did not stop with the idea of getting Chicanos elected, however; he wanted community control of educational and local government institutions so as to institute reforms. After all, this was what the WGP was all about. Ignacio Garcia explains:

> The school board already had some [Chicanos], a few changes had been made. It was MAYO's philosophy that reforms would come when the Chicano community had not only the votes to implement changes but also the strength to resist outside pressures to rescind them. Empowerment also called for a shake-up of the organizational structure and a changing of the guard in the school's administration.[2]

On January 17 more than 150 people attended a meeting for the purpose of forming a Chicano party in Zavala County. The people's response was favorable. Gutierrez describes their reaction at the meeting:

> Tremendous: Let's go. You are right. This business is not going to get us anywhere. What they couldn't understand was this Democratic party business. Why the Democrats were so bad, overall. You couldn't tell them that Kennedy was rotten. Locally, they could understand. That's all I wanted to do, was to get into the local issues . . . so it was endorsed readily and people started signing up.[3]

It was at this meeting that Gutierrez's dream of a Chicano party began to take form. County officers were elected and goals were set. Luz Gutierrez was elected as Zavala County chairwoman, precinct committeemen for the county's four precincts were elected, and the name of the party was approved.

The party name had been selected prior to the meeting. One afternoon in January, Gutierrez, Bill Richy, and Viviana Santiago were in the project's office when their attorney Warren Barnett called to inquire the name of the Chicano party-to-be. Gutierrez's choice was Mexican American Democratic party, but under Texas electoral laws the party names were limited to three words. Furthermore, the word *democratic* could not be used because it was already the name of the Democratic party. For hours the three argued as to what their new party should be called. Viviana and Bill pushed for RUP. Gutierrez disagreed on the grounds that the name RUP would tend to alienate people more than unite them. He felt people were not ready for it, especially the Mexican American middle class. After hours of dialogue and debate on the matter, however, Gutierrez acquiesced.[4] The selection of Raza Unida was also a strategic decision. The term was in vogue among Chicano activists across Aztlan, and MAYO had participated in the Raza Unida conferences of 1967 and 1968. Consequently, the recommendation was presented at the January 17 meeting, where it was approved.

On January 23 Gutierrez filed an application signed by eighty-nine persons for recognition of the RUP in Zavala County. In announcing the formation of the RUP, Gutierrez explained that the party was more than a movement against the unresponsiveness of the Democratic and Republican parties; rather, it was oriented toward making politics more effective for Chicanos. He announced that, as required by Texas election laws, the RUP would hold a nominating convention on May 2, 1970, to nominate candidates for the November general elections.[5] Concurrently, similar applications were filed in Dimmit, La Salle, and Hidalgo (a county outside the targeted Winter Garden area). Gutierrez's strategy called for establishing the RUP on a multicounty basis. Once successful, it would spread statewide, then regionally throughout Aztlan.

The announcement of the RUP's formation caused alarm, enthusiasm, and much debate throughout the state. The alarmists judged the RUP to be un-American, nationalistic, racist, and segregationist.[6] Chicanos argued heatedly over the merits of a Chicano political party versus the opportunities available to them as liberals in the Democratic party or as liberal Republicans. The reaction in Crystal City was positive. Those who were enthusiastic were confident that at last they had a chance of winning control of both the Crystal City City Council and the school board. The same people who participated in the walkouts were involved in the formation of the RUP. They perceived the RUP as the vehicle that would empower them and bring about social reform. Conversely, the gringos' reaction was generally one of apprehension and alarm. Insinuations that Gutierrez and the RUP were radical and communist were commonplace. In general, the reaction to the RUP within the targeted area was mixed— largely positive from Chicanos who had supported the boycott and negative from gringos and conservative Chicano Democrats.[7]

By February 1970 the RUP had filed for county and local offices throughout the three-county Winter Garden area and Hidalgo

County. By the filing deadline in early February, all county offices up for election were being contested by RUP candidates in Zavala, Dimmit, La Salle, and Hidalgo counties.[8] For example, in Zavala County eight Chicanos filed for county offices under the RUP's banner. Justice of the Peace Julian Salaz filed for county judge; Fidel Benavides and Carmen Flores sought the office of county treasurer; Isaac Juarez ran for county clerk. Candidates for county commissioner posts were Ramon de la Fuente for Precinct Two and Esteban Najera for Precinct Four. Manuel Palacios filed for justice of the peace of Precinct Two, while Pedro Contreras filed for justice of the peace of Precinct Three.[9]

CU also began accelerating its organizing efforts in preparation for the April electoral revolt that would give it control of Crystal City's school board and city council. The group's top priority was to recruit qualified, eligible, and willing Chicano candidates. Finding these candidates proved to be difficult. In the past, any Chicano candidate who opposed the interests of the gringo power holders was harassed, intimidated, and coerced. A common tactic of the gringo power holders was to have defiant Chicanos fired from their jobs. Interestingly, many Anglos favored the idea of taking power away from the gringos, but few wanted to participate in the electoral revolt as candidates. CU finally nominated Gutierrez, Arturo Gonzalez, and Mike Perez as its candidates to fill the three vacancies for the school board. Gutierrez amplifies on why he decided to run: "By February I had switched my position, I knew then that we were going to win and that I was going to be able to stay as an organizer behind the scenes. . . . There was going to be a lot of decisions that had to be made. A lot of raw guts to break through many of these barriers. So I decided then to be a candidate for office."[10] Arturo Gonzalez worked as a service station attendant through one of the local War on Poverty programs. Initially he had been asked to run for the school board by a group of students. Thereafter, at a CU meeting with only Gutierrez willing to run, he volunteered. It was also decided at the meeting that Mike Perez, a local radio announcer and businessman, be asked to run on the RUP slate for the school board, to which he agreed.[11] Perez's political assets were his popularity and the likelihood of getting some political advertising from KBEN, the local radio station he worked for.[12]

By this time Gutierrez had spread the empowerment and change gospel of the WGP and RUP to the two other targeted counties, La Salle and Dimmit. As CU selected its candidates, Chicanos working with Gutierrez in these two counties also decided to run candidates for the April elections. In Carrizo Springs, county seat for Dimmit, two Chicanos ran for the school board. In Cotulla, La Salle's county seat, two Chicanos decided to run for the board. Thus, the nascent RUP fielded candidates for the school boards in all three targeted WGP counties. Aggressive and ambitious, the RUP also filed candidates for city council in the three counties. In Cotulla it ran three Chicanos for the city council's three vacancies. In Carrizo Springs it ran two candidates for two vacant seats.

A takeover of the city council in Crystal City was not possible because of a city charter change adopted in 1969 that stipulated that elections were to be staggered. The rationale behind the charter change was to discourage, if not prevent, another electoral revolt like the 1963 PASO takeover. Pablo Puente and Ventura Gonzalez were the two RUP city council candidates. Puente, however, was temporarily disqualified because he was not a property owner (the city charter stipulated that any person wishing to run for the city council had to be a property owner). This was another form of keeping the Chicano majority disfranchised, for many of them were not property owners. Gutierrez, assisted by MALDEF attorneys, struggled in the courts to reverse the disqualification decision. The intervention of MALDEF was in itself a victory, considering that it had been politically spanked by Congressman Gonzalez for previously assisting MAYO. Gutierrez was able to convince MALDEF to provide legal assistance using the argument that it was not MAYO that was making the request for its intervention but the people of Crystal City under the guise of CU and the embryonic RUP. By March the RUP machinery was ready to initiate the second electoral revolt in Crystal City and the first in Cotulla and Carrizo Springs.

RUP's Electoral Revolt

In March the RUP intensified its political activity throughout the targeted three counties. The April elections were the final obstacle Gutierrez had to circumvent to realize MAYO's WGP and give impetus to the emerging RUP. Consequently, the Chicano communities of the area continued in a state of mobilization. The primary objectives behind Gutierrez's grassroots mobilization strategy were to win and secure control of the targeted local governmental and educational institutions and concurrently to launch the RUP.

There were other important but more specific tactical objectives to this strategy: (1) to ensure a large Chicano voter mobilization; (2) to force the opposition to make mistakes; (3) to use the election to further educate and politicize the people on the merits of both MAYO projects; (4) to remind and convince Chicanos that their enemies were the local gringo power holders; and (5) to rely for the mobilization on the extended family method of organizing.[13] The cardinal theme of the RUP campaigns was that Chicanos of the Winter Garden area possessed the capability to transfer power and control from the gringo minority to the Chicano majority.

The contagion of activism created during the school boycott grew in intensity and magnitude, which helped to produce this unprecedented mobilization. This second electoral revolt in Crystal City, however, proved to be different from the first in several ways: First, the scope of the revolt was much bigger, not only geographically, but in that it sought control of both city and school institutions. Second, the leaders of the second revolt were by far more sophisticated, capable, and well versed in the game of politics and the workings of government than were those of the first. Third, unlike PASO in 1963, CU was well organized and had a powerful grassroots base of support in the Chicano community. Fourth, there was an organizing strategy behind the effort to build a statewide Chicano political party. Finally, this time there was the fervor of a powerful and pervasive CM, unlike the first electoral takeover of 1963. Overall, the political situation of Texas in 1970 was influenced by growing activism among Chicanos throughout Aztlan. The boycott's success had served to reinforce the people's confidence in themselves. Moreover, it had raised the people's expectations for change and power.

Throughout March, in preparation for the elections, this enthusiasm was quite evident. Not since the electoral revolt of 1963 had Chicanos in Crystal City manifested so much commitment and willingness to become politically involved. Chicano students continued their activism beyond the boycott. Now organized through MAYO, they continued to support both projects by organizing voter registration and education drives. With a rapidly expanding membership base, CU was ready and eager to demonstrate its growing political muscle and mobilization capability. Gutierrez had worked hard preparing and organizing for the April elections in Carrizo Springs and Cotulla. There was an unprecedented popular fervor and spirit of hope, faith, and determination to break the shackles of powerlessness and disfranchisement.

The RUP's mobilization strategy took various forms. Countless rallies, meetings, and social fundraisers such as dances, dinners, and receptions were held for the RUP candidates. In organizing these events Gutierrez relied on a technique commonly used by Mexico's governing PRI (Partido Revolucionario Institucional): enticing people with free beer, food, and music. This technique helped to create a large pool of volunteers for the campaigns. With ample volunteers and organizing entities such as CU, MAYO, and others, the RUP ran a strong grassroots mobilization campaign: precincts were canvassed, literature was developed and distributed, a media blitz was activated, telephone canvassing was implemented, sound trucks were deployed, poll watchers were assigned, and precinct get-out-the-vote entities were established, giving the campaign the semblance of a well-organized political machine. In addition, in an effort to ensure a clean election, free of discrepancies, Gutierrez requested that federal observers be sent to the area. Within a few days of the request he was informed by the Texas Advisory Committee to the U.S. Civil Rights Commission that federal marshals would serve as observers.[14]

Initially the RUP's political development was not perceived as a serious threat by the local Gringo power holders.[15] With the success of the boycott and the continued political mobilization for the elections, however, the Anglos responded by reviving their old organization, Citizens Association Serving All Americans (CASAA), which had helped to dismantle the first electoral revolt in 1965. As in 1965, CASAA chose Mexican American candidates they considered amicable to their interests and safe to run against the RUP candidates.[16] As a coalition of gringos and a few Mexican Americans, they felt their strategy had worked well before and quite possibly could work again. Their candidates were provided with money and personnel. In a countermobilization CASAA volunteers distributed literature, manned the telephones, and sought to find ways to stop the RUP's growing ground swell of support.

As the elections neared CASAA intensified its character assassination of the RUP. The strategy was basically threefold: (1) to attack Gutierrez's credibility as a candidate; (2) to characterize the RUP's candidates as unqualified to hold public office; and (3) to threaten economic reprisals against Chicanos voting for the RUP. As the campaign progressed Gutierrez became the main target of CASAA's attacks. Nevertheless, although he was hated perhaps more than any other Chicano in South Texas politics, the opposition's attacks were never directed at his qualifications or leadership. Instead they chose to depict him as being un-American, a dangerous radical, and in fact a communist and an atheist. Some called him a potential murderer, in reference to his "Kill the Gringo" statement made in 1969.[17]

In the few days preceding the school board election, the attacks on Gutierrez became more intense and vitriolic. The March 26 issue of the gringo-owned Crystal City *Sentinel* included an article containing excerpts from a so-called militant speech given by Gutierrez a few days earlier in Odessa in which he attacked the Catholic Church for its contribution to the impoverishment of the Chicano community. The article accused Gutierrez of being an atheist attacking God for not helping the poor of South Texas. The *Sentinel's* publisher, Dale Barker, followed up with allegations that RUP supporters had sought to buy every copy to prevent their distribution to the electorate. Luz Gutierrez did not skirt the allegations. She said that they bought all the newspapers in an effort to provide an explanation to the people before they read the article.[18]

The day before the April 4 school board elections, in an act of desperation, CASAA had some two thousand leaflets dropped by an airplane over Crystal City. The leaflets contained excerpts from Gutierrez's Odessa speech that had been published earlier in the *Sentinel*. The leaflets also warned of impending economic stagnation and other problems if the RUP candidates won. CASAA's strategy against Gutierrez was to malign his character. By branding him a radical, an atheist, and a communist, CASAA hoped that the Chicano electorate, which was predominantly Catholic and religious, would reject his candidacy and those of the other RUP candidates who were associated with Gutierrez.[19]

The second aspect of CASAA's strategy was to attack the credibility of the other RUP candidates, claiming that they were unqualified to serve in public office because they were either inexperienced or uncommitted. Throughout the campaigns CASAA stressed the importance of supporting their own responsible, business-oriented candidates, who, the organization alleged, represented the interests of all the community. One political advertisement in the *Sentinel* emphasized the need for "Responsible Men for Responsible Jobs": "Education and City Government are big businesses that need proper management by competent and responsible people. It is important that you vote for men who offer business and professional experience and willingness to devote their time to representing the best interests of all citizens."[20]

The third aspect of CASAA's anti-RUP strategy was to utilize intimidation of various kinds. Gringo ranchers and farmers worked to persuade RUP supporters against voting for their candidates. If persuasion failed, the groups threatened them with unemployment if they continued to support the RUP. This tactic was not a new one. It had been used in the 1963, 1965, and 1967 local elections. Another tactic was to suggest that if the RUP candidates won, industry would never come to Crystal City.[21] The implication was obvious: if the people wanted more jobs, they had to vote for gringo candidates. The tactic did not work this time because of the scope and intensity of the Chicano community's mobilization. There were just too many Mexican Americans who could exert pressures of their own in different ways. In retrospect, CASAA's overall strategy served to heighten tensions and to cement the distrust that Chicanos had long felt for gringos.[22]

Gutierrez and the RUP responded to CASAA's vehement attacks and intimidation tactics by increasing the fervor and intensity of the campaign's organizing efforts. Author John Staples Shockley wrote that Gutierrez, in countering charges against him, appeared at RUP rallies with such things as autographed photos of senators Ted Kennedy and George McGovern and the invitation he had received in 1969 to the Nixon-Agnew inauguration. Furthermore, Gutierrez had prepared the people throughout the campaign by warning them about the virulent attacks that would be made on him and the RUP. As for the intimidations, the RUP campaign had succeeded in instilling in the people a feeling of confidence, pride, and hope. They were encouraged to express no fear and to persevere in their determination to realize the WGP goals and establish the RUP.

Just a few days prior to the elections the federal courts ordered Puente's name back on the ballot. After Puente had been disqualified by the city attorney because the city charter stipulated that any candidate for the city council had to be a property owner, Gutierrez had immediately arranged for Jesus Gamez, a MALDEF attorney, to file a suit appealing the action in state court.[23] The state's Fourth Court of Civil Appeals responded by ruling that the question of putting Puente's name on the ballot was moot because balloting had already begun. Shockley elaborated on the appeal efforts:

> Appealing to the federal court, attorney Gamez . . . claimed that such a decision by the court opened the door to fraud. Any community, he argued, could wait until just before the start of the absentee balloting to deny a candidate a place on the ballot for any number of clearly unconstitutional practices and could do so successfully because the question would immediately become moot.[24]

Gamez ultimately succeeded in his appeal efforts and the federal judge ordered that new ballots be printed. In return, Puente agreed to forfeit the 150 absentee ballots that had already been cast. The judge's decision came on April 3, barely in time to get Puente's name on the ballot.[25]

The school board elections were held in Crystal City and in Cotulla on April 4. In Crystal City the RUP had its political machinery staffed and ready to get out the vote. Scores of student and adult volunteers walked the precincts, which were divided into blocks and sections. Vehicles with sound equipment blasted exhortations to vote a straight RUP ticket. At the polls RUP voters were urged to remain at the polling places. Tables were set up and scores of people congregated. This tactic, conceived of by Gutierrez, was used to boost confidence and moral support. It was also used to induce people to vote for the RUP candidates. The presence of scores of known RUP supporters had a psychological impact on an undecided voter, especially if they were friends or relatives. A choice had to be made. Family and peer group pressure thus compelled the voter to vote for the RUP candidates.[26] The weeks of preparation paid off for Chicanos; their turnout was considerably higher than during the 1968 presidential election.[27]

Chicano political history was made. The RUP slate of Gutierrez, Gonzalez, and Perez achieved an unprecedented political victory. Perez was the top vote getter with a total of 1,397 votes. Gutierrez and Gonzalez each received 1,344 votes. CASAA's candidates polled the following: E. W. Ritche, 1,119 votes; Rafael Tovar, 1,090 votes; and Luz Arcos, 1,080 votes.[28] The RUP victory was impressive. The RUP candidates garnered 54 percent of the vote, and for the first time in the history of the school district a Chicano slate had ousted the local gringo power holders and their sympathizers.

The electoral revolt was also successful in Cotulla. Throughout the previous months Gutierrez had been assisting Chicanos in Cotulla prepare for both the school board and city council elections scheduled for April 4. Locally, a troika of RUP leaders consisting of Juan Ortiz, Arseno Garcia, and Raul Martinez did much of the political organizing. Raul Martinez was the RUP county chairperson for La Salle County. During January 1970 the RUP registered some two thousand Chicanos to vote in the county.[29] By the time of the elections, the contagion of activism and mobilization that had permeated Crystal City had spread to Cotulla.

The RUP machinery in Cotulla also scored unprecedented political victories. Alfredo Zamora, Jr., became Cotulla's first Chicano mayor in thirty years. He defeated incumbent mayor Paul Cotulla, of the family that had founded Cotulla. Zamora received 587 votes to Cotulla's 554 votes. Two of the three other RUP candidates for the city council won. RUP candidate Enrique Jimenez received 636 votes, while his opponent, Claude Franklin, Jr., received 493 votes. George Carpenter, Sr., RUP candidate, got 667 votes, and his opponent Ray Keck tallied 439 votes. The only RUP loss in Cotulla was that of Alfredo Ramirez, who garnered 530 votes to incumbent Arthur Hill's 575 votes.

The RUP victories also encompassed the school board elections.

RUP candidate Reynaldo Garcia defeated incumbent Chester Bell, Jr., with 667 votes to 536 votes, and RUP candidate Rogelio Maldonado got 693 votes to incumbent F. D. Henrichmans's 524.[30] In sum, the RUP political scorecard in Cotulla was three out of four seats in the city council and two out of two for the school board.

With political victories in Crystal City and Cotulla, the RUP next directed political mobilization efforts toward the city council elections scheduled for April 7 in Crystal City and Carrizo Springs. In Crystal City, with Pablo Puente back on the ballot, the RUP scored its second political triumph by an even greater vote margin than was expected. Ventura Gonzalez was the RUP's top vote-getter with 1,341 votes. Puente was second, with 1,306 votes. CASAA's candidates lost by a nearly 500 vote spread. Emmett Sevilla received 835 votes and Charles Crawford got 820 votes.[31] The RUP candidates won an impressive victory with 60 percent of the vote.

The school board and city council elections in Crystal City gave the RUP community control of those institutions. With the election of Gonzalez and Puente to the city council, Francisco Benavides, already a member of the city council, threw his support to the RUP, giving the RUP a three-to-two majority. By the same token, the three RUP school board victors were joined by Eddie Trevino, a holdover, giving the RUP a tenuous four to three majority over the CASAA opposition.[32]

In Carrizo Springs two RUP-supported candidates were also victorious. Rufino Cabello received 711 votes and Jesus Rodriguez polled 639 votes to defeat Mayor Joe Schmitt, who garnered 470 votes, and Eddie Leonard, with 423 votes. Initially both Cabello and Rodriguez were part of the RUP slate. One week prior to the election, however, both switched their status to independents, arguing that the campaigns against the RUP candidates in Crystal City were becoming so dirty and polarized that identifying with the RUP was going to hurt them politically. Even though they switched, the RUP political machinery in Carrizo Springs continued actively to support them.[33]

The RUP victories in Crystal City, Cotulla, and Carrizo Springs had unprecedented results for South Texas, as well as for the rest of Aztlan. Within the targeted three-county area, Chicanos were in a state of jubilation and euphoria. Gutierrez, who had engineered the victories, reacted by enthusiastically predicting that the RUP would create "Crystals" anywhere and everywhere Chicanos wanted them.[34] The victories in Cotulla and Carrizo Springs were perhaps more remarkable than Crystal City's in the sense that neither town had gone through the political mobilization that Crystal City had.

Such victories in nearby towns confirmed the belief that the strategies behind the second revolt were exportable to other South Texas communities.[35]

Throughout the targeted three counties the RUP leadership and machinery maintained their mobilization momentum. They moved aggressively to ensure that the people understood the significance of their victories. In an open letter in *La Verdad*, the RUP victors committed themselves to effecting major change within the city and school institutions. The letter, written in Spanish, read: "Queremos dar nuestras mas expresivas gracias a toda la gente que nos dio su apoyo y su voto. Porque sin su voto, nosotros no podriamos ganar. Ustedes los Mexicanos nos eligieron, y dentro del tiempo que serviramos a usted, haremos todo en nuestro poder para mejorar el sistema escolar y la ciudad [We want to give our most expressive thanks to all the people who gave us their support and vote. Because without their vote, we would not have won. You the Mexicans elected us, and during the time we serve you, we will do everything within our power to improve the educational system and the city]."[36]

The subsequent reaction of the gringo power holders to the RUP victories was one of cynicism and anger. Crystal City school board president E. F. Mayer said, "Other communities better wake up or they will be facing the same thing." He warned about the potential danger of the RUP disrupting both local and state elections.[37] Moreover, the second revolt created an exodus of gringo families from the area. The *Sentinel*'s publisher, Dole Barker, when interviewed by the San Antonio *News*, wrote that so many people had left Crystal City that the local Rotary Club was deactivated due to lack of membership. The Lions Club lost half its membership. Jack Kingsberry, local rancher and businessman, reported that two industrial firms that had been interested in locating in Crystal City decided not to because of the RUP victories.[38] Ignacio Garcia further explains the gringo power holders' reaction:

> Fewer than six years after the Anglos had recaptured Crystal City from Los Cinco [the five Chicanos elected in 1963], they were again out of power, but this time to a better organized and more astute opponent. Anglos soon realized after the election that the situation was different from the one in 1963. Although most of the voters were still illiterate and poor, they no longer seemed so afraid, and without doubt they were better led. The Chicano revolt of 1963 had been an uncontrolled flood of passions, but this one was a calculated barrage of blows from a wide-awake and power-hungry giant.[39]

Thus, the RUP victories served to further strain the relations between Chicanos and gringos in the Winter Garden area. Historian John Chavez describes the crux of the gringos' fear: "As the successes of Castro's Cuba promised to spread his revolution to the rest of Latin America, [gringos] feared the successes of Crystal City would spread similar revolts throughout the Southwest."[40]

The Decline of MAYO

The reverberations of the RUP's victories in the Winter Garden area were felt throughout Aztlan and beyond. The CM and CYM were both injected with increasing vitality. The cries for "Chicano Power" were no longer rhetorical phrases. In the Winter Garden area, thanks to the leadership of Gutierrez and MAYO, Chicano power had taken on a palpable reality. In particular, Crystal City became a symbol of empowerment—a mecca for activists who preached the political gospel of Chicano self-determination. Historians Matt S. Meier and Feliciano Rivera write of the significance of the RUP victories: "As a result of Raza Unida's vitality and commitment to political action, Crystal City has become a symbol to Chicanos of strength through Unity. . . . The political apathy that formerly was noted throughout the lower Rio Grande region is disappearing . . . from Crystal City, the spirit of *La Raza Unida* has already spread over the Southwest."[41] To many activists across Aztlan, Crystal City became a symbol of things to come. Its symbolism propagated like a prairie fire across Aztlan. Both in the urban and rural areas, Chicanos suddenly became more conscious of the importance of expanding the CM's agenda to include Chicano political empowerment.

As a result of the RUP victories, the CM from 1970 through 1972 developed a more pronounced political agenda. During the sixties the fuel that had propelled the CM's developing organizational machinery had been a variety of educational and social issues. Until this time electoral politics had not been a priority in the CM's agenda. The RUP victories not only served to galvanize the CM's activism but also, for the first time in its brief history, gave the CM a political focus using a third-party vehicle. Instead of relying on such political entities as the Political Association of Spanish-speaking Organizations (PASO) in Texas or the Mexican-American Political Association (MAPA) in California, Chicano activists in increasing numbers embraced the RUP, which, in turn, dared to challenge the omnipotence of the Democratic and Republican parties.

The CYM was not exempt from the positive fallout of the RUP's victories. Chicano students across the land likewise felt more energized toward the CM's growing political agenda. Students became exposed to new concepts of self-determination, community control, and empowerment. Years of socialization that had led them to believe in the viability of the two-party system in general and the Democratic party's commitment to the poor in particular were rejected and replaced with an awareness of the beginning of a new political era for Chicanos, one where Chicanos would control their own destiny through the RUP. As the RUP movement spread across Aztlan, the CYM became one of the pivotal sectors that gave it life and support.

The realization of the WGP's community control and empowerment goals and the establishment of the RUP affected the leadership of both the CM and CYM. With these two success stories, Gutierrez was catapulted to national leadership status within both movements. By the early seventies, numerous scholars gave him equal rank with Tijerina, Gonzales, and Chavez. In his book *Chicano Power,* Tony Castro wrote:

> Gutierrez is all these things—a planner, an organizer, a tactician, a realistic dreamer. . . . If any one man in the Chicano movement symbolizes the hopes of the party and the forces that will hold it together or split asunder, it is Jose Angel Gutierrez. He represents not so much the rise of a Chicano revolt as the decline of Chicano indifference to years of political frustration.[42]

Others described him as a protagonist imbued with the spirit of Machiavelli who perhaps was more politically adroit than any other leader in the CM. Even his adversaries did not underestimate his leadership and intellectual acumen.

For Chicano students Gutierrez became a symbol, a CM leader who had emerged from the CYM. Students gravitated toward him for various reasons. First, as one of the main leaders of the CM, he had emerged from the struggle of the CYM. Second, his reputation for being courageous, bold, and macho appealed especially to the young Chicano. Third, his staccato and fiery rhetoric coupled with his witty and at times obnoxious demeanor appealed to both students and barrio youth. Fourth, he was the youngest of the four most prominent CM leaders. These perceptions of Gutierrez spread with his numerous presentations at student campuses. The "Crystal takeover" made him a hot item on the speaking circuit. In such a demanding leadership role, Gutierrez quickly made the transition from a MAYO leader to the RUP's national leader.

The most powerful reverberation of the RUP's victories was the unleashing of dialectical forces that led to the demise of MAYO. With the RUP's success in the Winter Garden area, MAYO's WGP was well on its way. Gutierrez had taken the WGP and converted it into a success story. Concomitantly, he had also implemented his dream of a Chicano party. The empowerment movement that Gutierrez created with both successes had literally had its genesis in MAYO. The historical reality was that MAYO served as the precursor to the RUP in Texas. Like the fabled phoenix, MAYO burned itself to cinders so that out of its ashes the RUP would emerge. MAYO made the ultimate sacrifice—its own self-inflicted demise.

With its successes in the Winter Garden area, MAYO reached its pinnacle of success and notoriety. Ironically, at the height of its activity, MAYO began a precipitous decline in 1971, giving way to the all-consuming process of partisan politics.[43] MAYO would exist for a few more years, but without any of its major founders and few of its veteran trained cadre. Within those two years, virtually all of MAYO's leaders and cadre made their transition to the RUP. Mario Compean became the RUP's state chairperson in 1972, and in the same year Gutierrez became the RUP's national chairperson. Alberto Luera, who served as the last MAYO state chairperson in 1971, became a key organizer and technician for the RUP in Crystal City. Other MAYO notables such as Perez, Patlan, and Guerra likewise assumed major leadership roles with the RUP. Only a handful of MAYO leaders did not switch to the RUP.

Willie Velasquez refused to follow the rest of his MAYO cohort in the transition to the RUP. For three years Velasquez had been a major force behind MAYO, but with MAYO's increasing militancy in 1969 and its transition to the RUP in 1970 he pulled out of both groups. Ignacio Garcia explains the reason for Velasquez's decision not to support the RUP:

> An individualist with a flair for the dramatic, Velasquez did not share Compean's and Gutierrez's enthusiasm for the more ideological goals. While dedicated to working at the grassroots level, he believed in pluralistic participation rather than Chicano empowerment. An avid student of history, he concluded that ethnic movements and third parties were ill-fitted to survive in American politics. Velasquez later described himself as a Jeffersonian Democrat who believed in the system.[44]

Earlier, Velasquez, under pressure from other MAYO leaders like Compean, resigned his position with the Mexican-American Unity Council (MAUC). Prior to his departure he had told Gutierrez that the idea of forming a Chicano party was a mistake; he refused to raise money for an endeavor that was bound to fail. Moreover, Velasquez believed that the ignorance of MAYO leaders caused them to make rash decisions. "We didn't read enough," he said later. He also believed that there were provocateurs, some probably on government payrolls, who pushed MAYO toward a more militant role, one that took it away from any possible compromise with middle-class Chicanos, who tended to be dyed-in-the-wool Democrats.[45]

With the exception of Velasquez, few MAYO leaders opposed the transition to the RUP. For the next two years (1971–1972) MAYO chapters both within the universities and barrios of Texas actively worked to build the RUP into a statewide party. This became their paramount priority. Numerous MAYO members came and went to Crystal City as Voluntarios de Aztlan (Volunteers of the Southwest) to lend their support in implementing the RUP's peaceful revolution. Given the shortage of technicians, administrators, and teachers, MAYO became a major source for needed RUP personnel. MAYO was steadfast in supporting the RUP's peaceful revolution in Crystal City. After all, most of the changes being effected derived from MAYO's WGP. In other words, the RUP's peaceful revolution in Crystal City was the WGP in action.

MAYO supported the idea that Crystal City must be a model community with exportable qualities. In particular, Gutierrez devoted much of his time between 1970 and 1972 to transforming Crystal City into an oasis of prosperity and democracy in the midst of a desert of wretched poverty and powerlessness. In spite of stiff resistance from the gringo power holders and some disenchanted Mexican Americans, the RUP's peaceful revolution in Crystal City made significant changes in both school and city politics. The following items characterized the main thrust of the peaceful revolution during these two years: First, power moved from the gringo minority to the Chicano majority, giving Chicanos community control of both the schools and city government and removing a quasi-apartheid system of governing. Second, the transfer of power resulted in a real social and political democracy that allowed the poor to participate in the government and new organizations such as CU. Finally, the transfer of power effected numerous social, economic, and educational reforms that improved the people's quality of life by producing more jobs, affordable housing, better health care, Chicano businesses, paved streets, quality education, and numerous other changes.[46] With stiff gringo opposition to these reforms, MAYO continued to support the RUP's efforts to consolidate power in the Winter Garden area. Former MAYO leaders, now RUP officials, would periodically visit and attend rallies and other RUP events.

By the latter part of 1971, with Crystal City cast into a symbol, MAYO accelerated its efforts to organize the RUP into a statewide party. Gutierrez's success in consolidating the RUP's power base in Crystal City by defeating the electoral challenge of the gringo power holders in the April 1971 school board and city council elections let MAYO set the stage for the expansion of the RUP statewide. Up to then the RUP had been organized on a regional basis, namely in Zavala, Dimmit, La Salle, and Hidalgo counties. During the summer months MAYO leaders had debated the pros and cons of building the RUP into a statewide party. At a MAYO state board meeting held that summer at Garner State Park, two major concerns were addressed: the election of MAYO officers and the expansion of the RUP. With regard to the former, three prominent MAYO leaders were vying for the state chairperson's position: Alberto Luera, Carlos Guerra, and Rogelio Muñoz. Fearing a power struggle, Gutierrez intervened and brokered a compromise. Alberto Luera was elected MAYO state chairperson, and Carlos Guerra was elected to a newly created position, national MAYO chairperson (Gutierrez persuaded the MAYO leaders that MAYO was ready to go national). It was decided to postpone the decision of expanding the RUP into a statewide party until a subsequent RUP convention that would focus entirely on the matter of the RUP's future.[47]

The RUP convention was held on October 31, 1971, in San Antonio. This first official RUP convention drew some three hundred participants from some twenty counties throughout Texas. The issue at the core of the convention's agenda was whether to build the RUP into a statewide political party or to maintain it on a regional basis. The convention's forces were divided into two camps: the rural camp headed by Gutierrez and the urban camp led by Compean. The rural camp comprised delegates from various parts of South Texas, particularly from the Winter Garden area. They agreed with Gutierrez that the RUP should not go statewide.[48] Prior to the convention Gutierrez had argued that the conditions, circumstances, and timing were not auspicious for such a move. Initially, however, this had not been his position. After the RUP's electoral victories in November 1970, he had enthusiastically told the press: "We are capturing the imagination of the Chicano voter. This is the party that is finally opening up an avenue so they [Chicanos] can express themselves, their frustration, anger and aspirations. . . . With the 18-year-old vote and a place on the ballot for our party, the *Gringos* can kiss South Texas good-bye." In a state of euphoria, he also informed the press that work on the 1972 elections would begin in January 1971 and vowed that the RUP would be ready and on the ballot.[49]

By the time of the convention, however, Gutierrez had apparently done an about-face. Prior to the convention he had told some of his close associates about the importance of keeping the RUP at the county level, which had been the intent of MAYO's WGP.[50] He felt that going statewide was a serious mistake. The organizing ingredients such as money, a trained cadre of organizers, a strong grassroots power base, and viable Chicano candidates were essentially nonexistent. He believed that MAYO's statewide infrastructure and leadership were not ready or strong enough to take on such an endeavor, especially given that putting the RUP on the state ballot required a petition drive of some 22,000 signatures.[51]

At the convention Gutierrez exhorted the delegates to develop a strong community power base for the RUP prior to going statewide, particularly in the twenty-six South Texas counties where Chicanos clearly constituted the majority of the population.[52] Luera elucidates Gutierrez's position:

> He [Jose Angel] said that we couldn't do it, because we were trying to run before we knew how to walk. But most of the people wanted to run. . . . Some people made accusations that he was being selfish in not wanting the *partido* to go statewide, just because he had the *partido* in Crystal . . . nevertheless, he wanted to build a regional party first, then, after solidifying the power, expand.[53]

In essence, Gutierrez felt that MAYO as a whole was not ready to take on the organizing tasks of building a statewide party as well as the certain opposition from Mexican Americans Democrats, who would see themselves threatened by the emergence of a Chicano third party.[54]

Unfortunately for Gutierrez, the Crystal City takeover, coupled with his effective marketing of the RUP, had engendered in the urban areas of Texas a great interest in expanding the RUP statewide. Compean and other MAYO leaders from the urban areas ardently rebutted Gutierrez's arguments. To Compean, building the RUP into a statewide party would create a general mobilization of Chicanos throughout the state and would give further impetus to a moribund CM. Compean further felt that if the RUP went statewide, Chicanos would be in a position to run for state and federal positions.[55] Luera explained that Compean believed that the RUP was running out of time and that many counties were ready to pick up the RUP banner.[56] Ramsey Muñiz, who in 1972 ran for governor under the RUP label and who had been brought into the leadership ranks of MAYO, sided with Compean.

With Compean declaring, "We must go ahead. We can't just rely on Crystal for the rest of our lives," the convention delegates voted overwhelmingly to go statewide, much to the regret of Gutierrez. He explains why the RUP urban proponents won out in the matter: "The rural areas had been largely influenced by the successes of Crystal City, which had been a rural model. The urban areas had been looking for some sort of activity that they could rally around. Ramsey was an urban cat. He was very attractive to them. He was also very persuasive and so was Mario Compean. They were able to swing the effort."[57] Even though Gutierrez and his rural supporters lost the vote, they accepted and supported the majority's decision without question. MAYO's adherence to democratic centralism was carried over into the RUP.

With this issue resolved, the convention delegates elected provisional state RUP officers. Gutierrez was nominated for state chairperson but turned it down due to time constraints. During this time he was working on a doctorate in government at the University of Texas at Austin while concomitantly organizing the RUP, serving on the school board in Crystal City, and making speeches throughout the country. Still, the convention delegates wanted to recognize his leadership contributions and elected him convention chairperson by acclamation.[58] Provisional elections were held for the RUP's state executive committee, which included Mario Compean, RUP state chairperson; Efrain Hernandez, vice chairperson; Alberto Luera, secretary; and Jose Gonzalez, treasurer.[59] All four came from MAYO's leadership ranks. This was especially significant in that it established a bond in which MAYO's leadership, infrastructure, and networks became synonymous with those of the emerging RUP.[60] The convention delegates also began the process of developing a provisional party platform. Chaired by Joe Castillo from San Antonio, a resolution committee of ten members formulated and presented a multifaceted document covering seven major categories that made up the RUP's developing platform: education, the courts, national defense, voting, women's rights, public welfare, and natural resources.[61] The resolution committee was given the task of researching and documenting the principles of the RUP as dictated by the resolutions passed at the state convention. With the election of RUP provisional officers and the adoption of a platform, the convention served to accelerate the growth and development of the RUP in Texas and signaled the coming demise of MAYO.

What followed in the ensuing months was a major mobilization of MAYO and others to get the RUP on the state ballot. The original executive committee became the platform committee. Each county delegation was permitted to appoint one representative to the committee.[62] As part of the RUP statewide organizing effort, numerous meetings were held in communities throughout Texas to develop a people-oriented platform. The platform meetings were open to all who wished to attend. MAYO chapters became the cardinal organizing mechanisms in setting up these meetings. The platform took on a very populist and progressive perspective. The following quotation provides a synopsis of the type of goals formulated by the platform committee: "The party seeks political power for *La Raza*; social justice; preservation of our human and natural resources; freedom from exploitation, hunger, disease, cultural and physical genocide, poverty, ignorance, and oppression; re-distribution of economic resources; peace; self determination; and a tranquil future for all peoples."[63]

As the RUP platform was being developed, MAYO spearheaded organizing efforts to get the RUP on the state ballot for the 1972 elections. After the convention, as prescribed by the Texas election code, letters of intent were sent to the secretary of state indicating that the decision had been made at the convention to organize the RUP on a statewide basis. Moreover, the request was made that the RUP be placed on the ballot for the 1972 elections and stipulating that the convention delegates had opted for the convention method rather than the open primary for selecting its candidates.[64] The process of getting the RUP on the ballot was complex and required meeting various deadlines and requirements. Luera, who had been running the MAYO state office in San Antonio, for the next year became totally immersed in coordinating the petition drive and other activities designed to get the RUP on the ballot for the 1972 elections. "For weeks I lived according to the election code. Even though I was MAYO state chairperson, I didn't have the time for anything else but work on getting the *partido* on the ballot."[65]

MAYO chapters in both the universities and barrios joined MAYO's RUP organizing crusade. MAYO became almost totally consumed. The sole activity of the MAYO chapters was helping to organize the RUP on a county-by-county basis and to circulate petitions, with the objective of securing at least 30,000 signed and notarized signatures, although officially they needed only 22,000. It was during the months of October 1971 to August 1972 that MAYO's transition or absorption into the RUP took place. All MAYO's chapters moved to organize the RUP. In the process of doing so, MAYO members joined the RUP county and local organizing committees. Consequently, according to Luera, for all practical purposes, with some exceptions, MAYO by 1972 "ceased to exist."[66]

MAYO's state office in San Antonio was replaced with a RUP office that had the administrative responsibility of coordinating the petition drive. As the RUP was emerging, MAYO was being absorbed into its infrastructure.

This became very apparent with the recruitment of RUP candidates. By moving from being advocates on issues to recruiting political candidates, MAYO's leaders had made the quantum jump to the world of electoral politics. Gutierrez, Compean, and other MAYO leaders became directly involved in finding candidates who would be willing to run on the RUP ticket. Their search continued up to the filing date in February 1972. Initially they had sought to recruit prominent Mexican Americans to run for governor, including some who were not close to the RUP, such as Carlos Truan of Corpus Christi, a state representative; Hector Garcia, the founder of the American GI Forum; and Joe Bernal, state senator from San Antonio and a strong supporter of MAYO. All declined.[67]

With its failure to recruit a mainstream Chicano to run for governor, the MAYO leadership turned to its own leadership ranks. None of MAYO's main cadre leaders were interested in running, but after some difficulty a young lawyer from Waco named Ramsey Muñiz, who was an administrator in the Model Cities program, was chosen. Muñiz had been active in MAYO since 1968 and had served as one of its organizers in northern Texas. At the time Muñiz filed to run for governor, MAYO had yet to establish a state campaign committee, it had no money, and the RUP's platform had yet to be completed. Furthermore, MAYO's leadership was also having problems recruiting Chicanos to run for other state and federal positions.

Through a combined and coordinated recruitment effort initiated by Gutierrez, Compean, Luera, Guerra, and others, candidates were chosen. On February 9, 1972, MAYO's leadership held a press conference where Muñiz and a list of fifty-two other RUP candidates were presented. Joining Muñiz at the press conference were Alma Gonzales, candidate for lieutenant governor; Flores Anaya, a lawyer candidate for the U.S. Senate; Ruben Solis, candidate for state treasurer; Fred Garza of the United Farm Workers Organizing Committee, candidate for state railroad commissioner; and Robert Gomez, candidate for land commissioner. Also participating in the press conference was Compean, who informed the press that the RUP was fielding candidates for numerous other state and county offices in Hidalgo, Zavala, La Salle, Starr, Nueces, Victoria, McLennan, Tassant, and Bexar counties.[68] Several of the RUP candidates were MAYO members or supporters. These candidates had been officially nominated at the RUP state convention held in June 1972.

Many of the delegates at the state convention were from MAYO chapters, but by June other Chicanos who were not members of MAYO had joined the RUP bandwagon. The convention affected both MAYO and RUP. First, MAYO's transition into the RUP was enhanced and expedited, making the conversion from MAYO to RUP almost complete. Second, Muñiz became one of the main spokespersons for the RUP. Impelled by a profound sense of mission, he and his wife had traveled the state extensively, developing high name recognition and a substantial following. In a short period of time this politically inexperienced but charismatic man had been transformed into a formidable gubernatorial candidate. Whereas Compean was associated with MAYO and Gutierrez with Crystal City, Muñiz symbolized the RUP at the state level, principally because he was its standard-bearer but also because he found himself, as a dynamic campaigner, among a group of less than charismatic candidates.[69]

At the convention the delegates from throughout Texas elected permanent officers and approved the RUP's platform. Compean was elected state RUP chairperson. In addition, most of the other officers elected at the October convention of 1971 were reelected. With RUP's statewide candidates officially nominated, the convention turned to the adoption of the RUP platform. MAYO's influence on the development of the platform was especially evident in the area of education. With MAYO being at the vanguard of school boycotts and protests in Texas, the RUP's platform made education reform its top priority. It called for multilingual and multicultural programs at all levels of education, from preschool to the university; equal funding of school districts; proportional representation in school boards and administration; the elimination of standardized testing as a measure of achievement until the tests reflected the culture and language of those tested; and free prekindergarten education, including day-care centers.[70]

The rest of the RUP's platform followed a leftist-liberal direction. The delegates took a more pragmatic approach toward developing the platform. No reference was made to Chicano separatism. Chicano nationalism was toned down, and socialist rhetoric was avoided. The document reflected an effort by the old MAYO and the new RUP leaders to attract support from liberals and other progressive forces outside the Chicano community, such as the antiwar and civil rights movements. Besides containing a plank on education, the platform included thirteen other sections dealing with politics, welfare, housing, justice, international affairs, natural resources, transportation, and health. In general the platform called for free education; lowering of the voting age to eighteen; giving the right to vote to foreigners; breaking up monopolies; fair distribution of wealth; implementation of equal minority representation in the judicial system; abolishment of capital punishment; passage of the Equal Rights Amendment; removal of trade embargoes and economic sanctions against Cuba; the reduction of U.S. forces in Europe; [and] the abolishment of the Texas Rangers.[71]

After the RUP convention the nascent RUP organizing entities turned to the petition drive. In particular, Ramsey's campaign became a great mobilizer for volunteers for the petition drive. Added to this was Gutierrez's use of a quota system. Each county in which the RUP had a presence was assigned a certain number of petition signatures. The petition drive did especially well in the rural areas of South Texas. In a matter of weeks, and before the August deadline, the old MAYO chapters and the new RUP county and local structures had secured the required 22,365 signatures, consequently guaranteeing the RUP a place on the 1972 state ballot.[72] Besides the RUP candidates and Gutierrez, Compean and Luera played a major role in coordinating the petition drive.

The RUP's official place on the ballot in essence nailed the lid on MAYO's coffin. In the next three months MAYO as a state entity disappeared and was replaced by RUP structures. Its leadership became the RUP's leadership. Compean was Texas RUP state chairperson from 1972 to 1974. Although he resigned as RUP secretary in the summer of 1972, Luera became a major organizing force for the RUP in Laredo and other South Texas communities.

With the RUP becoming a major focus for the CM, Gutierrez in September 1972 moved to hold an RUP national convention in El Paso, Texas. After a lively internecine power struggle between Gutierrez and Corky Gonzales, the convention, attended by some three thousand persons representing eighteen state delegations, elected Gutierrez national RUP chairperson.[73] A platform similar to that of the RUP in Texas was adopted. No presidential candidate was endorsed. The convention delegates decided to focus on state and local races rather than on the presidential election. Ramsey Muniz's candidacy for governor of Texas was endorsed. Furthermore, a national RUP structure, a *congreso* of Aztlan, was adopted. Thus, with MAYO's main and secondary leadership now fully immersed in the RUP, MAYO's death as a statewide entity occurred in 1972 without any official board meeting, pronouncement, or ceremony. In other words, there was no official dissolution of MAYO; it simply was absorbed into the RUP.

Many MAYO chapters were transformed into RUP entities. A few MAYO chapters continued beyond 1972, but by the latter part of the seventies most had disappeared. The few that did survive continued to deal with educational and social issues. None, however, possessed the vigor, militancy, and notoriety of their predecessors. Without the dynamism of Mayo's original leaders, especially Gutierrez and Compean, there was no state leadership or structure to guide, direct, and motivate the young *MAYOistas* from the barrios and universities. MAYO's legacy of militant direct action was replaced by a modus operandi of accommodation and a growing conservatism. After MAYO's success in launching the RUP in Texas, no other Chicano organization came forward to fill the organizational leadership void left by MAYO.

In short, during its brief life span (1967–1972), MAYO was truly a unique CM and CYM organization that was able to coalesce youth from both the barrios and universities and forge them into a powerful cadre committed to bringing about social reform and empowerment for the Chicano community. For those who are cognizant of Chicano political history and who continue to struggle for change and empowerment, MAYO's legacy continues to live on.

Epilogue

In developing this case study on MAYO, I used a comprehensive, descriptive, and analytical approach to examine one of the leading organizations of the Chicano movement and Chicano Youth Movement. MAYO was a creation of a climate of change that was characterized by exogenous and endogenous antagonisms. These antagonisms molded MAYO's character, politics, and agenda, as both a student and a barrio youth change and empowerment organization. No other Chicano student group or Chicano barrio youth organization in Aztlan was as versatile, dynamic, pragmatic, and militant in its pursuit of extricating the Texan Chicano from what MAYO described as a "colonialist syndrome."

From its inception in 1967 to its demise in 1972, MAYO was the avant garde organization of the CM and CYM in Texas. With its relentless use of unconventional protest politics, MAYO was like David armed with the rock of organization, eager to take on the giant—the gringo power structure of Texas. And take it on it did, in the areas of educational reform, social issues, and Chicano political empowerment. In dealing with a variety of issues, MAYO's organizers were like the old television Western hero who lived by the words "have gun, will travel." But in the case of MAYO, the "gun" became "organization." MAYO organizers did indeed travel to all corners of Texas, especially South Texas, in the pursuit of justice and change, and they initiated school boycotts, demonstrations, marches, and other direct actions inherent to the group's protest strategy.

Without a doubt MAYO left an imprint on both Texas and Chicano political history. Even though MAYO's five-year life span was relatively short, no scholar looking at the years 1967 to 1972 could avoid examining MAYO as a political phenomenon in Texas. MAYO's role in the creation of the Raza Unida party (RUP) and its continuation as that entity beyond 1972 warrants this examination.

No other Chicano organization in the history of Texas was as bold and tenacious in challenging the racist policies of the gringo power structure as was MAYO. It uprooted old negative stereotypes of Chicanos and implanted new, more realistic images. MAYO left an unprecedented legacy of activism.

This study provides ample documentation of MAYO's legacy for the Chicano community of Texas and Aztlan. There is no doubt that MAYO will go down in Chicano political history as a major player that made a significant contribution to the development and radicalization of the CM. This is ascribable to MAYO's adherence to Chicanismo and its bold history of direct action against the gringo power structure of Texas.

In the course of conducting the interviews for this book, I asked MAYO leaders what they thought MAYO's most significant contribution to Chicanos in Texas was. Jose Angel Gutierrez's response best illustrates their responses:

A loss of fear. It means that we stopped being afraid of the gringo. We taught our parents to have courage like we did. We taught all those who were watching that you could confront the gringo[s] and beat them at their own games. All that violence that had accumulated over centuries we washed away with our activism, with our confrontations, with our bold pronouncements, and with our public postures of militancy.[1]

The remaining three members of Los Cinco echoed Gutierrez's analysis. Mario Compean stressed "the psychological liberation of the Chicano not only through rhetoric but through actual deeds."[2] For Nacho Perez, MAYO's most important contribution was the creation of human resources. "What spawned from MAYO was a legacy of leaders, organizations, and networks that to this day exist."[3] To Patlan, however, it was MAYO's impact on other existing Chicano organizations. "MAYO brought other organizations into the twentieth century."[4]

Other *MAYOistas* interviewed were in accord with the remaining four founding members of MAYO. To Luz Gutierrez, "MAYO lit the fire for the whole issue of who we were as a people. We actually opened people's eyes, including those of the *políticos,* that we wanted to have a say-so in running ourselves."[5] Choco Gonzales Meza emphasized how MAYO became a leadership training vehicle: "Without MAYO you would not have had such a young group of people to train themselves politically. The interesting thing is that . . . [they] have reached heights in politics and in educational institutions that I am sure they would not have reached without that kind of positive anger [MAYO] had."[6]

They also alluded to how MAYO provided some of the Chicano youth of the Texas barrios with a new sense of hope and pride that in turn resulted in a decline in Chicano gang violence. Viviana Santiago elucidates this point: "It got the youth organized. It got a lot of so-called troublemakers, gangs, potential gang members . . . involved in a political movement. MAYO expanded their minds from killing and maiming each other to doing something constructive for their people. It gave them an identity and pride. . . . We didn't have the degree of gang violence that we have today."[7] In buttressing Viviana's analysis, Rudy Rodriguez responded, "The greatest contribution MAYO made in Texas was that we gave La Raza in Texas a sense of pride . . . that you did not have to be ashamed of the color of your skin."[8] Carlos Guerra's perspective was one of a complete redefinition of the role of Chicanos in Texas society and politics.[9] Complementing Rodriguez and Guerra, Alberto Luera stated, "MAYO brought to the forefront in a very forceful manner the inequities of the system as it related to Mexicanos."[10]

All those interviewed saw MAYO as unique—a one-of-a-kind action organization. They alluded to the fact that because of the experience gained in working with MAYO, many of them had become successful in a variety of professions, as attorneys, businesspeople, bureaucrats, teachers, academicians, and journalists. They emphasized that many of the leaders who were active in MAYO or the RUP are today prominent leaders, influential within contemporary political and business arenas.

Illustrative of this is MAYO's founding and state leadership. All of Los Cinco have done well for themselves. Before his death in 1988 Willie Velasquez was the founder and president of the Southwest Voter Registration and Education Project. Jose Angel Gutierrez is now a successful academician and attorney. He is a professor at the University of Texas at Arlington and practices law in Dallas. Mario Compean is completing his graduate work for a Ph.D. in education and is employed by the Minnesota Spanish-Speaking Affairs Council as a policy research specialist. Ignacio Perez is the Texas coordinator for the Southwest Voter Registration Institute, Latin American Project. Juan Patlan is acting director of multifamily housing for the Resolution Trust Corporation. Carlos Guerra is a successful journalist, and Alberto Luera is the executive director of Centro Aztlan in Laredo. Other MAYO leaders and spokespersons (male and female alike) have also done as well socioeconomically.

Moreover, with the demise of the RUP, most of MAYO's leaders who were active with the RUP have returned to the ranks of the Democratic Party. In 1993 Jose Angel Gutierrez ran unsuccessfully for the U.S. Senate in Texas on the Democratic Party ticket. He returned to the ranks of the Democratic Party after so many years of being its relentless and acrimonious critic. Many other MAYO leaders have been key figures in the development of the most prominent Chicano political organization to date in Texas, the Mexican-American Democrats. To them, MAYO served the very important function of training organizers to be leaders.

When asked what MAYO's greatest mistake was, however, Jose Angel Gutierrez replied, "We stopped organizing. We never continued to replenish ourselves. . . . We went from project to project. When we ended up with the Raza Unida party, we stopped there. We never kept rejuvenating. We should have. With the creation of Raza Unida, there was no new MAYO. Everybody became Raza Unida."[11] What contributed to the decline of MAYO? Outside of answers that stressed the emergence of the RUP, the responses to this question were revealing. Juan Patlan explained: "My own theory is that movements and personalities are tied together . . . the reason MAYO died is because of personalities moving on and becoming involved in other things. Jose Angel went to Crystal City and organized Raza Unida. Willie Velasquez developed a voter registration project. And I took over the Mexican-American Unity Council and so on."[12] Luz Gutierrez's response was more pointed than Patlan's. She said, "I think people grow up. It is like aging. Frankly, many of the people outgrew MAYO. It served its purpose."[13] Daniel Bustamante attributed MAYO's decline to burnout. His perspective was that the transition from MAYO to the RUP was a welcome one because of MAYO's militant and radical image. MAYO increasingly was being depicted by its adversaries as communist. According to Bustamante, "People were scared."[14]

In the nineties, MAYO is but a few recorded paragraphs in the pages of Chicano history. Today, the dynamic activism of the CM and its progeny, the CYM, is almost nonexistent. Tijerina, Gonzalez, and Gutierrez are absent from the activist circuit, and Chavez, the nonviolent warrior for the campesino, died in 1993. No others have replaced them. In fact, this leadership vacuum constitutes one of the most serious problems Chicanos need to overcome if there is to be any serious effort to reanimate the CM.

The thunderous cries of "Viva La Raza," "Chicano Power," and "Si Se Puede" are somewhat muted. The marches, demonstrations, boycotts, and other forms of direct action are essentially gone. The people's growing frustration and discontent have yet to translate to the rebirth of the CM. With the end of the epoch of protest by the early seventies, the nation as a whole was swept by powerful currents of neoconservatism. The same occurred in the Chicano community.

Despite the fact that the crises plaguing the Chicano community during the sixties still existed throughout Aztlan, the activists of the epoch of protest were mellowed by the materialism, self-indulgence, and individualism of what can be described as the "Vivo Yo Generation," which emerged in the midseventies and reached its apogee in the eighties; vestiges of it still exist in the nineties. This new self-indulgent generation was conceived on the deathbed of the epoch of protest. With the end of the war in Vietnam came an end to the epoch of protest. This devastating war, which polarized American society and produced some 54,000 casualties, had been the primary antagonism that contributed to this nation's radicalization in the late sixties and early seventies. As the war wound down, so did the divergent protest movements, and the CM was no exception.

The "Vivo Yo Generation" of the seventies and eighties rejected the protest politics of the CM. Chicanos became Hispanics, or "Hi-Spanics," as Jose Angel Gutierrez labeled them. Corporate America and Hispanic leaders announced to the world that the eighties were to be the "decade of the Hispanic." For the most part, ballot-box politics replaced protest/confrontational politics. This meant that the demonstrations, marches, boycotts, and other direct action methods were superseded by such ballot-box methods as the running of Chicano candidates, voter registration, political education, and get-out-the-vote drives. This decade witnessed a dramatic increase in Chicano political representation. The cardinal focus became one of empowerment using a more mainstream approach. Change-oriented efforts now relied on the use of lobbying, letter writing, political action committee (PAC) formation, press conferences, and other conventional methods. This was also the era of lawsuits such as the Watsonville decision and the Victorville Five that relied on the benevolence of the courts rather than on the mobilization of the Chicano community.

With the decline of *movimiento* organizations, the eighties saw the return and rejuvenation of the more moderate Mexican American organizations such as LULAC, the GI Forum, and MAPA. Furthermore, with the end to the CM, numerous nonprofit service and development entities were formed. Concomitantly, other organizations that had their genesis during the late sixties and seventies, such as the National Council of La Raza, the Mexican American Legal Defense and Education Fund, the Southwest Voter Registration and Education Project, and the National Association of Latino Elected and Appointed Officials, began to take on a more regional to national organizational leadership role. A number of activists, perhaps tired of and frustrated with the politics of *el movimiento*, opted for the more lucrative politics of acquiring financial resources.

Some of these groups, however, became caught up in bitter conflicts among themselves to see who would control the scarce resources. All too often, the enemy was not the gringo or the system but themselves. The dictum "we have met the enemy and he is us" was applicable at times in describing the nature of these conflicts. There were exceptions, however, such as the Communities Organized for Public Services (COPS) in San Antonio, United Neighborhood Organization (UNO) in Los Angeles, some other Alinsky-oriented groups, and a few die-hard activists still trying to organize. For the most part, the "Vivo Yo Generation" was characterized by pronounced apathy, indifference, and complacency that permeated many of the barrios of Aztlan.

These attitudes were particularly evident among the Chicano youth. With the CM moribund in the seventies, a dialectical change occurred. During these years Chicanos in general evolved from the UFW generation to the BMW generation. More specifically, Chicano student groups discarded their berets, field jackets, and symbols of Aztlan and the CM and became immersed in the pursuit of a new life-style that was epitomized by three-piece suits, titles of importance, and escape from the barrio to the sanctuary of suburbia. In essence, they became "Chuppies" (Chicano Urban Professionals), counterparts to the Anglo "Yuppies." They embraced the neo-individualism of the Vivo Yo mentality.

This was especially true during the eighties. Many student groups rejected activism and began to resemble fraternities, at least superficially. Parties, conferences, and cultural events made up their menu of social activities. Some groups splintered into special interest groups with a much narrower vocational focus such as law, teaching, and medicine. Those few activist student groups that did exist and sought to rekindle the spirit of *el movimiento* were often plagued by ideological cleavages and self-destructive power struggles. While apathy and internecine conflicts beset the student sector, administrators of universities and colleges moved to dismantle Chicano studies programs and departments.

The nineties arrived and the crises that Chicanos had faced in the eighties became more acute. With massive emigration from Mexico and Central America and high fertility rates, Chicanos and Latinos were helping give impetus to the "browning of America." According to the U.S. Bureau of the Census, the 1990 census revealed that Chicanos and Latinos combined constituted 9 percent of the nation's population. This meant that there were some 22 million Chicano/ Latinos, of which 62 percent were Chicano/Mexicano. The "cactus curtain" separating Mexico from the United States was moving ever northward. Throughout the nation, particularly in Aztlan, a demographic transformation was in progress; within fifty years Chicanos/ Latinos would be the majority in many parts of Aztlan. Some nativist alarmists and Chicano activists have labeled this demographic reality the *reconquista*.

Chicanos in the nineties find themselves in a situation reminiscent of the one Charles Dickens wrote of in *A Tale of Two Cities:* the best of times, the worst of times. For Chicanos, however, the worst-of-times scenario is by far the dominant. Following an economic downturn, Chicanos find themselves relegated to the bottom of society's socioeconomic ladder. Across the board the barrios of Aztlan are victimized by increased poverty, unemployment, inadequate education, scarcity of affordable housing, crime, gang violence, drug and alcohol abuse, and numerous other problems. These social problems threaten to relegate Chicanos to a permanent underclass status. As if this were not enough, the economic downturn has created a powerful nativism that in the early nineties is sweeping much of this nation. In particular, its strong currents of racism, bigotry, and prejudice are directed at undocumented immigrants, principally those from Mexico. The Mexican illegal alien is being blamed by nativists for many of the socioeconomic ills confronting the nation. The undocumented, in short, have become the scapegoat for extremist right-wing nativist groups and Republicans and Democrats alike, who preach a similar nativist gospel that includes such xenophobic measures as militarizing the U.S.-Mexican border; issuing of national ID cards; denying citizenship to U.S.-born children of undocumented parents; withholding social and health services; and so on.

In 1993, while the United States and Mexico were negotiating the North American Free Trade Agreement (NAFTA), the United States was building a twenty-foot-high fence along the border between California and Mexico. The irony of this action by the United States is that while it supported and applauded the tearing down of the Berlin Wall, it was erecting its own "wall" along the border to stop what it calls the "silent invasion" of Mexican and Central American immigrants into the country. Although the cold war is over, nativists are creating their own war of vitriolic rhetorical attacks. This time their enemy is Mexico. To them, Mexico is the new "evil empire."

Adding to the scenario is the prospect that, if Chicanos' overall quality of life does not drastically improve in the coming years, they could very well be governed by a quasi apartheid in the twenty-first century. Nowhere is the possibility of this scenario more evident than in the schools of Aztlan. As the Chicano/Latino communities grow in population, so do the student populations. While de jure segregation no longer exists, de facto segregation is very much alive. The separate-but-equal doctrine has been superseded by an unofficial "separate and unequal" modus operandi. Schools in the barrios are poorer than others, often lack appropriate facilities and equipment, and are plagued by an absence of Chicano teachers and administrators. Bilingual programs are often targets of "English Only" nativist zealots who are unequivocally against cultural pluralism. Barrio schools are generally beset by high "push-out/drop-out" rates and functional illiteracy. In addition, Chicanos in the early nineties are not graduating from high school or going on to college in significant numbers. Nationally, only 45 percent of those Chicano/Latinos who enter kindergarten graduate from high school, and only 7 percent graduate from a four-year college.[15]

The ramifications of this educational crisis are devastating to the future of the Chicano community. The lack of a trained, prepared, and committed intelligentsia, coupled with the increasing "pauperization" of the barrios, makes the prospect of a South African syndrome more probable. While constituting an overwhelming majority in many communities, Chicanos will not have sufficient numbers of trained leaders or personnel to govern or administer their communities. This means that Chicanos will become increasingly dependent on other ethnic or racial groups to run their schools, local governments, businesses, and programs. The specter of such a reality is already unfolding in many areas of Aztlan, especially California and Texas.

For Chicanos this problem is further exacerbated by the growing interethnic and racial conflicts among Chicanos, African Americans, Asian Americans, and European Americans. The national economic crisis has spilled over, precipitating a struggle for control of shrinking resources and opportunities. Dangerous tensions exist among these competing groups. These tensions are intensified by increasing numbers of non-Latino businesses penetrating the barrios of Aztlan and threatening to control the barrios' already dependent and depressed economy. The South Central Los Angeles eruption of 1992 was a manifestation of the powder keg potential that exists in many of this nation's urban areas. Furthermore, these tensions produce a dangerous climate of violence that, if unmitigated, could very well "balkanize" American society. These conflicts and tensions are occurring at a time when Latino organizational and individual leadership is at its weakest.

The MAYO leaders interviewed were asked to state their perspectives and prognoses on the future of Chicanos in Texas. They qualified their responses by pointing out that because of MAYO's and the RUP's efforts, Chicanos today have more Chicano political representation. In 1991 there were 1,969 elected Chicano/Latinos in Texas, constituting 7.3 percent of the state's elected officials.[16] In 1993 Texas had five Chicano congressmen, one more than did California. Henry Cisneros, former mayor of San Antonio, was appointed U.S. secretary of housing and urban development by President Clinton. At the state level, Dan Morales was elected in 1990 as Texas's first Chicano attorney general. In spite of these significant inroads, however, the former *MAYOistas* tended to speak pessimistically. Juanita Bustamante summed it up with the following comment: "The situation in Texas today is worse, or at best the same as it was in the sixties."[17]

In the introductory chapter of this study I discussed the idea that social movements are conceived in the womb of discontent and nurtured by adversity and conflict. Such an analysis implies that American society today is ripe for the emergence of new movements and a new epoch of protest. In other words, the political ground is fertile enough to yield a new crop of activism. In 1993 this is very much the case with Chicanos throughout Aztlan. There is a growing restlessness and frustration among Chicanos, especially the youth. From California to Texas Chicano students are once again beginning to demand the reestablishment or establishment of Chicano studies programs, the hiring of Chicano faculty and administrators, and the recruitment of Chicano students. This was illustrated by the many student demonstrations that occurred at various universities such as the University of California at Los Angeles; University of Texas at San Antonio; University of California at Riverside; Claremont Colleges; and several others. Once again, if this activism continues, Chicano youth could be playing a major role in the development of a new *movimiento*. Only time will tell whether this renaissance of activism will create the climate of change necessary to resurrect the CM.

The resurrection of the CM must be guided by the strategic process of the three Rs: we must *recommit, reorganize,* and *remobilize.* We must learn from history so as to avoid repeating the mistakes of the past. The stakes have never been higher. Time and demographics are on our side. The only questions are when and how. The answer to "when" is "now," and the answer to "how" is zealous adherence to the strategic process of the three Rs. In addition, this reenergized CM must be broadened to allow it to coalesce with other Latinos and non-Latinos whenever it is mutually beneficial.

If we Chicanos are going to transform the nineties into a decade of change and progress for ourselves, then we must embrace the notion that no one is going to do this for us. We must do it for ourselves. Regardless of our burgeoning numbers, it is imperative to remember that power is never given, it is taken; that change is never realized without a struggle; and that unorganized masses do not constitute power. Thus, the challenge for Chicanos in the nineties is to work toward transforming potential to actual empowerment. In other words, we must strive to develop a "fear factor" of power, based on our ability to mobilize ourselves effectively within the electoral and pressure group arenas. Presently Chicanos suffer from what I call the "Rodney Dangerfield Syndrome"— we get no respect because we show no fear factor or power. Therefore, existing Chicano leaders must recommit. New leaders must emerge who are as committed and competent as were MAYO's Los Cinco. They must also be willing to reorganize the CM by revitalizing existing advocacy organizations and, if necessary, creating new ones that will exemplify the activist spirit and deeds of MAYO. As MAYO was able to create an unprecedented mobilization of Chicanos in Texas, Chicanos in the nineties must once again create a remobilization of the barrios of Aztlan. El futuro es nuestro, si nos organisamos (The Future Is Ours, If We Organize Ourselves).

Appendix 1. "El Plan Espiritual de Aztlán"

In the spirit of a new people that is conscious not only of its proud historical heritage but also of the brutal "Gringo" invasion of our territories: We, the Chicano inhabitants and civilizers of the northern land of Aztlan from whence came our forefathers, reclaiming the land of their birth and consecrating the determination of our people of the sun, declare that the call of our blood is our power, our responsibility, and our inevitable destiny.

We are free and sovereign to determine those tasks which are justly called for by our house, our land, the sweat of our brows and by our hearts. Aztlan belongs to those who plant the seeds, water the fields, and gather the crops, and not to the foreign Europeans. We do not recognize capricious frontiers on the Bronze Continent.

Brotherhood unites us and love for our brothers makes us a people whose time has come and who struggle against the foreigner "Gabacho," who exploits our riches and destroys our culture. With our heart in our hands and our hands in the soil, We Declare the Independence of our Mestizo Nation. We are a Bronze People with a Bronze Culture. Before the world, before all of North America, before all our Brothers in the Bronze Continent, We are a Nation, We are a Union of free pueblos, We are Aztlan. . . .

Program

El Plan espiritual de Aztlán sets the theme that the Chicanos (La Raza de Bronze) must use their nationalism as the key or common denominator for mass mobilization and organization. Once we are committed to the idea and philosophy of El Plan de Aztlán, we can only conclude that social, economic, cultural, and political independence is the only road to total liberation from oppression, exploitation, and racism. Our struggle then must be for the control of our barrios, campos, pueblos, lands, our economy, our culture, and our political life. El Plan commits all levels of Chicano society—the barrio, the campo, the ranchero, the writer, the teacher, the worker, the professional—to La Causa.

Nationalism

Nationalism as the key of organization transcends all religious, political, class, and economic factions or boundaries. Nationalism is the common denominator that all members of La Raza can agree upon.

Organizational Goals

. . . 2. Economy: economic control of our lives and our communities can only come about by driving the exploiter out of our communities, our pueblos, and our lands and by controlling and developing our own talents, sweat and resources. . . . Lands rightfully ours . . . will be acquired by the community for the people's welfare. . . .

3. Education must be relative to our people, i.e., history, culture, bilingual education, contributions, etc. Community control of our schools, our teachers, our administrators, our counselors, and our programs. . . .

6. Cultural values of our people strengthen our identity and the moral backbone of the movement. Our culture unites and educates the family of La Raza towards liberation with our heart and mind. We must insure that our writers, poets, musicians, and artists produce literature and art that is appealing to our people and relates to our revolutionary culture. Our cultural values of life, family, and home will serve as a powerful weapon to defeat that gringo dollar value system and encourage the process of love and brotherhood.

7. Political liberation can come only through independent action on our part, since the two-party system is the same animal with two heads that feed from the same trough. . . .

Action

. . . 7. Creation of an independent local, regional, and national political party. . . .

Liberation

A nation autonomous and free culturally, socially, economically, and politically will make its own decisions on the usage of our lands, the taxation of our goods, the utilization of our bodies for war, the determination of justice (reward and punishment), and the profit of our sweat.

El plan de Aztlan is the plan of liberation!

Source: Luis Valdez and Stan Steiner, eds., *Aztlan: An Anthology of Mexican American Literature* (New York: Vintage Books, 1972), 402–406.

Appendix 2. MAYO Membership Requirements

1. A sincere desire to help La Raza as well as self.
   A. When one progresses, not to forget one's fellow Chicano.
2. A basic knowledge of what the movement is about.
   A. Romantic people and people out for kicks or publicity are not helping any. This movement is serious business—not a game.
3. No qualms of being labeled a militant; radical; or other names for fear of losing job, prestige, etc.
4. A desire to put La Raza first and foremost. Can't belong to other political groups or owe allegiance to other philosophies—Young Democrats, Republicans, communists, etc.
5. Believe that all Chicanos have every right as human beings and that they are not inferior to any race or nationality.
6. Courage to follow orders as well as give them. When ordered to attack directly, must do so and he who gives the orders must be ready to lead.
7. Believe in the unity of the Chicano, La Raza Unida—not criticize other Chicanos in public—all internal problems to be solved at meetings.
8. Owe allegiance to no man but to the idea of justice for all the Raza—no idols, saviors, super Chicanos.
9. Support all fellow MAYO's in time of crisis. Wherever there is trouble everyone goes. All go to Del Rio, Kingsville, etc.
10. Age should be no factor—but must have an ability to think young.
11. An alert and open mind together with a closed mouth.
12. Knowledge of what one is saying, a desire to study, learn and articulate.

Source: MAYO document, no date, Jose Angel Gutierrez files, Crystal City, Texas, 1973.

Appendix 3. Crystal City School Walkout Demands

1. That all elections concerning the school be conducted by the student body. Concerning class representatives, the petition asked that the qualifications such as personality, leadership, grades be abolished. These factors do not determine whether the student is capable of representing the student body. The students are capable of voting for their own representatives. The representatives are representing the students, not the faculty. All nominating must be done by the student body, and the election should be decided by a majority vote.

2. The present method of electing most handsome, beautiful, most popular, and most representative is elected [sic] by the faculty. The method of cumulative voting is unfair.

3. National Honor Society—the grades of the students eligible must be posted on the bulletin board well in advance of selection. The teachers should not have anything to do with electing the students.

4. An advisory board of Mexican American citizens should be a part of the school administration in order to advise on the needs and problems of the Mexican American.

5. No other favorites should be authorized by school administrators or board members unless submitted to the student body in a referendum.

6. Teachers, administrators and staff should be educated; they should know our language—Spanish—and understand the history, traditions and contributions of Mexican culture. How can they expect to teach us if they do not know us? We want more Mexican American teachers for the above reason.

7. We want immediate steps taken to implement bilingual and bicultural education for Mexican Americans. We also want the school books revised to reflect the contributions of Mexicans and Mexican Americans to the U.S. society, and to make us

aware of the injustices that we, Mexican Americans, as a people have suffered in an "Anglo" dominant society. We want a Mexican American course with the value of one credit.

8. We want any member of the school system who displays prejudice or fails to recognize, understand and appreciate us, Mexican Americans, our culture, or our heritage removed from Crystal City's schools. Teachers shall not call students any names.

9. Our classes should be smaller in size, say about 20 students to one teacher to insure more effectiveness. We want parents from the community to be trained as teacher's aides. We want assurances that a teacher who may disagree politically or philosophically with administrators will not be dismissed or transferred because of it. Teachers should encourage students to study and should make class more interesting, so that students will look forward to going to class.

10. There should be a manager in charge of janitorial work and maintenance details and the performance of such duties should be restricted to employees hired for that purpose. In other words, no more students doing janitorial work.

11. We want a free speech area plus the right to have speakers of our own.

12. We would like September 16 as a holiday, but if it is not possible we would like an assembly, with speakers of our own. We feel it is a great day in the history of the world because it is when Mexico had been under the Spanish rule for about 300 years. The Mexicans were liberated from the harsh rule of Spain. Our ancestors fought in this war and we owe them tribute because we are Mexicans, too.

13. Being civic minded citizens, we want to know what the happenings are in our community. So, we request the right to have access to all types of literature and to be able to bring it on campus. The newspaper in our school does not carry sufficient information. It carries things like the gossip column, which is unnecessary.

14. The dress code should be abolished. We are entitled to wear what we want.

15. We request the buildings open to students at all times.

16. We want Mr. Harbin to resign as Principal of Fly Jr. High.

17. We want a Mexican American counselor fully qualified in college opportunities.

18. We need more showers in the boy's and girl's dressing rooms.

Source: MAYO document, Jose Angel Gutierrez files, Crystal City, Texas, 1973.

Appendix 4. "El Plan de Del Rio"

On this historic day, March 30, 1969, the Mexican American community of the United States of America stands in solidarity with the Mexican American poor of Del Rio, Texas. The infamy recently perpetrated upon them by local and state authorities has exhausted our patience. From throughout the country and all walks of life, we have come to join our voices with theirs in denouncing the forces that oppress them and us, and in demanding redress of their grievances and ours. We believe that both our denunciation and our demand are firmly in keeping with a country made up of minorities and committed to abide by democratic ideals.

Recent events in this city have made it amply clear that our minority continues to be oppressed by men and institutions using the language of democracy while resorting to totalitarian methods. A highly regarded OEO project of self-determination, the Val Verde County VISTA Minority Mobilization program, has been arbitrarily cancelled by Governor Preston Smith at the request of three Anglo county commissioners representing less than five percent of the population. The fourth commissioner, a Mexican American representing the rest of the citizens, while originally abstaining, joined his vote to that of the other three following the Governor's decree. The charges were pathetic—a reflection of nervous power-wielders who saw the growing assertiveness of the poor served by VISTA Mexican Americans as a threat to their traditional supremacy. A collusion was alleged between the VISTA volunteers and the Mexican American Youth Organization (MAYO), a local group of youngsters, mostly high schoolers, who frequently assail the injustices of what they call the "gringo system." Without bothering to consult with the local Community Action Program Board, or the Austin Regional OEO office, both of which continue to endorse the Del Rio VISTAs, the Governor sent wires to the National VISTA office and to all Texas judges in whose counties other VISTA programs are operating, informing them of the cancellation of the Val Verde County program, and adding, "the abdication of respect for law and order, disruption of the democratic process, and provocation of disunity among our citizens shall not be tolerated by this office."

A dispassionate analysis of this appalling misuse of power by both the Val Verde Commissioners and the Governor reveals it is they, not the poor, the VISTAs, or MAYOs who are guilty of "abdication of respect for law and order, disruption of the democratic process, and provocation of disunity among our citizens." Del Rio was no paradise of unity, before VISTAs and MAYOs arrived. Except for minor differences of detail, the list of local grievances they have dramatized parallel the experience of countless other communities where Mexican Americans are still treated as conquered people. We see our own conditions elsewhere as we review the sorry catalogue that our destitute Del Rio brothers have shared with us in describing the Anglo-controlled establishment:

1. It is they who built a multi-million dollar school for their children, then built barracks for ours.
2. It is they who stole our land, then sold it back to us, bit by bit, crumb by crumb.
3. It is they who speak one language and resent us for speaking two.
4. It is they who preach brotherhood and practice racism.
5. It is they who make much ado about equal opportunity but reserve it to themselves or their replicas.
6. It is they who proclaim concern for the poor through a welfare system calculated to keep our people in perpetual dependency.
7. It is their police system that harasses and over-polices our sons and daughters.
8. It is their educational system that violates the innocence of our children with required literature like *The Texas Story*, a book that caricatures our ancestors.
9. It is their double standard of justice—minimum penalty for Gringo and maximum for Chicano—that makes criminals of our young men.
10. It is they who denounce our militancy but think nothing of the legal violence they inflict on us mentally, culturally, spiritually and physically.

There must be something invincible in our people that has kept alive our humanity in spite of a system bent on suppressing our difference and rewarding our conformity. It is such an experience of cultural survival that has led us to the recovery of the magnificence of LA RAZA. However we define it, it is a treasure house of spirituality, decency, and sanity. LA RAZA is the affirmation of the most basic ingredient of our personality, the brownhood of our Indian ancestors wedded to all the other skin colors of mankind. Brown is the common denominator of the largest number among us—a glorious reminder of our Aztec and Mayan heritage. But in a color-mad society, the sin of our coloration can be expiated only by exceptional achievement and successful imitation of the white man who controls every institution of society. LA RAZA condemns such a system as racist, pagan, and ultimately self-destructive. We can neither tolerate it nor be a part of it. As children of LA RAZA, we are heirs of a spiritual and biological miracle where in one family blood ties unite the darkest and fairest. It is no accident that the objects of our veneration include the black Peruvian Saint Martin de Porres, the brown Indian Virgin of Guadalupe, the blond European madonnas, and a Jewish Christ of Indian and Spanish features.

We cannot explain our survival and our strength apart from this heritage—a heritage inseparably linked to Spanish, the soul language of LA RAZA. On this day we serve notice on Del Rio and the nation that for their sake and ours we are willing to lay down our lives to preserve the culture and language of our ancestors, to blend them with that which is best in these United States of America, our beloved country. Let no one forget that thousands of our Mexican American brothers have gallantly fought and died in defense of American freedoms enjoyed by us more in hope than reality. We shall escalate the defense of such freedoms here at home to honor those who fell for them yesterday, and to sustain those who live for their fulfillment tomorrow. We are committed to non-violence, even while living in the midst of officially tolerated violence. We are prepared, however, to be as aggressive as it may be necessary, until every one of our Mexican American brothers enjoys the liberty of shaping his own future.

We feel compelled to warn the Val Verde Commissioners and Governor Preston Smith that they are inviting serious social unrest if they do not immediately rescind their VISTA cancellation action. Likewise, we feel compelled to warn the United States Congress that unless legislation is enacted to protect the VISTA principle of self-determination from arbitrary termination by local and state officials, the entire concept of volunteer service, whether at home or abroad, will be prostituted in the eyes of those idealistic fellow-Americans who participate in it. Lastly, we feel compelled to warn

the whole nation that unless the ideal of self-determination is upheld with our poor at home, the entire world will judge us hypocritical in our attempt to assist the poor abroad.

On this day, Mexican Americans commit themselves to struggle
ceaselessly until the promise of this country is realized for us and
our fellow-Americans: one nation, under God, indivisible, with liberty and justice for all.

Source: Armando B. Rendon, *Chicano Manifesto* (New York: Collier, 1971),
332–336.

Notes

Preface

1. The definition and origin of the word *Chicano* are elusive and uncertain. No one knows its origin, although various theories exist. One theory ascribes to it a Nahuatl origin, suggesting that Indians pronounced *Mexicano* as "Me-shi-ca-noh." The first syllable was in time dropped and the soft "shi" was replaced with the hard "c" to form "Chi-ca-noh." Regardless of its origin, for decades the term has been commonplace to the vernacular of the barrio. With the cultural renaissance of the 1960s, activists of all ages rejected such terms as Mexican-American, Latino, Hispano, and others. They opted instead for Chicano and La Raza (the race or people) when referring to themselves and others of Mexican extraction. Thus, Chicano and La Raza will be used interchangeably throughout this book.

2. The term *Aztlan* is used to denote the point of origin of the Aztecs prior to their journey to Mexico; I will use it to refer generally to the Southwest.

Introduction

1. Herbert Blumer, "Collective Behavior," in Alfred McClung Lee, ed., *New Outline of the Principles of Sociology* (New York: Barnes and Noble, 1951), 166–222.

2. Rudolf Heberle, *Social Movements: An Introduction to Political Sociology* (New York: Appleton-Century Crofts, 1951), 6.

3. James L. Wood and Maurice Jackson, *Social Movements: Development, Participation, and Dynamics* (Belmont, Calif.: Wadsworth, 1982), 3.

4. John Wilson, *Introduction to Social Movements* (New York: Basic Books, 1973), 4.

5. Norman I. Fainstein and Susan S. Fainstein, *Urban Political Movements: The Search for Power by Minority Groups in American Cities* (New Jersey: Prentice-Hall, 1974), 239.

6. Wilson, *Social Movements*, 3–14. The author presents several definitions of social movements and differentiates them from related phenomena.

7. Carl Leiden and Karl M. Schmitt, *The Politics of Violence: Revolution in the Modern World* (New Jersey: Prentice-Hall, 1968), 37.

8. Karl Marx, *The Class Struggles in France 1848–1850* (New York: International Publishers, 1964), 120.

9. R. N. Carew Hunt, *The Theory and Practice of Communism* (Baltimore: Penguin, 1964), 63.

10. Alexis de Tocqueville, *The Old Regime and the French Revolution,* trans. John Bonner (New York: Harper and Bros., 1856), 214.

11. Crane Brinton, *The Anatomy of Revolution* (New York: Dodd, Mead, 1974), 250.

12. James Davies, "Toward a Theory of Revolution," in Clifford T. Paynton and Robert Blackey, eds., *Why Revolution? Theories and Analysis* (New Jersey: Schenkman, 1971), 178–179.

13. Ibid.

14. Ted Robert Gurr, *Why Men Rebel* (Princeton, N.J.: Princeton University Press, 1971), 13.

15. Eric Hoffer, *The True Believer* (New York; Mentor, 1958), 20, 22.

16. See Saul Alinsky, *Rules for Radicals* (New York: Vintage, 1971) and *Reveille for Radicals* (New York: Vintage, 1969), for an excellent analysis of the mechanics of community organizing and how discontent and frustration are integral to the process.

17. Lee Staples, *Roots to Power: A Manual for Grassroots Organizing* (New York: Praeger, 1984), 35.

18. Neil J. Smelser, *Theory of Collective Behavior* (New York: Free Press, 1963), 12–21, 270–381.

19. Wood and Jackson, *Social Movements,* 42.

20. Chalmers Johnson, *Revolutionary Change* (Boston: Little, Brown, 1966), 60.

21. Waltraud Q. Morales, *Social Revolution: Theory and Historical Application* (Denver: University of Denver International Studies, 1973), 19.

22. Ibid., 20.

23. Harry Eckstein, *Internal War: Problems and Approaches* (New York: Free Press, 1964), and Johnson, *Revolutionary Change.*

Chapter 1

1. Armando Rendon, *Chicano Manifesto* (New York: Collins, 1971), 18.

2. See Rodolfo Acuña, *Occupied America: The Chicano Struggle toward Liberation,* 1st ed. (New York: Canfield Press, 1972); and Mario Barrera, Carlos Munoz, and Charles Ornelas, "The Barrio as an Internal Colony," in F. Chris Garcia, *La Causa Política: A Chicano Politics Reader* (London: University of Notre Dame Press, 1974).

3. Acuña, *Occupied America,* 3.

4. Much of the analysis in this section is a product of my article "The Evolution of Chicano Politics," *Aztlan* 5, no. 1–2 (Spring/Fall 1974): 57–84.

5. David J. Weber, ed., *Foreigners in Their Native Land: Historical Roots of the Mexican Americans* (Albuquerque: University of New Mexico Press, 1973), 204.

6. Eric J. Hobsbawm, *Primitive Rebels* (New York: W. W. Norton, 1959), 23–24.

7. Carey McWilliams, *North from Mexico: The Spanish-Speaking People of the United States* (New York: Greenwood, 1968), 130.

8. Leonard Pitt, *Decline of the Californios: A Social History of the Spanish-Speaking Californians (1846–1890)* (Berkeley: University of California Press, 1968), 256.

9. For an excellent analysis of the impact of the *guerrilleros,* see Alfredo Mirande, *Gringo Justice* (Notre Dame, Ind.: University of Notre Dame Press, 1987), 50–99.

10. Weber, *Foreigners in Their Native Land,* 207–208.

11. Juan Gomez-Quiñonez, "Plan de San Diego Reviewed," *Aztlan: Journal of the Social Sciences and Art* 1 (Spring 1970): 124–128.

12. Weber, *Foreigners in Their Native Land,* 149.

13. Ibid., 213–216.

14. Refer to Jose Hernandez, *Mutual Aid for Survival: The Case of the Mexican Americans* (Malabras, Fl.: Robert E. Krieger, 1983). Provides an excellent case study of Chicano mutual benefit societies.

15. For a comprehensive analysis of the development of Chicano organizations, refer to the article by Miguel David Tirado, "Mexican American Community: Political Organization, the Key to Chicano Political Power," *Aztlan* 1, no. 1 (Spring 1972): 53–78.

16. Acuña, *Occupied America,* 153–186. Provides an overview of the participation and impact of Chicanos on the labor movement from 1900 to the 1930s.

17. Juan Gomez-Quiñonez, *Chicano Politics: Reality and Promise (1940–1990)* (Albuquerque: University of New Mexico Press, 1990), 45.

18. Ibid., 45–48.

19. Ibid., 63.

20. Guzman quoted in Eugene P. Dvorin and Arthur J. Murray, *California Politics and Policies* (Palo Alto, Calif.: Addison-Wesley, 1970), 354.

21. See Gomez-Quiñonez, *Chicano Politics,* 31–99. Provides an extensive analysis of many of these factors.

22. Ibid., 45–46.

23. Ibid.

24. Ibid., 57–60.

25. Joan Moore and Henry Pachon, *Mexican-Americans* (Englewood Cliffs, N.J.: Prentice Hall, 1976), 156.

26. Acuña, *Occupied America,* 3d ed. (New York: Harper & Row, 1988), 313–314.

27. McWilliams, *North from Mexico,* 52.

28. Moore and Pachon, *Mexican-Americans,* 25.

29. McWilliams, *North from Mexico,* 163.

30. Ibid.

31. Ibid., 54.

32. Ibid.

33. Abraham Hoffman, *Unwanted Mexican Americans in the Great*

Depression: Repatriation Pressures, 1929–1939 (Tucson: University of Arizona Press, 1974), 14.

34. Acuña, *Occupied America*, 2d ed. (New York: Harper & Row, 1981), 128.

35. Ibid., 133.

36. Hoffman, *Unwanted Mexican Americans in the Great Depression*, 31.

37. Moore and Pachon, *Mexican Americans*, 26.

38. Hoffman, *Unwanted Mexican Americans in the Great Depression*, 18.

39. Moore and Pachon, *Mexican Americans*, 26.

40. Matt Meier and Feliciano Rivera, *The Chicanos: A History of Mexican Americans* (New York: Hill and Wang, 1972), 159.

41. Acuña, *Occupied America*, 2d ed., 136.

42. Hoffman, *Unwanted Mexican Americans in the Great Depression*, 19.

43. Acuña, *Occupied America*, 2d ed., 138.

44. Meier and Rivera, *The Chicanos*, 161.

45. Ernesto Galarza, *Merchants of Labor: The Mexican Bracero Story* (Charlotte, N.C.: McNally and Loftin, 1964). Provides a comprehensive analysis of the workings of the Bracero Program from 1942 to 1962.

46. Ibid., 72–106. Chapter 8 provides an overview of how Public Law 78 was administered.

47. Moore and Pachon, *Mexican Americans*, 44.

48. Acuña, *Occupied America*, 3d ed., 267.

49. Meier and Rivera, *The Chicanos*, 231.

50. Moore and Pachon, *Mexican Americans*, 60.

51. Ibid.

52. Ibid., 54.

53. Ibid., 55.

54. Ibid., 66.

55. Acuña, *Occupied America*, 3d ed., 340.

56. Peter Nabokov, *Tijerina and the Court House Raid* (Albuquerque: University of New Mexico Press, 1969); and Richard Gardner, *Grito! Reies Lopez Tijerina and the New Mexico Land Grant War of 1967* (Indianapolis: Bobbs-Merrill, 1970).

57. Ellwyn R. Stoddard, *Mexican Americans* (New York: Random House, 1973), 195.

58. Ibid.

59. Ibid.

60. Tony Castro, *Chicano Power: The Emergence of Mexican America* (New York: Saturday Review Press, 1974), 112.

61. Stoddard, *Mexican Americans*, 196.

62. Castro, *Chicano Power*, 117.

63. Stoddard, *Mexican Americans*, 196.

64. Meier and Rivera, *The Chicanos*, 270–271.

65. Acuña, *Occupied America*, 1st ed., 238.

66. Quoted in John Chavez, *The Lost Land: The Chicano Image of the Southwest* (Albuquerque: University of New Mexico Press, 1984), 140.

67. Acuña, *Occupied America*, 3d ed., 340.

68. Chavez, *The Lost Land*, 140.

69. Acuña, *Occupied America*, 3d ed., 341.

70. Meier and Rivera, *The Chicanos*, 273.

71. Castro, *Chicano Power*, 123.

72. Meier and Rivera, *The Chicanos*, 273.

73. Ibid., 274.

74. Gomez-Quiñonez, *Chicano Politics*, 117.

75. Ibid., 118.

76. Ibid.

77. Acuña, *Occupied America*, 3d ed., 325.

78. Ibid.

79. Sam Kushner, *Long Road to Delano* (New York: International, 1975), 150–151.

80. Ibid.

81. Acuña, *Occupied America*, 3d ed., 325.

82. Ronald Taylor, *Chavez and the Farm Workers* (Boston: Beacon, 1975), 93–96.

83. Joan London and Henry Anderson, *So Shall Ye Reap* (New York: Thomas Y. Crowell, 1970), 147.

84. Jean Maddern Pitrone, *Chavez: Man of the Migrants* (New York: Alba House, 1971), 64.

85. Jacques Levy, *Cesar Chavez: Autobiography of La Causa* (New York: W. W. Norton, 1975), 175.

86. Pitrone, *Chavez*, 73.

87. Meier and Rivera, *The Chicanos*, 261.

88. Acuña, *Occupied America*, 3d ed., 325.

89. J. Craig Jenkins, *The Politics of Insurgency: The Farm Worker Movement in the 1960's* (New York: Columbia University Press, 1985), 143.

90. Ibid.

91. Acuña, *Occupied America*, 3d ed., 326.

92. Meier and Rivera, *The Chicanos*, 265.

93. Chavez, *The Lost Land*, 136.

94. Meier and Rivera, *The Chicanos*, 267.

95. Ibid.

96. Ibid.

97. *Los Angeles Times*, April 24, 1993.

98. Acuña, *Occupied America*, 3d ed., 328–329.

99. Meier and Rivera, *The Chicanos*, 268–269.

100. Ibid.

101. Kushner, *Long Road to Delano*, 193.

102. Levy, *Cesar Chavez*, 425–433.

103. Acuña, *Occupied America*, 3d ed., 326–327.

104. Levy, *Cesar Chavez*, 443–446.

105. Acuña, *Occupied America*, 3d ed., 369.

106. Taylor, *Chavez and the Farm Workers*, 289–290.

107. Ibid., 290.

108. Stan Steiner, *The Mexican Americans* (New York: Harper and Row, 1968), 380.

109. Acuña, *Occupied America*, 3d ed., 341.

110. Quoted in Steiner, *The Mexican Americans*, 380.

111. Castro, *Chicano Power*, 143.

112. Quoted in ibid.

113. Acuña, *Occupied America*, 3d ed., 341.

114. Chavez, *The Lost Land*, 142.

115. Ibid.

116. Meier and Rivera, *The Chicanos*, 275.

117. Quoted in Wayne Moquin and Charles Van Doren, eds., *A Documentary History of the Mexican Americans* (New York: Bantam, 1972), 488–489.

118. Ibid., 491.

119. Gomez-Quiñonez, *Chicano Politics*, 114.

120. Ibid.

121. Meier and Rivera, *The Chicanos*, 276.

122. Quoted in Luis Valdez and Stan Steiner, eds., *Aztlan: An Anthology of Mexican American Literature* (New York: Vintage, 1972), 402–403.

123. Carlos Muñoz, *Youth, Identity, Power: The Chicano Movement* (New York: Verso, 1989), 75.

124. Quoted in Acuña, *Occupied America*, 3d ed., 346.

125. Ibid.

126. Richard Santillan, *La Raza Unida* (Los Angeles: Flaquito, 1973), 19.

127. Ibid.

128. Ignacio Garcia, *United We Win: The Rise and Fall of La Raza Unida Party* (Tucson: University of Arizona Press, 1989), 96.

129. Ibid.

Chapter 2

1. Juan Gomez-Quiñonez, *Mexican Students Por La Raza: The Chicano Student Movement in Southern California 1967–1977* (Santa Barbara: Editorial La Causa, 1978), 1.

2. Carlos Muñoz, *Youth, Identity, and Power: The Chicano Movement* (New York: Verso, 1989), 20.

3. Darren L. Smith, ed., *Black Americans: Information Directory* (Detroit: Gale Research, 1990–1991).

4. Muñoz, *Youth, Identity, Power*, 21.

5. Carlos Muñoz, "Occidental's Barrio Boy," *Occidental College Quarterly* (Summer 1987).

6. Gilbert G. Gonzalez, *Chicano Education in the Era of Segregation* (Philadelphia: Associated University Press, 1990).

7. S. J. Holmes, "Perils of the Mexican Invasion," *North American Review*, 615–623.

8. House Committee on Immigration and Naturalization, Western Hemisphere Immigration, 71st Congress, 2d session, 1930, 75.

9. Holmes, "Perils of the Mexican Invasion," 615–623.

10. Gonzalez, *Chicano Politics in the Era of Segregation*, 136–156.

11. Rodolfo Acuña, *Occupied America: The Chicano Struggle toward Liberation*, 1st ed. (New York: Canfield Press, 1972), 316.

12. Muñoz, *Youth, Identity, Power*, 29.

13. Ibid., 30–31.

14. Gomez-Quiñonez, *Mexican Students Por La Raza*, 10.

15. Ibid.

16. Acuña, *Occupied America*, 316.

17. Ibid., 317.

18. Gomez-Quiñonez, *Mexican Students Por La Raza*, 10.

19. Muñoz, *Youth, Identity, Power*, 33.

20. Gomez-Quiñonez, *Mexican Students Por La Raza*, 10.

21. Muñoz, *Youth, Identity, Power*, 42.

22. Ibid., 42.

23. Gomez-Quiñonez, *Mexican Students Por La Raza*, 11.

24. Ibid., 11–12.

25. Muñoz, *Youth, Identity, Power*, 51.

26. Ibid., 53.

27. Muñoz, *Youth, Identity, Power*, 52.

28. Ibid.

29. Munoz, *Youth, Identity, Power*, 51–52.

30. Interview with Jose Angel Gutierrez, Crystal City, Tex., May 16, 1973.

31. Acuña, *Occupied America*, 3d ed. (New York: Harper & Row, 1988), 334.

32. Matt Meier and Feliciano Rivera, *The Chicanos* (New York: Hill and Wang, 1972), 250.

33. Muñoz, *Youth, Identity, Power*, 128–130, 142–143.

34. Gomez-Quiñonez, *Mexican Students Por La Raza*, 29.

35. I selected "Chicano Youth Movement" rather than the commonly referred to "Chicano student movement" as being more inclusive of all the youth who participated in the CM. This chapter will treat both models of youth groups. However, it is my contention that the student subsector was the more prominent of the two.

36. Gomez-Quiñonez, *Mexican Students Por La Raza*, 19.

37. Meier and Rivera, *The Chicanos*, 251.

38. Gomez-Quiñonez, *Mexican Students Por La Raza*, 19.

39. Ibid.

40. Since the focus of this study is on MAYO, I will elaborate subsequently on MAYO's development.

41. Acuña, *Occupied America*, 3d ed., 336.

42. Gomez-Quiñonez, *Mexican Students Por La Raza*, 20. Due to the limited availability of research on UMAS, much of my analysis was taken from Muñoz, *Youth, Identity, Power*; and Acuña, *Occupied America*, 3d ed.

43. Acuña, *Occupied America*, 3d ed., 335.

44. Muñoz, *Youth, Identity, Power*, 66.

45. Quoted in ibid., 67.

46. Ellwyn Stoddard, *Mexican Americans* (New York: Random House, 1973), 203.

47. Gomez-Quiñonez, *Mexican Students Por La Raza*, 27.

48. Muñoz, *Youth, Identity, Power*, 64.

49. Acuña, *Occupied America*, 3d ed., 336.

50. Muñoz, *Youth, Identity, Power*, 64.

51. Acuña, *Occupied America*, 3d ed., 337.

52. Ibid.

53. Muñoz, *Youth, Identity, Power*, 65–66.

54. Acuña, *Occupied America*, 3d ed., 335–336.

55. Stoddard, *Mexican Americans*, 215.

56. Tony Castro, *Chicano Power* (New York: Saturday Review Press, 1974), 315.

57. Quoted in "Black Beret Organization," in Chris Garcia, *La Causa Política: A Chicano Politics Reader* (London: University of Notre Dame Press, 1974), 405–408; quotation on 408.

58. Castro, *Chicano Power*, 135.

59. Juan Gomez-Quiñonez, *Chicano Politics: Reality and Promise, 1940–1990* (Albuquerque: University of New Mexico Press, 1990), 120.

60. Acuña, *Occupied America*, 3d ed., 337.

61. Elizabeth Martinez and Enniqueta Vasquez, *Viva La Raza: The Struggle of Mexican American People* (Garden City, N.Y.: Doubleday, 1974), 302–306.

62. Stoddard, *Mexican Americans*, 215.

63. Ibid.

64. Castro, *Chicano Power*, 136.

65. Gomez-Quiñonez, *Chicano Politics*, 136.

66. Acuña, *Occupied America*, 3d ed., 337.

67. David Sanchez, *Expedition through Aztlan* (La Puente, Calif.: Perspective Publications, 1978). Sanchez provides his own account of the Brown Berets' history, development, and orientation from its inception in 1967 to its formal demise in 1972.

68. Ibid., 202–297.

69. Muñoz, *Youth, Identity, Power*, 86.

70. Gomez-Quiñonez, *Chicano Politics*, 120.

71. Martinez and Vasquez, *Viva La Raza*, 306.

72. Sanchez, *Expedition through Aztlan*, 34.

73. Ibid., 5.

74. Ibid.

75. Ibid.

76. Gomez-Quiñonez, *Chicano Politics*, 120.

77. Martinez and Longeaux y Vasquez, *Viva La Raza*, 251.

78. Quoted in Luis Valdez and Stan Steiner, eds., *Aztlan: An Anthology of Mexican American Literature* (New York: Vintage, 1972), 402–403.

79. Ibid., 39.
80. Muñoz, *Youth, Identity, Power*, 76.
81. Barrera, *Beyond Aztlan*, 39.
82. Ibid., 41–44.
83. Gomez-Quiñonez, *Chicano Politics*, 79.
84. Muñoz, *Youth, Identity, Power*, 79.
85. Ibid., 80.
86. Ibid., 194.
87. Gomez-Quiñonez, *Chicano Politics*, 123.
88. Muñoz, *Youth, Identity, Power*, 84–93.
89. Ibid., 129–134.
90. Ibid.
91. Meier and Rivera, *The Chicanos*, 254.
92. Ibid., 254.
93. Muñoz, *Youth, Identity, Power*, 142.
94. Meier and Rivera, *The Chicanos*, 253–254.
95. Ibid.
96. Acuña, *Occupied America*, 3d ed., 345.
97. David Gomez, *Somos Chicanos: Strangers in Our Own Land* (Boston: Beacon, 1973), 157.
98. Acuña, *Occupied America*, 3d ed., 367.
99. Gomez-Quiñonez, *Chicano Politics*, 136–137.
100. Muñoz, *Youth, Identity, Power*, 86–87.
101. Gomez-Quiñonez, *Chicano Politics*, 119.

Chapter 3

1. Ignacio Garcia, *United We Win: The Rise and Fall of La Raza Unida Party* (Tucson: Mexican-American Studies and Research Center, 1989), 15.
2. Interview, Jose Angel Gutierrez, Crystal City, Tex., May 16, 1973.
3. Telephone interview, Ignacio "Nacho" Perez, September 15, 1993.
4. Interview, Gutierrez, May 16, 1973.
5. Telephone interview, Juan Patlan, September 4, 1993.
6. Jose Angel Gutierrez, "Notes from Jose Angel Gutierrez: Presently in Self-Imposed Exile" (unpublished position paper), January 1969, 2.
7. San Antonio *Express*, April 16, 1969.
8. Interview, Mario Compean, San Antonio, Tex., May 15, 1973.
9. San Antonio *Express*, April 16, 1969.
10. Gutierrez, "Notes from Jose Angel Gutierrez."
11. Garcia, *United We Win*, 16.
12. Interview, Perez, September 15, 1993.
13. Compean quoted in Garcia, *United We Win*, 16.
14. Interview, Patlan, September 4, 1993.
15. Interview, Perez, September 15, 1993.
16. Ibid.
17. Jose Angel Gutierrez, "Aztlan: Chicano Revolt in the Winter Garden," *La Raza* 1, no. 4 (1971): 34–35.

18. Interview, Compean, May 15, 1973.

19. Interview, Gutierrez, May 16, 1973.

20. The term *power holders* is used to denote either Chicano or Anglo elected officials or heads of agencies and programs whose power and influence is predicated on the position they hold. Also, the term will be used to denote individuals who wield substantial economic power.

21. Garcia, *United We Win*, 18.

22. Ibid., 18–19.

23. Interview, Gutierrez, May 16, 1973.

24. Garcia, *United We Win*, 17.

25. Interview, Patlan, September 4, 1993.

26. Ibid.

27. Interview, Gutierrez, May 16, 1973.

28. Interview, Jose Angel Gutierrez, Crystal City, Tex., April 11, 1973.

29. Ibid.

30. Gutierrez, "Notes from Jose Angel Gutierrez."

31. Jose Angel Gutierrez, "Gringos" (unpublished position paper), no date given, 1.

32. Interview, Jose Angel Gutierrez, Crystal City, Tex., June 2, 1973.

33. Jose Angel Gutierrez, "MAYO" (unpublished MAYO position paper), November 1968.

34. Ibid.

35. Interview, Gutierrez, May 16, 1973.

36. Ibid.

37. MAYO's constitution and bylaws of the board, section 11, no date.

38. Ibid.

39. MAYO, informational pamphlet, no date.

40. Interview, Compean, May 15, 1973.

41. Interview, Gutierrez, May 16, 1973.

42. Pamphlet, "MAYO," no date, 3.

43. Saul Alinsky, *Rules for Radicals* (New York: Random House, 1971), 4.

44. Interview, Gutierrez, May 16, 1973.

45. Alinsky, *Rules for Radicals*, 12–13.

46. Ibid.

47. Telephone interview, Carlos Guerra, September 1, 1993.

48. Gutierrez, "Gringos" (position paper).

49. Jose Angel Gutierrez, "*La Raza* and Political Action" (position paper), no date, 3.

50. Interview, Gutierrez, May 16, 1973.

51. Interview, Alberto Luera, Crystal City, Tex., April 18, 1973.

52. Ibid.

53. Interview, Compean, May 15, 1973.

54. Interview, Luera, April 18, 1973.

55. Interview, Gutierrez, May 16, 1973.

56. Interview, Guerra, September 1, 1993.

57. Telephone interview, Daniel Bustamante, September 7, 1993.

58. Interview, Garcia, 25.

59. Interview, Daniel Bustamante, September 7, 1993.

60. Interview, Patlan, September 4, 1993.

61. Alinsky, *Rules for Radicals*, 4.

62. Interview, Guerra, September 1, 1993.

63. Michael Lipsky, *Protest in City Politics* (Chicago: Rand McNally, 1970), 2.

64. Peter Eisinger, "The Conditioning of Political Behavior in American Cities," *American Political Science Review* (March 1973): 14.

65. Jerome H. Skolnick, *The Politics of Protest* (New York: Simon and Schuster, 1969), 5.

66. Gutierrez, "Notes from Jose Angel Gutierrez, January, 1969."

67. Alinsky, *Rules for Radicals*, 126.

68. Ibid., 127–130.

69. Interview, Patlan, September 4, 1993.

70. Interview, Gutierrez, May 16, 1973.

71. *American Opinion*, April 16, 1969.

72. Ibid.

73. Rodolfo Acuña, *Occupied America*, 1st ed. (San Francisco: Canfield Press, 1972), 234.

74. Interview, Gutierrez, May 16, 1973.

75. San Antonio *Express*, April 16, 1969.

76. Garcia, *United We Win*, 21.

77. Interview, Compean, May 15, 1973.

78. Minutes, MAYO state meeting, October 10, 1969.

79. Ibid.

80. Interview, Compean, May 15, 1973.

81. Ibid.

82. MAYO's constitution and bylaws of the board, section 7, policy, no date.

83. Ibid., section 3.

84. Ibid., section 7.

85. Ibid., sections 4 and 5.

86. Telephone interview, Lupe Youngblood, September 13, 1993.

87. Interview, Daniel Bustamante, September 7, 1993.

88. Interview, Patlan, September 4, 1993.

89. Interview, Perez, September 15, 1993.

90. Telephone interview, Rudy "Flaco" Rodriguez, September 6, 1993.

91. Interview, Youngblood, September 13, 1993.

92. Minutes, MAYO state meeting, May 10, 1969.

93. Interview, Gutierrez, May 16, 1973.

94. Minutes, MAYO state meeting, May 10, 1969.

95. Interview, Gutierrez, May 16, 1973.

96. Telephone interview, Mario Compean, April 26, 1993.

97. Ibid.

98. Minutes, MAYO state meeting, May 10, 1969.

99. Ibid.

100. Ibid.

101. Telephone interview, Edgar Lozano, September 4, 1993.

102. V. I. Lenin, *Collected Works*, vol. 4 (New York: International Publishers, 1929).

103. Interview, Youngblood, September 13, 1993.

104. Interview, Compean, May 15, 1973.

105. Interview, Perez, September 15, 1993.

106. Telephone interview, Jose Angel Gutierrez, August 31, 1993.

107. Interview, Patlan, September 4, 1993.

108. Telephone interview, Mario Compean, September 8, 1993.

109. Interview, Guerra, September 1, 1993.

110. Interview, Rodriguez, September 6, 1993.

111. Telephone interview, Luz Gutierrez, September 9, 1993.

112. Telephone interview, Choco Meza, September 21, 1993.

113. Telephone interview, Juanita Bustamante, September 7, 1993.

114. Telephone interview, Viviana Santiago Cobada, September 7, 1993.

115. Telephone interview, Rosie Castro, September 15, 1993.

116. Interview, Gutierrez, September 9, 1993.

117. Ibid.

118. Interview, Meza, September 21, 1993.

119. Interview, Bustamante, September 7, 1993.

120. Interview, Gutierrez, September 9, 1993.

121. Interview, Castro, September 15, 1993.

122. Interview, Santiago Cobada, September 7, 1993.

123. Interview, Compean, September 8, 1993.

124. Interview, Guerra, September 1, 1993.

125. Lenin, *Collected Works*, 87–88.

126. San Antonio *Express*, April 12, 1969.

127. Ibid.

128. Ibid.

129. MAYO, position paper on its philosophy, no date.

Chapter 4

1. Joan Moore and Harry Pachon, *Mexican-Americans* (New Jersey: Prentice-Hall, 1975), 65.

2. Ignacio Garcia, *United We Win: The Rise and Fall of La Raza Unida Party* (Tucson: Mexican-American Studies, 1989), 29.

3. Interview, Mario Compean, San Antonio, Tex., May 15, 1973.

4. Garcia, *United We Win*, 29.

5. Telephone interview, Alberto Luera, January 26, 1993.

6. Garcia, *United We Win*, 29.

7. Interview, Luera, January 26, 1993.

8. Telephone interview, Edgar Lozano, September 4, 1993.

9. Garcia, *United We Win*, 32.

10. *Monitor*, November 24, 1968.

11. Ibid., November 7, 1968.

12. Edinburg *Daily Review*, November 15, 1968.

13. *Monitor*, November 7, 1968.
14. *Monitor*, November 6, 1968.
15. Letter sent to parents by school district, November 15, 1968.
16. *Monitor*, November 6, 1968.
17. *Morning Star*, November 13, 1968.
18. *Monitor*, November 14, 1968.
19. Ibid.
20. Ibid.
21. Edinburg *Daily Review*, November 15, 1968.
22. *Morning Star*, November 19, 1968.
23. Corpus Christi *Caller*, November 15, 1968.
24. Edinburg *Daily Review*, November 15, 1968.
25. Edinburg *Daily Review*, November 19, 1968.
26. Corpus Christi *Caller*, November 19, 1968.
27. *Morning Star*, November 19, 1968.
28. Corpus Christi *Caller*, November 21, 1968.
29. Corpus Christi *Caller*, November 27, 1968.
30. Ibid.
31. Ibid.
32. Ibid.
33. MAYO document listing demands, April 9, 1969.
34. San Antonio *Express*, April 15, 1969.
35. Corpus Christi *Caller*, April 15, 1969.
36. MAYO letter, April 23, 1969.
37. Ibid.
38. San Antonio *Express*, April 17, 1969.
39. MAYO letter, April 23, 1969.
40. San Antonio *Express*, April 17, 1969.
41. MAYO document, "Chronology of Events," no date.
42. San Antonio *Express*, April 17, 1969.
43. San Antonio *Express*, April 18, 1969.
44. Kingsville *Record*, April 20, 1969.
45. San Antonio *Express*, April 20, 1969.
46. *Morning Star*, April 17, 1969.
47. Interview, Jose Angel Gutierrez, Crystal City, Tex., May 16, 1973.
48. Corpus Christi *Caller*, April 21, 1969.
49. San Antonio *Express*, April 22, 1969.
50. San Antonio *Express*, April 23, 1969.
51. MAYO document, no date.
52. Interview, Alberto Luera, Crystal City, Tex., April 18, 1973.
53. Interview, Gutierrez, May 16, 1973.
54. Kingsville *Record*, April 20, 1969.
55. Interview, Gutierrez, May 16, 1973.
56. Telegram sent to MAYO by Corky Gonzales, chairperson of the Crusade for Justice in Colorado, April 16, 1969.
57. Interview, Gutierrez, May 16, 1973.
58. John Shockley, "Crystal City: La Raza Unida and the Second Re-

sult," in *Chicano: The Evolution of a People,* ed. Renato Rosaldo et al. (Minnesota: Winston Press, 1973).

59. "U.S. Journal: Crystal City, Texas," *New Yorker,* April 17, 1971, 102.
60. Shockley, "Crystal City," 120.
61. Zavala County *Sentinel,* May 1, 1969.
62. Ibid.
63. Shockley, "Crystal City," 317.
64. Ibid.
65. Ibid.
66. Interview, Jose Angel Gutierrez, Crystal City, Tex., May 24, 1973.
67. Shockley, "Crystal City," 318.
68. *Texas Observer,* January 2, 1970.
69. Crystal City School Board Minutes, November 3, 1969.
70. Interview, Gutierrez, May 24, 1973.
71. Crystal City School Board Minutes, November 3, 1969.
72. Interview, Gutierrez, May 24, 1973.
73. Ibid.
74. Ibid.
75. Jose Angel Gutierrez, "Aztlan: Chicano Revolt in the Winter Garden," *La Raza* 1, no. 4. (1971): 34–35.
76. Shockley, "Crystal City," 318.
77. Interview, Gutierrez, May 24, 1973.
78. Interview, Luz Gutierrez, Crystal City, Tex., May 9, 1973.
79. Interview, Gutierrez, May 24, 1973.
80. Gutierrez, "Aztlan," 34–35.
81. Crystal City School Board Minutes, December 8, 1969.
82. Zavala County *Sentinel,* December 11, 1969.
83. Interview, Gutierrez, May 24, 1973.
84. Ibid.
85. Zavala County *Sentinel,* December 11, 1969.
86. George Sanchez, "The Crystal City School Boycott: 1969" (unpublished paper), 6.
87. Shockley, "Crystal City," 319.
88. Ibid.
89. Interview, Gutierrez, May 24, 1973.
90. Sanchez, "The Crystal City School Boycott," 8.
91. Shockley, "Crystal City," 319.
92. Ibid.
93. Zavala County *Sentinel,* December 18, 1969.
94. Corpus Christi *Caller,* December 17, 1969.
95. Sanchez, "The Crystal City School Boycott," 10.
96. Jose Angel Gutierrez, lecture given at a seminar to high school teachers, Crystal City, Texas, April 11, 1973.
97. Interview, Gutierrez, May 24, 1973.
98. Corpus Christi *Caller,* December 17, 1969.
99. Sanchez, "The Crystal City School Boycott," 10.
100. Interview, Gutierrez, May 24, 1973.

101. Ibid.

102. Shockley, "Crystal City," 319.

103. San Antonio *Light*, January 6, 1970.

104. San Antonio *Light*, January 8, 1970.

105. Ibid.

106. Sanchez, "The Crystal City School Boycott," 14.

107. Ibid.

108. Michael Lipsky, *Protest in City Politics* (Chicago: Rand McNally, 1970), 2.

109. Interview, Gutierrez, May 24, 1973.

110. Gutierrez, "Aztlan."

111. Ibid.

112. Gutierrez, lecture, April 11, 1973.

113. Ibid.

Chapter 5

1. Interview, Mario Compean, San Antonio, Tex., May 15, 1973.

2. Interview, Luz Gutierrez, Crystal City, Tex., May 9, 1973.

3. Saul Alinsky, *Rules for Radicals* (New York: Random House, 1971), 99.

4. Interview, Gutierrez, May 9, 1973.

5. Rodolfo Acuña, *Occupied America*, 1st ed. (San Francisco: Canfield Press, 1972), 226.

6. Interview, Compean, May 15, 1973.

7. Armando Rendon, *Chicano Manifesto* (New York: Collier-Macmillan, 1971), 130.

8. Ibid., 134.

9. Interview, Compean, May 15, 1973.

10. Ibid.

11. Ibid.

12. *Texas Observer*, April 11, 1969.

13. Interview, Compean, May 15, 1973.

14. Interview, Gutierrez, May 9, 1973.

15. Interview, Compean, May 15, 1973.

16. Interview, Jose Angel Gutierrez, Crystal City, Tex., May 16, 1993.

17. Interview, Gutierrez, May 9, 1973.

18. San Antonio *Express*, April 15, 1969.

19. Rendon, *Chicano Manifesto*, 134–135.

20. San Antonio *Express*, April 15, 1969.

21. Interview, Gutierrez, May 9, 1973.

22. San Antonio *Express*, April 19, 1969.

23. Ibid.

24. Ignacio Garcia, *United We Win* (Tucson: Mexican American Studies and Research Center, 1989), 23.

25. San Antonio *News*, May 18, 1970.

26. Ibid.

27. Ibid.
28. Letter sent to Jose Angel Gutierrez by Pete Tijerina, April 9, 1969.
29. Memorandum from Pete Tijerina to Jose Angel Gutierrez, no date.
30. Garcia, *United We Win*, 23.
31. Ibid.
32. Texas Observer, April 11, 1969.
33. San Antonio *Express*, March 19, 1969.
34. *News World*, March 14, 1969.
35. San Antonio *Express*, March 14, 1969.
36. San Angelo *Standard Times*, March 14, 1969.
37. *Texas Observer*, April 11, 1969.
38. San Antonio *Express*, March 14, 1969.
39. Interview, Gutierrez, May 16, 1973.
40. San Antonio *Express*, March 16, 1969.
41. San Antonio *Express*, March 23, 1969.
42. San Antonio *Express*, March 16, 1969.
43. Ibid.
44. San Antonio *Express*, March 23, 1969.
45. Rendon, *Chicano Manifesto*, 334.
46. Interview, Compean, May 15, 1973.
47. MAYO press release, March 18, 1969.
48. San Antonio *Express*, March 23, 1969.
49. San Antonio *Express*, March 29, 1969.
50. Ibid.
51. Ibid.
52. San Antonio *Express*, March 31, 1969.
53. Ibid.
54. Ibid.
55. Laredo *Times*, March 31, 1969.
56. San Antonio *Express*, March 31, 1969.
57. San Antonio *Express*, April 10, 1969.
58. San Antonio *Express*, April 2, 1969.
59. "Race Hate," *Congressional Record*, April 3, 1969, 8590.
60. San Antonio *Express*, April 4, 1969.
61. San Antonio *Express*, April 8, 1969.
62. San Antonio *Express*, May 8, 1969.
63. San Antonio *Express*, April 8, 1969.
64. Ibid.
65. San Antonio *Express*, April 15, 1969.
66. Washington *Post*, November 2, 1969.
67. Acuña, *Occupied America*, 273.
68. San Antonio *Express*, March 18, 1970.
69. San Antonio *News*, April 11, 1969.
70. Interview, Gutierrez, May 16, 1973.
71. San Antonio *Express*, April 11, 1969.
72. San Antonio *News*, April 11, 1969.
73. San Antonio *Light*, April 11, 1969.

74. Interview, Gutierrez, May 9, 1973.

75. Garcia, *United We Win*, 28.

76. Ibid.

77. Ibid.

78. Del Rio *News*, May 16, 1969.

79. Ibid.

80. *Monitor*, May 18, 1969.

81. Ibid.

82. San Antonio *Express*, November 16, 1969.

83. San Antonio *Express*, November 13, 1969.

84. Interview, Gutierrez, May 16, 1973.

85. San Antonio *Express*, December 1, 1969.

86. Ibid.

87. Ibid.

88. Washington *Post*, January 11, 1970.

89. Ibid.

90. *Monitor*, December 30, 1969.

91. Washington *Post*, January 11, 1970.

92. Interview, Alberto Luera, Crystal City, Tex., April 24, 1973.

93. Ibid.

94. Interview, Gutierrez, May 16, 1973.

95. Interview, Luera, April 24, 1973.

96. Telephone interview, Alberto Luera, July 29, 1994.

97. Interview, Ignacio Perez, Los Angeles, July 30, 1994.

98. Ibid.

99. Interview, Luera, July 29, 1994.

100. Interview, Perez, July 30, 1994.

Chapter 6

1. Interview, Mario Compean, San Antonio, Tex., May 15, 1973.

2. Ibid.

3. Ibid.

4. Interview, Luz Gutierrez, Crystal City, Tex., May 9, 1973.

5. Ibid.

6. Ibid.

7. Interview, Jose Angel Gutierrez, Crystal City, Tex., May 16, 1973.

8. Interview, Gutierrez, May 9, 1973.

9. Interview, Gutierrez, May 16, 1973.

10. Ibid.

11. Jose Angel Gutierrez, "La Raza and Political Action" (position paper), no date.

12. Interview, Gutierrez, May 9, 1973.

13. Ibid.

14. Interview, Compean, May 15, 1973.

15. Ibid.

16. Ibid.

17. Interview, Gutierrez, May 16, 1973.

18. Interview, Compean, May 15, 1973.

19. Ibid.

20. Interview, Gutierrez, May 9, 1973.

21. San Antonio *Express*, April 12, 1969.

22. Ibid.

23. Interview, Gutierrez, May 16, 1973.

24. Interview, Compean, May 15, 1973.

25. Interview, Gutierrez, May 9, 1973.

26. Interview, Gutierrez, May 16, 1973.

27. Rodolfo Acuña, *Occupied America*, 1st ed. (San Francisco: Canfield Press, 1972), 234.

28. Interview, Gutierrez, May 16, 1973.

29. Ignacio Garcia, *United We Win* (Tucson: Mexican-American Studies and Research Center, 1989), 40.

30. Interview, Jose Angel Gutierrez, Crystal City, Tex., April 12, 1973.

31. Ibid.

32. Summary report of collected data and mental health program for the seven-county Winter Garden Area, submitted by Jose Angel Gutierrez et al., May 31, 1973.

33. John Staples Shockley, *Chicano Revolt in a Texas Town* (London: University of Notre Dame Press, 1974). An excellent study on the 1963 Chicano electoral revolt and on the forces that gave rise to the second electoral revolt of 1970.

34. Jose Angel Gutierrez, "Aztlan: Chicano Revolt in the Winter Garden," *La Raza* 1, no. 4 (1971): 34–35.

35. Interview, Virginia Musquiz, Crystal City, Tex., April 13, 1973.

36. Crystal City Internship Program Proposal for Municipal Management and School Administration, prepared by Francisco Rodriguez, City Manager, and Angel N. Gonzalez, Superintendent, Crystal City Public Schools.

37. Ibid.

38. Gutierrez, "Aztlan."

39. Robert Blauner, *Racial Oppression in America* (New York: Harper and Row, 1972). An excellent study that posits that Chicano, African American, and Native American experiences are explainable in the context of internal colonialism. Subsequently, Chicano scholars such as Rodolfo Acuña, Mario Barrera, Carlos Muñoz, Charles Ornelas, and others have used it in their work on Chicano history and politics.

40. Colonialism traditionally refers to the establishment of domination over a geographically external unit, most often inhabited by people of a different race and culture, where this domination is political and economic and the colony exists subordinated to and dependent upon the mother country. Typically, the colonizers exploit the land, the raw materials, the labor, and other resources of the colonized nation; a formal recognition is given to the difference in power, autonomy, and political status, and various agencies are set up to maintain this subordination (Blauner, *Racial Oppression in America*).

41. Gutierrez, "Aztlan."

42. Ibid.

43. Ibid.

44. Ibid.

45. Ibid.

46. Ibid.

47. Ibid.

48. Interview, Gutierrez, April 12, 1973.

49. Jose Angel Gutierrez, diary, 1968–1969.

50. Ibid.

51. Interview, Luz Gutierrez, May 9, 1973.

52. Gutierrez, diary.

53. Ibid.

54. Interview, Gutierrez, May 24, 1973.

55. Interview, Gutierrez, April 12, 1973.

56. Ibid.

57. Gutierrez, diary.

58. Interview, Gutierrez, May 24, 1973.

59. Gutierrez, diary.

60. Garcia, *United We Win*, 43.

61. Interview, Gutierrez, May 24, 1973.

62. Ibid.

63. Gutierrez, diary.

64. Ibid.

65. Interview, Gutierrez, May 24, 1973.

66. Ibid.

67. Ibid.

68. Ibid.

69. Ibid.

70. Julian Zamora, *La Raza: Forgotten Americans* (London: University of Notre Dame, 1967), 54.

71. Interview, Gutierrez, May 24, 1973.

72. Ibid.

73. Ibid.

74. Gutierrez, diary.

75. Ibid.

76. Ibid.

77. Ibid.

78. Ibid.

79. Interview, Gutierrez, May 24, 1973.

80. Gutierrez, diary.

81. V. I. Lenin, *Collected Works*, Vol. 4 (New York: International Publisher, 1929).

82. Interview, Ignacio Lozano, Crystal City, Tex., May 21, 1973.

83. Interview, Gutierrez, May 21, 1973.

84. Interview, Gutierrez, May 24, 1973.

85. Interview, Lozano, May 21, 1973.

86. Ibid.

87. Interview, Gutierrez, April 12, 1973.

88. Ibid.

89. Gutierrez, diary.

90. Ibid.

91. Shockley, *Chicano Revolt in a Texas Town*, 182.

92. Cuidadanos Unidos constitution and bylaws pamphlet, no date.

93. Ibid.

94. Interview, Gutierrez, May 24, 1973.

95. Ibid.

96. Interview, Alberto Luera, Crystal City, Tex., April 18, 1973.

97. MAYO press release, December 31, 1969.

98. Ibid.

99. Interview, Luz Gutierrez, May 9, 1973.

100. Interview, Gutierrez, May 24, 1973.

101. Gutierrez, diary.

Chapter 7

1. Interview, Jose Angel Gutierrez, Crystal City, Tex., May 24, 1973.

2. Ignacio M. Garcia, *United We Win: The Rise and Fall of La Raza Unida Party* (Tucson: University of Arizona Press, 1989), 57.

3. Interview, Gutierrez, May 24, 1973.

4. Telephone interview, Viviana Santiago Cobada, May 28, 1973.

5. Zavala County *Sentinel*, January 29, 1970.

6. Interview, Gutierrez, May 24, 1973.

7. Interview, Luz Gutierrez, Crystal City, Tex., May 9, 1973.

8. Gutierrez, "Aztlan: Chicano Revolt in the Winter Garden," *La Raza* 1, no. 4 (1971): 34–35.

9. Zavala County *Sentinel*, February 10, 1970.

10. Interview, Gutierrez, May 24, 1973.

11. Interview, Mike Perez, Crystal City, Tex., April 13, 1973.

12. Interview, Arturo Gonzalez, Crystal City, Tex., May 22, 1973.

13. Interview, Gutierrez, May 24, 1973.

14. San Antonio *Express*, March 23, 1970.

15. Interview, Dale Barker, Crystal City, Tex., April 17, 1973.

16. John Staples Shockley, *Chicano Revolt in a Texas Town* (Notre Dame: University of Notre Dame Press, 1974), 142–143.

17. Ibid., 146.

18. Interview, Gutierrez, May 9, 1973.

19. Ibid.

20. Zavala County *Sentinel*, April 2, 1970.

21. John Staples Shockley, "Crystal City: La Raza Unida and the Second Revolt," in *Chicano: The Beginnings of Bronze Power*, ed. Renato Rosaldo et al. (New York: William Morrow, 1974).

22. Garcia, *United We Win*, 59.

23. Shockley, *Chicano Revolt in a Texas Town*, 142.

24. Ibid.

25. Gutierrez, "Aztlan."

26. Interview, Gutierrez, May 24, 1973.

27. Shockley, *Chicano Revolt in a Texas Town*, 147.

28. Zavala County *Sentinel*, April 1, 1970.

29. *La Verdad*, February 1970.

30. San Antonio *News*, April 15, 1970.

31. Jose Garcia, thesis, 1971, Trinity University, Tex.

32. Ibid.

33. Interview, Gutierrez, May 24, 1973.

34. San Antonio *News*, April 16, 1970.

35. Shockley, *Chicano Revolt in a Texas Town*, 148.

36. *La Verdad*, April 1970.

37. San Antonio *News*, April 16, 1970.

38. Ibid.

39. Garcia, *United We Win*, 59.

40. John R. Chavez, *The Lost Land* (Albuquerque: University of New Mexico Press, 1984), 145.

41. Matt S. Meier and Feliciano Rivera, *The Chicanos: A History of Mexican Americans* (New York: Hill and Wang, 1972), 278–279.

42. Tony Castro, *Chicano Power: The Emergence of Mexican America* (New York: Saturday Review Press, 1974), 166.

43. Garcia, *United We Win*, 56.

44. Ibid., 61–62.

45. Ibid.

46. For more specific information on the various reforms initiated by the RUP, refer to my dissertation, "El Partido de La Raza Unida in Crystal City: A Peaceful Revolution."

47. Telephone interview, Alberto Luera, March 2, 1993.

48. Ibid.

49. *Militant*, November 20, 1970.

50. Garcia, *United We Win*, 71.

51. Zavala County *Sentinel*, November 4, 1971.

52. Interview, Gutierrez, May 9, 1973.

53. Interview, Luera, March 2, 1993.

54. Garcia, *United We Win*, 72.

55. *Sentinel*, April 2, 1970.

56. Interview, Luera, March 2, 1993.

57. Interview, Gutierrez, May 9, 1973.

58. Interview, Jose Angel Gutierrez, Crystal City, Tex., June 2, 1973.

59. *Sentinel*, April 12, 1970.

60. Interview, Luera, March 2, 1993.

61. *Sentinel*, April 2, 1970.

62. "Texas Raza Unida Party," unpublished paper, no date.

63. "Eleven Questions about the Raza Unida Party," unpublished paper, no date.

64. Interview, Luera, April 24, 1973.

65. Ibid.

66. Ibid.

67. Garcia, *United We Win*, 73.

68. Ibid., 79.

69. Ibid., 83.

70. Ibid., 84.

71. Ibid.

72. San Antonio *Express*, August 9, 1972.

73. Press release by Jose Angel Gutierrez issued at the first national RUP convention held in El Paso, Tex., September 4, 1972.

Epilogue

1. Telephone interview, Jose Angel Gutierrez, August 31, 1993.

2. Telephone interview, Mario Compean, September 8, 1993.

3. Telephone interview, Ignacio "Nacho" Perez, September 15, 1993.

4. Telephone interview, Juan Patlan, September 4, 1993.

5. Telephone interview, Luz Gutierrez, September 9, 1993.

6. Telephone interview, Choco Meza, September 21, 1993.

7. Telephone interview, Viviana Santiago Cobada, September 7, 1993.

8. Telephone interview, Rudy "Flaco" Rodriguez, September 6, 1993.

9. Telephone interview, Carlos Guerra, September 1, 1993.

10. Telephone interview, Alberto Luera, April 18, 1993.

11. Telephone interview, Gutierrez, August 31, 1993.

12. Telephone interview, Patlan, September 4, 1993.

13. Telephone interview, Luz Gutierrez, September 9, 1993.

14. Telephone interview, Daniel Bustamante, September 7, 1993.

15. Joan Moore and Harry Pachon, *Hispanics in the United States* (Englewood Cliffs, N.J.: Prentice-Hall, 1985), 65.

16. Harry Pachon, *An Overview of Hispanic Elected Officials in 1991* (NALEO Educational Fund, 1991), 12.

17. Telephone interview, Juanita Bustamante, September 7, 1993.

Index

A Fairy Treasure Hunt

Chloe
the Topaz Fairy

Amy
the Amethyst Fairy

The Jewel Fairies

Scarlett
the Garnet Fairy

India
the Moonstone
Fairy

Sophie
the Sapphire
Fairy

Lucy
the Diamond Fairy

Emily
the Emerald Fairy

Library of Congress Cataloging in Publication Data is available.

ISBN 978-0-545-43684-7

10 9 8 7 6 5 4 3 2 1   12 13 14 15 16 17/0

Printed in the U.S.A.   40
This edition first printing, January 2012

A Fairy Treasure Hunt

by Daisy
Meadows

SCHOLASTIC INC.

New York Toronto London Auckland

Sydney Mexico City New Delhi Hong Kong

The morning sun shines on Fairyland.
The Jewel Fairies are excited.
"I can't believe today is the day!" says India.

"Our Fairy Test is finally here," Sophie agrees. "We've been training for so long."

Sophie looks around the cottage at
her sisters.
They are all fairies in training.
Once they pass their Fairy Test, they
will be full fairies.

"I wonder what our challenge will be,"
Sophie says.
"There's only one way to find out,"
says Emily.

After breakfast, the fairies fly
to the royal meadow.

As soon as they arrive, sparkles swirl in the sky. Queen Titania lands in front of them.

"Welcome to your Fairy Test," the queen says. "Your challenge will be a treasure hunt!"

"I will hide each of your jewels somewhere in Fairyland," the queen explains.
She twirls her wand, and the seven gems magically appear.

"Believe in yourselves and help one another
find the jewels," she says.
Then the colorful gems disappear right
before the fairies' eyes.

"Find your seven jewels and you will pass the test."

The queen smiles at the young fairies.

"Soon we'll be full fairies!" Sophie whispers to herself.

"Remember, the magic is inside you," the queen says. "Good luck, Jewel Fairies!" The wise fairy twirls her wand and disappears.

"Where should we start?" Emily asks.

"She didn't give us any clues," Scarlett adds.

"Yes, she did," says India. "She said the magic is inside us."

"Maybe our magic will help us find our jewels," says Emily.

"But how?" asks Sophie.

"Just trust your magic," says India. "Come on!"

India grabs Sophie's hand, and all the Jewel Fairies fly into the air.

Their wings sparkle in the sunlight.

"I see something!" Chloe yells with delight.
"There are golden sparkles in that tree."
Chloe dives over for a closer look.
"My jewel is hiding in a bird's nest," she says.

The fairies split up to search for the
other gems.
India follows a trail of pale pink sparkles
into the castle.
"My moonstone was under the queen's pillow!"
she says with a giggle.

Amy and Scarlett see sparkles in the royal garden.
Scarlett finds her red jewel in the strawberry patch.
Amy's purple jewel is in a lilac bush.

Sophie searches the palace grounds, but she does not see blue sparkles anywhere.

"Look how the fountain glitters," Lucy says.
"It must be fairy magic."

Lucy zips down and plucks her jewel from
the top of the fountain.
"Hooray!" she exclaims.

The fairies fly to the Fairyland Forest.
Sophie and Emily are still looking for
their gems.

Emily spies a swirl of green sparkles coming
from a hole in an old log.
She peeks inside.

"Well, hello there!" Emily says to a rabbit
family. "Thank you for keeping my jewel safe."
Emily gives each rabbit a pat.
Then she takes her green gem.

"We only have to find one more jewel," Chloe
says.

The fairies turn to Sophie.

"I haven't seen blue sparkles anywhere,"
Sophie says. "Maybe I don't have any magic
inside me."

"You just need to believe in yourself," says Amy.
"What's your favorite part of being a fairy?"
Scarlett asks.
Sophie thinks for a moment. "I love to make
wishes come true," she says.

"Maybe you need to make your own wish now," Emily suggests.

Sophie takes a deep breath. "I'll try. Will you help me?" she asks.

The sisters nod and form a circle.

Sophie recites her wish. It sounds like a song.

"Magic might, magic may,
Be with us this very day.
In a circle fairies bow,
May magic grant my wish right now."

The fairies touch their wands together.
A burst of blue sparkles appears.

"Look, the sparkles make a path," India says.
The Jewel Fairies follow the trail.

"The sparkles lead through here," says Sophie as she pushes back some leafy branches. Sophie gasps with surprise.

Queen Titania is standing in the clearing, and she has Sophie's blue jewel in her hands!

"Congratulations on finishing the treasure hunt!" the queen exclaims. "You found all the jewels. This calls for a celebration!"

Now the fairy sisters are full fairies.
The queen gives them necklaces.
Hanging from each necklace is the special
jewel each fairy found.

"This has been a magical day," says India.
"Yes," Sophie agrees. "It's been like a wish
come true!"

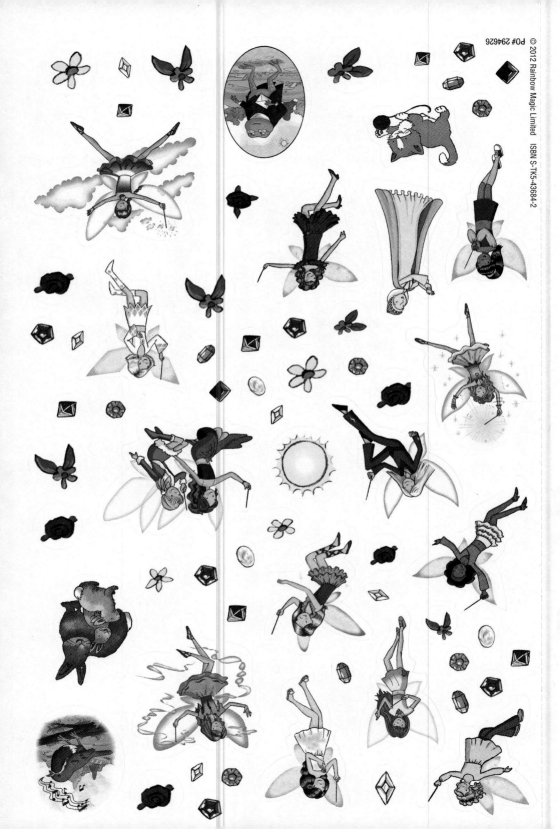

The Weather Fairies bow, and the Fairy
Godmother hurries onto the stage.
"What a beautiful ballet!" she exclaims.
"We did it!" Goldie says to her fairy sisters.
Crystal smiles. "Yes, we danced straight
from the heart."

The music fills their hearts, and they
pirouette around the stage.
With a swirl of their wands, the sky
lights up with weather magic!

The seven fairies dance onto the stage for
the finale.
Their wings sparkle under the starry sky.

The music grows soft.
Giant, glittery snowflakes begin to fall.
Crystal floats onto the stage, whirling
around with the snowflakes.

It's time for her big jump. Crystal leaps
into the air. When she lands, she's so
happy, she glows.

Abigail wears a crown of acorns, and
skips as she throws leaves in the air
like the autumn breeze.

Then Evie dances onto the stage, slow
and graceful, like a misty dream.

Hayley wears rain
boots and dances
with an umbrella,
twirling in a dizzy
spin.

Storm's dance is like
lightning: bold, fast,
and flashy.

Pearl bounds in
next, flipping from
one fluffy cloud to
another.

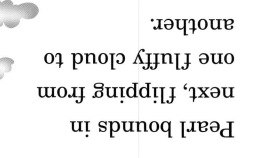

The fairy orchestra starts to play the ballet music.

Goldie is the first to go on. She does a dance of the rising sun. At first, the stage is dark. Then rays of light burst from Goldie's wand as she dances.

The Weather Fairies wait for their turn
backstage.
Crystal peeks out from behind the curtain
and crosses her wings for good luck.

The night of the Fairy Godmother's party arrives.
There is a big outdoor stage.

The guests sit on blankets under the stars.
The Fairy Godmother, King Oberon, and Queen Titania are there.

Then they meet with the fairy orchestra.
A ballet needs music!

The Weather Fairies practice and practice.
They also design and sew their costumes.

Abigail helps the snow fairy up.

"Don't worry about them," Evie suggests. "When you dance from the heart, you won't even know the crowd is there."

"I've seen you do that leap hundreds of times," Hayley says. "You just have to believe in yourself, like we believe in you."

Crystal nods and starts her dance again.

"I'll never get it right," Crystal says with a sigh. "I can't dance in front of the king and queen."

When it is Crystal's turn, she is nervous. Before her big leap, she stumbles and falls.

The fairies start to practice.

They help one another with their dances.
Each one is different, but they all tell a story
about weather.

Each fairy plans a special dance for her kind of weather.

Then they all work on the grand dance that comes at the end of their ballet.

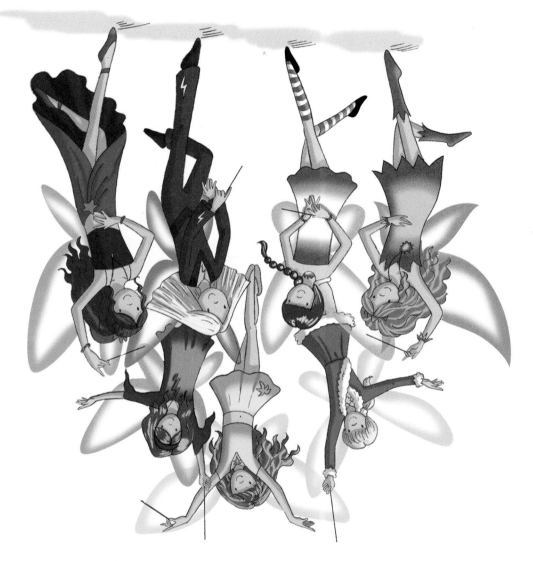

"We're all in the finale," Hayley says. "Because it's a gift from all of us."

"We'll practice. We're all in this together."
Crystal tries to smile.

All the fairies are excited, except Crystal.

"I'm not so sure," Crystal says quietly.

"But why?" Storm asks. "You love to dance."

"I like to dance for me," Crystal explains.

"But what if I mess up?"

"You'll be fine," Goldie insists.

"How?" asks Storm.

"We can dance to show everyone how weather makes us feel," says Goldie.

"We can create a ballet!" Evie exclaims.

"I love to hear the breeze whisper," Abigail says.
"I love how things look magical in the mist,"
says Evie.

"Well, *I* love snowflakes," says Crystal.
"When I watch them whirl around, I want
to dance."
"We all love weather," Goldie says.
"Maybe that can be our gift."

The bird chirps and flies toward the forest.
The fairies follow.

Outside, the fairies see a bird.

"Was that your pretty song?" Pearl asks the bird.

Just then, a beautiful song dances
through the window.
"Let's go outside," suggests Crystal.
"We do our best thinking there."

"I can't believe we have to perform for the king and queen," says Crystal.

"We'll think of something," Goldie says.

"It has to be from the heart," Hayley reminds them.

The Weather Fairies look at one another.
"Have a good day," Bertram says. "See you at
the party."

"The Fairy Godmother wants the guests to perform for the king and queen," Bertram explains. "That will be your gift. Remember, it needs to be from the heart."

"Oh, it sounds wonderful," sighs Hayley.

"But what about the gift?" Abigail asks.

Goldie opens the envelope and reads:

Dear fairies and friends:
Come one, come all!
In Fairyland, we will have a ball.
With songs and skits
for the king and queen,
it will be a celebration
like you've never seen.
Please be sure to prepare your part.
Bring a gift straight from your heart.
It's a night of fun for all to share.
I hope that I will see you there.

Always,
Fairy Godmother

"Hello, Weather Fairies," Bertram says.
"I have an invitation from the Fairy
Godmother for you."

"The Fairy Godmother?" gasps Evie.

Storm opens the door, and a frog strides in.
It's Bertram, the royal messenger.

It's early morning in Fairyland, and the
Weather Fairies are just waking up.
There's a loud knock at their door.
"Who could it be?" Crystal wonders.

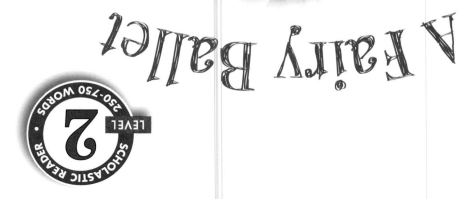

A Fairy Ballet

by Daisy Meadows

SCHOLASTIC INC.

New York Toronto London Auckland
Sydney Mexico City New Delhi Hong Kong

SCHOLASTIC READER • LEVEL 2
250-750 WORDS

The Weather Fairies

Crystal the Snow Fairy

Hayley the Rain Fairy

Abigail the Breeze Fairy

Pearl the Cloud Fairy

Goldie the Sunshine Fairy

Evie the Mist Fairy

Storm the Lightning Fairy

Library of Congress Cataloging in Publication Data is available.

ISBN 978-0-545-43684-7

10 9 8 7 6 5 4 3 2 1   12 13 14 15 16 17/0

Printed in the U.S.A.   40
This edition first printing, January 2012

A Fairy Ballet